WATERLOO
DIAMONDS

WATERLOO
DIAMONDS

RICHARD PANEK

St. Martin's Press
New York

Design by Sara Stemen

LIBRARY OF CONGRESS CATALOGING-IN-PUBLICATION DATA

Panek, Richard.
    Waterloo Diamonds / Richard Panek.
        p.   cm.
    ISBN 0-312-13209-3
    1. Waterloo Diamonds (Baseball team)—History.
    2. Minor league baseball—Iowa—Waterloo—History.
    I. Title.
    GV875.W33P36   1995
    796.357'64'09763—dc20   95-7935
                                                     CIP

First Edition:June 1995

10 9 8 7 6 5 4 3 2 1

For Meg Wolitzer, with love

Acknowledgments

Hundreds of people contributed to the research of this book, and all deserve thanks. Many are mentioned in the course of the book, though such an accounting is hardly representative of who helped most. Those who aren't named in the book but whose generosity of time, hospitality, knowledge, and resources nonetheless proved especially and specifically valuable are listed below, though this accounting is, in some ways, equally incomplete. Suffice it to say that I owe an enormous debt to the people of Waterloo, the staff of the Waterloo Diamonds, and the fans and staff of minor league baseball clubs in cities throughout the midwest.

Certainly this book would not have been possible without the cooperation of two groups in particular. Those members of the board of directors of Waterloo Professional Baseball, Inc., who do not appear in the book but deserve formal recognition are: Rich Blumeyer, Lyle Buhr, Fred Hahn, Patty Huffman, Fred Kezar. Likewise, those players on the Waterloo Diamonds who do not appear in the book but deserve formal recognition are: Jared Baker, Chris Benhardt, Tim Goins, Larry Hawks, Jeff Huber, Ryan Ivie, Tom Martin, Rusty Silcox.

In addition, these individuals each merit mention for their generous cooperation: Rose Angel, Dave Austin, David L. Backmann, Linda Baker, Steve Batterson, John Baxter, A. Craig Bemson, Michelle Boswell, Jay Brazeau, Randy Brown, Kathy Buhr, Patrick Daly, Rich Fanning, David Fisher, Andy Graykowski, Tonya Harmel, Bob Heaton, Dr. James Kenyon, Pat Kinney, Wally Krouse, Scott Krusinski, Bill Kuehn, Bill Larsen, Jim Lawrence, M. Mark, Paul Marshall, Jim Maxwell, Bill McKee, Jeffrey Miller, Todd Natenberg, Mike Nelson, Bob Neymeyer, Susan Otolski, Dan Pawlak, Curt Rallo, Don Richards, Jack Roeder, Fred C. Rose, Milton Roth, George Saucer, Russ Smith, Marty Strasen, Mike Tatoian, Don Temeyer, Kevin Temperly, Phil Theobald, Gene

Thorne, John Tull, Dave Tyler, Larry Underwood, Dave Van Dee, Don Wade, Dave Walker, John Waller, John Wendel, Fred White, and Richard White.

Among written sources, several were useful in particular areas of research: for the history of the minor leagues, *The Minors,* by Neil J. Sullivan (St. Martin's Press, 1990); for the history of Waterloo, *Waterloo: Factory City of Iowa,* by Barbara Beving Long (Historic Preservation Commission, City of Waterloo, 1986) and *Cities on the Cedar,* by Glenda Riley (Mid-Prairie Books, 1988); and for the history of the minor leagues in Waterloo, *A Love Affair with the Minor Leagues,* by Steven Maravetz (a paper submitted to the English Department at the University of Northern Iowa, 1977). In addition to those sources cited in the book, the following deserve formal acknowledgment: Harvey Frommer's *Primitive Baseball* (Atheneum, 1988); Joel Garreau's *Edge City: Life on the New Frontier* (Doubleday, 1991); David Gebhard and Gerald Mansheim's *Buildings of Iowa* (Oxford University Press, 1993); Bill James's *The Bill James Historical Baseball Abstract* (Villard Books, 1986); Arthur T. Johnson's *Minor League Baseball and Local Economic Development* (University of Illinois Press, 1993); the National Association of Professional Baseball Leagues' (Robert Finch, L. H. Addington, and Ben M. Morgan, editors) *The Story of Minor League Baseball* (The Stoneman Press, 1952); Jack Sands and Peter Gammons's *Coming Apart at the Seams* (Macmillan Publishing Company, 1993); Neil J. Sullivan's *The Diamond Revolution* (St. Martin's Press, 1992); Loren Thomas's *T Remembers* (Spectrum House U.S.A., 1986); James V. Young and Arthur F. McClure's *Remembering Their Glory* (A. S. Barnes and Company, 1977); Andrew Zimbalist's *Baseball and Billions* (Basic Books, 1992). Numerous articles in *Baseball America, The Des Moines Register, USA Today Baseball Weekly,* and, especially, *The Waterloo Courier* were invaluable.

For their expert editorial advice, I thank Adam Gopnik, Jesse Green, James Ledbetter, and Stacy Schiff.

George Witte, this book's editor, deserves special thanks for his early grasp of the book's scope and for his subsequent guidance and patience. Henry Dunow, my agent, performed far beyond the call of duty, and for that I feel particularly fortunate and especially grateful. Finally, there would be no book if it weren't for Bryan

Oettel, a friend and editor who, having listened to my descriptions of attending professional baseball games in Iowa in the early 1980s, called one day and asked if I'd ever given any thought to writing about minor league baseball in the midwest.

I

MEET THE DIAMONDS

WATERLOO—We are writing this to inform the people who were driving a vehicle on the right side of the street facing in front of our house who fired two bullets into our home on Dec. 30. One bullet went into the wall of the living room. Another went into a window of a bedroom also facing the street. The bullet crossed the room diagonally above the bed where a person was sleeping and into the wall directly 2 feet above the person's head.

The bullets were found, so there's proof of the type of gun that was used and the caliber of the bullets.

You committed a crime by shooting at our house and very nearly committed a murder.

What was the motive of this type of act on innocent people?

Mr. and Mrs. H. G. Allen
1717 Mitchell Ave.

—*Waterloo Courier,* Jan. 26, 1992

1

The Iowa sky, when its clear, will carry signs of the outside world: white vapor trails that trace the progress of planes on routes as true to the cardinal points of the compass as the roads below. On a good day they might number half a dozen or more at any one time—New York to Los Angeles, San Francisco to Chicago, Boston to Denver, Minneapolis to St. Louis, Los Angeles to New York—and although they rarely occasion any comment, their nearly constant companionship can't help serving as a reminder, however remote, of the area's physical remove. They punctuate the landscape. Vapor trails may be visible elsewhere, but they assume a greater prominence in a land where the eye will search the horizon for relief and, finding none, drift up.

Iowa soil is another matter. A geologist might look at it and count three distinct varieties: the black alluvial soil that fingers outward from the Mississippi and Missouri rivers along the state's eastern and western borders, as well as from their many tributaries; glacial drift soil, a clay, sand, and gravel combination that in most places is buried under a layer of black loam a foot or more thick; and loess soil, a mixture of clay, sand, and silt that is slightly lighter in color than the others, yet often no less fertile. An immigrant or explorer would have seen it and thought: Life. For here was some of the richest soil in the world. By an accident of geography, Iowa has lain in and under the paths of commerce—the trails cleared by the first westward settlers, the railroads that followed them, the highways and interstates and flight patterns that followed *them*—but the soil has also made this land a destination in itself. It excites the senses; it invites inspection, and a certain respect. The temptation is to take handfuls of so much satiny blackness and looseness, to sift it and squeeze it and breathe it, and then to put it back: to get out of its way, to give it as much room as it needs, setting aside a corner somewhere only for the occasional white house and red barn that will anchor a homestead, or the grain elevators and church steeples that will come to mark a town from a distance, or, intermittently but inescapably, the smoke-stacks and modest skyscrapers that pass in these parts for a city.

Waterloo in 1992 was one such city. For hundreds of miles in any direction, it was surrounded by farmland. Rivers, too, towns, roads, a few hills, some lakes—but farmland mostly, a gridwork of county roads and cropland that stretched right to the Waterloo city limits, and then inside them, where the square-mile–square perfection at last broke down. To a traveler, the isolation of Waterloo might have made its abrupt appearance on the prairie seem unlikely, but in fact it was to that isolation that the city owed its existence. As recently as the 1970s, it was common for area residents to claim, with a kind of perverse pride, and in the gentle accent of the region—a peculiar penned-in flatness—that here was "the largest city in the country not being served by a major interstate." By 1992, though, the attempts to reverse that isolation were everywhere evident—the massive concrete T-frames of the interstate extension that forever changed the landscape along the southern city limits, or the elevated highway, then still under con-struction, that city planners had deliberately routed right through the heart of town rather than around it, so that the outside world would have no choice but to wonder, if only in passing, what Waterloo might have to offer.

For more than a century, Waterloo had stood at the geographic if not the economic center of the northeastern quadrant of Iowa, its forces of commerce serving as the conduit between the eight million enveloping acres of farmland and the outside world. If those forces were fewer or less formidable or more prosaic now— if many of the downtown shops had shuttered for good or moved to the malls along the highway at either end of town, if factories had closed or drastically downsized, if the National Cattle Con-gress had altered its mission over the course of the century from an annual exhibition of livestock to a showcase for the latest in flail shredders, manure spreaders, and slurry pumps—those forces still existed in sufficient numbers and exerted enough influence to lend Waterloo considerable regional majesty. Waterloo—accent on the final syllable, and often followed in local conversation by "Iowa," as in "this little town of Waterloo, Iowa"—was still a city. The Waterloo area was home to one television station, ten radio stations, and one afternoon newspaper (a morning edition wouldn't reach first-shift workers before they left the house); it was host to three commercial rail carriers and several airlines for which the local airport served as a satellite to hubs in St. Louis, Minneapolis, and Chicago; and what Waterloo had to offer, among the cultural and recreational amenities that might come under the "Quality of Life" heading in a Chamber of Commerce economic development brochure, were eight museums, one symphony orchestra, a community theater, greyhound racing, semi-pro hockey, and, on a tract of parkland along the east bank of the river that divided Waterloo in two, in a corner lot defined by a railroad track on one side and a cemetery on the other, minor league baseball.

The 1992 season of Waterloo Professional Baseball, Inc., took shape in a room at one end of a cinder-block bunker under a concrete-and-steel grandstand. The hours the members of the front-office staff kept during the winter were business hours, and many of the tasks they performed were business tasks, but when they pulled their cars into the lot outside their place of employment under a crystalline nine A.M. sky, or locked the office door under cover of five o'clock darkness, where they were was a ballpark. It was almost too good to be true: the candy store after closing; the amusement park in the middle of the night; the ballpark in winter. During business hours they might busy themselves in this office with bookkeeping, invoicing, or preparing a budget, but at least twice a day they got to experience the ghostly thrill of drifting past shuttered concession stands, of rolling aside the chain-link gate at the entrance, of passing directly underneath the greeting on the back of the grandstand that read, in white letters on a field of blue,

MUNICIPAL STADIUM
HOME OF THE

"It's crunch time!" the assistant general manager for sales and marketing announced one day from a desk in a corner of this room. Jeff Nelson swiveled in his chair to face an unmoving back hunched over a desk in another corner of the room. "How much are you willing to accept?"

David Simpson, the general manager of the organization, hesitated. He was staring down at the paperwork he'd been filling out, his pen hovering perhaps half an inch off the page. "A thousand," he finally drawled.

The third man in the room piped up. Brian Pfaltzgraff was the assistant general manager for stadium operations, and he was designing the layout for the upcoming season's souvenir program on a computer that he'd rigged to the screen of a black-and-white television on his desktop. "Why don't we just put an ad in the paper?" he said, working the keyboard, watching the screen. " 'We're having a sale on our back cover, limited time only.' " The screen went blank. Pfaltzgraff stared at it a moment, then slapped his hand against the side of the set, and it blinked back. "Clapper TV," he said and resumed typing.

It was still winter by the calendar, but a scrawl on the erasable acrylic plate hanging over Nelson's desk was perhaps more to the point: "Opening Day 25 Days!!!" At the moment, a Monday afternoon in March, the three men were estimating that they had forty-eight hours to secure an advertiser for the back page of the upcoming season's souvenir program before the ball club would have to forgo the $1,200 it might otherwise collect. As crises go, this one hadn't yet reached the critical stage; it demanded immediate attention, and Nelson, whom Simpson had hired only six weeks earlier for the purpose of finding new advertisers, had been devoting his day to it, flipping through the yellow pages and cold-calling potential customers, his expansive salesman's rap filling the office: "Jeff Nelson here, Waterloo Diamonds! How are you? Super! Listen! . . . Yeppers! . . . Hey! I understand! . . . You bet!" But other concerns kept intruding, and in such close quarters, the front-office staff found them impossible to ignore.

The three desks faced three walls. A reception counter faced the fourth. The room measured twelve feet by twenty-one, and at the moment its other furnishings included: a sometimes functional photocopier; a fax machine that frequently jammed; a four-drawer metal filing cabinet; a number of cardboard boxes, on the floor and the reception counter and the floor under the reception counter, to handle the overflow from the filing cabinet; a wooden panel that, when open, functioned as the ball club's ticket window; another wooden panel that could function as the ball club's

second ticket window if the need ever arose; several overhead par-
ticleboard shelves buckling under manuals, rule books, and souvenir programs from other ball clubs; shipping crates of souvenirs
and merchandise that lately had been arriving daily by United Par-
cel Service; two space heaters; a pea-green shag rug that years of
overcrowding had matted as flat as Formica; a tangy mix of after-
shaves; the trilling of phones; the nonstop chatter of three men
doing their jobs. This afternoon, Pfaltzgraff called a volunteer
who was performing carpentry duties for the ballpark and asked if
the Sno-Cone booth and raffle box would be ready by opening
day. Simpson advised an applicant for the groundskeeper's job,
who had called offering to come out today and paint, that he
didn't want to start paying a groundskeeper two weeks before the
ballpark needed one. Nelson dunned a deadbeat advertiser who
still owed $1,500 from two seasons earlier. Before he made that
call, he announced to the office, "It's now been turned over to Jeff
Nelson Collections. That's why I'm going to leave the message,
'Jeff Nelson *representing* Waterloo Baseball.' " When he was
done with that call, he announced, "I love my job!" Then Nelson
got up from his desk, opened the Dutch door that led into the
adjoining room—the concession stand that occupied the rest of
the cinder-block bunker under the grandstand—and disappeared.
When he returned a couple of minutes later, he had changed out of
his gray pin-striped double-breasted suit into a pink T-shirt, a pair
of paint-splashed jeans, and an ESPN gimme cap. "If you need
me," he announced, waving a paintbrush and heading around the
counter toward the door to the concourse, "I'm going to be playing Bob Vila out here."

Business hours were ending. At 5:00 P.M., Nelson positioned a
ladder against one of the girders in the concourse under the grandstand, balancing a paint tray in one hand and a brush in the other,
and started climbing. Like many businesses, baseball was seasonal. The carnival atmosphere at a ballpark on a humid midsummer evening—the giveaways at the gate, the hot dogs and beer,
the between-innings contests, the postgame fireworks—depended
on the foresight of the front-office staff at a time of year when
home plate might well be invisible under a fresh fall of snow. That
was true at the major-league level as well, but in the minors the
division of responsibilities was pronounced: Roughly, the respon-

sibility for what happened on the field (players, uniforms, bats, balls) belonged to the major league affiliate with which the ball club had signed a Player Development Contract, in this case the San Diego Padres; what happened off the field (stadium staff, concessions, the playing facility itself) belonged to the minor league franchise, in this case Waterloo Professional Baseball, Inc. But there was a third entity, too, a name that came to encompass both ends of the operation, the team on the field as well as the behind-the-scenes personnel, and that name in this case was the Waterloo Diamonds.

In the hierarchy of minor league baseball, the Waterloo Diamonds occupied a position rather nearer the lowest rung than the highest. The Diamonds belonged to the Midwest League, a fourteen-team Class-A division that spanned Iowa, Wisconsin, Illinois, and Indiana, and that was one of nineteen minor leagues comprising the National Association of Professional Baseball Leagues. Above Class A, in ascending order of classification, were Class A-Advanced, Class AA and Class AAA. Below it were only Short Season A and Rookie, neither of which started playing until June. Still, it was professional baseball, a fraternity whose exclusivity was perhaps best appreciated by the people who belonged to it in any capacity. For four years, Nelson had worked as an umpire in professional baseball, advancing, just as the players do, from the lowest level upward. He'd stalled, however, at the Midwest League—just as players do—and after last season, he'd received his release. He'd headed home to Salt Lake City and secured a front-office position with the local pro hockey club, but he found he couldn't let go of baseball; during the off-season he'd called the president of the Midwest League, a friend from his umpiring days, and asked if he'd heard of any openings. He had: Waterloo. Nelson knew Waterloo well; he remembered the time last year that he'd complained to the general manager, a soft-spoken guy from Kentucky, about the airlessness inside the umpires' dressing room, and then he'd come to work the next day and found a window fan waiting. Despite Nelson's occasional grousing—"Hey," he'd tell friends on the phone back in Salt Lake City, "it could be worse. I could be in some Appalachian League town where the one promotion a month is Hard Liquor and Handgun Night"—he was, in fact, grateful to be back. It was Nelson who had hung up the erasable acrylic plate when he'd arrived here at the start of February and who dutifully updated it every morning, though as the number preceding "Days!!!" kept dropping, the three exclamations he'd originally appended in a burst of enthusiasm and anticipation had started to acquire a slightly hysterical cast.

So here he was, after the close of business for the day, painting a girder royal blue. At this level of the minors, it was understood, everybody did anything: whatever it took, and no exceptions. But that's why he was here—to learn every aspect of a professional baseball organization. Nelson painted, and he kept painting, climbing down, refilling his tray, climbing up, painting, until nine that evening, when a storm broke, and arcs of lightning the likes of which he'd never seen chased one another across the broad and black midwestern sky.

The next morning, Nelson didn't have any new thoughts for the back page of the souvenir program, but he did have an idea for a promotional gimmick. He'd been thinking that there must be something he could do to publicize Waterloo's traditional rivalry with the Cedar Rapids Reds, seventy miles to the south. What was pure Iowa? Cornfields? *Field of Dreams?* The movie had been shot just sixty miles east of here down U.S. 20; the ball field itself was still intact, a shrine of sorts that most everyone who came out to this ballpark had visited at least once. What were those sayings from that movie? "If you build it, they will come." "Is this Heaven? No, it's Iowa." That one was promising. That one was everywhere in this part of the world: T-shirts, bumper stickers, gimme caps. But then Nelson had it. It was so simple, it was perfect, if he said so himself: pigs. He picked up the phone and called the Cedar Rapids front office and made the following proposition to the GM and assistant GM there, both acquaintances from his umpiring days: that the front-office staff of the losing ball club in the season series of fourteen games between the two teams shall appear before a game in the opposing team's park and kiss a pig.

A pause. "Okay," he heard. "It's a bet."

Nelson slammed down the phone and announced, "I love it! I love it! This is what makes minor league baseball great!"

It wasn't until the following morning, two days after he and Simpson and Pfaltzgraff had agreed that emergency measures were necessary, that inspiration struck. Nelson remembered a phone conversation the previous week with a representative from Ferrara Pan candies, who said he advertised only with ball clubs that sold his line of products, which Waterloo didn't—*yet*, Nelson thought now. Nelson found the salesman's business card, reached for the phone, and made the quickest sale of his young career.

Nelson announced that this deserved a celebration, and he disappeared through the Dutch door into the concessions area. When he returned to the office, he was holding a freshly heated brat in a bun. He asked Pfaltzgraff if there were any mustard packets in the office and, while Pfaltzgraff rummaged among the file cards and paper clips and staple centipedes in his desk drawer, Nelson stood in the center of the office and recounted the sale.

"He goes, 'Any full-page color?' I go, 'They're all gone but the back page.' 'How much?' 'A thousand dollars.' 'Done.' Ha!" Then he instructed Pfaltzgraff to call the Ferrara Pan distributor in Rock Island, Illinois, and start ordering Lemonheads.

Simpson had been listening to all this from his desk, nodding his head. Now he said, softly, "You could have gotten the twelve hundred."

Nelson turned and stared, sickly, then saw that Simpson was trying to hide a smile.

"*Fifteen* hundred," Simpson drawled.

Nelson broke back into a grin and said, "Hey, you want the page? Six thousand dollars!" He laughed heartily.

Pfaltzgraff waited for him to come up for air, then asked if he'd accept a yellow Magic Marker instead of mustard.

Nelson started laughing heartily again, then stopped, as if struck by a vision, or a coronary. He dropped into his chair and called the manager of the local Bonanza franchise and for $250 offered a space on the scorecard insert that would go into every souvenir program all season long. He hung up.

"In . . . the . . . bag!" He high-fived Simpson. Then he announced that in the past ten minutes he'd made $125 in commissions. Then he took a generous bite of his brat.

"Do you have renewed faith in me now?" he said to Simpson.

"No," said Simpson, "I never had faith in you."

Nelson threw his head back and laughed heartily.

A short while later, the office received a visit from a traveling salesman. He introduced himself as Dean Himelick, account manager for Midwest Embroidery in South Bend, Indiana, and he brought from his car trunk a collapsible metal clothing rack that, when unfolded and strung with samples of shirts and sweatshirts and T-shirts, reached the width and length of the remaining floor space, from Pfaltzgraff's desk to the photocopier, from the front counter to the swivel chairs where Nelson and Simpson sat, appraising the merchandise. While Himelick delivered his pitch, Nelson made low, approving noises. Simpson sat in silence. When he was done, Himelick paused and said, "Come on, don't spoil my perfect record. You're my third stop of the day, and I did a little business with all of you."

Nelson looked to Simpson. Nelson raised his eyebrows, bared his teeth in a mockery of a winning grin, mouthed the word, "Please." Simpson didn't look at Nelson. Instead, he hesitated a long time before delivering his verdict: No. The product, he said, wasn't right for this market. Then, with hardly a hitch of a shoulder, he turned back to his desk and resumed his paperwork. While Himelick dismantled the rack, Nelson continued talking to him, assuring him that the rejection was no reflection on the quality of the merchandise, and that he himself would have approved the purchase, if it were within his authority. The moment Himelick had squeezed his metal tubes and merchandise out the door, Nelson dropped to his knees in the space formerly occupied by the samples rack.

"Pleeease!" he said. "It's only six for one hundred seventy-five dollars!"

"You give me one hundred seventy-five dollars right now," Simpson said, not looking up, "I'll do it."

"But you'll make your money back!"

"And who's going to buy?"

Nelson raised his hand. With his other hand he thumped his thumb against his chest. He adopted his pleading grin again.

Simpson glanced up. He blinked. "Who else?" he said, looking back down.

Nelson dropped his hands to his sides in a pantomime of exasperation and got to his feet. "You won't *know,*" he said, "until April eleventh"—the date of the home opener.

"If they're not going to buy a twenty-dollar item," Simpson

said, speaking evenly, "they're not going to buy a fifty-dollar
item."

"You're wrong," snapped Nelson. "Apples and oranges. This is
a quality item. Somebody like me isn't going to buy a twenty-
dollar shirt because I know it can't be good quality. But I *will*
spend fifty dollars for a quality item."

"But you gotta remember." Now Simpson laid down his pen.
He turned from his desk and faced Nelson fully. The deliberate-
ness of his manner suggested that he was about to impart an important lesson, and Nelson drew back. For nearly two months,
Nelson had been working in this office, and while his enthusiasm
was evident, and his salesmanship laudable, it was Simpson who
had spent a full season here, who had talked to the advertisers and
sat among the fans and figured out a way to make a profit for this
ball club during a year it just as easily could have gone out of
business, who had lived through two winters now in Waterloo,
Iowa.

"This is a blue-collar town," he said to Nelson. "You don't *git*
the fifty-dollar consumer here."

Everyone over a certain age in Waterloo and throughout much of
northeast Iowa had seemingly the same memory of what the city
used to be. Again and again they would relate to one another the
same story in much the same words: how the Fourth Street bridge
used to choke with traffic; how lines of cars would stretch in either
direction from the Cedar River, block upon block, up and down
Fourth Street; how a trip downtown would involve parking the
car some ways away and then walking a great distance; how the
corner of East Fourth and Sycamore saw more traffic, foot or
auto, than any intersection for perhaps a hundred miles in any
direction; how no visit downtown was complete without a stop at
Black's, the famous department store at that famous intersection;
how no visit to Black's was complete without a stop at the famous
tearoom on the top floor; how no day in downtown Waterloo was
complete without an evening at one of the city's many movie pal-
aces, most likely the Paramount, an elaborate and fanciful river-
side structure where architectural flourishes along the walls and
on the ceiling of the auditorium conspired to create the illusion of
an evening under a Moorish sky, right down to the stars, which

twinkled. It was a prosperous time. In those days, they'd say, the factories never closed; shift followed shift, around the clock, and bowling leagues ran right through the night. "Back then," they'd say, "this town *smoked*."

In July 1845 a family from Illinois settled along the Cedar River, and forever after local schoolchildren had learned to think of Mary Melrose Hanna as the "Mother of Waterloo." The area had been acquired by the United States government in 1804 as part of the Louisiana Purchase, and Daniel Boone's son, among other explorers and pioneers, had camped along the Cedar River in the 1830s, sending word back east about the region's natural beauty and economic potential, but the future site of Waterloo didn't have a permanent settlement until Mary Hanna arrived on the Cedar's eastern shore, surveyed the gentle hills across the river, and declared to her husband, two children, and brother, "This is the place—we shall stay here." The next day, she changed her mind, deciding that, in fact, she might prefer the other, western side of the river, and in the short history of Waterloo it has ever been thus.

The Cedar divided Waterloo from the start in a fashion both literal and symbolic. In the era before car travel and a dependable bridge could make each side equally accessible to the other, a rivalry developed that took the form of a kind of civic sibling squabbling. Each side wanted whatever the other side got: parks, government buildings, transportation systems. When the philanthropy established by Pittsburgh steel magnate Andrew Carnegie to bestow public libraries on towns across the country approached Waterloo, Waterloo wanted two, and for a time the Solomons of the city even considered splitting the difference and building one big library on a bridge over the river, but in the end the Carnegie representatives wearied of the bickering, threw $40,000 at the city (this was in 1904), and said, in effect, do with it what you will. Waterloo built two libraries.

The rivalry between east and west in Waterloo, however, also arose out of a deeper, though perhaps no less natural, division. From the start, the area east of the river and beyond downtown was abandoned, by those downtown and west of the river, to the less affluent. This settlement pattern wasn't exceptional in cities; summer winds tend to rise out of the south and west, transforming neighborhoods to the north and east into repositories for an entire area's airborne industrial waste. The dividing line in Waterloo became even more conspicuous in 1911, when the Illinois Central Railroad offered free transportation to African-Americans from Mississippi who were willing to work up North; only on their arrival did the new employees discover that they would be functioning here as de facto strikebreakers. Not surprisingly, they stayed close to the tracks, which were on the east side of town. The river's role as arbiter wasn't absolute; the boundaries sometimes blurred; a type of residence even developed that captured the dichotomy: the so-called double house, a two-family unit owned by a white-collar family, which lived on one side and rented to a blue-collar family on the other. Still, the geographical division held generally true enough that it became, for the people of Waterloo, a truism—even though all a river could do, really, was make manifest the class divisions already inherent in a city, which in the case of Waterloo were appreciable.

For few cities embraced industrialization with the zealotry of Waterloo. Local civic leaders of the late nineteenth century perceived manufacturing to be Waterloo's chance at a prosperity, and even a possible magnificence, that might endure long into the next century. Some industries they courted from out of town, some came to them unbidden, and others arose out of local ingenuity and resourcefulness in order to meet the needs of a booming community. By the 1920s Waterloo had succeeded in reinventing itself from a fairly typical, somewhat sleepy county seat into a manufacturing center with a population of 36,000 and industrial plants numbering more than 160. The city acquired the amenities and necessities commensurate with its newfound status: office buildings and hotels eight and ten stories high; a railway system extensive enough to accommodate seventy-one passenger trains alone in and out of town every day; department stores that offered the most elaborate array of fineries between here and Chicago, though none so elaborate or fine as that at James Black's Dry Goods Store; and an annual National Cattle Congress—a kind of county fair to end all county fairs that reinforced Waterloo's stature as a national headquarters for the dairy industry. Other Iowa cities were emerging at the same time as agricultural-industrial centers—Cedar Rapids, Fort Dodge, Ottumwa, Sioux City—but none to match Waterloo's rate of growth. Waterloo boosters laid claim, with ample justification, to the slogan "The Factory City of Iowa."

At the height of its powers—a period that began after the Depression and World War II had claimed all but the fittest of economic enterprises, and that lasted roughly until the late 1970s—Waterloo drew its identity from two industries in particular. Both were agricultural, of course, and both had arisen during the fin de siècle fever of expansionism. Following an aggressive recruitment campaign by local civic leaders, Rath Packing (as well as the wealthy Rath family) had relocated to Waterloo in 1891 after fire destroyed the company's headquarters in Dubuque, Iowa. That same decade, a local inventor started the Waterloo Gasoline Traction Company, which eventually ended up manufacturing the immensely successful "Waterloo Boy" tractor and, in 1918, being acquired by the John Deere Company of Moline, Illinois. John Deere, at that time already a major presence in farm equipment production throughout the Midwest for more than three-quarters of a century, kept expanding the Waterloo facility until it had become the largest of the fourteen in the Deere system. There were other successful businesses—Warren Transport, a trucking firm and locally owned, Chamberlain Manufacturing, a machine-parts manufacturer and locally owned, Hoxie Fruit Company, a canning firm and locally owned—scattering over the landscape around Waterloo proper and into the outlying communities. But by midcentury it would have been no exaggeration to say that the slaughterhouse and the tractor factory—Rath and Deere, Deere and Rath, and said in a single breath—accounted for the local economy, period.

Half a mile down the Cedar River from downtown, hugging the eastern shore, Rath Packing's 150 buildings sprawled across 40 acres. Half a mile upriver from downtown, hard by the west bank, John Deere's tractor works' 2.5 million square feet of factory devoured 137 acres. Foundries fired the night sky like a false dawn, smokestacks pounded dusky clouds across the noon-whistle sun, and when the wind was out of the south or west and you could see the August heat rising off the sidewalks of Fourth Street, what you were seeing were remnants of blood and grease, a mixture that created a not-altogether-unpleasant odor—heady, intoxicating

even—when you were trying to decide whether to shop at J. C.
Penney, Montgomery Ward, or Sears before heading over to
Black's, where from behind either the marble railing on the mez-
zanine level that overlooked the main shopping floor or the
arched windows of the tearoom that overlooked the entire city,
you would observe the habits and customs of your fellow citizens,
and you stopped to consider that this was the smell of success.

The formula for this success was simple: "Corn for steel." In
practice it was more complex than that, and it involved many variations, but in essence this equation was the foundation of whatever prosperity Waterloo enjoyed during the twentieth century.
The agricultural resources that left Waterloo by rail returned by
rail as the raw materials that would become the farm implements
that would help bring more agricultural resources to market. It
was a perfect circle—farm to city to world to city to farm—and a
model of self-sufficiency, and it was a formula that locals long
afterward repeated with a respect bordering on disbelief, an air of
Imagine that! as if in awe that once something so pure could have
existed here, or anywhere: "Corn for steel."

This self-sufficiency, however, also bred insularity. For a quarter of a century, voters in the northeast corner of the state kept
returning to Congress a Waterloo broadcaster who embodied a
local brand of grass-roots populism that would have been impossible without a thriving local economy. His was a no-nonsense
approach to taxation: the less, the better—and no pork. But the
practical effect was that when the opportunity arose for his fellow
members of Congress to pass out packages of federal largesse, the
Third District of Iowa went wanting, especially in highway development. Not that the locals necessarily minded—not as long as
the trains full of corn and steel kept crossing paths in the East Side
switching yards. Isolated from the rest of the world by design as
much as default, Waterloo came to assume the role of Iowa's necessary evil, the incarnation of everything that the surrounding
countryside was not: a city of factories; a city of Negroes; a city.

Certainly some of the indignities that Waterloo suffered were
peculiarly urban. Long and even violent lockouts and labor strikes
became part of the city's economic rhythm, as contracts at Rath,
Deere and other manufacturing plants came up for renewal every
few years. Racial tension sparked, flared, burned, even receiving

national attention in a 1967 *Wall Street Journal* article headlined "Why Would Negroes Riot in Waterloo?" (The answers: segregation in housing, education, and employment.) Downtown declined, as a host of national chains and local shops flocked to the controlled-climate, parking-lot convenience of the new malls at the city's outskirts. Black's lingered in its stately old headquarters at Fourth and Sycamore, was sold to an out-of-state interest, changed names, went out of business. Hoxie Fruit, Chamberlain Manufacturing, Warren Transport—many of the city's most familiar names—all sold to outside interests.

Other old manufacturing and agricultural cities across the country were enduring similar traumas at the same time, but Waterloo's dependence on two industries left it especially vulnerable. Deere, after expanding extensively in the Waterloo area throughout the 1970s, building several plants and adding employees until the payroll reached 16,000, laid off nearly 10,000 workers. Rath, which in its heyday had a payroll of 7,000, cut back to 2,500 employees, who, in the latest of numerous last-ditch efforts to save the company, ended up owning it as it went out of business. Waterloo scrambled to reverse its earlier insularity, plowing tax money into roads that would either put the city back on the map of interstate commerce or, as skeptics feared, provide a faster route out of town.

The exodus was singular. During the 1980s, the population of Waterloo proper dropped from 75,985 to 66,467—in terms of percentage loss of a city's population, the thirteenth worst in the country. But if a city's population is said to include all the people in the outlying area who call it home—the suburbs of Cedar Falls and Hudson, the small towns of Finchford and Dunkerton, the six streets of Dewar and the rural routes and, especially, the family farms that once checkerboarded the landscape—then Waterloo came in dead last. Waterloo, Iowa, had turned into one of those cities where the local joke went, *Will the last person to leave please turn out the lights?*

What went wrong depended on who was doing the blaming. For decades Waterloo had operated under a tacit understanding. The laborers on the vertical kill at Rath or the assembly line at Deere might have been able to shut the city down from time to time through the brute force of their greater number, but the real

power in Waterloo had rested with the neighbors, business partners, country-club confederates, and tireless civic boosters who
resided in the spacious houses beyond the long lawns behind the
ancient trees lining Prospect Boulevard, on the city's Southwest
Side. Still, there would have been as much sense in the majority
trying to recast the natural order of things as there had been in the
suggestion somebody once made to reroute the Cedar around the
city and fill the dry riverbed with railroad tracks. In the privacy of
their downtown offices, community leaders left little doubt as to
who they held responsible for Waterloo's circumstances ("What's
changed is that instead of people having nineteen dollars-an-hour
jobs and buying boats and campers, they have nine dollars-an-
hour jobs and they're not buying boats and campers. This area
used to have the highest percentage of boat owners in the state of
Iowa—but no lakes. All that's gone is that luxury. Boats!" and
"My father ran the beef operation at Rath. He ran it. He was *it*.
And let me tell you I saw reports that that union was the highest in
pay and the lowest in productivity of any beef union. The worst of
both worlds!"), while the rank and file learned to pride themselves
on their proficiency at packing the chamber and hallways and
front lawn of City Hall whenever the matter of taxes appeared on
the agenda ("There are always chronic complainers, but Waterloo
seems to have had more of them. I don't know why. And it's gotten a lot worse!" and "You wouldn't guess it by the number of
voters at the polls, but the ones who do get involved are highly
vocal—*very* highly vocal. Waterloo is a sociologist's dream. It's a
little bit of Americana!").

Fairly or not, by the 1991 mayoral election the three-term incumbent Bernie McKinley had come to embody in the minds of
many Waterloo voters "the Prospect Boulevard crowd." He and
his wife of more than thirty years didn't in fact live on Prospect
Boulevard, but in an even more exclusive enclave, a community
consisting of one circular street ringing a private lake at the southern edge of the city; signs at the entrance to the development announced the names of the ten or so families residing therein, as
well as a warning to unauthorized vehicles to keep out. By contrast, his challenger in the 1991 mayoral race lived in a bungalow
on the opposite end of town, in a racially mixed Northeast Side
neighborhood where the front yards sported old appliances and

the back yards, boats. Al Manning, a third-shift bakery supervisor, was among those who made a habit of visiting City Hall on Monday nights, charging that Bernie McKinley and his seven-member City Council had lost touch with the needs of the people. "The mayor tries to tell people that they should be happy," Al Manning said, early in his campaign. "You know if you're happy or not."

Despite the presence of working farms well within the city limits; despite the county zoning code that in its first line set aside prime land (that which has a Corn Suitability Rating above 50 on a scale from 0 to 100) for "only agricultural uses or those uses incidental to agriculture"; despite the fact that in warm, dry weather, the topsoil circulating in the air over the countryside continued to filter the sunsets to spectacular, lingering effect, or that in cool, wet weather, the rain passing across the cropland continued to sweep the sweet-and-sour smell of manure and silage along the city streets—despite all the evidence that had always sufficed, it was becoming increasingly difficult for the people of Waterloo to summon the conviction that their city was one more farming community, a small town in all ways but size. In the *Courier,* the city's daily newspaper, drought and flood predictions shared space with coke and crack arrests. In the summer of 1991, arson visited more than a dozen downtown buildings and East Side houses, not all of them vacant. An arrest outside an East Side nightclub was attended by accusations of police brutality, then a riot. Students by the dozens at Waterloo High—East *and* West— were getting suspended for weapons possession. An elderly woman and her retarded brother were stabbed to death in their home. And, in one of those incidents that forever changes the way a community conceives of itself, gang recruits who were instructed as part of an initiation rite to drive across town and kill a white person, did: a twenty-four-year-old man out for an evening stroll with his fiancée, one block from her parents' house, on Prospect Boulevard.

Rather than fretting about what the city might want in the next century, Al Manning charged, the mayor should be trying to figure out what Waterloo needed now. Manning criticized the combination of higher taxes and cutbacks in essential services. He criticized the use of tax incentives to lure low-paying employers.

He criticized renovations at City Hall, decorative streetlights downtown, and the arrogance of a City Council that voted pay raises for itself and the mayor one month before the election. Then, during a radio debate one week before the election, he criticized the ongoing renovation of the baseball stadium. It was, he said, precisely the kind of expense the city could no longer afford. "We're spending over half a million dollars on improvements," the challenger said. "Is that something really needed at this time?"

"Baseball fans," the incumbent replied, "I hope you heard that."

"Over half a million dollars": It certainly sounded like a lot. Yet even if the amount were accurate, it still wouldn't be enough. What would, nobody knew.

For most of that winter, David Simpson had inhabited the front office at the ballpark alone, filling it with classical music from the radio, fielding phone calls, adjusting the setting on the space heaters. The winter had been mild, by Iowa standards: long sunless periods, more than a week at a stretch, of temperatures in the forties and a fog that wouldn't lift, punctuated only occasionally by the more predictable overnight foot of snow or sixty-below windchill. Simpson was more fortunate this winter than last, when unrelentingly low temperatures and the punishing prairie winds had forced him to evacuate the cinder-block insulation of the ballpark for a rented office downtown. There was no question that the conditions in Waterloo were primitive, even by the minimal standards of Class A professional baseball. When he was with the Fayetteville Generals, the front office had been located in a trailer, but at least it had partitions, and you never would have seen the general manager counting box office receipts in full view of the rest of the employees, as happened here every night. Still, he'd known what he was getting into when he accepted the job in Waterloo, and it was part of what had attracted him: the chance to make a minor league operation professional in more than name alone.

His arrival in Waterloo had coincided with a new Professional Baseball Agreement. In late 1990, the contract that governed every aspect of the relationship between the majors and the minors expired. In the end, the two sides renewed the agreement, but only after months of rancorous and fractious negotiations that built on decades of mutual resentments and that at times seemed to threaten the existence of the minors altogether. The result was a new PBA that radically restructured numerous financial arrangements between the majors and the minors, mostly at the minors' expense. At the Class A level, the new PBA would be costing each ball club at least $20,000 during the first season alone. For an organization such as Waterloo, where annual operating expenses ran about $300,000, such a substantial shift from one side of the ledger to the other could have proven fatal. Previously, the owners of the Diamonds, a group of fifteen Black Hawk County residents who ran the ball club more or less as a public service, had routinely put whatever money was left over at the end of the season back into the operation, but otherwise had contented themselves with breaking even. Now what the ball club needed, the owners decided, was a general manager who thought in terms of the bottom line.

David Simpson had wanted to be a stockbroker. He'd earned a bachelor's degree in political science at the University of Kentucky, but then he'd taken a stockbroker certification test, and he soon found work at a firm in Louisville, his hometown. In August 1984, he married; that same month, the stock market dipped. Simpson had been the most recent hire at the firm, and now it dawned on him that he could easily be the first out the door—just like that. It was not in his nature to take risks—even the simplest of questions could elicit a substantial pause while he considered all his options and, inevitably, selected the safest—yet the vocation he'd chosen was predicated on volatility. What had he been thinking? Whatever it was, the fluctuation in the Dow brought him back to his senses. The stock market, of course, more than recovered from whatever doldrums it might have experienced in that long-ago summer at the end of the first Reagan term, but by then Simpson had found another job, this time in the more pastoral field of baseball, with the Memphis Chicks. After three seasons in the front office there, he entertained an offer from Fayetteville, North Carolina, to become the assistant general manager there. It would represent a professional advancement, and yet how could he be sure that this was the job for him? After his interview in Fayetteville, he called his wife, Trish—six years his junior and, as most everyone who met the two of them couldn't help commenting, not as prone to circumspection as her husband—to ask what she thought he should do. "Take it! Take it! Take it!" she told him. Three years later, he was entertaining another offer in another city, this time to be the general manager in Waterloo. He met with several of the owners, and after his interview he'd gone back to his hotel room and called Trish and said that the board members had told him they wouldn't be making a decision until the middle of the following week, and that they were still seeing other candidates, some from the Midwest League. A half hour later, he called Trish back: The job was his—if he wanted it. Did he want it? The ball club was owned locally, which he liked, and he'd have a chance to start virtually from scratch, which was a challenge he could appreciate, but he had no guarantee that this was the opportunity that would work out best for him, and, besides, it was 70 degrees back home in Fayetteville, and there was snow on the ground here, and—

"Take it! Take it! Take it!"

In his first year in Waterloo, Simpson made money for the ball club. He managed to maintain revenues at the same level as the previous, pre-PBA season, while lowering expenses. Not everyone agreed with his methods—winnowing away free nights for customers, refusing to cut desperation deals with advertisers—but in the end it worked, somehow. Now Simpson would have to perform the same miracle again, only this time while overcoming a further obstacle: In 1992, according to the PBA, minor league franchises would have to tithe 5 percent of their first $200,000 in ticket revenues to Major League Baseball.

Even so, these financial headaches weren't the worst of it. The new PBA, for the first time, imposed uniform standards on the quality of the playing facilities themselves: lighting, clubhouses, field conditions, and so forth. In the past, all it took for a minor league facility to pass muster was the say-so of a major league parent, and sometimes not even that. Now, under the new PBA, each minor league ballpark would have to meet an extensive and highly rigorous series of structural requirements by April 1, 1994, or else—what? Nobody could say for sure; the situation had never arisen. The franchise would lose its Player Development Contract before the 1994 season? After the season? Would a show of good faith—blueprints in hand, pledges of funding—be enough? Or would every one of the hundreds of architectural and engineering details have to meet spec? In the year since he'd come to Waterloo, David Simpson had spent countless hours addressing precisely this topic. He and the president of the organization, Dan Yates, had attended numerous meetings with other Midwest League general managers and presidents. On other occasions, they'd conferred with representatives from other minor league teams in Iowa, and then traveled with them to Des Moines to meet with state legislators. They had endured numerous Park Board meetings; would endure more. (Then the following afternoon, Simpson would add one more *Courier* clipping to the bulletin board above his desk: "Park Officials Throw Heat at Baseball Board," "Park Board Says No to Diamonds' $75,000 Request.") And at each of these meetings the question inevitably arose: What did this new PBA mean, exactly? By the midpoint of the upcoming season, inspectors would be visiting every minor league ballpark in order to quantify precisely each facility's shortcomings. In the meantime, one of the few things that anyone familiar with both the demands of the new PBA and the state of Waterloo Municipal Stadium could say with any certainty was that the city's current commitment of $325,000 was, at best, only a beginning.

That winter, Waterloo Municipal Stadium was in the third year of a four-year renovation project. When the City Council, acting at Mayor McKinley's behest, and over the severe objections of the regular battery of City Hall critics, had entered into that agreement in 1989, the rationale was that the stadium improvements would satisfy the needs of the major leagues once and for all, or at least for the foreseeable future. But the following year, with the adoption of the new PBA, those requirements changed—and now, one of the mayor's most severe critics had himself become mayor.

The Honorable Al Manning mumbled. He'd taken the oath of office as the thirty-second mayor of Waterloo on January 2, 1992, and within the week Simpson and Yates paid him a courtesy call in his City Hall office. Manning wore a thick slash of a mustache across a pasty oval face, and when he spoke, he lowered his head and tucked his chin. He found public speaking painful, and he exhibited every indication that he considered private meetings, such as the one with the ball club's representatives, only slightly less pernicious a form of torture. He alternated nervous tics—a chronic clearing of the throat, a sometime half smile, the occasional cough into a clenched fist—while Simpson and Yates tried to explain, to the best of their understanding, the PBA deadline. The major leagues had changed the rules, they said. It wasn't their fault; they didn't even like the majors. But the fact was that if somebody didn't come up with the money for the improvements out at Waterloo Municipal Stadium—a city-owned facility, they reminded the mayor; a city-owned facility, moreover, that the landlord had neglected for more than four decades—then the city might well lose professional baseball. And could Waterloo really afford to lose a small business that brought $2.495 million into the city's economy every year?—and Simpson and Yates said they had the figures to back it up. For his part, the mayor tried to assure his visitors that he wasn't flatly "anti-baseball." He wasn't a fan of the sport, either, he said, or of sports in general, but he said that he certainly appreciated the value to the community of inexpensive family entertainment. Then he said, "These improvements are nice. For the players especially, and the fans in some regards. But"—he cleared his throat; he coughed—"can we really afford niceties when we're cutting back on necessities in other parts of the city?"

So there it was: their answer: no. The mayor was going to be true to his campaign rhetoric. If the ball club were to survive, it would have to seek money elsewhere—which didn't necessarily mean outside the city coffers. Just because this mayor wouldn't be helpful didn't mean that some branch of government couldn't find a way to invent a new source of revenue, or that the members of the City Council—who, after all, had run on an opposition slate—couldn't find a way to circumvent his wishes. Across the country, local governments were in effect bidding for the privilege of hosting minor league baseball; were bailing out old facilities with $2 million face-lifts; were building state-of-the-art stadiums for $6 million, $8 million, $10 million. In the Midwest League, Fort Wayne, Indiana, was doing it: building a ballpark, getting a ball club. In Iowa—Iowa!—Des Moines was doing it: rebuilding Sec Taylor Stadium from the ground up, keeping the Class AAA Iowa Cubs. It was nearly inconceivable to someone with Simpson's background in baseball that Waterloo couldn't come up with a measly half a million.

In the meantime, Simpson had a ball club to run. It wasn't his job to make the people of Waterloo appreciate what they already had. If they couldn't do that on their own—and if they wound up losing professional baseball from their community in the bargain—then so be it. He had his own future to worry about. And so he proceeded to prepare for the coming season with the same attention to fiscal responsibility he'd demonstrated the previous season, only more so. He attended the baseball Winter Meetings in Miami and placed thousands of dollars in orders for the souvenirs and promotional giveaways that were the lifeblood of any professional baseball organization; he signed up Captain Dynamite and his exploding "Coffin of Death" for a personal appearance on the night before the Fourth of July; he interviewed prospective employees for the upcoming season; he invested in the little improvements that he thought would streamline the operation and ultimately make it more profitable; he mapped out advertising schedules in the newspaper and on the radio; and when these tasks became too time-consuming, he hired an assistant.

It was a difficult balance to strike: the need to appear professional, the need to provide the kind of hokey entertainment that brought audiences out to the ballpark and kept them coming back, and the need to save money. He rejected a deal Nelson set up with the local cable company for a preseason show on public-access TV that would have cost the ball club nothing. ("How many people watch it? Ten?" "But that's ten people!" "But it's cheesy! And I don't want anything that's gonna look cheesy.") Then that same day he raised the idea of having a funny-nose-and-glasses giveaway—a thousand sets at 67 cents each, enough to outfit most customers, all employees, and even the umpires and managers during the exchange of lineups at home plate. ("It'd be *funny,*" he insisted, when Nelson and Pfaltzgraff didn't immediately respond.) The decision to hire an assistant itself had met with resistance from some of the ball club's owners, who saw only the certainty of the short-term expense and not the potential for long-term revenue—and who didn't seem to understand that there were franchises even at this lowly level of pro ball, even in the Midwest League, that routinely kept eight or ten full-time employees on the payroll, year-round. Waterloo, Simpson had known when he came here, wasn't that kind of club; but he still couldn't comprehend how anyone could expect a GM to run a professional operation without an assistant. ("I'm takin' a chance on you," he sometimes announced to Nelson, who sometimes answered, "I left a good job in Salt Lake City to come out to Waterloo, Iowa, for $1,000 a month, and *you're* taking a chance on *me?*") And every step of the way he had to ask himself: Was this it? Was this the expense that would prove to be his professional undoing? Was this pizza warmer, this mesh behind home plate, this hot-dog grill or reduction on the price of an ad or lumber for a Sno Cone booth going to make the difference between a profit and a loss?

In time, the preparations acquired a momentum, an inevitability, all their own. By late winter, the T-shirts and caps and pennants that Simpson had ordered in Miami, the squeeze bottles and canteens and seat cushions, the sunglasses and batting helmets and magnet schedules—the accessories of high summer—were arriving by the boxload. Pfaltzgraff tasted the six varieties of candy samples that Ferrara Pan sent to the office and decreed that the ballpark would stock Jaw Breakers, A&W Root Beer Candy, Atomic Fire Balls with the RED HOT Flavor!, Gummi Baby Bears, and, of course, Lemonheads, but not Boston Baked Beans. Nelson negotiated a straight trade, facsimile machine for fence sign: a $2,400 fax for $250 worth of paint. Simpson hired a groundskeeper, fired him for hanging around the office chewing the fat, hired another. Then he hired an assistant groundskeeper, too. He also hired an intern and a full crew of concessionaires and a ticket seller and a ticket taker—about three dozen employees in all. DIAMONDS filled the blank following HOME OF THE.

Then, one night, they tested the new lights. The city's $325,000 worth of improvements included a set of $120,000 lights for the ballpark. Fortunately, when the city parks director was ordering the lights, he had insisted that the grade of lighting surpass the major-league standards then in effect; as a result, the lights met the standards *now* in effect. Without a doubt, the lights were the one part of the PBA inspection that the ballpark was going to pass with flying colors. It was Bill Boesen, one of the ball club's owners, and a retired electrician and former steward of the International Brotherhood of Electrical Workers, who had arranged for some of his friends from Local 288 to volunteer to help city crews install the lights in the off-season, and now it was Boesen who performed the honor of flipping the switch in the groundskeeper's cage under the first-base bleachers. The union volunteers, the city crew, and the ball club's representatives then gathered in the infield to stare skyward and wait for the bulbs to burn to life. Slowly they glowed. It took about twenty minutes for the lamps to fire up to full capacity, but nobody minded waiting. The sudden yet gradual brightness was harsh and artificial, but it seemed to warm the men against the night chill, to ward off the dew. In this light, the grass looked greener, healthier, than during daylight; the stands cleaner; the infield dirt purer. Suddenly spring seemed feasible, and baseball a distinct possibility. At one point Nelson proclaimed that he'd seen every ballpark in the Midwest League, and these lights were the best by far. But for the most part everybody simply stood on the ground around where second base soon would be, squinted up, and went, "Wow."

Second base itself was problematic. Three days before the players and coaching staff were to show up at the ballpark, fully expecting a playable ball field, the two members of the grounds crew were still trying to locate the bases. They ransacked the cranny behind the souvenir stand; they rummaged among the mounds of spare dirt under the bleachers; they foraged through every storage area in the concession stands and locker rooms and front office, finally narrowing their search to one locked crate, which not even Brian Pfaltzgraff, eight-year employee and keeper of ancient keys, could open. So they sought out the president of the ball club, who was in the visitors' clubhouse using a razor blade to scrape the crud off the sink. Dan Yates, thin, unfailingly courteous, and attired in a crisp shirt and creased slacks despite his chore—already the new employees had taken to calling him "Rowdy" Yates—listened patiently to their story. Then he told them that if they'd looked everywhere and they couldn't find the bases, and the only place they hadn't looked was one last box, then he'd have to say the bases were in that box. Break the lock, he commanded, and so they did, and there they were: white, square, pristine pillows of cloth, touching softly, like hibernating critters. The groundskeepers carried the bases into the daylight. They succeeded in securing first and third without incident, but when they got to second they couldn't find the anchor—the metal latch in the ground that kept the base in place. They dug a small hole where they thought second should be: still no anchor. Again they eyeballed home, first, and third, aligned themselves accordingly, and dug. Again, no anchor. Now Nelson sauntered out to help them eyeball, align, dig. Eventually the search party located the anchor—more than a foot from where they'd thought it would be—but not before they'd excavated a hole as wide and as deep as a shallow grave.

At that moment, the product around which all these preparations would coalesce and through which, with luck and timing, they'd pay off—the team—was some 1,500 miles away, in Yuma, Arizona, at the San Diego Padres spring training camp. For Simpson, and for general managers of minor league franchises everywhere, the impending arrival of the players precipitated one final financial concern before the start of the season. Like other seasonal businesses, baseball tended to create a cash-flow problem: money going out for inventory and payroll, nothing coming in until the season hit. Now, when this situation was at its most precarious, the ball club suddenly had to commit itself to more than $1,000 for the team's arrival: the bus transportation from the airport in Cedar Rapids, 70 miles south of Waterloo, and the hotel rooms for two nights, and the three vans that the players would use their first two days in town while they looked for housing. The major league affiliate would pay back the money—promptly, perhaps, or not, in which case the governing body of the minor leagues would have to intervene, as was the case with San Diego the winter that Simpson arrived—but in the meantime the minor league club was providing what amounted to a short-term loan at no interest. And all this at a time when the majors were contending, through the strong-arm tactics of the PBA, that they wanted more responsibility for and authority over the minors. Simpson would not have been alone among minor league operators in daydreaming about how great this business would be, if only it weren't for the baseball teams.

So incidental were the players even at this late date in the preseason that Simpson hadn't bothered even to call Yuma for the roster. After all, it wasn't an allegiance to particular players that would generate revenue at the box office. A team's turnover from season to season, or even within a season—what with players getting promoted, if they were lucky and talented, or retiring at the age of twenty-one, if they weren't—guaranteed that fans would be able to follow a favorite player just long enough to be able to say, one day, maybe, that they knew him when. Instead, what would generate revenue was something even less tangible than talent: a happy confluence of front-office ingenuity and merchant support and fan spirit; that potentially lucrative point on the graph of commercial ventures where civic pride intersects the National Pastime.

On Sunday, April 4, in the middle of the afternoon, a young woman wearing a sundress walked into the front office, introduced herself as the wife of a player, and said that she and her mother had just driven up from Oklahoma in anticipation of her husband's arrival. In this manner, those members of the ball-club staff who cared learned for the first time the name of a player on this year's Waterloo Diamonds: pitcher Joe Waldron, 10–6 with a 3.73 ERA and a 141/147.1 strikeouts-to-innings ratio at Charleston, South Carolina, the previous season—as they ascertained from the San Diego Padres media guide the moment Jackie Waldron left the office. The players would be flying into Cedar Rapids at 11:30 that night, and Nelson wondered aloud whether Robbie Beckett, a first-round draft choice in 1990 and a pitcher with a notorious control problem, would be among them.

"We need somebody to play 'Wild Thing' for," Pfaltzgraff said. Then he lamented that nobody would be there to greet the players at the gate. "We'd have met them ourselves," he said to Nelson, "if they were landing during daylight."

"What did we do last year?" Nelson said.

He turned to Pfaltzgraff. Pfaltzgraff turned to Simpson. Simpson hesitated.

"They all drove up," Simpson finally said. "We didn't have to worry about it."

"So what do we do now?" Nelson said. "Rent vans and get reimbursed?"

This time Simpson didn't hesitate. "Reimbursement, *bullshit*," he said.

*

Several weeks before the start of the season, Nelson accepted a dinner invitation at the home of Dan Yates. The meeting was more than a formality, a courtesy extended by an organization's president to the newest member of the executive staff. Yates recognized in Nelson the kind of newcomer's enthusiasm that might prove contagious. He also suspected that he could impress on Nelson the urgency of the situation. Over the course of the evening, the two men arrived at the idea of having a "Meet the Diamonds" event—an informal gathering a couple of days before the start of the season where the media and fans could mingle with the members of the team. Nelson immediately replied that he'd seen the concept in action. Each of his three seasons as an umpire in the Midwest League, he'd worked Opening Day in Peoria, and although he'd never attended any of the "Meet the Chiefs" nights, he'd arrived in town just in time to read the favorable coverage of the event in the *Journal-Star*. Yates said that here in Waterloo the club used to host a "Meet the Indians" night, back when the franchise's affiliation was with Cleveland, and it had always generated a fair amount of fan interest and media attention. This year, though, such an event could serve a third purpose: as a fundraiser. Even if the modest donations that the club collected at the door wound up covering nothing but the evening's expenses, the fact of the event would illustrate to the city that the ball club took seriously its commitment to its nonprofit arm, the Waterloo Diamonds Baseball Association.

The next morning, Nelson informed Simpson that the club would be sponsoring a "Meet the Diamonds" promotion.

"Well," said Simpson, "that's an expense."

Nelson drew a breath heavy enough that Simpson was sure to hear it. He understood how from Simpson's point of view it might appear that Yates and Nelson, his superior and his subordinate, had usurped his contractual right to "determine and schedule all promotions throughout the baseball season." But Nelson also understood this: The president of the board of directors of Waterloo Professional Baseball, Inc., had assigned him the task of successfully launching "Meet the Diamonds."

He picked up the phone and left a message for his contact at the Ramada Inn to call him back. When he got off the phone, he said,

"The Peoria Chiefs do it, and it's huge. It's *huge.* Three, four hundred people. Hey, you can take the expenses out of my salary. *Oops,*" he added, "there's nothing left."

By the end of the day, Nelson had heard back from his Ramada Inn contact, who agreed to donate a banquet room on the evening of April 7, and who suggested that they reserve a smaller room in case of a sparse crowd, then rebook a larger room, if necessary. Brian Pfaltzgraff, the only member of the front-office staff who had grown up in the Waterloo area, threw out from memory the names of all the local media contacts Nelson would want to call.

"Dan Yates will make his little speech," Nelson said now. "Then the manager: 'Hey, we got a great team this year.' Even if we suck, you know he's going to give that speech."

Simpson joined in. " 'Our pitching looks good, hitting looks good. We got a lot of exciting prospects. We're gonna hit 'em where they ain't. It's great to be here.' Same speech," Simpson drawled, "being given in a hundred and sixty-two places across America on April seventh."

If Simpson were harboring any hard feelings about Yates's giving Nelson this assignment, he wasn't showing it. Nelson mentioned again how successful Peoria had been with similar ventures. Then he went on to say that he saw this event as just the beginning of a successful fund-raising drive; the trick, he said, was getting people to recognize that the ball club was, in fact, raising money. "Hey, you know what we could do?" he said. "Take ten cents out of every ticket and put up a thermometer at the entrance."

Simpson didn't respond at first. Then he said, "I'm confident we'll make money, but I don't want to take ten cents out of every ticket if that ten cents is the difference between us making money on the year and not. There is another thing," he went on. "We don't want to be a charity. We are a for-profit organization. I don't want to bend over. I don't want to beg."

Nelson said he'd beg. "Hey, otherwise we'll be out there at the Winter Meetings looking for a job." He laughed, but he didn't smile.

Suddenly Simpson stood up; it was precisely 5:00. Nelson and Pfaltzgraff stood up then, too. Nelson kept on talking.

"We got the team involved. We got the hotel. We're eighty percent there. The rest is publicizing the shit out of it." He spread his arms in the air, as if describing a billboard, or a banner trailing a plane across the endless Iowa sky. " 'Keeping Diamonds baseball where it belongs—in Waterloo.' I want people to be asking themselves, 'Why doesn't the city want them when they want to be here? Why are they fighting to stay when the city doesn't want them?' And," he added, pulling on his coat and tugging at its generous lapels in an approximation of annoyance, "I'm asking myself that right now, anyway."

Simpson was heading for the door. Nelson followed him around the counter, still throwing out suggestions. He said maybe the city could agree to match whatever funds the ball club would raise. He said maybe the city could hold a referendum on renovating the stadium. Simpson wasn't answering.

"Let the people decide!" Nelson boomed. "If they don't want us, then we don't want to be here, anyway!"

"You got that right." Simpson nodded his head once and disappeared out the door.

"Hey," said Nelson, pausing to pitch a question over his shoulder to Pfaltzgraff, "is this Heaven?"

"No," Pfaltzgraff said, and he sighed. Then he turned out the lights. "It's Waterloo."

2

"I hope those trees turn green," the baseball player was saying, " 'cause this scenery is killin' me."

He had sprawled the length of the backseat of a passenger van. When he'd first settled himself onto the cushion, he'd assumed an attitude of hands-on-knees alertness. But as morning turned into afternoon, as this single day of freedom slipped away in a succession of cheerless errands, as the scenery started repeating itself—motel, highway, ballpark, highway, motel, highway again: heading across town for the third time today and he'd been awake maybe, barely, three hours now—he had sunk lower in the seat until at last he'd leveled himself, experiencing little but the light-headedness that comes from watching the world go by upside down. Clusters of brown and gray branches, clouds of boughs, floated across his sky.

"Everything looks *dead,*" he said.

Nobody answered. Other players on other seats had similarly spread their arms and stretched their legs. The bus transporting them from the Cedar Rapids airport had arrived at the motel well past midnight, and on the flight east from Arizona they'd lost an hour, and the day before that they'd lost another hour in the seasonal change to daylight savings time, but the fact was, time didn't mean much anymore anyway. For as long as they could remember, their own daily routines as well as their families'—meals and vacations and jobs and dates and studying—had pivoted on the demands of their practice schedules and game times, but that single-mindedness paled next to the regimen they'd been following for the past three weeks in Yuma: baseball, baseball, baseball, baseball, baseball. And not just the game of baseball that had inspired them as kids, but that baseball and only that baseball which immediately, personally, professionally concerned them now. In the motel lobby earlier this afternoon, while the players were waiting for the vans to arrive, a TV hanging in a corner of the reception area had been showing a major league baseball game. "What game's that?" one player said. "Opening Day?" said a second. "Today Opening Day?" said a third, not waiting for the answer, pushing open the glass lobby door and stepping out to the parking lot and the weak midday sun.

Three vans were circulating throughout the city now. The drivers, veterans of last season's Diamonds who now knew their way around town, honked hello to one another from their high perches whenever their vans crossed paths. An informal shuttle system had developed, players hopping from one van to the other at the motel, the ballpark, the real estate office, or whatever rental opportunity outside of which the drivers happened to find themselves at the same time. Some players had gone to hunt apartments first; others had headed to the ballpark to drop off their equipment, more eager to see the facilities where they'd be playing for the next five months than the four walls where they'd be sleeping. "Better than Spokane," one of them reported later, during a van ride. It had to be a joke. Whatever the ballpark in Waterloo might turn out to be, it couldn't possibly be an improvement on the one in Spokane, a Padres farm club where many of these players had spent part of their pro careers last season or the season before. Interstate Fairgrounds, home of the Spokane Indians, once had served as a Class AAA stadium. It seated 7,000 and sometimes sold out; it was located in a booming college town; the clubhouse had carpeting. "Spokane," another player said, shaking his head, "was awesome." Then he said, "Honk."

A young woman, overweight, was walking along the sidewalk ahead of the van. The driver honked. The woman turned. The players laughed as the van rolled past.

The cruelty was thoughtless, literally; not a thought accompanied these actions. They were impulsive, reflexive. They were what one did under the circumstances—no more, no less. If the endless accommodations of their families, acclaim of their peers and attentions of a major league organization—scouting, recruiting, drafting, ponying up a bonus, paying airfare and meals and motels, studying a pitcher's stretch or a hitter's stance for a telltale hitch—had communicated to them that they were somehow special, it was only because it was so: They were special. People paid good money in hard times to watch them play. Strangers approached them for autographs. Women waited outside clubhouses. Vans materialized. The players were simply going along for the ride, passengers on a vehicle that was drifting through a subdivision near the outskirts of a city in the middle of nowhere, sleepily circling Melissa Lane and Sonya Drive and Tami Terrace, stopping, finally, to discharge its godlike human cargo on Joan.

At any moment, they could count themselves among the five thousand or so best baseball players in the country. For many of the players, Iowa had been little more than a rectangle on a television weather map, one of those states up north where the winters bring temperatures they'd never experienced and couldn't imagine. More often than not, baseball players hailed from warm-weather states; California, Florida, and Texas often were referred to as "baseball factories," and of the twenty-six players on the Waterloo roster, fourteen had rolled off the high school or college baseball-program assembly line in those three states alone. Still, it wasn't just the tans they'd cultivated under the Arizona sun, a ripeness that contrasted with the sickly gray of the Iowa foliage and sky and skin; it wasn't the Styrofoam cups they'd collected from the coffee counter in the motel lobby to carry throughout the day as impromptu spittoons for their tobacco juice; it wasn't the earrings or the Oakleys or the "X" caps alone. It was in their attitude; it was the way they carried themselves that announced their distinctness. Even in repose, their athleticism showed. They might slouch and slump and gaze lazily, but theirs was the effortlessness of entitlement, a shrugging acceptance of their gift, and with it their common lot. They had earned this. This was theirs. They had arrived—even if where they'd arrived was a city where the trees hadn't turned green even by April. Twenty-four hours earlier, they had been so many members of the San Diego Padres organization, mercenaries awaiting assignment. Now, they were Waterloo Diamonds.

"Aggh!" said Kyle Moody.

The van had turned down an access road. Two players were aboard at the moment, infielders who knew each other from the University of Texas baseball program. Scott Pugh, a pug-nosed squinter, was behind the wheel; he'd gotten the promotion to Waterloo from Spokane last year for the final month of the season. Earlier today, he'd driven Moody past the place he'd lived then, a leaning two-story clapboard house where he'd shared a couple of un-air-conditioned bedrooms with four other players, and every time one of them took a shower, the poor guy who lived below them got wet. "Jeez," Moody said when he saw the house, but then he'd looked away, set his jaw, and declared, "I've lived in plenty of dumps." And they'd looked at an apartment a teammate had seen and sort of recommended—"They're all dumps but this one"—only to leave muttering, "Where's *he* from?" Even when the neighborhood appeared promising, the buildings run by the rental agency always turned out to be the one "dump" on the block. But nothing Moody and Pugh had seen today prepared them for this: a row of low apartment buildings whose only adornment seemed to be the color of the siding: airport-motel aqua for the first two buildings, army-barracks green for the second two. To one side the buildings faced the back end of a lumber warehouse; to the other, an open field, wild with bent grass and weeds.

"Wow," said Pugh, easing the van forward. "Wow."

The address they wanted turned out to be the middle unit on the ground floor of the last building on the left, where the access road met the countryside. Pugh tugged on the screen door; the lower panel swung free, then slapped back into place, then swung free again. The two men considered this flapping fragment for a moment before continuing inside. They passed together through the living room and split up at the two bedrooms in back. They took turns looking out the windows at the view of the field. On their way back, they each stepped into the bathroom to give the taps a perfunctory twist, then into the kitchen to give the refrigerator door a perfunctory tug. About half a minute after they stepped into the apartment, they met back in the living room.

"I like this one better," said Moody.

It was settled, then. Pugh pointed to a wall of the living room. "TV here." He pointed to the opposite wall. "Couch here."

"That's all we need."

Pugh nodded and walked outside. He stood in the parking lot and surveyed the landscape beyond the wooden fence that separated their parking lot from the parking lot of the lumber supermarket. "We're in a pretty good spot," he called back to Moody.

"Hotel's right there. Fast food. Country Kitchen." He was turning in a semicircle to take it all in. Moody opened the screen door, let it smack shut behind him, and joined Pugh in the parking lot. The afternoon had turned unseasonably warm and fragrant, a first burst of spring. One hand Moody pushed into his pants pocket; the other held the cup, into which he now spit. "Wal-Mart for cheap stuff," Pugh said.

When he was back in the van, Moody reached to the dashboard for the day planner that his girlfriend had given him as a Christmas present. At first he hadn't understood the gift, but over the past few weeks he had found himself filling pages with the phone numbers of friends, some in pro ball. When he'd settled down somewhere, he would call their parents and find out where their organizations had assigned them.

"Okay," he announced, turning to a blank page and starting a list. "We need two beds. A TV."

"Couch," said Pugh.

"Pillows, blankets." Moody had to write quickly to keep pace. "God, a lot of this stuff you take for granted."

"Table to put the TV on," said Pugh.

"Phone."

"Fuck."

"We can just buy paper cups," Moody offered. He scribbled until he caught up, then stopped. Pugh had guided the van toward a shortcut he remembered from last year. In the farthest reaches of a mall parking lot, the van was snaking between two grass medians immaculate from the lack of pedestrian traffic. Improbably, at that moment a young woman was walking across these flawless lawns, apparently making her way from the fast-food places along the highway on the left to the discount shops in the mall on the right.

"I'll tell you something," Pugh said. "That place was probably thirty times better than the place last year." He honked the horn. The young woman turned. "Just wanna look at you, darlin'," Pugh purred, more to himself than to her. Then he and Moody rode in silence, except for the occasional spurt of tobacco on Styrofoam.

"We got burnt-orange carpet," Pugh said, after a while.

*

Early one morning in that week before the season opened, Keith Champion, the new manager for the Diamonds, arrived at the ballpark front office to join Jeff Nelson for a promotional appearance at a local school. Nelson had dressed in a gray pin-striped double-breasted suit. Champion was wearing a windbreaker and running pants. He rested a cup of coffee on the reception counter, gingerly lifted the plastic lid, and nodded crisply to Nelson, who boomed back from his desk in the far corner of the office a hearty *"Gooood* morning!"

Champion sipped the coffee, narrowing his eyes against the steam. "What time's this thing?" he said.

"Eight-seventeen."

Champion's eyes flicked toward the clock on the wall. His head didn't otherwise move. "Eight-seventeen," he said. "Can't be fifteen. Can't be twenty. Got to be eight-*seventeen*. Fucking typical." He took another sip.

"One thing," Nelson said.

"Hmm."

"They asked us, I mean, they really made a point of it, they even put it in a letter"—Nelson produced a piece of stationery off his desk and rattled it in the air—"they said just make *sure* we tell these kids it's important to stay in school. Sports are fun and all that, but they've got to stay in school."

"Hmm." The manager swallowed more coffee, then replaced the lid on the cup and headed out with Nelson into an early-morning drizzle. Over the past decade, Champion had played in the Midwest League, he'd coached in the league, and two seasons earlier, he'd returned to this league as a manager. You tell him "Waterloo in April," and what he would picture was precisely this: clouds close to the ground, breath you could see, and a steady pelting pebble rain. It was the kind of day, he said, where in the middle of the afternoon he'd get a call at the motel telling him they've still got the tarp down on the field and nobody knows if there'll be a game tonight—only now, he supposed, that call would be coming to him at home.

Keith Champion and Jeff Nelson already knew each other from their earlier incarnations. When Nelson had phoned Champion in Yuma to invite him to this career day, they'd reminisced about an Opening Day a couple of years earlier in Peoria, when Nelson was umpiring and Champ, as everyone in baseball who knew him called him, was managing the visiting Springfield club, and the wind-chill temperature at game time had been all of nine degrees Fahrenheit. Now, as they made the five-minute drive to the junior high, on the same side of the river as the ballpark, Nelson explained that it was, in fact, an item in the *Courier* about his own change of careers that had prompted a teacher to invite him to school this morning. She thought that Nelson's example might be useful both to illustrate the importance of having something to fall back on and to disabuse students of the notion that sports were an easy way to make a living.

"Hmm," said Champ.

At the school auditorium, a teacher directed them to one of the tables in front of the stage; up on the stage were several other tables. Champ picked up a sheet of paper that the teacher had left on their table, a "Planning Now for the Future" worksheet listing the questions the students would have to answer about their career-day guests, and sniffed it. "It's 1992," Champ said, letting the sheet slip back to the table. "Why are they still using mimeograph machines?" After a few minutes, a teacher on stage introduced the students to the career representatives at the various tables, then instructed the kids to break up into groups. Ten boys descended on the professional sports table; on the stage, nine girls gathered around cosmetology.

Champ started the discussion. His seeming disinterest had been an illusion; like any professional athlete, he had developed the habit of conserving his energy until he needed it. Now he animated himself, leaning forward in his chair, making deliberate eye contact with the boys, launching into a pep talk about how fortunate he had been to attend college on a sports scholarship. Then he hesitated. He asked if everybody here knew what a scholarship was. No hands went up.

"If you're not familiar with a scholarship," Champ said, "it's paying you to go to school and play baseball. It helps you, and it helps Mom and Dad, because school's expensive."

Then it was Nelson's turn. He said that even if a student had a great deal of athletic talent, he should still stay in school. He said that in the minor leagues, managers and coaches and umpires, even ball players, had to hold jobs in the off-season. He said that being in the minor leagues was no guarantee of advancement. As an example, he used himself. He had been an umpire in the minors, and he knew for a fact that 98 percent of umpires don't make it to the majors. He said this with extra emphasis: *"Ninety . . . eight . . . percent!"*

"Man!" said one kid. Other kids whistled and shook their heads.

Champ looked at Nelson.

"Of course," Nelson said quickly, "it's the greatest job in the world, too. There's nothing like the thrill of being on the field. Or around the game," he added.

A boy was making a point of manipulating around his mouth a free sample that he'd picked up at the nursing table. As Nelson continued his pitch, the puckering and slurping only grew louder. Still Nelson tried to ignore him. Finally Champ addressed the boy directly.

"What's your name?" Champ said.

"Jason."

"Jason. What are you chewin' on, Jason?"

Jason pulled the plastic apparatus out of his mouth. "This respirator thing."

Champ nodded his head and let his gaze wander to the back of the auditorium. Nelson tried to return to his talk, but when he got to the part about going to umpire school, Jason spoke up.

"Where in Florida?"

"Fort Lauderdale," Nelson said.

"Females!" said Jason.

Nelson adopted a tone that suggested bemusement. "I guess that's an advantage," he said. "Spring break *is* going on during spring training."

"You mess with them college girls?" said Jason.

Nelson looked at him.

"I'm just asking questions," Jason said. "That's why we're here, to ask questions."

Now Champ spoke up. "Jason," he said, "what do you want to do when you grow up?"

"Marry me a Puerto Rican!"

Every few minutes, the students rotated among the tables. At the John Deere table, an engineer was distributing copies of a comic book, "The Amazing Spider-Man: RIOT AT ROBOT-WORLD!," published by the National Action Council for Minorities in Engineering, Inc. "People think robots do whatever they want," the engineer said. "It's not true. Robots are programmed and controlled by us." Then he passed around Polaroids of other engineers, men and women sitting in cubicles staring into computers. Onstage, at the cosmetology table, a representative of the La James College of Hairstyling started off her sessions by asking how many students had relatives who were hairdressers. In one group of six, three students raised their hands. She nodded briskly, then got down to the business at hand: answering the questions from the worksheet. " 'What is the salary range?' " she read aloud. "Okay. The national average is $15,000—and *up*. But the important thing to understand is you're going to be in a career, not a job. *Jobs* pay by the *hour*." She looked at the sheet again. " 'What is the attendance/tardy policy?' It's simple. If you're off and you don't call in, they'll kick you out of school." She waited for this hard fact to sink in. "All we're doing is grooming you for the real world. This isn't a game. It's a career." She returned to the sheet. " 'What are the advantages of a career in this field?' After you build your business, you can set your hours. And not just in a salon, either. You have limitless career opportunities." She looked down again. " 'Are there any disadvantages? If so, what are they?' Yes. People might be dissatisfied. It's *true*," she said, as if one of the students had challenged her. "And then what? Someone looks in the mirror and hates what you've done to their hair, what are you going to do—sit down and bawl? No. You try to make it better because your client is your walking advertisement. And remember: The customer is always right. And you're wrong."

Back at the professional sports table, Nelson was running through the statistical improbability of anyone advancing to the major leagues. "You read the papers," Nelson was saying. "You see what these guys make. Five million dollars to what? To play a game. But—keep in mind: There's only one Ryne Sandberg." He held up a forefinger and pointed it with emphasis. "*One* Darryl Strawberry. *One* Ken Griffey, Jr."

A boy spoke up. "That's what I was just thinking," he said, looking mournfully at the floor.

For some time now Champ had been sitting still, hands in his pockets, legs straight out, eyes blankly staring at the bank of empty seats rising toward the back of the auditorium. He had grown up in the Midwest, in an industrial suburb of St. Louis on the Illinois side of the Mississippi, the son of a high school physical-education instructor, and he couldn't remember a time that he didn't want to spend the rest of his life around the game of baseball. As a boy, he'd wanted to be a first baseman. When that turned out not to be enough, in Little League, he'd learned how to be a catcher. When that wasn't enough, as a college junior, he'd learned to switch-hit. When that wasn't enough—when he'd spent three years as a player in the St. Louis Cardinals organization without advancing any higher than Class A—he'd offered to coach. He became what baseball people call a "good organization man": a player perhaps lacking the skills to make it to the major leagues, yet possessing the know-how and leadership and loyalty and patience and intellect to cultivate, in scouting or coaching or managing or whatever capacity the organization saw fit, the skills of those more naturally gifted. And when he saw *that* wasn't enough, he'd jumped organizations. Now he leaned forward in his chair with a suddenness that commanded attention.

"But, *hey,*" he said to the boy, "you can be that one person." The boy looked up from the floor. "Okay, maybe you can't be Darryl Strawberry. Darryl Strawberry was *born* a millionaire. That's just talent. I could do all the things he could do at the same age he did them, but he's who he is today because he's got more talent. Throwing a ball hard isn't something you can learn; it's something you have or you don't. But," he went on, "you can still be in baseball. So I'm not Darryl Strawberry, but I'm still playing the same little-kid's game. It's a *hobby*—only now I'm getting paid. I don't want to work nine to five. I don't want to go out in the real world and do the jobs these people do." His gesture encompassed all the other career tables in the auditorium. "What I do *beats* going to school. It *beats* going to work."

On the drive back, when they reached the parking lot of the ballpark, Champ asked what the story was on the paint job. Nelson explained that the ball club had traded advertising for paint, and that they'd painted until they used it all up.

"Half blue," Champ said, looking out his window, through the streaking rain. "Half rust."

The sign on the door read "Meeting Room," but except for the tables and chairs that occupied the central patch of wall-to-wall carpeting where a bed otherwise might have been, Room 130 looked like any other room at the Heartland Inn. Sofas hugged the walls, end tables supported lamps and telephones and a plastic ice bucket, and, beyond the venetian blinds on the windows, highway traffic schussed past. Usually the members of the Waterloo Professional Baseball, Inc., board of directors would conduct their monthly meeting at the VFW Hall downtown, or, during the season, at the ballpark on a night the team wasn't playing, either up in the grandstand or down in one of the two clubhouses, but they'd agreed to convene their last couple of meetings at the Heartland Inn because their general manager had negotiated free use of the room as part of the group-rate package deal for visiting clubs, and because, as their president advised them, "It's the way to do business."

Down the hall, or out in the parking lot, they couldn't help noticing that this year's players had arrived in town, lumbering back to their rooms from the fast-food joints in the area, gripping their tidy white paper sacks. The players, however, were of no concern tonight. Neither was the new manager—though, over the winter, the owners had studied closely the article in the *Courier* ("A Champion, and a winner?") announcing a replacement for last season's seemingly capable but ultimately embattled skipper. Whatever magic might attach to this year's edition of the Waterloo professional baseball team, individually or collectively, would have to wait at least the three days to Opening Day, if not several weeks into the season. Once the campaign was under way, there would be plenty of time for a closer observation of the game. Tonight, however, was for business.

At 7:00 P.M., Dan Yates, the president of the board, took his place at the head of the U-shaped arrangement of tables and called the meeting to order. He began by summarizing the situation facing the ball club's owners. He'd talked to Waterloo's new mayor. He'd talked to the City Council. He'd talked to the Park Board and he'd talked to the parks director and he'd written a letter to the *Courier,* and the response all around, to say the least, had not been encouraging. For that reason, he said, it was his opinion that they should announce that the ball club was for sale.

Yates was tall and trim, and he had sallow cheeks and a high forehead that on another person might have seemed severe. He looked strikingly like the Iowa farmer in Grant Wood's *American Gothic,* only grinning, and he spoke in a speedy, chipper manner that worked equally well conveying contagious enthusiasm or grave concern. Formerly in Christian-radio broadcasting, and currently working in public relations for the Black Hawk County Sheriff's Department, Yates had served his fellow owners for six years now as a reliable and diplomatic interpreter of whatever information he gleaned through his ongoing discussions with representatives of the major league parent club, his fellow ball club presidents in the Midwest League, city officials, their own front office staff, and themselves. Yates had let his fellow Waterloo stockholders know in advance what would be on tonight's agenda, and the subject was bound to arise sooner rather than later anyway. Even so, it carried considerable weight when he said that the time had come to think the unthinkable.

"Owners," "stockholders," "board of directors": The formality of the official titles might have been misleading. Fifteen area residents did own stock as board members of Waterloo Professional Baseball, Inc., but they were also the fans who'd happened to come out to the ballpark with such frequency that at some point each of them had crossed the line between partisan and participant. Most of them had been attending games in Waterloo since they were kids, an allegiance that, for a few of them, dated to the 1930s, back when the ballpark was still a wooden bandbox and the pro club was a truly local and independent affair, free even of affiliation with a major league organization. One day complaining about the long line at the beer bar, the next day working the bar; or, one day overhearing the GM moan about a shortage of baseballs for batting practice, the next day bringing from home several dozen batting-practice foul balls and home runs collected over the course of a season: They'd joined, just like that. They'd taken tickets, worked the scoreboard, sold souvenirs. A few had housed players. They had volunteered their services to the professional baseball team in Waterloo simply because they thought that professional baseball was something a city such as Waterloo *had*.

Since 1904, Waterloo continually had found the wherewithal to host a professional baseball team, going without only ten seasons in all, owing to two World Wars, one Great Depression, and a couple of times when the inherently precarious machinations of minor league baseball simply had gotten the better of the ball club, most recently in 1957. On that occasion, it had fallen to a group of local boosters—the spiritual ancestors of the present board of directors—to secure the return of professional baseball, and then, in succeeding seasons, to ensure its survival. This organization, as it evolved, had been informal in the extreme. Some people joined the Jaycees; others the Rotary. For the purpose of getting together with neighbors and having a beer or two (or more) while also performing a public service, this group of thirty or forty or even fifty—the number varied from year to year and often meeting to meeting—had the ball club. Members met on a regular basis, elected officers, took votes on such matters as raising ticket prices or hiring a new general manager, and divided among themselves the responsibility for pressing season tickets or booster buttons upon friends, neighbors, business associates, and those children's friends' parents who previously had pressed upon *them* raffle books and Girl Scout cookies. When dignitaries from the major league affiliate came to town, the ball club dispatched a delegation of its own, and if a parent club decided not to renew its affiliation with Waterloo, the ball club's directors took appropriate emergency measures, and every few months the ball club's president attended a meeting with other presidents of Midwest League ball clubs, and every off-season the Winter Meetings themselves. The organization was operational, certainly. It was its official status that remained questionable.

"Who *owns* this club?" a new Waterloo president had asked in 1984 at a Midwest League meeting. Those days, it was a question that minor league operators everywhere were sitting around tables asking one another. The operation of a ball club was self-evident, tautological even: the operator of a ball club was the person who operated the ball club: each of the people sitting around this table. Ownership, however, was another question. By the early 1980s, the minor leagues, experiencing their first growth in popularity in decades, had begun expanding, and with the new ball clubs had arrived lawyers and contracts and certificates of ownership. In the presence of paperwork, the absence of same could be unsettling.

Who owned this ball club? What did ownership even mean? Whatever it was, this wasn't it. If the Waterloo ball club wasn't legally or literally an abandoned business, it had come close to functioning—or not functioning—like one. In order to protect their right to operate the franchise, the members agreed to incorporate themselves, a commitment that would cost each "stockholder" the token amount of $50: fifty shares of Waterloo Professional Baseball, Inc., at $1 per share. A number declined the opportunity; a dozen didn't. (Three others joined later.) If anybody had been in it for the money, this would have been one of the shrewdest investments of a decade remarkable for the potential to reap windfalls. The value of minor league franchises soon skyrocketed in general, and by the time of the monthly board meeting in April 1992, a franchise such as Waterloo's was worth, on the open market, $1 million, maybe more: $1 million, split fifteen ways.

Call it the *Bull Durham* effect. The success of the minor leagues was a genuine phenomenon. Over the past fifteen years, annual national attendance had more than doubled. In the previous season, it had reached 26 million for the first time in forty years. This renewal of fan interest in the minors had been documented in and reinforced by magazine articles (*Sports Illustrated* put the "Minor Miracle" on its cover), newspapers (the circulation of *Baseball America*, the biweekly bible of minor league baseball, grew exponentially in less than ten years, from 6,000 to 60,000), and, most influentially, a movie that a Hollywood producer was inspired to make through his own part-ownership of the Durham, North Carolina, Bulls. The success fed itself. Leagues expanded to accommodate the demand, while individual clubs increased in value and eventually became objects of speculation. The Midwest League itself, in the previous ten years, had gone from eight clubs to fourteen, while one franchise had risen in value during that same period from $40,000 to $2.7 million.

The ball club was theirs to sell, technically. But a technicality was what that possibility had always seemed to the Waterloo owners: a fact of law more than a fact of life. After the reincorporation of the ball club, they began running a statement of principle in the annual souvenir book sold at the ballpark: "All officers and members of the board serve without remuneration and for the sole purpose of preserving baseball for this community." Technically, the ball club was a for-profit enterprise, but practically, the owners ran it as a not-for-profit community service, making enough money to cover expenses, and putting any profits back into the operation. This model of ownership was far less common than it used to be; the economic changes that the minors had undergone in recent years had seen to that. For this reason alone, the owners in Waterloo tended to greet with suspicion any pressure to depart from the style of operation they knew best. Not that they didn't accommodate change; they did, but only after subjecting it to lengthy scrutiny and debate. Even the choice of meeting site these days had met with resistance. Some of the owners with memories of monthly get-togethers in the old days had walked into a motel room filled with framed prints of rustic scenes on pastel walls and wondered, Where's the fun?

Their ranks included a school attendance clerk, a study-hall monitor, a truck driver, an apartment-building desk clerk, a retired electrician, and a retired drive-in movie theater short-order cook. Even those with a potentially greater sophistication in business matters—a bookkeeper, a couple of English professors from the local state university, a junior-high teacher who also held an interest in a sporting-goods store, a salvage-company operator, the eponymous owner of Patty's Hairstyling—would never claim to know as much about the business of baseball as their president. If Dan Yates said that their situation was dire, then their situation, no doubt, was dire. Their situation may well have been worse than ever. Even in 1984, when the local economy was collapsing under the loss of thousands of jobs, the city had found money for ballpark renovations. Since then, however, as the cost of keeping professional baseball had continued to grow and the resources of the local economy had continued to shrink, the sense of civic solidarity between the ball club and the community had diminished. Just that afternoon, the *Courier* had printed the results of a public-opinion poll on the future of the franchise in the weekly "Your

Views" column, a call-in survey that was unscientific but nonetheless significant, if only because everyone in town would see it. Of the 105 responses, 71, in fact, had been in favor of city funding for ballpark renovations, but it was the accompanying article that provided coverage of a kind that never used to commemorate the approach of Opening Day. "Tuesday, Sept. 1," it began.

> Baseball fans might want to circle that date on their calendars. It's the last home game of the 1992 season for the Waterloo Diamonds, the second half of a two-game series with the Clinton Giants.
>
> But if the relationship between the Diamonds and the city doesn't improve, it may be the last game the team plays in Municipal Stadium.

Throughout the minors, owners were facing the same predicament. Hardly a month passed that *Baseball America* didn't report the sale of some franchise somewhere. Here in the Midwest League, the Waterloo owners had watched in recent years as one franchise after another had changed hands: Davenport, Iowa, sold by a group of local owners like themselves to an outsider; Wausau and Wisconsin Rapids, sold by locals to outsiders, who then uprooted the franchises for potentially more lucrative markets; Kenosha, sold just this past off-season, and destined to move. Pressure to address the issue in Waterloo had been building at least since the majors and the minors had signed the 1990 Professional Baseball Agreement, if not, as any of the owners who had involved themselves even glancingly with the politics of baseball might have argued, for years. First came the extra expenses imposed on individual franchises; David Simpson had proved last year that Waterloo could survive them—not happily, and maybe not forever, but at least for now. Then came the new stadium standards, the uniform requirements that every minor league ballpark in the country had to meet by April 1, 1994. It was to underscore the importance of this deadline, now less than two years away, that Yates wanted to announce that the ball club was for sale—though, as he emphasized, not necessarily for the purpose of selling it. He simply wanted to make a point with the city. "We just want to scare 'em!" Yates said. "No one is taking us seriously.

Everybody thinks baseball is one of those things that goes on and on, and you never have to think about it."

But what if the city didn't scare?

In that case, Yates acknowledged, they might have to sell the club.

Back in 1984, the city had seemed doomed and they themselves didn't even own the paperwork to prove they existed, and they'd survived. Only a little over a year ago, Yates had returned from the Winter Meetings wringing his hands and warning of bankruptcy, and they'd survived. They had accommodated themselves to the formal incorporation of the ball club; they had accommodated themselves to the necessity of hiring a general manager who thought in terms of generating a profit. They'd even accommodated themselves to meeting in a Meeting Room, as if they were any other board of directors. Now, no doubt, they would accommodate themselves to some new compromise. Yet even if they couldn't quite imagine the circumstances under which the present situation would resolve itself, neither could the owners imagine the circumstances under which it wouldn't.

In the end, only one other owner agreed with Yates that putting the ball club up for sale was a chance worth taking. The owners then framed and passed unanimously an alternative motion, not only formalizing the informal policy they'd been following all along, but entering it into the record with renewed vigor: "that it be the policy of Waterloo Professional Baseball, Inc., that 100% of all revenue left over after annual operating expenses be directed to stadium improvements each year, and that all other energies of Waterloo Professional Baseball, Inc., be devoted to fund-raising for stadium improvements."

One final item of business then remained: a vote on whether to move the board's future meetings from the Heartland Inn back to the VFW Hall. This time the sentiment of the owners wasn't as easily discernible. The vote ended in a tie, and it fell to Dan Yates, as president, to cast the deciding vote.

The motion failed.

The windows along one wall of the reception room on the top floor of the Ramada Inn afforded a panoramic view of a purpling city: highway construction immediately below, its earth-moving machinery dormant for the day; a tidy congregation of downtown office structures farther away, lights starting to snap off; and, rising above the horizon, a smokestack, smokeless, the letters "R-A-T-H" running earthward. At 6:00 P.M. on the Tuesday before the season opened, the starting time for the ball club's "Meet the Diamonds" fund-raiser, Jeff Nelson stood before the windows, regarded the view, and announced to anyone within earshot, "You know, the city looks kind of nice from up here."

Nelson and the GM had disagreed on how best to promote the event in advance. Nelson had argued that the more advertising, the better, while Simpson, ever mindful of his budget, demurred, but in the end, about a hundred fans showed up—enough, with the addition of the players, the players' wives and girlfriends, the owners, and the media, to fill the room. The *Courier* had assigned a photographer and a reporter, and some radio reporters were working the crowd, too. In addition, television stations from Waterloo and Cedar Rapids had sent crews, and one would be doing a live remote during the six-o'clock news. From time to time a television light clicked to life and washed one end of the hall in an indiscriminate white bath, erasing the view of the city from the windows and, like a mirror doubling the size of a room, replacing it with a reflection of a celebration that gave every appearance of being a success.

First Dan Yates took the stage. He reminded the fans, and he made a point of informing the players, that this season would mark the eighty-eighth anniversary of professional baseball in Waterloo, and the thirty-fifth in the Midwest League. Then David Simpson gave a little speech that consisted, almost in its entirety, of "We got a new manager, Keith Champion, and we think he's going to do a good job for us." Next Nelson took the stage, thanking the mayor for showing up—Al Manning was standing against a wall toward the back, wearing a smile that suggested he'd prefer not to be called upon to speak—and plugging Magnet Schedule Day on Saturday, the home opener against the Cedar Rapids Reds. He also explained the wager he'd made with the Cedar Rapids front-office staff. "Not to put down any pork producers here," he added, lowering his tone, "but I don't want to smooch a porker." Then, raising his voice, Nelson turned to the manager and said of Saturday's home opener, "We'll be two-and-oh by then. Right, Keith?"

Champ wore a wry smile beneath a trim mustache. His build was compact, and his assessments of his squad's prospects blunt. "To be honest, most of these guys are new to me," he said. He explained that he was at a disadvantage not only because he was in his first year with the Padres organization, but because a possible trade involving San Diego's All-Star starting catcher Benito Santiago had delayed final roster assignments throughout the farm system right up to the weekend. "It's been hard to get a good read on the team," he said. He also said, "I think we won't be exceptional in any particular area—hitting or pitching." Finally he offered, almost as an afterthought, "But I think we'll be a very sound team with talent at every position." Then it was time to introduce the team. Champion began reading the names on his roster, and only then did the players venture across the room and into the spotlight.

The players had passed the evening huddling among themselves at one end of the room. Fresh from the ballpark shower, their hair slick and their cologne potent, they, too, had visited the windows to take in the view, then withdrawn to the several circular tables along the opposite wall, insufficiently impressed, perhaps, or unwilling to make even so nominal a commitment to their new home. They laughed softly, playfully punched shoulders, and allowed the outside world—or Waterloo, anyway—to come to them. When it did, the players complied graciously, even respectfully, with all requests. They signed autographs, spoke into reporters' recorders. But when they turned back to the circle of familiar faces, what they said to one another, shrugging, was "It's in our contract. We've got to do publicity."

"Any you guys gonna make it to the pros?": It was probably the question most commonly asked of a ball player by well-meaning if ill-informed fans. One answer was: These *are* the pros. Earlier in the day, the players had attended their first practice at Municipal Stadium. They'd sat in front of their lockers and pulled off their jeans and mesh T-shirts and pulled on their jerseys, and that's when it happened, really. They put on their uniforms and walked out on the field and it happened. Out there, beyond the walls of this ballpark and any others in which they would find themselves for the next five months, they were mere mortals, however taper-torsoed. Even within these walls, the stack of ramshackle folding chairs and the particleboard-and-chicken-wire lockers and the peeling ceiling all had communicated something less than an over-whelming welcome. Forget Spokane. Municipal Stadium was in-ferior to the facilities that most of these players knew from college or even high school. But out here, on this field, before this grand-stand and between these bleachers, a transformation occurred. They were professional baseball players now, and anyone needing confirmation only had to glance at the grandstand, where, every so often, one or another member of the ballpark staff would emerge from the darkness of the concourse and stand in the blue afternoon shadows and simply stare down at the spectacle the players were creating, in their white uniforms, out here.

"Don't be too hard on me," Champion said to the crowd, when the last of the players had stepped to the stage, "if I don't send the runner home from third. Just have another beer."

The manager smiled. The fans laughed. The players shifted, as if struggling slightly under the weight of a burden.

It was a tableau that would have been equally and instantly familiar to earlier generations of Waterloo fans. In that moment, before the team clambered off the stage, the television lights blinked off, and the reflection of the room vacated the windows, it seemed reasonable to believe, if not impossible to refute—it seemed at least forgivable to expect—what generations of fans and players and managers and owners gathering together on simi-lar occasions in hundreds of cities dating back to the early years of the century had firmly held: that the presence of a professional baseball club endowed its surroundings with a dignity, grace and professionalism all their own. In that moment, all slates were clean, everything old was new again, and anything was possible.

The season slipped into existence a few minutes after seven on a damp Thursday evening in Davenport, Iowa. Drizzle filled the bowls of the box seats, and small crowds huddled under the grandstand roof, but, in the best entertainment tradition, the show went on. A white stretch limousine rolled into foul territory and deposited the new mascot for the newly christened Quad City River Bandits, Rookie the Raccoon. A moment of silence followed, honoring an alderman who had advocated city funding of stadium renovations. Then a skydiver dropped into right field. Another parachuted near first base. A final one, bearing a giant American flag, tried to land directly on home plate and came pretty close, considering. At this point, a lone patron in the box seats behind home, braving the light rain in a poncho, cupped his hands around his mouth and bellowed, "Just get the goddamn ball game started!"

The beginning of a baseball season is, almost without exception, unexceptional. Despite the pregame hoopla—however many parades and ceremonial first pitches and moments of silence a front office can concoct to lend the occasion a balance of frivolity and gravity—in the end it still comes down to this: a pitch. One player faces another from a distance of sixty feet, six inches, and throws a baseball, executing a movement that each team will see repeated approximately forty thousand more times over the course of the coming season. One pitch, and then another, their number ultimately finite yet seemingly inexhaustible, like heartbeats in a lifetime, the only difference between this pitch and all the others being that it's the first, because one of them has to be.

Fastball, low and away. Shad Williams to Scott Bream, for the record.

The game that followed, under clearing skies, was typical Class A–caliber baseball, especially so early in a season, when the players wouldn't have developed the reflexes and dexterity that come only from playing day after day for a long period, and the new teammates wouldn't have yet figured out one another's rhythms, and the managers and coaches would have barely begun to absorb their squads' limitations and strengths, individually or overall. A catcher's throw to second landed in medium center field. A pitcher's throw to first wound up in the bullpen. Two Quad City base runners found themselves easy pick-off victims in consecutive innings. The Diamonds committed four official errors, while Quad City committed a few errors of the kind that don't appear in the box score: the batter in the bottom of the ninth swinging mightily in a futile effort to break the tie score and end the game with a home run, having not yet learned that the riverfront fog of Davenport wouldn't be as conducive to a baseball's trajectory as the thin mountain air of Boise, Idaho, where he had spent the previous season; or the batter in the tenth, with the bases loaded, jumping out of the way of an inside pitch that, had it but brushed his uniform, would have won the game.

The bellowing fan who'd booed the pregame ceremonies was missing the point: In the minors, the games were only part of the fun. In order to compensate for the frequently questionable quality of play, especially at this level, management had to entice the audience to the ballpark with a promise of sideshows, contests, and as many other amusements as staff, budget, and ingenuity allowed. In Quad City, the promotions tonight and every night included: Best Seat in the House, sponsored by a furniture company ("Enjoy the game in the comfort of a four-person couch"); Call of the Game, sponsored by a cellular-phone company ("Make a free ten-minute call to anywhere in the continental United States from your seat at the ballpark"); Dice Game, sponsored by a casino on the Mississippi River ("Follow the giant dice as they roll off the stadium roof . . . the better the roll, the better the prizes"); Dirtiest Car in the Lot, sponsored by a car wash ("Free car wash for the owner of the dirtiest car in the parking lot"); Fan of the Game, sponsored by a national pizza chain ("One lucky fan receives a pizza delivered to his seat"); Jackpot Inning, sponsored by another casino on the Mississippi River ("A progressive contest . . . the longer the club goes without hitting a home run in the sixth inning, the bigger the cash prize"); Mascot Race, sponsored by a restaurant ("Race Rookie the Raccoon to home plate and win"); Move of the Game, sponsored by a moving-and-storage company ("Move from general admission seats to box seats and win prizes"); and more than half a dozen others— enough, even not including the obligatory lucky-number prizes in the souvenir program, to keep the ballpark's loudspeakers blaring without interruption between half-innings, and sometimes between pitches, through a regulation nine-inning game.

The score was tied, 1–1, going into the top of the ninth, but more important, as far as this crowd was concerned, was the time: 9:30 on a school night. Fully half the crowd—the announced attendance was 3,172—went home. Before the bottom of the ninth, the score still tied and the home team coming up to bat with a chance to win the first game of the season right then and there, another half left. The crowd continued to halve itself every half-inning, until, by the middle of the eleventh, only a few dozen die-hards remained, buried under blankets or deep inside down coats.

In the bottom of the eleventh, Waterloo manager Keith Champion made a move that from the stands might have looked like one more mental lapse, but from the dugout could be seen only as an act of mercy peculiar to the lower levels of pro ball. The inning started with Kyle Moody, a late-inning defensive replacement at third, fielding a ground ball and throwing low to first, where the ball exploded out of the dirt and off the forehead of Waterloo's first baseman, and Moody's roommate, Scott Pugh. One throwing error later—this time by the pitcher, trying to pick the runner off first—Quad City had a runner on third with no outs, and Champ had a tough choice.

In the majors, or even the higher levels of the minors, this situation would call for a simple execution of a textbook strategy: intentionally walk the bases loaded, thereby setting up a force at any base, and pull the outfield in, thereby conceding the long fly that would score the runner from third, anyway. At this level of the minors, however, standard considerations didn't always apply. In the dugout, Champ conferred with his pitching coach. The pitcher, Todd Altaffer, was already erratic, walking two batters in the previous inning, then committing a throwing error in this inning. If Champ ordered Altaffer to walk the bases loaded intentionally, and then Altaffer gave up an *un*intentional walk to lose the game, what would it do to him—and on the first day of the season? "His asshole's already this small," Champ said, making a miniature OK sign. "We walk the bases loaded, it's gonna be like *this*." He squeezed the OK sign until it shrank to nothingness.

Champ waved his outfield in, but he didn't order any intentional walks. Altaffer walked the next batter anyway, unintentionally. Then he surrendered a fly to the outfield, deep enough to land beyond the right fielder's reach and to register as the winning hit. The runner from third stepped on home, and the game ended: the Quad City River Bandits over the Waterloo Diamonds 2–1 in eleven innings, for the record, the only difference for the Diamonds between this loss and any others to come being that this was the first, because one of them had to be.

*

The first call to the Diamonds front office on the morning of Saturday, April 11, concerned the possible availability of free tickets. Nelson patiently informed the caller that no ball club would schedule a free-ticket promotion for the *home opener*. A few minutes later, the phone rang again. Again Nelson answered.

"Any free tickets to today's game?"

On the wall, the countdown calendar had stalled at "Opening Day 10 Days!!!" but this was it: the day that the staff of the Waterloo Diamonds would get a preliminary indication of whether all the work of the off-season was going to pay off. The team was returning to town with an 0–2 record, and the weather was overcast and bitterly cold, but neither factor would necessarily affect how many fans showed up at a home opener. Attendance might dip precipitously for the second home date—in Davenport, for a game that had ended when a thunderstorm broke in the bottom of the fifth with the River Bandits leading 4–2, turnout had fallen by two thirds from one day to the next—but the home opener would draw enough of the core audience to provide a reasonably reliable harbinger of the kind of support a franchise could expect once the season had hit its hot-dogs-and-beer midsummer stride.

The chain-link gate at the ballpark's entrance rolled open at 2:00 P.M., one hour before the scheduled starting time. Dan Yates, stationing himself next to the young woman who was taking tickets and selling souvenir programs, handed out free magnet schedules and called a greeting to each customer: "Hello. Welcome to Municipal Stadium. Hello. Welcome to Municipal Stadium." At one point, a line threatened to form, and he ran back into the front office, yelled, "We need more programs!" and grabbed a box. When he returned to his post, he spotted a woman carrying a heavy blanket. "Hey, this is no first-and-ten weather," he called to her. "This is strike-three weather!"

"Honey," she answered him, "you come prepared."

For the opening weekend, Jeff Nelson had negotiated a trade with a formal-wear shop for himself and the other members of the front-office staff, and a little past 2:30, he walked onto the field in black tie to preside over the pregame festivities. As the public-address announcer introduced the players by name and hometown, they emerged from the home dugout on the third-base side, lined up along the foul line, and faced the fans—at the moment, maybe twenty minutes before the first pitch, all 107 of them. In the faint light of an overcast afternoon, the two sides sized one another up. "It's cold up here, ain't it?" somebody called out to Kyle Moody of Plano, Texas.

Then came the ceremonial first pitch, an honor to be shared by sales representatives from the cosponsors of the magnet schedule giveaway, Wal-Mart and radio station KOEL, whom the club had invited, and a first-term congressman from a neighboring district, Jim Nussle, whose staff had asked the club to invite him because in the fall, he'd be running for reelection in a redrawn district that would include Waterloo. This afternoon he showed up under the grandstand shaking hands and smiling, at least until he'd walked up a ramp to get a look at the size of the crowd.

Every day a series of faxes arrived in the front office from Howe Sportsdata International, a Boston firm that compiled the official statistics for most of professional baseball, including the Midwest League. These league stats sheets featured a wealth of such on-the-field information as the previous day's results, that day's pitching match-ups, overall standings, and leaders in any number of hitting and pitching categories, organized both by individual and by team; but only one off-the-field statistic: daily and cumulative attendance for every ball club in the league. If a glance at the standings provided a quick assessment of how each team was doing on the field, a glance at the attendance figures provided a quick assessment of how each franchise was faring off the field. Among Midwest League franchises, Simpson couldn't hope to compete with the bigger-market, better-financed, and larger-staffed operations in Kane County or Quad City, both of which had drawn more than 3,000 to their home openers. But Simpson could hope at least to compare favorably with Kenosha and Burlington, which were bringing up the rear with opening day totals fewer than 600 each.

The promotions today and every day at Waterloo Municipal Stadium would be a trivia contest sponsored by Chi-Chi's Mexican restaurant, a "Guess the Strikeouts" contest sponsored by the Maple Lanes bowling alley, and a hitting contest sponsored by the Sky Room Comedy Club, in addition to several souvenir program lucky numbers, Ballpark Bingo (three cards in every program, three winners a game, $5 a winner), and a free game of bowling for everyone in the park if the Diamonds' pitching staff combined for twelve strikeouts, sponsored by Cadillac Lanes bowling alley. Opening Day passed mostly in silence, except for these occasional echoing, metallic public-address announcements, as well as the usual batters' names and pitching changes. The chamber effect was enhanced by a nearly complete absence of bodies in the grandstand portion of the ballpark, behind home plate; early in the game, the combination of concrete underfoot and shadows cast by the overhang had forced the few fans who had chosen to sit there to seek what warmth there was in either set of open-air bleachers along the foul lines. By the sixth inning, the concession stand had run out of hot chocolate. When the PA announcer said that the last of the three winning bingo cards had been claimed, the crowd noticeably thinned. In the end, the Diamonds won, 3–2, and even as the remaining fans were filing out of the ballpark the Cedar Rapids Reds, still in uniform, were hustling out to the idling bus in the parking lot without bothering to shower in the underheated visitors' clubhouse.

When Nelson walked into the front office, the first thing he asked about was the attendance. Brian Pfaltzgraff answered that it was 728, including 63 no-shows. Nelson's shiny tuxedo shoulders sagged.

"That sucks," he said.

Simpson shrugged. "We'll be third from the bottom, anyway," he drawled.

Nelson's arrival had brought the number of employees in the front office to thirteen. Simpson, wearing his tuxedo and counting money at his desk, hadn't stepped out of the office all game; Pfaltzgraff hadn't even had a chance to change into his tux. The floor was littered with staff workers rummaging through boxes, organizing inventory, counting tickets. Nelson silently picked a path through the bodies to his desk. Simpson asked Pfaltzgraff to fax the attendance to the league president. Pfaltzgraff said he'd already done it. "Radar," said Trish, Simpson's wife. Nelson said that his patent-leather rental shoes were pinching his feet and maybe he wouldn't be wearing his tux tomorrow after all. Suddenly a cry went up from the souvenir-program seller, and all work stopped.

She said she'd just uncovered the box of programs from which, prior to the game, she'd randomly chosen that afternoon's lucky-number winners. She must have been selling out of the wrong box all day, she said. She must have mixed up the right box with the box that Yates, in a panic, had lugged out there. Everybody stared at her.

"No wonder we didn't have any winners," said Pfaltzgraff, and everybody went back to work.

A short while later, Nelson suddenly brightened. He straightened his shoulders and barked instructions. Then he called for quiet. He picked up the phone, dialed the number of the front office in Cedar Rapids and, after waiting for the beep, said that this was Jeff, up in Waterloo, and that he had a message. Then he held the receiver up in the air.

"Oink!" everybody screamed. "Oink! Oink! Oink! Oink! Oink!"

I s there a sight more forlorn than a professional ballplayer window-shopping at Florsheim's? Windmilling one arm, working his way from storefront to storefront as slowly as possible, Cameron Cairncross was killing time during a rainout on a Monday evening in downtown Clinton, Iowa. Most of the stores on the block were closed for the day; those that weren't, were defunct. Not that Cairncross minded. Some of his teammates had taken advantage of the night off to board a casino floating on the Mississippi River, which was speeding along thickly at full spring-thaw tilt only a couple of blocks east of here. Others had settled into the downtown Travelodge that the Diamonds were calling home for the night to order pizza and watch cable. A few were nursing beers at a bar around the corner. But as a native Australian more than 9,000 miles from home, Cairncross was enjoying the early-season luxury of regarding every stop in the league as a new adventure. *I seen the Mississippi River,* he told himself. *I seen some shit.*

Rainout, in this instance, was an imprecise term. As what would have been game time neared, the occasional fat windblown raindrop did plop to the sidewalks from a sickly yellow sky, but the weather was otherwise amenable to baseball. A more precise reason for calling the game would have been "wet grounds." The rain that had collected on the grass and dirt under the tarp the previous Friday, when the understaffed Clinton grounds crew couldn't cover the infield quickly and thoroughly during a sudden downpour, had still been standing today, when the crew had lifted the tarp. The Clinton general manager had decided to reschedule tonight's game as part of a doubleheader the following night, and for the third time in the season's first eleven games, the Diamonds had found themselves—in one more variation—"weathered out."

"I don't mind doubleheaders," Keith Champion was saying. "The way minor league schedules are, I'll take any off day I can get." The manager and his staff had settled into a booth at a tavern a block from the team motel. Dean Treanor, the pitching coach, and John Maxwell, the trainer, were sitting across from Champ. All three had turned in their seats so they could see the television hanging over the bar. Up there, a baseball game was about to start. Down here, they were killing time, waiting for 7:00 and the movie theater down the block to open. Champ, Treanor, and Maxwell would be seeing *Basic Instinct;* a group of five players standing around a table across the bar, *Wayne's World.* Earlier, Champ had sent two pitchers of beer their way. "It's what, five o'clock?" he'd said then. "Hell, they'll need a couple beers to go to sleep. I understand that." The Diamonds previously had been "colded out" on the second home date of the season, and rained out, for real, in Burlington last week. Their won-lost record now stood at 4–4, an almost-meaningless statistic in the face of 62 more games in the first half of the season alone, and 132 more over the full season.

During the first week and a half of the season, the Diamonds' road schedule had described an informal tour of the Midwest League's surviving Mississippi River cities—first Davenport, then Burlington to the south, now Clinton to the north. The cities themselves dated from 1836, 1834, and 1855, respectively; their involvement in professional baseball from 1879, 1889, 1895. They could trace their origins to the first wave of settlement in the region, steaming up the Mississippi out of the South: riverboat landings at the height of the era of water commerce. Those cities that survived and prospered were the ones that had risen at an intersection with the next wave of settlement, barreling across the river from the East: station stops at the height of the era of rail commerce. (Some cities, among them Clinton, had been platted to lie in the path of the onrushing railway system; where city planners had guessed wrong, the embryonic towns had vanished, and now were buried under fields and farmland.) As the economic fortunes of individual communities had fluctuated, so had their ability to maintain minor league franchises. At various times, the ranks of Mississippi River cities hosting professional baseball had included Moline, Quincy, and Rock Island, Illinois; Dubuque and Keokuk, Iowa; Hannibal, Missouri. By 1992 they numbered precisely three.

These, then, were the stalwarts, the minor league cities that had always been aboard, or, when not aboard, at least lurking on shore, waiting for word of a berth in an existing league, or for the arrival of a whole new league. But that's where present similarities ended. Like Waterloo, Clinton and Burlington were "mom-and-pop operations"—a common sobriquet for those organizations still run by and for the community. In the history of minor league baseball, the term had come into use relatively recently, and, as was generally the case, a particular way of doing business hadn't seemed especially mom-and-pop until an alternative arrived. In Davenport, the new era was inaugurated when the ballclub caught the attention of a Chicago sports investor with a growing port-folio of minor league baseball holdings.

And no wonder: When Rick Holtzman bought the franchise, in September 1987, the Davenport area represented the largest Class-A market in the country. At that time, Holtzman was in the midst of an eighteen-month, five-club minor league buying spree. After completing almost every purchase, he pursued a strategy that he was hardly alone in using in the minors during this early boom period, but one new enough, and one he used often enough, that in minor league circles it became nearly synonymous with his name: Pressure the local government into building a better sta-dium; failing that, find a city that would.

From the start, the Quad Cities (the perennial subject of a trivia question among bored Midwest League players; the answer was: Moline and Rock Island, Illinois, and Bettendorf and Davenport, Iowa) had enjoyed the natural advantage of rising along the shores of not one river but two—the Rock emptying into the Mis-sissippi. The major railroad routes followed, of course, and so, in time, did Interstate 80, the coast-to-coast thoroughfare connect-ing New York City and San Francisco by way of Chicago. The four cities spread together, and together spread in every direction. When Holtzman went shopping for a ball club in the Midwest League in 1987, he would have been looking, in part, at whether a market had an untapped profit potential, not to mention the ca-pacity to underwrite a new ballpark once he'd explained that po-tential to the right civic leaders—which was to say there was no choice. The metropolitan area populations of Burlington and

Clinton, for instance, were each under 40,000. The Quad Cities, however, stood at a quarter of a million.

Another common term for mom-and-pop ball clubs was "glorified American Legion," and in fact Community Field in Burlington *was* owned by the Legion, which leased it to the city for the use of professional baseball. Community Field used to have a roof, but it and the stands burned down in 1970. What the ballpark had now was overhead netting that showed numerous holes, and wooden backless benches that, the year after the fire, had been imported from a fairgrounds being displaced by a new freeway. Clinton played at Riverview Stadium, a tiny, vaguely Art Deco, jewel-box ballpark built under the Works Progress Administration in 1937. It was architecturally striking but starting to show its age. In recent years, the Burlington ball club, like Waterloo, had succeeded in securing new lights from the city government, while Clinton had received a new home clubhouse.

In Davenport, however, John O'Donnell Stadium was now as good as new. It dated from 1931, but since 1989 it had been undergoing a series of renovations costing more than $3.2 million. Gone were the three meager rows of box seats and the wooden benches and the free-standing ticket booth out front. In their place came eight rows of theater-style box seats, blue plastic grandstand benches, and an interior ticket booth, as well as an entire front-office complex folded up within what used to be the open space of the rafters under the grandstand. The facade was new. The field was new. The parking lot and the electronic marquee blinking high above it were also new. The press box and the clubhouses and the picnic areas were all new, and an exploding scoreboard was due any day now. Just about all that remained from the ballpark's old incarnation was the view.

John O'Donnell's greatest draw had always been its site. The Mississippi rolled right past the right-field wall; from most any seat a fan could see both the river and the arched bridge that spanned it in Bunyanesque leaps and bounds. The bridge lights, the triple-decker steamboat lights, the distant lights of Illinois, and then, without warning, from the darkness behind the grandstands, the wail of a train whistle: out of settings such as this must have arisen the enduring romance of baseball: innocence by association.

"I knew I was back in the Midwest League when I heard a train whistle," Champ said now to his staff. He had decided to try to instill in his two season-long companions some enthusiasm for the charms of his native Midwest. He described the walk he'd taken around downtown Clinton that afternoon. "It's just these two blocks here," he said. "I like old towns like this. That Woolworth's luncheonette—whenever I come back I have to make sure it's still here." He grinned. "I wouldn't mind a milkshake in a metal container."

Maxwell smiled grimly and nodded. Treanor grunted his agreement and checked his watch: 4:45. Maxwell and Treanor, the trainer and the pitching coach, side by side, could have been "before" and "after" shots for a life in the California sun. Maxwell, at twenty-eight, possessed the blond locks and unlined open face of a surfer; Treanor, at forty-two, a reptilian hardening. Above a white dress shirt that he'd buttoned to the collar, his face burned a dark hole in the darkness of the booth. While neither of them might have known what to make of the Midwest, it was Treanor who kept his watch set two hours earlier, on San Luis Obispo time.

Maxwell said that he'd spent the afternoon in his room. Treanor said that he'd stayed in his room, too, watching ESPN. Champ sighed and allowed as to how when he got back to his motel room from his walk downtown he'd watched a little TV, too, an interview with a game-show spokesmodel who had fallen off a stage and was suing the network.

Maxwell smiled crookedly. "I don't know," he said. "That dugout in Waterloo, those steps can get pretty slick." He shook his head and tsk-tsk-tsked. "Some of those wooden slats look ready to break."

Champ shrugged. "I like those dugouts."

Treanor finally lowered his gaze from the television. He gave Champ a look a ten-year-old boy might give another boy who had just admitted that he liked girls.

"You see those major league dugouts?" Champ nodded up at the screen. "They're all concrete, and they're sunk down, and they've got netting all over the place."

Treanor blinked and turned back to the television, shaking his head to himself. A tornado warning was crawling along the bottom of the screen.

Maxwell said, "Who're you gonna sue anyway? The Padres?"

"Sue the Diamonds," said Treanor, indignantly.

"Don't sue the *Diamonds*," said Champ. "There's nothing to sue for. You'll wind up owning the club."

"Owning the *ballpark*," Treanor snorted.

"It could be a neat place," Champ said.

Treanor gave him another look.

"It could be a really neat place." Champ shrugged. He'd played in John O'Donnell years earlier. He knew what was possible. "It'd take work, but it could be like Quad City."

Treanor continued looking at Champ, then gave another small snort and consulted his watch: 4:55. He finished his beer. At the table across the room, the players were finishing theirs. Then the eight tourists walked out of the bar and down the block to the movie theater to do what there was to do at seven on a Monday evening in downtown Clinton, Iowa.

At that moment, approximately 150 miles northwest of the theater into which the players and staff of the Diamonds were filing, another kind of audience was assembling in a room at one end of the second floor of the Waterloo City Hall. Bowling leagues, greyhound races, movies at the mall, even baseball games—to the short list of nightlife attractions in Waterloo had been added in recent months the Monday-evening City Council meetings. Funding for ballpark improvements would be among the items under discussion tonight, and Dan Yates, who was away on business, had asked one of the other ball-club owners to represent him. As Yates's immediate predecessor as president of the organization, Mildred Boyenga would have been the logical replacement, anyway, but in fact she'd welcomed the chance to assess the situation for herself. At the most recent owners' meeting, Yates had argued that the city's relationship with the ball club had deteriorated so much that it warranted putting the ball club up for sale, and now, two weeks later, as Mayor Al Manning opened the City Council meeting to public comments, Boyenga was still asking herself: Could Dan Yates possibly have been right?

A woman named Kathy Oberle was first. "I think," she began, stepping up to the microphone before the mayor and the seven members of the Council, "it's about time that you begin to realize that it's the citizens of this community that have to pay for the ongoing projects." She explained that she wasn't necessarily objecting to these specific renovations at the ballpark, or even to city funding of baseball in general, but to the funding of baseball as representative of any number of civic improvement projects. "I think you really have to begin to look at what is the end cost that the citizen has to bear for all this," Oberle went on. "I guess I'm uncomfortable with you sittin' around here spending my money so quickly, and I think it's time that we have to make our own decisions. And I mean, this is not a decision that I think I elect you to do. Now, I want a positive direction here from the mayor as well as the Council; I think for the past six or seven, eight, nine, ten years, you *have* been spending money that we *really* don't have. And I think it's time that we say, 'Stop. And let's take a look at what you're doin' here.' Have you *seen* this long list?" She held up a copy of the agenda from that night's Council meeting. "If you have an item that's gonna cost millions—and I don't care if you cut it in a pie of seventy-five thousand dollars for ten years—at the beginning of that cut of the pie, I want to be the person that says, along with everybody else out here, I want to have the opportunity to say yes or no. So, I mean, now is the time for leadership." One member of the audience started to clap . . . clap . . . clap. "Now is the time for all of us to stand up and be counted, and I'm talkin' about the people that are watchin' and sittin' at home." More applause. "It's time they get their little royal scenarios down here and start makin' the important decisions to help you." Now the applause was joined by barrel-chested cheers. "You don't have to do that," she shot over her shoulder. "I think it's about time that we help you," she said to the Council. "Let's get it all out on the table. Let's play ball."

It was the kind of diatribe that any observer of government bodies sees all the time. Oberle herself frequently appeared in these chambers in the guise of gadfly; two years earlier, in fact, she'd organized a successful challenge to the city budget. For years Al Manning had been just like Oberle—more polite, perhaps, and unfailingly respectful, but, still, a burr, a blister: pestering the powers that be about the crack on the sidewalk in front of his house, or presenting a petition protesting a cutback in the number of days animals must stay at the humane shelter before being put to sleep. It was in part the treatment he'd received while standing before the same microphone now projecting Oberle's breathy expressions of indignation that had prompted him to run for mayor. From that vantage point, down there, Mayor Bernie McKinley hadn't seemed like such a nice guy. Oh, Manning was willing to grant that McKinley was probably nice to his friends and to people he liked; but to someone he didn't like, he could be "rude" and "abrasive," and "come off like he didn't care." So Al Manning had fought City Hall—and won.

It had been Manning's great leap of insight to understand that he could run for mayor all by himself. In an effort to free local proceedings of allegiances to state and national political organizations, City Council and mayoral candidates in Waterloo didn't announce party affiliations; instead, they ran as a single coalition, presenting a united front that theoretically crossed party lines, bridged class divisions, and reflected ideological consensus. In the 1991 election, on the way to what was widely presumed would be a fourth mayoral term for its leader, The McKinley Team had raised $11,332 in contributions from more than seventy sources, including most of the area's business luminaries. Manning, running alone, had raised $718 in cash contributions from two sources, one of whom was himself. In addition, he'd taken out $1,300 in personal loans. Manning offered no opposition slate. He offered only opposition.

On the morning of the mayoral election, in early November, a freak storm had slicked city streets with a sheet of ice, and in the days following Al Manning's upset victory, the speculation around town was that the weather had kept home all but the most motivated of voters. The weather, however, couldn't account for another recent election result: The woman who had served as the new mayor's campaign manager—a frequent accomplice of his at City Council meetings and an outspoken and controversial exponent of the Christian right—had won a seat on the Waterloo School Board only two months earlier. Nor could the weather account for the fact that voters had returned to office the seven members of the City Council, all of whom had run under the banner of The McKinley Team, but not Bernie McKinley himself. And sleet alone couldn't explain the lopsided margin of victory: 57 percent to 43 percent. Not that Al Manning was foolish enough to mistake his majority for a mandate. "I had a feeling people were ready for a change," he told the *Courier*. "I don't know if just any unknown could have done it, but I wasn't much more than that." What he was, as one write-in voter put it, was "Anybody but Bernie."

In the six months since Manning's election, public interest in the weekly City Council meetings, already high during McKinley's tenure, had only heightened. Thanks to cable television, the entire city had gotten to witness the humiliation of the new mayor every Monday night, to see him squirm and cough and clear his throat as he searched in vain for the proper way to move the meetings along, while the Council members sat and watched and waited and, in their own good time, threw him a procedural lifeline. For some observers, it might have been reminiscent of a trick that labor used to play on management during the final and most desperate period at Rath Packing, just to show who was boss: sabotage a piece of machinery, step back, and watch the foreman with the baby-fat fingers try to fix it. Only now it was the city elite sabotaging the underdog; the roles had reversed. Or had they?

Although mayoral and City Council candidates in Waterloo didn't announce party affiliations, allegiances were nonetheless evident. It was widely assumed that no mayor in recent memory had taken office without the blessing of the small circle of business interests that wielded the real power in town. Furthermore, the boundary between the two wards that together encompassed nearly the entire southern half of the city, a predominantly middle-class setting, zigged and zagged in precisely a manner that would allow two representatives from the exclusive Prospect Boulevard neighborhood to sit on the Council (including, at the moment, the cochair of the county Republican Party). But now Waterloo had a mayor from the "wrong" side of the river—from the same neighborhood as the ballpark, in fact (and a ward that was represented in the City Council by a member of the Democratic Party). How did Al Manning's ascendance reflect on the several members of the Council who had always cast themselves as defenders of the little guy, yet had run for reelection as loyal members of The McKinley Team? The retiree from John Deere's component works, or the former student protester and longtime critic of institutionalized East Side neglect—had they now evolved into the elite, if not by casting their lot with a white-collar candidate who had become (in the minds of many) a living symbol of business-as-usual, then by gumming up the procedural works for the blue-collar bumbler who had no idea how to run a City Council meeting, let alone a city of 66,000? These were unsettling—if unspoken—questions, and they did nothing to relieve the increasingly dizzying sensation, among Council members in the chamber and the citizenry watching at home, that the old roles no longer applied.

The Council gave the guy a break. Whether out of concern for the greater good of the community or guilt at their own possible complicity in the continuing fragmentation of Waterloo, by the time of their April 20 meeting, the Council members had achieved at least a public showing of shoulder-to-shoulder fellowship with their new mayor.

As bad as the city's financial problems had been when Al Manning took office, they had worsened significantly since then, though not through any fault of his. Within weeks of his inauguration, the city had outlined two options in forming the next municipal budget: cuts in essential services or higher taxes. The fire chief responded by claiming that funding cuts would force the closing of two fire stations, while the police chief released a report warning of the presence of four hundred members of national street gangs in Waterloo, and promised that revenue loss in his department would necessitate laying off nine officers. A month prior to this evening's meeting, when the Council members had taken their customary seats in this chamber in order to debate the new budget, they found themselves facing an overflow crowd protesting the proposed cuts—several hundred angry residents filling the room, spilling into the hall, and standing on the sidewalk just below the meeting-room's windows, chanting. "Ultimately, we have to increase taxes to protect ourselves," Kathy Oberle had told the Council that evening, as a representative of the all-volunteer Citizens Budget Review Committee. "The people out here don't mind paying a little more if they know what they're getting." The evening ended, after a four-and-a-half hour public debate, with Council members promising to return with a budget incorporating a 7 percent property-tax increase and no service cuts.

When Council members arrived at City Hall a week later, they found themselves facing another overflow crowd of several hundred angry residents, this time protesting the proposed tax increase that had placated the last angry overflow crowd. "Mr. Mayor," the owner of a Waterloo engineering firm said at one point, "we read your lips, or we attempted to read your lips, before the election. We still believe we made the right decision. I guess you'll have to prove us wrong." At the end of the evening, the no-new-taxes contingent had won. The city would dodge the most egregious service cuts in part by dipping, for the first time, into money left over from previous budgets—a resource the city traditionally had set aside in case of an emergency. In the small hours of the morning, the Council passed a $66 million budget that would maintain the old property-tax rate, and Waterloo had come to a place in its history where any riot, any arson outbreak, any bookkeeping error or act of God could bring the whole house of cards crashing down. *Angry,* Council members said to one another, and the mayor said it, too, and in so saying they found at least one topic on which they were in complete agreement: They'd never seen people so *angry.*

It was in this emotional environment that, three weeks later, the City Council turned its attention to the final, $65,000 installment on the four-year, $325,000 program of improvements to Municipal Stadium. The Council's vote was a foregone conclusion. The money was already there; Bernie had seen to it. This particular funding, in fact, barely affected the ball club. The $65,000 would allow the Park Commission to meet safety-code and engineering requirements at the ballpark—legal obligations it would have had to satisfy even if the Diamonds were no longer a tenant. But the original purpose of the $325,000 four years earlier had been to guarantee professional baseball's future in Waterloo, which it hadn't done. If nothing else, tonight's meeting would provide both sides of the stadium issue with one more opportunity to enter into the public record their opinions on the city's further commitment to baseball.

Mildred Boyenga was no stranger to this chamber. "Good

things come in small packages," began her bio in the souvenir program sold at the ballpark in the summer of 1984, "and our new president, Mildred Boyenga, is a prime example. At 5'2" and less than 90 lbs., she is a bundle of energy with a knack of getting things accomplished." Boyenga had assumed the presidency of the ball club at a time when the local economy was collapsing—Deere downsizing, and Rath, her own place of employment, breathing its last—yet immediately she had approached the mayor and Council and convinced them to commit the city to improving the ballpark. It had been under her stewardship that the ballpark had received its first series of significant renovations since it opened in 1946, and it had been at her instigation that the ballpark had continued to undergo renovations over the past eight years.

It wasn't quite true that the ballpark had been receiving an annuity from the city, a rubber-stamp renewal of funding for whatever construction the ball club or the major league parent saw fit. Boyenga herself could attest to that. Still, the widespread impression that Bernie McKinley routinely conferred just such a consideration on any number of projects had helped Al Manning win office, and it was an impression from which the new mayor had been at pains to distance himself. At one point in tonight's City Council meeting, Manning tried to reassure Oberle that the $65,000 represented a commitment both essential and finite—an effort "not to meet any baseball requirements, but to maintain the structural integrity of the facility, whether it's used for professional baseball or amateur baseball—"

"And there's another amount next year," Oberle cut him off, "and another amount *next* year—"

"No, no, no, no," said Manning.

Under the circumstances, Boyenga had little choice but to mount a defense that was purely financial. She followed Oberle ("Thank you. And I'll be back"), and she began her comments by citing the various salaries that the ball club contributed to the city's economy: the players, a manager, a coach, a trainer, a general manager, office staff, and the workers at the concession stands, the beer bar, and the souvenir booth. "The players alone bring in $30,000 in salary every month," she said, "and believe me, every cent of that money is spent in Waterloo. These kids eat here, they sleep here, they rent apartments, they buy cars, they buy gas, they go to the mall." In addition, visiting teams stay and eat and recreate in Waterloo, as do the families and friends of the Waterloo players who come to visit, often for weeks at a time. "I think it's very shortsighted to look at sixty-five thousand dollars as a big amount of city expenditure, when the city itself gets so much more in dollar turnover," she said. "Any city that is clamoring to get minor league baseball and is putting up five-, six-million-dollar stadiums knows this. It's a plus for the community. Let's not lose it. Thank you."

One person applauded.

"If we commit the sixty-five thousand dollars," the mayor said hesitantly, "you think that'll be sufficient then?"

She was old enough to be his mother. In fact, Boyenga worked with Al Manning's mother at Miller Medical Service, where she had found a job in bookkeeping after Rath folded. She understood that she and the mayor belonged to different generations. His lack of appreciation for what the ball club represented to the city didn't surprise her, but his lack of understanding of even the fundamental issues did.

"It won't be sufficient, *no,*" said Boyenga. "But I hate to see quibbling over such a small amount each year, because you're right, down the road we're gonna have to put more money in the stadium."

"Well, I guess what we have to look at—really, all we're addressing here is the sixty-five thousand dollars," the mayor said. "But I think you're talkin' about a long-term commitment—"

"That's right. There's gonna have to be if we're gonna keep it."

"—and when we get into that, I guess we need to hear from the public: If we have to put eight hundred dollars to one million dollars into the stadium, where do you want us to cut back on something else?"

That wasn't the point—not to Boyenga, anyway. Over the years, appearing before one city meeting after another, she had learned to pursue whatever economic argument anyone wanted to make. But economic arguments went only so far. She couldn't justify a $1 million investment in the ballpark—not when she well knew that the contribution of the ball club to the city was more than purely economic. So: enough about economics. Boyenga switched now to the argument that had always informed her participation in the ball club and that used to be the only argument she needed to make, back when she was president of the organization: the ball club as a civic institution.

Mildred Boyenga had been coming out to the ballpark since the 1930s, when she was a little girl living in the nearby town of Stout, and the team was playing at the old Waterloo Stadium on Westfield Avenue, on the future site of the John Deere Tractor Works. When she and the other owners talked about what going out to the ballpark meant to them—well, they *didn't* talk about it, or at least they didn't use to. At the most recent board meeting, however, when the subject of selling the club came up, they had found themselves trying to put into words what baseball contributed to the community, and what they'd talked about was how their parents had taken them out to the ballpark when they were children, and they'd talked about how they'd taken their own children out to the ballpark, and they'd talked about how now their children wouldn't have a place to take *their* own children.

"You talk about the future of the city," Boyenga said now. "We have a lot of kids come out to the ballpark. We have a lot of families come out. In fact, I'm glad you were out there, Al." Two days earlier, the mayor had visited the ballpark to throw out the first ball, then stayed to watch the game with his wife, Becky, and infant daughter. "I talked to Becky," Boyenga went on, "and she enjoyed the game Saturday, and I think it's great to have people come out, and I wish more people did. And in the summertime, it's a great family entertainment."

But that wasn't the point, either—not to Manning, anyway. "I don't think anybody is arguing with that," he said. "You know, right now, the city is having some difficult financial times, and we need to set priorities . . . ," and that was it. He continued on in that vein, and then—after Boyenga had said, "Thank you," and Manning had made sure to answer, "We're happy to hear your input, though"—so did everyone else.

"I was listenin' to her," one man said, gesturing toward Oberle, "sittin' in front of my television, and she said get off your butt and get down here. We just got through a meeting three weeks ago and left the budget alone. . . . This city is not equipped to put a million dollars into a stadium. It becomes a—it just becomes a thorn in the city. . . . You tell us we can't lose police, we can't lose fire; and now you're telling us we can't lose that. When are you going to stop issuing bonds? Why don't you pass legislation to stop bond issuing for one year? See if you can live without bonds. Because you don't need a stadium. That doesn't bring in that much money. The city's in deplorable condition because of its roads, and then you're worried about a stadium?" Then another man said, "Maybe something to look at would be to have a study to see what the economic impact is of the team," but then the mayor said to him, "You yourself, during the budget hearings, were telling us our taxes are too high, and yet now you're sayin' maybe we should spend that eight hundred thousand dollars or one million dollars?" and then a City Council member said he seemed to remember there being a study on the ball club a few years earlier that showed an annual economic impact of "over a million a year," and the parks director said that the result in fact had been much higher but that he himself thought the dollar-turnover rate in the study should have been much lower so that an economic impact of "two-point-five million dollars quickly becomes, uh, three hundred thousand dollars," and the City Council member challenged *that* figure, and the parks director said, "Fine. I'm not an economist."

Finally the discussion turned to Sammie Dell. Dell was an at-large Council member who lived in the same ward as the ballpark, and for the past several years Dell had served as the informal liaison between the City Council and the Park Board whenever stadium funding needed a little push on either front. He had grown up on the East Side, and graduated from East High. Since becoming the first African-American to hold a citywide elected post in Waterloo, in 1987, he had used his platform to serve as an advocate for his side of town—or, perhaps more accurately, as an opponent to the neglect he felt it received from the power brokers who ran the rest of the city. Municipal Stadium was one of the few communitywide institutions to which the area north and east of the river and beyond downtown could lay claim, and often, when Dell had addressed the issue of what might become of the ballpark, he'd made it clear that he didn't want to see the structure standing abandoned, an invitation to vandals—"another blight on the north end of Waterloo." If anybody had shared Boyenga's belief over the years that what the ball club offered to the city couldn't be measured only in dollars and cents, it was Sammie Dell. Now, as he began speaking, Boyenga tilted her head and raised her chin.

"I personally don't feel we're going to be able to afford baseball in Waterloo," he said.

Boyenga shut her eyes. She lowered her chin.

"Somebody has to pay for those million-dollar new showers," Dell went on. "I think Kathy's right. Before we spend any significant money, I think the people ought to decide if they want to do it or not. Everybody's got their own opinion about it, but lookin' at that stadium, lookin' at baseball, there's two things: Either we fix the thing, or we raze it."

Two afternoons later, Jeff Nelson emerged from the front office in Waterloo wearing his calf-length Padres thermal overcoat, placed a thermometer on the lid of a metal trash barrel in the concourse, and continued walking until he'd reached the right-field foul territory, where the fence-sign painter had parked his truck. "We can't have a truck in the playing area!" Nelson yelled at him. "This is professional baseball!" Then he spun and strutted toward the infield, where the groundskeeper, Jim Van Sant, crouching in the muck near third base, was trying to rig a plow to the back of a small John Deere tractor. Champ was standing on the grass nearby, watching Van Sant manipulate the plow so that its spikes pointed toward the sky, which at the moment was a churning gray: the last of the late-winter skies, with luck.

"You might want to reverse the plow," Champ suggested.

Van Sant was not a groundskeeper by trade; he was a student at the University of Northern Iowa who, while interviewing for an intern's position, had happened to mention that he used to do grounds work for Little League. As a teenager, Van Sant had lost an eye in an accident. He squinted up now, adjusting his glasses.

Champ explained that the teeth on the plow should be pointing toward the soil so that, rather than smooth it down, they churn it up. Van Sant straightened and looked from Champ to plow and back again. "The wind's what you need to dry it," explained Champ. "You don't have sun, right? So you need *wind*."

Van Sant cocked his head, nodded, and bent back to his task. Champ looked around for his pitching coach, mouthed a "Wow," and decided that the time had come to set to work himself. From the various tools lying on the grass, he selected a hoe, pointed the handle toward the shortstop's position, and said, "Get me a shovel. I'm gonna fill that hole before Scott Bream breaks his ankle." Then he marched over to the pitcher's mound and started turning over dirt.

For the third time in as many days, the Diamonds were threatened with the cancellation of a game in weather that was seemingly playable. The Clinton GM had called off the previous day's make-up doubleheader even before the Diamonds had left the motel for the ballpark; a combination of overcast skies and cold temperatures hadn't given the field a chance to dry, and the Diamonds had found themselves boarding the bus back to Waterloo barely twenty-four hours after they had arrived in Clinton, and without having touched any equipment except the orange-and-blue Padres-issue canvas bags they'd unloaded from, then reloaded into, the luggage compartment.

Like their manager, the players would prefer a night off and a doubleheader the next day, or, better yet, on a later, warmer date. Even given a choice between nine innings of cold today and fourteen innings of mosquitoes later (doubleheaders in the minors consisted of seven-inning games), the players would take the mosquitoes, assuming that the GM could reach today's decision promptly. A week ago Sunday, on the afternoon of the second scheduled home game of the season, Simpson had waited until just minutes before the first pitch before deciding to call the game on account of the cold. The temperature had stalled literally at the freezing level; on the ground next to the home dugout lay a cooler's worth of ice that the batboy had dumped the previous afternoon. The Waterloo players, however, already had changed into their uniforms, and by the time word came that the game was off, they were taking turns trying to stay warm by sitting on the clothes dryer in the clubhouse. The Cedar Rapids players had fared even worse. Their driver had vanished from the premises, taking the transportation with him. While the Reds, still in uniform, paced along the concourse, it fell to Dan Yates to sequester himself in the front office with the yellow pages, calling every restaurant in the greater Waterloo area and asking whoever answered the phone to look in the parking lot and see if they saw a bus.

"Forty-one degrees!" Nelson announced now, banging open the office door and holding aloft the thermometer he'd retrieved from the trash barrel. Simpson glanced up from his corner desk, where he'd been stenciling a sign for the front entrance of the ballpark: "PROGRAMS $1.25." Like the manager, and like the players, the GM wouldn't particularly disavow the advantages of an occasional day off, either. On that first freezing Sunday of the season, the number of fans in the stands at game time had numbered exactly seventy; on a night like tonight, it wasn't as if the ball club were going to draw enough of a crowd even to justify the expense of opening the gates. Officially, the decision belonged to the home-team GM, at least until that moment the managers handed their lineup cards to the home-plate umpire (after that, it was the ump's call), but in the end he would have to supply a reason to the major-league front office: too cold, too wet, whatever. Forty-one degrees, however, was borderline: warm enough to play if the game were now, but who knew how far the temperature might drop once the sun went down? After a while, Simpson asked Van Sant to call the ball club's contact at the local office of the National Weather Service, and Van Sant reported back that a band of showers was visible on the radar, but it didn't look to be moving any farther north than Iowa City, nearly 100 miles south of Waterloo. Simpson decided to call off tonight's game, to schedule a doubleheader for the next day, and to leave the tarp off until then, in the hope that the night air, however cool, might dry the field.

The thunderstorms that rolled through Waterloo late that night and well into the morning were heavy, drumming, punishing thunderstorms, truly torrential. By the time the rain had stopped and the staff could assess the damage, the dirt area of the infield lay mostly under water—a sea lapping against archipelagoes of mud. There was nothing to do but spade, hoe, plow, dump bag after bag of the infield-dirt enhancer Turface, and, every so often, step back and exclaim.

"This field is the worst I've ever seen it," Champ said.

"I've never seen it this bad," agreed the assistant groundskeeper

Craig Pfaltzgraff, Brian's brother and better known as Rollo.

"I've never seen puddles this big," said Champ.

The managers might not mind the occasional night off, and the players might prefer muggy heat to brittle cold, and the local front-office folks might welcome a reprieve from another night of empty stands and idle concession workers, but major league executives in Chicago or St. Louis or Minneapolis or San Francisco held a different set of priorities. For them, the minors existed for one purpose only—player development—and an effective realization of that goal was predicated on proper conditioning and reliable evaluations. During the night, a fax had arrived in the Diamonds' office at the ballpark, and in the offices of all the franchises throughout the Midwest League, from the league president. "I have been receiving calls from GM's, Mgr's, and Farm Directors that the tarps are not being used," the note read, in part. "This is professional baseball, please make a better attempt to save games."

Throughout the Midwest League, teams were falling behind in their schedules. South Bend had played all thirteen scheduled games so far, but Burlington, for instance, had been weathered out six times, and Appleton seven. In Waterloo, the team had missed five of thirteen games, and, depending on what the grounds crew and front-office staff and, by the end of the afternoon, a couple of the team's owners could accomplish through vigorous and judicious tilling, tonight's ball game might make it six of fourteen. The team hadn't managed even batting practice in five days. Not only had the weather problems destroyed any semblance of a playing rhythm or training schedule, but they had made a mockery of future player evaluations by creating a backlog that would necessitate five doubleheaders in eight days at the end of May. Under these conditions, a farm director or big-league general manager trying to coordinate a minor league system from a distance of several hundred or several thousand miles was reduced to guesswork. Tonight, however, one such executive, the senior vice president and director of player personnel for the California Angels, parent club to the visiting Quad City River Bandits, would be in attendance.

Whitey Herzog was, as the following day's *Courier* would report, in an interview accompanying a four-column color photo of him on the front page of the sports section, "a nationally known face in the stands at Waterloo Municipal Stadium." He arrived at the ballpark about an hour and a half before the scheduled 6:00 P.M. start of the make-up doubleheader, and members of the local media, whom Nelson had alerted, encircled him on the walkway between the grandstand and the first-base bleachers. Herzog said that the moment he entered the ballpark today he remembered the last time he'd been here, forty years earlier, as a player for Quincy, Illinois. He talked about his years of service to the Cardinals organization, about managing the Cardinals to a World Series victory in 1982, about his hopes for building a pennant winner for perpetually pennant-hopeful Angels owner Gene Autry. Then, as soon as the reporters had disappeared back down the ramp, Herzog announced, "All these guys writin' articles, they want me to write the fuckin' things for them. You want to write an article, *write* the fuckin' thing. Right?"

He was directing this question to Champ, who knew Herzog from their years together in the Cardinals organization, and who had been waiting at the wall along the field to pay his respects. Champ winced and tried to smile and managed a shrug. Two of the ball club's owners and several fans had wandered over to welcome their visitor, too. Already Herzog was moving on to other topics.

"Why are the minors worth so goddamn much?" Herzog wondered aloud. "Is it supply and demand?" He said that it was he who ten years earlier had talked August Busch III into buying the Class A club in Springfield, Illinois, for the St. Louis Cardinals organization. At that time, Herzog said, the Anheuser-Busch company had embraced a business philosophy that demanded a certain annual rate of return on each of its holdings, and he had encountered great resistance to the idea of acquiring a property in a traditionally marginal industry; in the end, Herzog had prevailed, and the organization had paid a few thousand dollars for a franchise now worth at least a million, and he said he supposed it was safe to assume that the MBAs at Anheuser-Busch had met their profitability quota on *that* acquisition.

But they had gotten something else in the bargain, too, something that they wouldn't appreciate because it didn't show up on ledgers, but that, among the baseball people in the operation, constituted an immeasurable advantage: a compact farm system. When a major-league GM thinks of a farm system, what he sees (and they were all, and always had been, men) is a map—and not just a map of the cities in the system, but a map of the cities connected by spokes to the major-league affiliate, and connected by arrows to one another in order of ascension, from Rookie League through Short-Season A and so on, all the way up to the Show. St. Louis now had a Class A team just up the interstate in Springfield, its Double A affiliate in nearby Arkansas, and its Triple A club in equally nearby Louisville, Kentucky. "Good for players with wives," Herzog said—a player moving up through the system could settle in one central location and never be far from home—"and good for travel"—players could shuttle freely, as could scouts, coaches, roving instructors, and various front-office figures. By contrast, the farm system that Herzog now oversaw from Anaheim, California, progressed from Rookie League Mesa, Arizona, to Short-Season A Boise, Idaho, to Class A Davenport, Iowa, to A-Advanced Palm Springs, California, to Double A Midland, Texas, to Triple A Edmonton, Alberta. Herzog squinted now at the infield in Waterloo, where the reclamation efforts were reaching newly frantic levels. He was breathing through his mouth. Clouds rose in front of his face. "Four times this month they were snowed out in Edmonton!" Herzog thundered. "We don't need to be in goddamn *Edmonton!*"

It was Whitey Herzog, more than anyone else, who had championed a particular remedy to these cold, wet periods of prolonged inactivity in faraway places: complex ball. Eliminate the Class A and Rookie levels of the existing minor leagues, consolidate those players into their organizations' spring-training facilities, and what you'd have was a controlled environment that would allow the majors to observe, instruct and discipline on their own terms. Up at seven, ball game at nine, back in the dorm by noon. No fans; no umps; no rainouts. No distractions. No junk food. A road trip? A crosstown bus ride. "Robot ball," its opponents called it. "Dollars and cents," responded its proponents—Champ, for one. Last season Champ had managed the Cardinals club in the Rookie level Arizona League, one of two complex-ball leagues in operation. (The other was in Florida.) Yesterday afternoon, sitting in his office after Simpson had called off the game and after he'd heard that Herzog would be here today, Champ had quickly risen to the defense of complex ball against Treanor's skepticism. "Double A and Triple A, you definitely need fans," Champ had said. "But A ball, all you're doing is evaluating talent, letting the players show who can play. The last thing on our minds is fans. The point is, do they ever have a chance to make the major leagues? We're here to make major leaguers. We're not here to make minor leaguers." He shrugged. "Besides, if the majors get a ton of money, and they don't want to have complex ball, then great. Then the players can play in front of fans. But if the majors want to cut"—another shrug—"then this seems like the likeliest place." His spread-armed, open-palmed gesture had seemed to take in a good deal more than Waterloo Municipal Stadium— and, in fact, during the negotiations leading up to the 1990 Professional Baseball Agreement, the majors had threatened to dissolve dozens of their minor league affiliations and simply transform the whole shebang into complex ball.

Whose minor leagues were they, anyway? Virtually since the start of professional baseball, more than a hundred years earlier, the minors' autonomy from the majors had been a source of constant conflict. The introduction of the farm system in the 1920s by a GM with Herzog's old organization—Branch Rickey, of the St. Louis Cardinals—had gone a long way toward resolving the issue by formalizing the minors' subservient status. To the minors, the 1990 contract negotiations with the majors had seemed like another incursion, one more attempt to wrest away control of the minors, possibly once and for all. To a major league organization, however, each minor league affiliate represented an average annual investment of $600,000. In addition, some of the players would have cost hundreds of thousands of dollars—if not, in a few cases, more than a million dollars—to sign. Even a player who cost next to nothing might one day emerge as the cornerstone to a major league club. From that perspective, why shouldn't the major leagues have a say in the quality of the playing conditions? By threatening to convert much of the minors into complex ball, the major league owners had succeeded in getting the message across to their farm system counterparts: The minors as you now know them—as you now run them—are expendable. If nothing else, this threat had laid the groundwork for the eventual outcome of the 1990 negotiations: a new way to run the minors, effective April 1, 1994: the ballpark standards set forth in Articles 11, 12 and 13 of Attachment D of the Professional Baseball Agreement.

Herzog retired to the press box to await the possible start of the games. The press box at Waterloo Municipal Stadium was a flimsy wooden wind trap that occupied the last row of the grandstand directly behind home, a narrow aerie tucked under rust- and birdshot-spotted girders that supported an equally blemished corrugated metal roof. Here Herzog perched. The 6:00 starting time came and went. Some fans in the first-base bleachers stood and salaamed in Herzog's direction, chanting, "Whitey! Whitey! Whitey!" Then 7:00 came and went. But soon the PA announcer broadcast the starting lineups, and it began to look as if an evening of baseball would take place, after all. Where seven hours earlier had rolled oceanic puddles, there now lay a plain of sandlike substance. The managers even had handed their lineups to the home-plate ump. It wasn't Simpson's call now—though he was down there on the field with the umpires and the managers, because it was still his ballpark, and because there was still some question whether his customers were going to get a show tonight. But it wasn't his decision anymore; he'd made his decision by letting matters progress this far. It was the umps' call. And the umps wanted to know: What did the managers think?

Champ, for one, didn't know what to think. The situation had progressed past the point where he and his players could use a night off. He thought that enough was enough—that the Padres deserved to start seeing some results for their investment. But he also thought that he didn't want to get a call from someone in San Diego asking why a player whose future had been entrusted to Champ's care had sustained a career-ending ankle snap in the Waterloo slop.

The umpires waved everyone off the field.

In the grandstand, Nelson had stopped in an aisle when it appeared that a decision was imminent. Now he glared at the figures leaving the field and, addressing nobody in particular, spat out the words, "Keith Champion is a fucking no-good whiny motherfucker." Van Sant, standing nearby, snorted. "I could have told them at nine this morning," he said, shaking his head, turning away. "Fuck this bullshit!" said a fan, slamming against a fence on the third-base side the glove he'd brought to the ballpark in hopes of catching a foul ball.

It wasn't just profitability; it wasn't just proximity. What had motivated Herzog in his initial crusade for complex ball—and what was galling him even now, as he squeezed sideways along the length of the press box in Waterloo, his team not having taken on-field batting practice since a week ago Sunday, his trip to Waterloo not having yielded one single piece of insight into any player's development, the players' development not having *existed* for days on end—was professionalism. You couldn't stop snow from falling in Edmonton in April. And you couldn't maintain at every ballpark in the country the same water-sprinkler-green desert perfection of suburban Phoenix. But you could put down a tarp when it rained—unless you didn't have enough personnel, equipment, or experience. In which case, maybe—just maybe—you didn't belong in *professional* baseball.

The architect from Gould Evans Associates of Lawrence, Kansas, showed up at 5:15 on Tuesday, April 28, right around the time everybody in the front office was getting ready to give up and go home. In a letter, Mark Belford had specified that he'd need to see the field under lights, so it had been safe to assume that he'd show up on the late side, but 5:15 was pushing it. The last-minute off-season front-office crush was past, and on nights when the team was out of town, the staff was trying to return to some semblance of standard business hours. Game days were bad enough, starting at nine in the morning and running through midnight or beyond, without off days stretching into "overtime," too. But the PBA inspection was simply one of those things, like an early-morning Park Board session or a late-evening board of directors' meeting. Belford apologized, saying that he'd left his hotel at four, but he'd kept getting lost. He brushed the sandy hair off his forehead and offered a shy, sudden smile. What he didn't say was that earlier in the afternoon he had gone for a run, and he couldn't believe what he'd seen, and the same had been true during the hour-and-a-quarter it had taken him to navigate the one-and-one-half miles to the ballpark. He was eager to get to work and make up for lost time, but he was also eager to satisfy his urban-planner's curiosity about Waterloo: What had happened here?

Simpson called his wife and said he'd be late for dinner. Belford pulled up a chair to face Simpson, placed a clipboard on his lap, and started asking questions. What was the seating capacity? How many grades of seating? How many public phones? How many drinking fountains? Was there a turnstile or an open space at the entrance? Any handicapped parking? Simpson answered them all, patiently, wearily, even sorrowfully. Was there a stadium club? No. A picnic garden? No. Law enforcement to direct traffic? No. Hitting and pitching tunnels? Parking for players? A waiting area for girlfriends and wives? No. No. No.

"Is there a security command post?"

"Uhh," said Simpson, "this office."

"First-aid station?"

"We use that." Simpson waved past Belford's shoulder. "The concession stand."

"Do you know the square footage of the front office?"

"No."

"That's okay," said Belford. "I can just count the ceiling tiles." He did so. "And this is everything?"

"Unfortunately," said Simpson, "yes."

For several minutes thunder had been booming nearer and nearer, occasionally overwhelming their dialogue and causing them to glance uncertainly at the ceiling. Now the storm broke; rain beat violently on the roof and walls. The wooden ticket windows shuddered.

"You're the Astros?" Belford said, raising his voice.

"No. The Padres. When do you think we'll be done? I'm not hurryin' you, or nothin'."

"Depends on how bad this storm is." Then Belford said he was finished with the front office and suggested that the inspection move to the concession stands and whatever other parts of the facility were protected from the rain. Simpson, Nelson, and Belford filed out of the office into the crisp, burnt air of the thundershower. For a moment they stood at the ballpark entrance and stared into the rain, thick enough to obscure the far end of the parking lot. Then they walked along the concourse.

Belford measured the length of the concession stands, and he counted toilet stalls and sinks, and he took a picture of the interior of the press box. As he worked, Belford tried to pass the time with

Simpson and Nelson by telling them that the weather this spring had been hurting him, too; back home in the Kansas City suburb of Lawrence, he explained, he was a Little League coach, and his team had had to practice in the cold and rain. As he moved around this ballpark, Belford seemed especially attentive to the weather, and not just because it would affect whether he could complete his work tonight. His were careful observations, offered with a smile that vanished as suddenly as it appeared, as if he were embarrassed at his architect's appreciation for, and delight in, what's in the details.

"Well, I hear birds," he said when he reached the door to the visitors' locker room. "That's encouraging. Maybe the rain's lettin' up." He went inside and measured the clubhouse, noting the absence of a manager's office as well as a training room. Then he walked along the concourse to the home clubhouse, where he measured the coaches' office, the training room, and the players' locker room, and counted shower heads and inspected the Jacuzzi and toilets. When he stepped outside again, the rain had stopped. He asked Simpson to fire up the ballpark's lights. By the time he was done with the infield measurements, he said, the lights would be warmed up enough that he could get his readings. As Belford walked out on this field for the first time, he glanced up at the sky. Already a pinkish sunset had replaced the earlier darkness. The storm clouds were breaking up. At first the clouds appeared to be unnaturally still, but Belford found that if you stood in one spot and looked hard enough, you could see them moving, third base to first. Then the ballpark lights started to glow dimly, and Belford blinked and set about planting the measuring stakes.

The team was nearly 300 miles away tonight, in Appleton, Wisconsin, playing in another old ballpark near another set of railroad tracks that ran along one more Midwestern river. When a train passed, the grandstand shivered. Paper mills fed the local economy, which was hurting, and the prognosis for that franchise's future was not good, either. On the one hand what an architect from Gould Evans was doing in Waterloo tonight, and in Appleton one of these days, and in Clinton and Burlington and every other minor league ballpark around the country by the All-Star break, was nothing short of revolutionary. Without these measurements, the PBA deadline of April 1, 1994, would be meaningless, and the wholesale movement of franchises and the dramatic shift in power and the end of minor league baseball, as everyone now knew it, would become, if not moot, at least less enforceable. On the other hand, all Belford was doing out on this field was confirming what everybody already knew. For a long time, Simpson and Nelson stood behind the first-base foul line several yards apart, squishing from foot to foot on the soggy ground, but otherwise watching in silence. A cardinal started warbling somewhere in the grandstand. Belford soldiered on, setting up stakes and laying surveyor's lines and making notations in his notebook.

"This is what my life has come down to," Nelson eventually said. "I'm standing on the field at seven o'clock, on a night when there's no game, in Waterloo, Iowa. Shoot me." Suddenly he spun and shouted up into the grandstand. "Shut up!"

The cardinal fell mute for a moment, then started up again. Nelson turned back to the field and resumed his silent vigil. Simpson stuffed his hands deeper in his pockets and studied the sky.

"Lookee that," he said. "Clouds ain't movin'." Then he called out to Belford. "Ninety feet down the lines?"

Belford laughed. "No," he called back. He pointed to first base. "Ninety feet, four inches." He pointed to third. "Ninety feet, five inches." He waved at the dirt between third and second. "Eighty-eight feet, seven inches." Then second and first. "Eighty-nine feet, ten inches. You must have the fastest team in the minors." He smiled. Simpson and Nelson had edged forward now, a combination of amazement and amusement on their faces, to join him on the infield grass. Belford studied their faces for a moment, then continued. "And the *mound*," Belford went on. "Instead of sixty feet, six inches from home, it's sixty feet, one-half inch. And it's supposed to be ten inches higher than home plate. Yours is *nineteen*."

The three men stood there for a moment, looking first at the stakes rising out of the pitching mound, then at one another. Then Simpson nodded decisively. He smiled. He shrugged. He asked if Belford would mind staying alone and locking up the ballpark after himself, and Nelson said he was running late for dinner, too.

"I have one more question," Belford said before they could turn away. He hesitated. He seemed to be choosing his words with care. "What's the economic base of this city?" he finally said.

Belford received the standard answer about John Deere then, John Deere now, and Rath Packing. Belford nodded, thanked them, and assured them that he'd lock the place up securely. When Simpson and Nelson left the ballpark, Belford set out on his final task, planting orange flags to mark the points where he would measure the new lights.

So that was it, Belford thought. He'd wanted to ask about the city because he hadn't been able to make sense of it. Waterloo didn't fit any model he knew. From what he'd observed this afternoon, jogging or driving in circles, he'd never seen a town so working-class and poor. He'd grown up in St. Louis; his father was a cop; he used to go for rides in a squad car. He knew urban blight. And of course he'd seen plenty worse than what he'd seen today. But what struck him—what he had never seen before— was the *proportion.* The ratio of working-class and poor to the rest of the community was all wrong. It must have been—he was guessing here, and perhaps guessing wrong, since he was basing his guess on the unscientific sampling of a lost traveler; but it was nonetheless the guess of an educated outsider, and it was certainly the impression that Waterloo was leaving on a disinterested observer—80 percent.

Belford was walking along the outfield grass now, planting an orange flag every few feet, following a diagram in his notebook. When he had driven into Waterloo from Des Moines this afternoon, and he'd had to approach the city on a two-lane road, he'd sensed something was wrong. Why was there no highway connecting a city of this size with the state capital? And where was the other cross in the crossroads? Most cities of this size grow up around a natural crossroads—the confluence of two rivers, for instance. This city hadn't, which made it, according to everything he'd learned, the wrong size.

These were principles he hadn't thought about since college. They were right out of Urban Planning 101, a textbook exercise every student knew. You could almost predict the size of cities by setting them on a graph: Every 10 miles there needed to be a city of a certain size to meet the needs of a 10-mile radius; every 20 miles a larger city to meet the needs of a 20-mile radius; every 50 miles, a so-called 50 city that incorporated a 20 and a 10; and every 100, a 100 that incorporated a 50, a 20, and a 10. Now that Belford had asked about the economic base of this place, the whole picture made more sense. Waterloo wasn't really a 100 at heart. It didn't lie at that point on the graph where there should have been a 100; it hadn't evolved out of a natural crossroads. There was a river, all right, but then there was only John Deere—an artificial force of nature that had fostered a growth beyond the city's predictable size. And now Waterloo was paying a price for those years of plenty.

When Belford had planted the last of the flags, he turned to consider his handiwork. He had succeeded in imposing a perfect grid on the diamond, and in so doing, he had transformed it. It was no longer a field of grass and dirt, of green and brown; it was, overwhelmingly, a field of orange: plastic flags reflecting the artificial brilliance of the brand-new lights. He didn't dally on this singular sight; it was one that he'd become accustomed to seeing in the course of this project. But the same thought came to him then, as he started moving from flag to flag, taking the light readings, that always occurred to him when he confronted a minor league ball field: scale, in the architectural sense of the word. The scale here, it seemed to him, was human. Back home, watching a game in the modern stadium in Kansas City was like being— what? A candy wrapper in a dugout? A blade of grass on the field? But in a park like this, you could sit behind the visitors' dugout and make out the face of someone sitting behind the home dugout, and chances were, it was someone you knew. Belford understood that the tasks he'd performed here tonight might well seal the fate of this facility, at least as far as professional baseball was concerned. And yet—and yet he couldn't help also thinking that this seemed to be a city that needed a lot of other things before it needed a new ballpark.

Shortly after nine, he was done. He harvested his flags. He turned off the ballpark's lights. He rolled the front gate shut, snapped the padlock, and drove back across the river to his hotel. Waterloo, as far as he could see, was just a 50 that got lucky.

II

THE NATURE
OF THE BEAST

WATERLOO— This is to the lady who took the sack on the cosmetics counter at Younkers on March 29.

The sack had two craft items in it that I bought from the College Square Mall craft sale. Why didn't you turn the sack in to the clerk? I called the store, but no sack was turned in. I know for sure this is where I left it. I just wanted to let you know that I bought that bunny necklace for my daughter, who is just 2 years old. It was going to be from the Easter bunny, and she would have been so pleased.

If you have any conscience at all, please put the two items in the mail. I'll pay the postage when it arrives at my house. If you have no conscience, just remember when every Easter comes around what you stole from a 2-year-old girl.

Carla Manahl
2411 Wenner Drive

—*Waterloo Courier,* April 10, 1992

4

Cap Anson played here. It was June of 1867, and the future Hall of Fame first baseman for the Chicago White Stockings was then a fifteen-year-old center fielder for an amateur team from Marshalltown, Iowa, some 60 miles to the southwest. Baseball was young then, and so was Waterloo. It had been twenty-two years since a group of New York City gentlemen who liked to play the game on the Elysian Fields of Hoboken, New Jersey, organized themselves as the sport's first amateur team, the Knickerbocker Base Ball Club. Likewise, it had been twenty-two years since Mary Melrose Hanna had first set foot on the future site of Waterloo. It would still be another year before the town would incorporate itself as the "City of Waterloo," and two years before the Cincinnati Red Stockings would start paying players and charging admission, thereby inaugurating the era of professional baseball. The coincidence of dates between the ascendancies of Waterloo and baseball wasn't entirely coincidental; the same would have held true, with slight variations, for any number of cities on this side of the Appalachians. What had begun as a pastime for a wealthy Eastern elite had spread to the campsites of the Civil War and from there to virtually every outpost in the massive migration to the West, where the ability of a frontier settlement to field a credible squad had become one measure of its stature among neighboring towns and cities. In their three meetings with the Marshalltown Marshalls in the summer of 1867, the Empires of Waterloo lost 28–25, 40–22, and 76–29 (the game would undergo numerous rule changes and several structural innovations before becoming fully recognizable as the sport played in the twentieth century, though even at this early date the diamond of four equal ninety-foot sides was intact and already apparently inviolable), but no matter: Cap Anson played here.

Luis Aparicio played here, too. Not just in Waterloo, but here, at Municipal Stadium. The year was 1954, and the future Hall of Fame shortstop for the Chicago White Sox was then a twenty-one-year-old prospect with the Waterloo White Hawks. He played in 94 games for the White Hawks that year, hitting .282 and producing 47 RBI and 26 extra-base hits, including 4 home runs. And not just Luis Aparicio: Willie Wilson. Reggie Smith. Norm Cash. Von Hayes. The *arm* on Von Hayes! And not just the home team: Danville's Carl Erskine, Michigan City's Juan Marichal, Burlington's Paul Molitor. . . . The list could go on and on, as it could in any minor league ballpark of a certain age, as it did: the names that were invoked on any day at any game at all those ballparks by the faithful who had witnessed it for themselves, or, at any rate, had heard tell: History happened here.

It was spring now. The weather system that had settled on the Upper Mississippi Valley, trapping it for weeks in tornadoes and thunderstorms, had lifted, scattered, cleared. The trees ringing the outfield walls had filled out. Days were lengthening. Shadows were shortening. Every evening the ritual of turning on the lights—the dark outline of the grandstand roof inching across home plate from the third-base side, the umpire facing the press box and signaling with upraised finger and circling hand, the announcement over the public-address system, "Lights, please; may we please have the stadium lights?"—arrived a few minutes later. Turnouts were still small, the same one, two or three hundred fans game after game, but at least now the evenings were mild enough to allow them to move about, to stroll, to visit, to take in the ballpark: Jeff Nelson surprising one of the player wives with a birthday bouquet of balloons; Dan Yates grabbing fans along the concourse and pointing excitedly up to the girder under the grandstand where a robin had built a nest of twigs and napkins; Champ wandering over to the box seats outside the home dugout before a game just to say hello.

"Those fans bothering you?" a woman said.

Champ glanced over at the bleachers. Last year the *Courier* had quoted the manager as saying that the third-base bleacher fans were so verbally abusive he wouldn't be surprised if they started throwing things at him. The next day, the offending group showed up in caps bearing the logo "SNIPER FANS." That manager was gone now, promoted to High Desert; the caps, and the glares under them, remained.

"I threw a ball up there a couple weeks ago," Champ said, turning back to the fans in the box seats. He leaned against the mesh, gripping it with both hands at eye level. He was smiling. "Maybe that cooled 'em off."

"Last year," the woman said, "his wife and baby would be sitting here, and his wife would be saying, 'They're yelling at my husband.' It hurt her." She shook her head. "Everybody has the freedom to do what they want, but I don't know. It *hurt* her. What if we don't have a team—who are you going to yell at then?"

"Maybe I'll have to keep throwing 'em balls every once in a while." Champ winked and pushed off the mesh.

Then Jeff Nelson stepped down from the aisle into the box seats and started handing out free passes to Waterloo Diamonds Night at the Sky Room Comedy Club, a promotional event he'd arranged for the Saturday of Memorial Day weekend.

"Just don't send your boss," another woman said. "We'd rather have nobody."

Both women nodded their heads emphatically. They had been the core of the Booster Club, an organization of fans, common in the minors, that provided players with a place to stay, supplied them with cooking utensils and bedding, threw them barbecues, and organized bus trips to watch them play on the road. The Booster Club in Waterloo, however, had disbanded for this season, partly because a few of the members who had heckled last year's manager had responded to their fellow Boosters' reprimands by demanding a return of their ten dollars in dues, and partly because the remaining Boosters were unhappy with general manager David Simpson. One of the Boosters lowered her voice now and said that a player who roomed at her house last year told her how in Charleston the players would show up at the park and find that night's promotional giveaway in their lockers, and how it meant a lot to them. "I thought that was a great idea," she said, "and I told Dave, and he said, 'The players don't do anything for me; why should I do anything for them?' They're the ones who bring people to the park! But he could care less about them."

Nelson gave his head a shake of sympathetic disgust and

stepped up to the aisle, squeezing past the designated hitter's wife, who was leaning across the railing to say that she'd finally gotten around to trying a recipe for Swiss steak. "But I put in cream of broccoli," she added sheepishly.

"Well, that's *okay,*" the first Booster said, patting her shoulder. "You don't have to follow my recipe."

Just then something brushed the Wife's bare arm. She jumped, then realized that the Photographer was trying to hand her some pictures. By day the Photographer worked at John Deere as an environmental engineer; at night he served as the ball club's semi-official documentarian. He waited now, trying to hide a smile, his tongue bulging his cheek, as the Wife examined his work.

She shrieked.

He smiled.

"I sneaked 'em," he said.

"You must have! I didn't see you!"

The two Boosters had half risen out of their seats to get a look at the pictures, which showed the Wife sitting with the other player wives and girlfriends on a grandstand bench a few days earlier, just as Nelson had arrived with a bouquet of balloons. "I have a stroganoff recipe," one of the Boosters said, when the photographer had glided away. "I know how much you and Shawn like sauerkraut. Get a pork roast, cook it until it gets really done and brown, break it into pieces, add water to the natural juice, add sauerkraut, and cook some more."

"Well!" said the other Booster. "Here comes the chicken-pox kid!"

It was a pitcher's daughter, being wheeled in a stroller by her mother, a statuesque Southern belle for whom the two Boosters had thrown a baby shower last year, who always dressed the daughter in a matching hair bow and dress (today's color was purple), and who now stopped in the aisle and cried, "Ah can't get the calamine lotion out uh her hay-ir!"

At this point in the season, the stands resembled nothing so much as a small-town Main Street. The ballpark had three tiers of seating—box seats and wooden benches with backrests in the old covered grandstand behind home plate, and metal backless bleachers down either foul line—that ranged in price from $4.50 to $2.50 (though a season's pass to the bleachers for seventy home dates was available for as little as $90), but the effect in the end was overwhelmingly democratic. Neighborly visits were the norm. The regulars all had favorite seats, and they had all been coming here long enough to know the location of all the other regulars' favorite seats, and in these weeks before the Memorial Day weekend and, presumably, the arrival of summer-size crowds, the ballpark belonged to them.

The owners might not see one another all winter long, except at monthly meetings, and often not even then; now they renewed acquaintance on an almost nightly basis. And not just the owners. There was the Bugler, an auto-salvage-yard-and-body-shop employee who was, to be accurate, a cornetist, and who sat in the grandstand behind third and played the Budweiser theme between batters. There was Tex, a tall, bearded specter who worked at the Salvation Army store downtown, wore cowboy boots complete with jangling spurs, and always sat in the back row, and alone. There was the Zoo Crew, an assortment of Deere retirees and Rath veterans who sat in the first-base bleachers, and there was Kelly the Deejay, who'd given them their nickname during the ball club's experimental return to radio a couple of seasons back, and who himself always sat with his father and brother in the grandstand just to the right of home plate. There was Russ the Official Scorekeeper, who in the '30s had worked the scoreboard controls at the previous ballpark, who started writing for the *Courier* while sitting out World War II with a disability, who eventually had risen to the post of *Courier* sports editor before retiring three years earlier, and who always said, whenever Dan Yates stopped by the press box to remind him that the job of official scorekeeper was his as long as he wanted it, "I'd be out here anyway. I may as well be doing something." (It was entirely likely that Waterloo was the only franchise in professional baseball employing both a one-eyed scorekeeper and a one-eyed groundskeeper.)

Stronger than any presence, however, was the absence of John Shannon. A John Deere retiree, Shannon had attended every home game for decades until May 5, 1990, when he died. It was commonly said that the only game he missed in all those years was on the day of his wife's funeral. "Ai-yi-yi!" was his signature cry, audible throughout the park, famous throughout Waterloo, and infamous throughout the league for rattling the opposition. Cedar

Rapids was a favorite target of Shannon's, stemming not so much from the two cities' traditional rivalry as from the time he attended a game there and got slapped with a racial slur. (He never went back.) Even two years after he'd watched his last game in Waterloo Municipal Stadium, Shannon was routinely invoked by fans as if he were still sitting there, several rows back in the grandstand, slightly on the first-base side—how he'd bring fresh-baked cookies for the home team ("Cookie Man," the players called him), or how his heckling would follow a player on the opposing team into the dugout ("Throw youse helmet all youse want to do, but youse is o-u-t *out!*"), or how he'd try to bribe the home team into a rally ("Dollar for a hit!" or "Five dollars for a home run!"

"And he'd *pay!*"

"And they'd *take it!*")

Waterloo Municipal Stadium belonged squarely to a mid-century style of ballpark architecture, all steel girders and poured concrete, that was as blunt and functional as the city itself. It did the job. For years it had occupied not only a position of some prominence within the community, but quite literally a central place. The people who worked *there* (the factory behind the grandstand and across the river) would go home *there* (the neighborhood beyond the left-field fence and across the railroad track), then, with the whole family, walk over *here.* (And sometimes go to their final reward over there—the cemetery that sloped up from the right-field fence.)

Fans over a certain age in the city and throughout much of northeast Iowa had seemingly the same memory of what professional baseball in Waterloo used to be. Again and again they would relate the same story in much the same words: how the '47 club won the Three-I League (as in Iowa, Illinois, Indiana) championship; how on a day the White Hawks were playing at home you couldn't walk downtown without seeing hand-lettered signs announcing that night's game; how a season's coverage in the *Courier* would include daily "Know Your White Hawks" profiles ("George moved to the 2nd sack slot after being a 3rd sacker . . . Gained nickname 'Scooter' by way he scoots around the keystone sack!!"); how it sometimes got so you'd have to call for tickets days and weeks in advance; how for three seasons running, '47, '48, '49, attendance topped 170,000, or an average of more than 3,000 fans per game; how KXEL radio, covering the action from a makeshift booth behind the first-base bleachers and broadcasting clear-channel from high atop the old Russell Lamson Hotel, conveyed the glory of Waterloo to an audience that theoretically stretched from the Rocky Mountains to the Atlantic Ocean; how such national stature seemed only fitting for a city that, in 1949, was the site of a franchise in the inaugural season of the National Basketball Association, competing against the likes of St. Louis, Boston, Philadelphia, Chicago, and New York.

Another city in the NBA that first season was Denver, then not much more than a mountain town with possibilities. Denver, of course, had boomed, and by 1992 had secured a National League expansion franchise for the following season. And Waterloo's NBA franchise had lasted only one season, eventually winding up as the Hawks in Atlanta, another twentieth-century boom city and, back in 1969, another major-league-baseball expansion city. Still, it wouldn't be fair to say that Waterloo hadn't boomed and to leave it at that. By 1992, Waterloo—home to pro ball on and off, but mostly on, since 1904, for a total of seventy-seven years— ranked third on the active list of cities with minor league associations, after Rochester, New York (1900, eighty-nine years), and Portland, Oregon (1904, eighty-four years). It was true, the stands at Municipal Stadium might never see 170,000 people in one season again. But it was also true that this was still professional baseball, and that this was still professional baseball in *Waterloo*.

The fans brought testimony to the ballpark. The two pages in the baseball oral history *The Glory of Their Times* in which Rube Marquard described arriving at the Illinois Central station in Waterloo in 1906 to play for the local pro team and finding that the ball club's owners were the guys who ran the smoke shop; a scorecard from the 1940s discovered while rummaging through old papers in an antique shop; the city centennial edition of the *Courier* that devoted column after column to the history of professional baseball in Waterloo—game after game, fans showed up with one keepsake or another and, gingerly, passed it along. Then they returned it safely home, where they stored it in a place of honor with all their other baseball memorabilia. Sometimes this devotion took the form of two informal shrines: one to the long-time employer—a vacuum-packed 48-ounce can of Rath Black

Hawk Honey Glazed Ham on a shelf in a corner of the basement, or a scrapbook of *Courier* clippings documenting the death throes at Rath ("Rath production at virtual standstill"), or the Rath nutritionist's desk in the guest bedroom of a former plant watchman who hadn't driven past the front entrance of the factory since the day it closed; and one to baseball—box after box of clippings, programs, photographs, old Booster Club buttons ("Diamonds Are Forever"), even baseball cards of seemingly obscure major-league players from the '50s and '60s, just as long as they carried, somewhere among the career stats on the reverse side, the word "Waterloo."

Jack Kuper was one such fan. Days he'd worked at Rath, to which he'd devoted one corner of his basement; evenings and weekends he'd worked for baseball, to which he'd devoted the rest of his basement, as well as his garage. He'd been coming out to the ballpark since his parents started bringing him here in the 1940s, he and his wife had been running the Waterloo Optimist Clubs for more than thirty years, his son had played amateur baseball, his daughter had married a former Midwest League player (with Wisconsin Rapids), and he probably would have crossed the line long ago between passionate observer and passionate participant—between fan and owner—if his wife, Barb Kuper, a regular ever since *her* parents starting bringing her out to the ballpark in the 1940s, hadn't already beaten him to it. The two of them were Zoo Crew fixtures in the first-base bleachers, always easy to spot, even from across the field in the opposite bleachers, with their matching white hair and perfect postures. In 1966, he wrote a letter to the Chamber of Commerce, which at that time was more or less responsible for the operation of the ball club, complaining, "Our fine stadium is a little lacking in the groundskeeping dept." "A well dragged and chalked field makes the field look more professional," his letter continued. "We are in professional baseball and lets keep our baseball field looking like a pro. field, not a bush-league field like it is most of the time now. . . . I know this all means effort and work, but golly, wouldn't it be worth it to see it pay off and see our bleachers full of enthusiastic fans." In 1985, Kuper got his chance. Rath had closed during the off-season, and in the process he'd lost the only job he'd held since high school. When Jack Kuper, after thirty-two years in the extreme heat and stink of a smokehouse, heard through Barb that the ball club was looking for a new groundskeeper, the prospect of spending a summer out of doors didn't seem like a bad idea. He reported for work at seven in the morning if the manager requested it, he drove to the park and put down the tarps in the middle of the night if he saw a storm approaching, and, when he discovered that the ball club's lawn mower didn't perform up to his standards on the infield grass, he brought his own mower from home. That year a number-one draft pick named B. J. Surhoff made a much-publicized professional debut at Municipal Stadium, playing for Beloit, a Brewers' farm club. Years later, Kuper introduced himself to Surhoff at County Stadium in Milwaukee, saying he had the lineup card from Surhoff's first game in pro ball. Surhoff gave Kuper a quizzical look at first, but then he brightened. "Waterloo!" he said, to Kuper's immense satisfaction.

The intimacy with other fans that the ballpark afforded was only part of its attraction; of at least equal importance to the regulars was the proximity to the game itself. Nowhere did the grandstand or bleachers rise more than sixteen rows from the field. Even in what passed for the ballpark's deepest recesses, in the shadows of the uppermost grandstand bench, back against the rusted wire mesh that kept children and drunks from falling to the pavement out front, it was still possible to hear the chorus of *Baaack!* from the dugout alerting a base runner that the pitcher was throwing to first, or the pillow-punch of a catcher's throw to third when it missed the mitt and hit the bag, or that distinctive deadened thud of horsehide upon lumber when a fly ball whumped the outfield fence. At this range, fans could study the game in a way that wasn't possible on television or at a major league stadium. Here they could learn to *see* a player's development—to appraise talent at first glance, to watch adjustments week by week, to witness progress over the months of a season. To be a part, maybe, of history in the making.

By May the ballpark regulars had seen enough of the players to begin to recognize individual styles: outfielder Shawn Robertson's caveman drag of the bat as he approached home plate; the Australian Cameron Cairncross's pickoff move to first, nailing base runners who sometimes didn't even see the ball coming; Robbie Beckett's habit of pitching five or six innings of no-hit or one-hit ball and still giving up two or three runs on a combination of walks and wild pitches. Beckett's outings, in particular, were wonders to behold. When he lost his concentration, often in the first inning, sometimes with the first batter, he'd visibly unravel, shaking his head, taking more and more time between pitches, prolonging his agony in a misbegotten effort to shorten it. His falling apart—his inability to hold himself together—was no secret in the stands, no secret in the opposing dugout, and certainly no secret in the batter's box, where, after a while on certain nights, all a hitter had to do to reach first base was walk up to the plate and wait four pitches.

But it was Jason Hardtke who immediately distinguished himself as a prospect. What the San Diego organization thought of this switch-hitting second baseman was clear from the circumstances of his mid-April arrival: acquired in a trade with Cleveland almost straight up for a major leaguer, Padres outfielder Tom Howard. (Another minor league player was to be named later.) But even without those credentials, his talent would have been evident at a glance. Hustling a routine single into a double, then scoring on the next hit, when most any other player only then would be pulling into second; grabbing a grounder backhand behind second and flipping to the shortstop for the force, and making it look effortless; hitting for average and power from both sides of the plate: *The kid has a shot,* the whispering went, *the kid has a shot.*

Statistically, the most common estimates of a Class A player's chances of one day making the majors, even if only for the proverbial late-season "cup of coffee" single at-bat, ranged from one in nineteen to one in ten. But a more accurate estimate was: It depends. Assemble a squad of All-Stars and the chances improved. In 1975 the Waterloo Royals went 49–13 over the first half of the season and set the professional baseball record for best split-season won-lost percentage ever—.790—not only breaking the old mark set by the 1934 Los Angeles team in the Pacific Coast League, but cementing most of the Kansas City Royals starting lineup that would win the American League pennant five years later. But, really, all it took was one—one player to make a season stand out, to leave Waterloo behind, bound for glory two years down the road, or next year, or even this year.

It can happen. In 1986 Greg Swindell, a twenty-one-year-old left-handed pitcher who had been picked second overall in that year's June draft, held out until the end of July before signing (for $165,000) with the Cleveland Indians, who assigned him to Waterloo. In three starts he went 2–1, striking out 25 over 18 innings, and compiling a 1.00 ERA. The Indians organization promptly promoted him to Double A. This was on a Monday. That Thursday, early in the morning of what would have been his Double-A debut, Swindell received a phone call from the brass in Cleveland: That night's scheduled starter on the major league roster, Phil Niekro, was out with a sore elbow, and the only available backup pitcher would be going on the disabled list that same day with a sore neck. And so, on the evening of August 21, three weeks after signing with the Indians organization and joining his Waterloo teammates on the road in Appleton, Swindell found himself on the mound in Cleveland, pitching against the then-mighty Boston Red Sox. He wound up lasting three and two-thirds innings, giving up six runs (four earned) on six hits, three walks, and a run-scoring balk, and picking up the loss; and the Indians went on to lose the game 24–5, yielding the most runs in a game in franchise history; but: Swindell had made the jump from Waterloo to The Show, and in only three weeks, and in years to come he'd established himself as one of the game's premier pitchers. It *happened.*

And it happened *here*—in part, anyway. Forever after, no full accounting of Greg Swindell's professional baseball career could appear without at least a mention of Waterloo. Of course, anybody could have predicted that Greg Swindell would wind up in the majors; he arrived with massive fanfare, and he departed amid more of the same. But sometimes it was trickier: a name glimpsed in the sports section several years hence, a scratch of the head, a sudden recollection: Oh, *right*—the one with the caveman drag of the bat; the one with the unbeatable pickoff move; the one who couldn't get the ball over the plate if his career depended on it, which it did. And then Waterloo would have one more claim on immortality: the Waterloo Boy tractor that first rolled off the assembly line in 1914; the Dillinger henchman who during the Depression met his end in a hail of bullets on a downtown street; the five Sullivan brothers, who went down together on the same ship in the Pacific during World War II, and who became the subject of a Hollywood biography; Rath Packing, which over the decades must have placed the Waterloo name on millions of kitchen counters; the .282 hitter with four home runs in 1954 who, in retrospect, would turn out to be probably the greatest baseball player ever to call Waterloo his former home.

One afternoon in the spring of 1992, a baseball fan from Massachusetts, finding himself in Cedar Rapids on business, made the drive up to Waterloo just to see the ballpark that he used to hear about in Boston, in 1946, as a seventeen-year-old listening on the radio in his bedroom to clear-channel KXEL. He found his way to the home-manager's office, where he spent an hour chatting with Champ, and then Champ led him through the clubhouse and out to the field, where one of the ball club's owners, raking the dirt near first base, took him by the elbow and directed his attention around the park: Luis Aparicio played there. Willie Wilson played there. See that woman raking the dirt behind home? Where she's standing is where Carlton Fisk caught his first professional baseball game ever. "You've seen how small that tunnel is," the owner said, directing the visitor's attention to the home dugout and the doorway that led to the clubhouse. "Can you imagine Fisk having to fit through there?"

They laughed, and then they turned elsewhere, but before they did they stood there a moment, not moving, not speaking, simply staring into the darkness of the clubhouse tunnel, as if, any moment now, a future Hall of Famer might emerge.

The last thing a Waterloo Diamond would see before disappearing down the tunnel to the dugout were a couple of hand-lettered signs on the clubhouse wall. "To play this game you must have that fire in you," read one, "and there is nothing that stokes fire like PRIDE." Beneath this lettering, the word "PRIDE" was repeated in six-inch letters. The second sign said, "WINNING IS NOT EVERYTHING. IT IS THE ONLY THING."

In fact, it wasn't. The signs were remnants from another season, but they could have been relics from another era. By now, winning had long since ceased being the only thing in the minor leagues, and player development, if not the only thing or even everything, had become the most important thing by far. This was a fact of minor league life that every player learned soon after signing a pro contract, and this was a fact of minor league life that every player kept learning for the duration of his career. This year, for the Waterloo Diamonds, it was a lesson that their manager had made sure they heard fresh the first week of the new season.

"Okay!" Champ had begun. "Listen up!" It would have been an otherwise unmemorable occasion: immediately following the fourth game of the season, and the third loss, no Opening Day jitters or distractions now, just a chilly Tuesday night in Burlington, Iowa, in front of a couple of hundred customers, some in woolen hats. The players stopped what they were doing—sitting, stripping, trying to decide whether to shower here in this low concrete locker room or to wait until they were safely back in the warmth of their motel rooms—and faced their leader. Champ started slowly, admitting a mistake of his own, a botched signal he'd sent from the coach's box at third. "I fucked up," he said. "I admit it. But look, if you see me doing something that makes no fuckin' sense, tell me. Ask me to repeat the signs. Ask me, 'Hey, Champ, what are you fuckin' doin'? You're putting a fuckin' *bunt* on with two outs and two fuckin' strikes?' " Then he lectured a little on fundamentals: the importance of the leadoff hitter reaching base ("Get a walk, or get a hit, or *get* hit"); the importance of hitting to right ("You're not gettin' to the majors on your ability to bunt"). Then Champ turned to Kevin Farlow and asked why he'd thrown to second base in the first inning.

Farlow, lanky, heavy-lidded, was the starting second baseman. In the bottom of the first, with the bases loaded and nobody out, he'd chased a fly ball into foul territory near the Waterloo bullpen. On the run, Farlow had tucked one leg, slid in the mud, caught the ball, and in the same motion come up throwing . . . to second base. The runner on third tagged up and scored what would be the only run in a 1–0 game; the infield hit that had opened the inning, in fact, would turn out to be Burlington's only hit all night. It had been a tough loss for the Diamonds, and a tough loss for starter Cameron Cairncross, but winning or losing wasn't the point. It had been an *unnecessary* loss.

"I'm not sayin' it was right or wrong," Champ prompted Farlow about the throw to second. "I just want to know why."

Farlow didn't answer at first. He was now marking his second consecutive season in Waterloo: not a good sign. He straightened in his chair, took a deep breath, and said, all in a rush, "I was heading toward the bullpen and didn't see the play, so I had to take what I could find when I turned around."

"That's right!" said Champ. He swung away from Farlow. "Bullpen! Where were you? That's your job! You gotta say, 'Home! Home!' You gotta be in the game. Dean and I"—pitching coach Dean Treanor—"are out there goin', 'Shit, you hear anything?' 'No, I didn't hear anything.' " Champ lowered his voice. "You're here to go to the big leagues, and the way to get there is to learn from your mistakes. Work on your weaknesses. Don't worry about whether your buddy is goin' up. What are you going to do when they call you up, say you're not going unless they take your buddy?" He paused. "That's the toughest thing about baseball. We have to work as a team, but we're here as individuals. So do what it takes. *Fuck it.* Because either you're goin' to the big leagues, or you're goin' home."

In a way, the minor leagues acted as a series of chutes. As players advanced through a major league organization's development system, they found themselves herded through narrower and narrower passages. Those who managed to squeeze through one would emerge on the other side into a more privileged holding pen; those who didn't were shunted off to slaughter, so to speak. At the farthest reaches of the system, nearest the major leagues, the chutes were narrow indeed: Each major league club kept exactly one Triple A and one Double A affiliate—only twenty-three to twenty-five players at either level of development. For this reason, it was generally believed that the most difficult promotion for a player to get—the one that represented both the most marked difference in talent between two levels of the minors and the greatest commitment from the major league front office to a player's prospects—was into the Double A elite from the wide, wandering Class A hordes.

The designation Class A actually encompassed several levels: A-Advanced, A and Short-Season A. That single "A," additionally, encompassed two informal levels, by general agreement: "middle" (Midwest League) and "slow" (South Atlantic League). Unlike the uniform ratio of one major league organization to one minor league affiliate at both the Double A and Triple A levels, organizations forged affiliations with Class A clubs in whatever combination suited front office philosophy. Some organizations kept two A-Advanced clubs, for instance, and some none. Most included a Short-Season club; six didn't. The San Diego Padres were unusual, though not unique, in that they financed a club at each of the four Class A levels, plus an entry-level Rookie League club to boot.

As a rule, by the time a player in the Padres system reached Waterloo, he already would have spent at least part of a season at a lower level. Players drafted out of high school were most likely to land in the Arizona League, one of five Rookie leagues in the minors that stressed the baseball fundamentals and extra-baseball maturity that a player presumably would have learned had he continued on to college. (The Padres team even played at a community college, in Scottsdale.) Those players drafted out of college were most likely to start their professional careers at Spokane in the Northwest League, one of two Short Season-A leagues in the minors. After this initial June-through-August exposure to pro ball, a player's first full-season stop in the Padres' system would be Charleston, South Carolina, in the "slow A" South Atlantic League. Then came Waterloo.

Of the twenty-six players on the opening day 1992 roster of the San Diego Padres' "middle" Class A affiliate, exactly half had followed some variation on one or the other of these paths. They were the draft class of '90: first assigned to Scottsdale or Spokane, promoted to Charleston in '91, promoted to Waterloo in '92. The rest of the squad was split more or less between the draft classes of '89 and '91. It said something about the '89 draftees that in all this time they hadn't advanced past Waterloo, just as it said something about the '91 draftees that already they had attained this level—though what it said, in each player's case, wasn't necessarily what it seemed to say. Had he been drafted out of high school? College? Had there been an injury? How high had he been drafted? And what *about* the class of '90—how high had they been drafted? What about him? And him? And *him?*

What about me?

Already the A-ball shuttle had begun. Less than two weeks into the season, on the night the team returned from the washed-out series in Clinton, Champ had called Kyle Moody into his office.

"Sometimes I gotta sugarcoat," Champ had said, "but not in this case." Moody was going to Charleston—a demotion, technically. The previous year, Moody had been drafted in the forty-eighth round and assigned to Spokane, where he'd hit a respectable-though-hardly-remarkable .260, so the assignment this year to the Padres' middle-level A club had come as somewhat of a surprise. In most games, though, he'd checked the starting lineup that Champ posted in the dugout and found his name near the bottom of the sheet, as first-base coach. In fact, the only time he'd appeared in a game had been as a late-inning defensive replacement in the season opener, when he'd committed the throwing error that set up the winning run. He hadn't even gotten to bat. In Charleston, however, Moody would be getting the chance to play nearly every day. The morning after Champ broke the news to him, Moody hopped in the car his father had driven up from Texas over the weekend, and lit out of Waterloo before dawn.

Jason Hardtke, the player who had come from the Cleveland organization in a trade virtually straight up for a San Diego major league starter, replaced Moody in the apartment share with Pugh. He also replaced Farlow at second base. Farlow shifted to third. Dave Adams, a forty-first-round pick in 1990 with a .229 career batting average, shifted from third to the utility-infielder role that Moody, in theory, had occupied.

It was a curious position to be in, the professional ballplayer's. He was at once central to the operation yet peripheral, both the center of attention and very nearly incidental. Without him, of course, there would be no games, no entertainment to sell, no industry—no minor league franchise to run, no major league farm system from which to recruit. But the fact was inescapable that the "him" out there didn't have to be him specifically—didn't have to be him stepping into the spotlight at "Meet the Diamonds," didn't have to be his name in the box score, didn't have to be his face on the front of a trading card. On the afternoon in Beloit that the Diamonds had gotten their pictures taken for Best baseball cards, the team's designated hitter, Shawn Whalen, had approached the photographer in the shade of the dugout and said, "How come we don't get paid for this?"

"You'll have to ask Best," the photographer answered.

"The majors do," Whalen said.

"I don't work for Best," the photographer said. "I'm self-employed. You get a raise this year?"

"No." This was Billy Johnson, a pitcher who was sitting down the bench.

"Me, neither," the photographer said. "In fact, I'm working more just to make the same amount of money."

"I been wearin' the same underwear for two months," said Johnson.

"Me, too. You want to trade?"

"Mine got skid marks."

"Mine, too."

"Not that I'm sayin' I want more money," Whalen said. "It's just I been askin' this for the past three years, and I never get an answer." He shook his head and bounded up the steps to field level. "I think it's just another one of them minor league hang-with-'ems."

They were apprentices, was what they were. For $1,000 a month they were getting on-the-job training. They knew this; they accepted it. It was part of the bargain. High school graduates put college plans on hold; college students interrupted their studies; newlyweds left a bedroom full of gifts back at the parents' house; fathers said good-bye to wives and children or figured out a way to bring them along; but none of the players was suspending his life so much as pursuing a continuation of the only life he'd ever known. Once, a long time ago, when the minors were young and independent of the majors—when winning really was the only thing—a minor leaguer could have played as long as his stamina and desire allowed, without necessarily worrying about the major leagues. Players had made careers out of the minors, and in some cases the minor leagues had even paid more than the majors. Now, however, the sole goal was The Show.

One day toward the end of spring training, Shawn Whalen had gotten word that Ed Lynch, the Padres' minor league director, and Tom Gamboa, the minor league field coordinator, wanted to see him. He knew what that meant. In 1989 Whalen had been the Padres' fifteenth-round pick, bypassing short-season ball altogether that year and immediately placing at Charleston, where he had struggled through 62 games with a .182 batting average. Still, the following season, he'd gotten the promotion to Waterloo. The year after that, he'd remained in Waterloo. Now he'd been in pro ball for three seasons, he'd had the benefit of playing college ball and, under those circumstances, he was getting old—twenty-four—not to have advanced past Class A. He understood that at a certain point an organization had to get rid of those players who had demonstrated beyond a doubt they didn't have what it takes to make the majors in order to clear space for younger players who—who knew?—might. So Whalen bade his roommate farewell, then sought out Bryan Little, his manager at Waterloo the past two seasons, and offered a handshake and his heartfelt thanks. Little looked at him quizzically for a moment, then broke into a smile and explained that all Lynch and Gamboa wanted to know was whether Whalen would be willing to go back to Waterloo one more time, with the understanding that he would be moving up sooner rather than later. After recovering his composure, Whalen said he'd have to think about it. Baseball organizations didn't have forever to invest in some ballplayers, but some ballplayers didn't have forever to invest in baseball, either: Whalen and his wife were expecting their first child in October. Whalen returned to his room and called her. After debating the pros and cons for a while, she ended the discussion with one comment. "If it's what Jesus wants," she said.

So Whalen was in Waterloo, to his surprise. So was Robbie Beckett, to his. Apparently, being even a first-round draft selection offered no guarantees. In 1989 the White Sox, picking seventh in the first round, had drafted Frank Thomas; on the very next pick, the Cubs had taken Earl Cunningham. By mid-May 1992, Thomas was starting at first base for the White Sox in Chicago, while Cunningham was returning to Peoria from the Cubs' A-Advanced farm club—and facing him on the mound was Beckett, the Padres' own example of first-round frustration and proof that being a high draft pick wasn't even necessarily a status to envy. There was the money, yes—in Beckett's case, a signing bonus of around $150,000; and then there was the pressure. Everywhere Beckett went, it seemed his name couldn't be mentioned or written without the words "former first-round draft pick" preceding it. As a high-school pitcher in Austin, Texas, he'd developed a reputation for an overpowering 88 mph fastball and a formidable slider, but also for wildness—a tendency that only compounded itself under the constant scrutiny that went with being a first-round pick. The outing in Peoria was typical: He pitched four and two-thirds innings of no-hit ball before Champ yanked him—not because he'd given up three runs on nine walks, but because he'd reached his pitch count, as dictated to Champ from the front office back in San Diego. "Worst fuckin' feeling in baseball," Beckett raged to himself after the game, pressing his face against the webbing of the batting tunnel outside the clubhouse, obsessively shredding a strand of elastic while his teammates, at a safe distance, pretended not to watch, "to know they're takin', and you still can't throw a strike. Fuck!"

Seemingly the ideal position to be in was as a high prospect with good numbers, a slot that on this season's Diamonds was filled only by Jason Hardtke. Yet even he'd had a run of unfortunate luck lately. The Cleveland organization had drafted him in the third round in 1990, out of high school in San Jose, California, and assigned him to Rookie ball. The next year, predictably, he'd proceeded to slow-A Columbus, Georgia, where, over the course of 139 games, he led the league with 155 hits, batting .290 with twelve home runs, eighty-one RBI, and—his specialty—twenty-six doubles. Those stats and a batting average over .500 this past spring had earned him a promotion to A-Advanced Kinston, North Carolina, amid strong hints that a further promotion past the magical Double A barrier wasn't far away. Then came the trade. His new organization had assigned him to the middle-A affiliate—bit of bad luck number one—because the Padres were stocked with prospects at his position, second base—bit of bad luck number two. Now, whenever Hardtke looked up the organization to High Desert, there was Billy Hall batting .376, Billy Hall batting .393, Billy Hall batting .406.

So Hardtke was here, too. They were all here, A-ball players one and all—and any player who doubted it only had to look around.

"Don't get caught up in what town you're in," Champ had cautioned the team at the start of the season. "Charleston, Waterloo, High Desert—they're all A." In a sense, it was true. Very little differentiated one level of full-season A-ball from the next, and players often shifted between levels for any number of reasons, only one of which was talent. Still, there was A-ball, and then there was A-ball. Where was the Booster Club? In Charleston, the local newspaper had run profiles on them—why not here? In Cedar Rapids, a plaque at the ballpark entrance listed former players who'd made The Show—it had to help the Reds, showing up at the ballpark and seeing that incentive. But in Waterloo, after the "Meet the Diamonds" night—nothing. And the assistant general manager marching through the clubhouse a month and a half later handing out free passes to a Waterloo Diamonds Night at a comedy club where they would have to pay for their own drinks didn't count. Then there was Waterloo Municipal Stadium itself. As Scott Pugh had said, the night he'd arrived in Waterloo from Spokane late last season, during his almost-daily phone call home, "Well, Daddy, I'm in the minors now."

But it wasn't only the town. It was them. Errors, walks, balks, passed balls, missed signals, and all-around boneheadedness: games that staggered, games that sped, games that stretched and stopped and sputtered long into the night: games that breezed at a brisk two-hour clip, games that wheezed long past the three-hour mark: all the hallmarks of inexperience and inconsistency and incompetence, all in one place, and sometimes all in one night: the marathon in Beloit that lasted three hours and fifty minutes; that eventually spent itself before exactly 35 frigid souls; that featured seven errors by the Diamonds, four errors by the Brewers, two hit batsmen, two wild pitches, one balk, one passed ball and, in the top of the ninth, the old hidden-ball trick. With two outs, the bases loaded, and the score tied, the Brewer third baseman conferred with the pitcher, returned to his position and, when the Diamond runner on third wandered off the bag toward home, produced the ball from his mitt to make the tag. While Champ argued the call, the Diamonds didn't even take the field for several minutes—not so much because they had any legitimate protest, or because their manager had any legitimate argument, as out of stunned embarrassment at having fallen prey to the oldest trick in the book. It simply didn't get any more bush league than this.

Any you guys gonna make it to the pros? One answer was, These *are* the pros—but that wasn't *the* answer because the question wasn't *the* question, which was the question that the San Diego brass asked about them, and that they asked about one another, and that they asked of themselves. Naturals all, these players had exhibited a talent at an early age, and their parents had adjusted accordingly, apportioning time and money for the ball player in the family. On sandlots and in schoolyards and at ballparks where the bleachers were only half a dozen rows deep, their friends and teammates had acknowledged them as the best in the neighborhood, the best in Little League, the best in their whole high school. Scholarships or signing bonuses had followed, the competing seductions of college recruiters and major-league scouts. Eventually, the mammoth screening machinery of major-league baseball—the directors of player development and scouting for the twenty-six (and counting) major-league organizations, the vice presidents of scouting, the scouting coordinators, the directors of national scouting, the directors of international scouting, the national cross-checkers, the national supervisors, the regional supervisors, the special-assignment scouts, the consulting scouts, the *scouts,* not to mention the communally funded Major League Scouting Bureau—had narrowed its sights, elevating them to the elect ranks of the professional ball player. But that didn't change the answer: *I don't know.*

"Am I going to have to get a *job?*" said the outfielder and self-described beach bum to himself in the middle of the night, staring at the ceiling of a bedroom within walking distance of a cornfield, more than 1,000 miles from the nearest ocean.

"I'll be twenty-five next year," said the relief pitcher, on the phone at three in the morning to the girlfriend he met last season, over the bullpen fence in Erie, Pennsylvania. "I'll be *twenty-five* next year."

"Get outta my bed!" said the infielder, flat on his back on the sidewalk outside a college bar, balling his fist and roundhousing the night air. "*Get outta my bed!*"

All of which was all well and good in the minor league scheme of things, part of what major league player-development personnel inevitably like to call "the maturing process." It was perfectly natural for a player to wonder if, having come so far, the end was near—just so long as by morning he believed it wasn't. Because if he couldn't adopt that attitude—if he no longer could summon the belief that had sustained him this far: that, despite the evidence of his physical limitations or the pressures of his outside commitments or simply the overwhelming odds, he still had a shot, however remote—then he might as well go home.

*

Late one night Champ got a call at his apartment. It was from Billy Johnson, the pitcher who'd had nothing on the ball in relief in that night's game. He said that he was calling from a convenience store—his apartment didn't have a phone—and that he'd packed his bags and wanted to go home.

This was never an easy task for a manager. The hard fact was, Billy Johnson was battle fodder. There were only so many genuine prospects in any minor league system, and everybody at the uppermost levels knew who they were. When major league front-office executives looked at the outcome of a minor league game half a continent away, what they were seeing wasn't a battle between two teams but a game situation for, say, the two potential major leaguers on their own team and the three on the other. On the Diamonds, those prospects included Hardtke, Beckett if he ever got his head screwed on straight, possibly Cairncross, plus a couple of long shots. What these players needed most at this point in their careers were playing conditions to develop their game skills on a daily basis, and it was the job of the Billy Johnsons of the world to complete the field. It was their job to be in uniform, until the moment somebody in San Diego decided it wasn't. Somebody in San Diego: not a kid at a pay phone at a 7-Eleven; not a manager at a Class-A club in Waterloo, Iowa. Still, Champ couldn't blame him. At twenty-four, in his fourth year with the Padres, Johnson had compiled a career won-lost record of 9–22 and an ERA pushing 6.00, and he hadn't advanced past the organization's middle-A affiliate. Just battle fodder: Over two innings tonight, he had given up nine runs, seven earned, on seven hits and five walks. Oh, yeah—and a hit batsman. Champ had to wonder if Johnson might be better off hearing him say, "Go." But, then again, maybe what the kid wanted to hear was "Don't go," because here he was, calling Champ; here he was, not going home.

So Champ said what he had to say and hung up the phone. A manager's day was never done. This was always the case in pro ball, but Champ was finding it to be especially true this season. He'd wake up at 10:00 in the morning, and already he'd be juggling lineups in his head. Then he'd go for a run or a workout at the Y, all the while still rethinking possible lineups and pitching rotations, then over to his ballpark office by 1:30 or 2:00 to go over paperwork, maybe call San Diego, and suit up. Then BP at 4:15, infield at 6:00, game at 7:00. With luck the game would be over by 10:00, and then he and pitching coach Dean Treanor, eating hot dogs and sipping beer from the top of a cardboard box in the middle of their office, would have to fill out the postgame reports to fax to San Diego. By then it might be 11:00 or midnight. "Fuckin' long-ass day," he'd say and, as often as not, ask if anybody wanted to meet him at Toad's.

Toad's was a bar on Main Street in downtown Cedar Falls, safely away from the players' hangouts by the university. From the ballpark Champ had a choice of two routes: a direct path through Waterloo down the University Avenue commercial strip and its succession of stoplights, each seemingly more insidiously timed than the last, or a more circuitous route through the farmland on the far northern end of town. Early on, Champ had determined that the latter route, though longer in distance, was faster, and from that evening forward his choice never varied. Often his was the only car on that dark highway, out there where the temperature always seemed ten degrees cooler than in town, and he'd roll down the window and push the limit, just him and his headlights and the rushing country air under an impossibly starry sky, plus the satisfaction of knowing he was making good time.

Efficiency pleased Champion. He had studied graphic design at Southwest Missouri State, and his first job out of college, four days after a December 1981 graduation, was in the graphics department of CNN, back when it was a fledgling operation and Ted Turner himself would show up at the monthly parties. It wasn't something he discussed much, but privately Champion prided himself on his attention to detail, his knack of knowing a straight line at a glance, his natural affinity for order and composition. One off-season, he'd worked as a Housing and Urban Development inspector back home, testing low-income residences for carbon monoxide levels. On the coldest days, he would schedule his appointments so that he had to drive his truck from one corner of the county clear to the opposite corner, then to a third corner and across to its diametric opposite, and only then to the interior of the county, deliberately devising an itinerary that would allow him to remain within the warmth of the cab as long as possible. Even Champ's inefficiency was efficient.

But the ballpark—what was the excuse there? Champ would lean against the wall down the third-base line before a game and wonder why nobody had noticed that some of the outfield signs had so much lettering that the name of the advertiser wasn't legible from the stands. Forget about the big projects: replacing the many missing box seats, finishing the paint job, creating an even remotely appealing color scheme in the grandstands behind home, which at the moment consisted of a low green wall, a silver ledge, yellow box seats, brown metal chairs, blue rails, and red benches. What about the *dandelions?* Not a day passed that Champion didn't walk up to the front gate of the ballpark and ask himself how much effort it would take for someone—the city, the ball club, groundskeepers, volunteers, anyone—to weed the plot of grass that was a customer's first impression. And why was the ball club invisible? You go to Davenport, you see billboards for the River Bandits. Here, nothing. One night, he and Treanor had stopped at a sports bar, the kind of place where the walls are crowded with uniforms and pennants and framed photographs of local sports legends; nowhere was there a shred of evidence that within the same city that housed this establishment—this *sports bar*—there existed a professional baseball team. Finally they'd called over the bartender and asked her why there wasn't anything from the Diamonds on display.

"What," she'd answered, agreeably, "are the Diamonds?"

By the time Champ would get to Toad's, the marquee on the movie theater in the next block was always dark; when the rest of the world had finished its evening relaxation, he was just beginning his. It was like working the second shift, and in fact one of the things that Champ liked about Toad's was how much it reminded him of the bars where he grew up, in Granite City, Illinois, outside East St. Louis. "The town used to have five mills going," he said one night to John Maxwell, the trainer, who was sitting next to him at the bar. "Now they're down to half a mill." Champ nodded across from where they were sitting—the bar described a rectangle in the center of the room—at a bearded, potbellied man, possibly in his early thirties, wearing a red flannel shirt that was open most of the way down his chest. "The bars are full of guys like him," Champ said, his voice low. " 'As soon as they open that mill back up, I'm fifth on the list. Number *five!*' "

Maxwell smiled grimly and nodded. They looked back at the televisions hanging over the bar. It was Johnny Carson's final week on *The Tonight Show,* and at the moment the several screens were showing a close-up of a man, playing a horn, with his name underneath. Maxwell remarked that he must be in the band.

"The band?" said a woman from the far end of the bar. Champ and Maxwell turned toward her.

"Johnny Carson band," said Maxwell.

"Band," she said. "They're talkin' about the Johnny Carson band." In this light, and with her hair collapsing across her face, it was difficult to discern her age or her looks. She had both elbows on the bar. Vaguely, she waved a cigarette at them. "They're talkin' about a band over here. Got guys over here *love* the Johnny Carson band."

She leaned back on her stool and looked to either side, as if to see what anyone else might want to make of this information, but nobody in the bar seemed to be paying attention to her, except for Champ and Maxwell.

They went back to looking at the televisions. Champ himself had never worked in the mills. His athletic ability had been his ticket out: scholarship to Southwest Missouri, All-American honors twice, draft pick of his hometown St. Louis Cardinals, the organization that had employed him for ten years as a minor league player, coach and, most recently, manager. Last year, however, a friend from the Cardinals, Jim Riggelman, had accepted a managing position in the San Diego organization at the Triple A level, and Champ had sensed an opportunity. He'd always felt a great deal of loyalty to the Cards, but in the end Champ felt more loyalty to himself. He wasn't a kid anymore, and while he was doing what he'd always wanted to be doing, he didn't want to end up doing it like Dean Treanor: forty-two years old, divorced, two kids he rarely saw, didn't own a car, lived in a motel room, and when they went out to eat on the road, he'd study the menu and study the menu, mentally doing the math on the dinner specials, until Champ would have to restrain himself from saying, "Here's the money. Take it. It's worth it to me just so I can *eat.*"

At thirty-two, Champ was no longer young to be a manager. Especially at the lower levels of the minors, it wasn't unusual to find managers in their twenties; Champ himself had started managing at the age of twenty-eight, in Savannah, Georgia, in the South Atlantic League. The minors functioned as training grounds and tryout camps for managers, too, and after five seasons managing with the Cardinals organization, Champ hadn't advanced past the Midwest League. Last season, in fact, he'd found himself returning to the Rookie level; he was going backward. Not that he would ever admit to caring about advancement, exactly. Like any student of a steel-mill town, he'd learned that sometimes it was accomplishment enough just to *get out.*

When Champ had interviewed for this job, the Padres had given him two warnings: one, that they were planning to divide their A-level talent between the High Desert Mavericks in the A-Advanced California League and the Charleston, South Carolina, Rainbows in the slow-A South Atlantic League, in effect experimenting with keeping only two clubs at the Class-A level, and more or less leaving Waterloo to develop the players to feed them; and two, that he'd be in *Waterloo.*

The team was working out pretty much as Champ had expected. At the end of April, the team's record had stood at two games over .500 and the pitching staff was leading the Midwest League with a composite ERA hovering around 2.00. But cold and wet weather early in the season always favored the pitching, the especially sloppy playing conditions this season only exaggerated the advantage, and a few victories had simply been gifts: the Appleton shortstop's error in the ninth inning that set up a two-run, game-winning rally, or the time that the Peoria second baseman, with two outs in the bottom of the ninth of a scoreless game and Scott Pugh running from third, dropped a routine pop fly. The Diamonds' current standing, three weeks into May—five games under .500, seven games out of first, and a staff ERA over 4.00 that ranked as the third worst in the league—was more like it.

Still, it was Champ's job to tell the players that they were better than their record, to reassure them that they were capable of achieving more despite mounting evidence to the contrary, to guide them, gently, toward tapping some previously unknown potential, or at least toward believing that it existed. This wasn't always easy. Only the day before, he had lectured the team patiently about how important it remained, even in the middle of trying to master complex baseball principles, not to lose sight of such fundamentals as keeping your eye on the ball. Then, in the top of the ninth, he'd had to watch his center fielder let a routine single skip past his glove and roll all the way to the wall, putting what should have been an easy victory in jeopardy. "Fuck! Fuck! Fuck!" Champ had roared in the dugout, while the players sat very still. Fortunately, the Diamonds held on to win the game, and by the time Champ reached the clubhouse a few minutes later, he'd regained his composure. "I'm not askin' you to turn the double play while leapin' in the air and turnin' around," he'd told his players. "I'm just askin' you guys to make the plays you're capable of making. We learn that and we'll get better. And we *will* get better. Good job tonight."

San Diego didn't expect him to win. The minors weren't about winning, anyway. They were about letting the players get their hits, letting them get their innings. Champ was under orders from San Diego to play Scott Bream, a third-round draft pick from 1989 with a career .179 average, and Jerry Thurston, a third-round draft pick from 1990 with a career .186 average, every day, and to keep Robbie Beckett not only in the starting rotation, but in the ball game until he'd reached his pitch count, no matter what, because San Diego had money in them. So every day, even before the game started, Champ felt as if he were playing seven against nine; and every fifth day, the question wasn't if Champ would have to go to his bullpen down by a few runs but *when*. Yet, working within those restraints, Champ nonetheless would try to win, because it was a measure of professionalism, because it was a matter of pride—both of which seemed to be in short supply around Waterloo.

"Inefficiency," Champ said now. "That's what this organization has come to represent to me."

Maxwell smiled grimly and nodded.

"I know what they'd say if I went into the front office and complained," Champ said. " 'Ahh, he's just complaining 'cause his team is losing.' But it's more than that," he went on. "It's pride. I take pride in my work."

"What kind of music you like?"

It was the woman from the other end of the bar again. Maxwell and Champion exchanged glances. She was waiting. Her legs were crossed. Her posture suggested she had all day.

"R.E.M.," said Maxwell.

"I like Queensryche," she said. "Not their later stuff. The early stuff. You know it? It's the greatest. Very angry-young-man." Suddenly she frowned, as if seeing them for the first time. "Where you from?"

They looked at each other again. Then they told her. For some reason, their answers—St. Louis and San Diego—seemed to satisfy her.

"I'm from Cedar Falls myself," she said, shrugging. She said that she'd tried going to the university, but some of the classes were too big, *hundreds* of students, so she'd switched to Hawkeye Tech. She said she'd be done with her classes next year. "I'm from Cedar Falls," she said again, "but I'm getting out of here. Everybody does."

After a moment, her attention drifted again. Champ went on. "This is the sorriest organization in professional baseball," he said. "It is. You go to the ballpark, you want to put things out of your mind. But you come out here, it's all worries."

It wasn't the quality of the team that was consuming Champ this year. The day-and-night juggling of lineups and pitching rotations, the pep talks and reports, the long hours and late-night phone calls—those were all part of the job. What wasn't was coming out to the ballpark and doing somebody else's job.

The groundskeeping situation simply wasn't getting any better. Once he'd had to instruct assistant groundskeeper Rollo Pfaltz-graff that the white chalk lines should run flush with first and third bases, not on the outside of the bags. Another time he'd approached head groundskeeper Jim Van Sant about cutting the infield grass. "But," Van Sant had answered, "I already cut it once this week." The team would take the field for batting practice and the bases wouldn't be there, so Champ would have to go looking for the grounds crew himself, and finally he'd follow Rollo's spookhouse laugh—"BOO-hahaha!"—up to the press box, where he and Van Sant would be sitting and talking. *What about the bases?* Champ would ask. *Oh, yeah!* they'd answer. *We forgot!* How many times had he grabbed a rake and gone out there before the game, even in front of the fans, to try to make the mound vaguely mound-shaped? Or after the game, he and Treanor would be out there, working on the mound under the stadium's utility lights. "Some of these guys might be making millions in a few years," Champ would say, his lips thin. "We could have a Ryne Sandberg out here, and he'd be pitching off a pimple."

And then there was the time the Peoria manager refused to let his team take the field in Waterloo because, he claimed, the infield dirt was full of bolts and glass. A great deal of pointing at dirt, picking at dirt, and general jawboning ensued. In the end, some fifty-five minutes beyond the ball game's scheduled starting time, and only after a phone call from the umpires to the president of the Midwest League, the Peoria manager allowed his team on the field, but not before he'd taken Polaroid snapshots of the dirt, collected soil samples complete with alleged foreign objects, and insisted that the two managers, two umpires, and general manager sign a paper stating that the field was "playable but possibly unsafe."

Every few days, Champ would be on the phone to the executives in San Diego, and sooner or later, the conversation would turn to the field conditions, and Champ would try to convey what he felt was the severity of the situation. *But don't take my word for it,* he'd tell them. *Come out here. See for yourself.* The one satisfaction Champ had was knowing that before the season was out, they would.

Still, it wasn't as if Champ hadn't known what to expect. Over the years he'd come to regard Waterhole, as the stop was known on the circuit, as the worst baseball town in the league. "Meet the Diamonds," for instance: It might have looked impressive to someone who didn't know better, a decent crowd in a small room, and plenty of media. "But even with all the publicity," Champ had predicted over dinner with Maxwell and Treanor in a downtown Chinese restaurant on the evening after the home opener, "you'll get 105 people at 'Meet the Diamonds' and 107 at the ballpark a week later, and it'll be all the same people." It wasn't the fans' fault, he said. "Sure, you can say it's only $4.50"—or $3.50, or even $2.50—"but if you don't have it, you don't have it." And even those who did come out—that group who sat in the boxes by the home on-deck circle, the ones he'd chatted up the other afternoon? He *had* to come out to the ballpark. What was their excuse? "They're nice people," Champ said now to Maxwell. "But you've got to ask yourself, Why every night? I mean, would you come out every night? The atmosphere is dead, the games are boring, the facility is falling apart."

"Fuck these people!" It was their friend, the blonde. She wasn't talking to them now, or anyone else. She was just talking. "Fuck this place!"

Champ and Maxwell looked at each other. Then Champ said, "It doesn't get any lower in the minors than Waterhole." Maxwell smiled grimly and shook his head, and they agreed that it was time to go home.

Maybe it was competition from an antique-car parade in downtown Waterloo. Or maybe it was confusion over the message on the answering machine in the front office. "The Diamonds' game Saturday, May 22, was rained out," Simpson's voice informed potential customers on the morning of Saturday, May 23, presumably referring to the Friday-night ball game that had indeed been rained out. But ten minutes before the start of a doubleheader on a 60-degree afternoon at the beginning of the Memorial Day weekend, under a luxuriously azure sky spotted with home-uniform-white cloud puffs, Champ could poke his head out of the dugout and count forty-two patrons in the ballpark. "I'm not counting Beckett," he added, "because he's on my team."

Shortstop Scott Bream, sitting on the bench and shaking his head, was watching Rollo chalk the foul lines. "This is the worst infield in professional baseball," Bream said.

"Forty-two!" Champ repeated, stepping back down into the dugout, also shaking his head. He laughed. "This is *my town!*"

The Diamonds' season had reached a turning point of sorts, a convergence of two equally quirky happenstances that nobody could have predicted. Over the past thirteen games, the Diamonds had lost eleven, and their record now stood at 15–21. Over the next thirteen games, the Diamonds would be playing five doubleheaders, the fallout from the bad weather early in the season. It was precisely at this conjunction of frustration over the recent past and dread of the immediate future that Jeff Nelson had scheduled the Waterloo Diamonds Comedy Night at the Sky Room Comedy Club.

All week Nelson had been trying to drum up enthusiasm for the event among the fans, the ballpark staff, and, especially, the players, passing through the locker room plying them with free passes, and inviting Cameron Cairncross to serve as the emcee. The players' contractual obligation to participate in publicity events was imprecise. If their manager had instructed them to attend the Comedy Night, or even had appointed an emcee and a contingent to make a token appearance, the situation would have developed differently. But all week Champ had indicated nothing, which was all the indication the players needed. Minutes before the start of the doubleheader, Nelson visited Champ in his office and asked if Cairncross, the starting pitcher in the first game, could leave the ballpark before the end of the second game and act as the evening's host. Champ had stared blankly for a moment, then offered Nelson only a terse "We'll see."

In the first game, Cairncross took another hard-luck loss, 1–0. Over five and a third innings he gave up four hits, walked two, and struck out five. At the end of this respectable performance, his ERA for the season stood at 2.86 and his opponents' batting average around .240, and he was throwing better than one strikeout per inning. His won-lost record, however, reflected none of these accomplishments: 0–4. In the fifth inning of the second game, Nelson approached Cairncross, who by now had showered and found a seat on a grandstand bench.

"All ready?" Nelson boomed.

Cairncross winced. "Actually," he said, "I'm not feeling well."

Before the start of the season, Nelson had envisioned the Comedy Night as the culmination of two months of fun. By Memorial Day weekend, he'd figured, players and fans would know one another well enough to be ready to cut loose together. The idea for the promotion had occurred to Nelson one morning in the week before Opening Day, when he stopped by the comedy club office to finalize plans for a nightly hitting contest. In the fifth inning of every home game, a lucky fan would get three swings against pitching coach Dean Treanor; the farther the batter hit the ball, the better the prize: two passes to the Sky Room just for competing, six passes for hitting a fly ball to the outfield, and twenty for hitting a home run. After the start of the season, Nelson had arranged for another on-field promotion, the "Mama Nick's Give It A Spin Bat Race," sponsored by a local pizzeria: two children would stand near home plate, place their foreheads against upright bats and spin around in circles, then drop the bats and race, crazy-legged, for first base, where Nelson would be waiting to raise the arm of the winner and face the cheering crowd. Nelson had observed both promotions at other ballparks in previous seasons, some part of his brain apparently squirreling away ideas for that time, God forbid, his umpiring days would be behind him.

"I'll always be an ump!" he'd declared, downing beers with the groundskeeper one night before the start of the season; or, collating tickets with an intern in the concession stand one afternoon, he'd moaned, "I love being on the field!" At the University of Utah, Nelson at first had majored in acting. ("Can you cry?" the intern had asked him, wide-eyed. "Sure," he shrugged. "It came in handy with girls." "I think that's sad when a guy cries," she said.) When he'd noticed that even the students he considered talented were graduating without finding instant fame and fortune, and after considering the visibility and salaries of network anchors, he'd switched majors to broadcast journalism. For Nelson, the subsequent postgraduate shift into umpiring—at the urging of an umpire he met one night while tending bar at his parents' tavern in downtown Salt Lake City, a couple of blocks from the local minor league ballpark—was not without a certain show-business logic. This year, he'd worried what it was going to feel like when Opening Day arrived and he wasn't part of the game, but then he'd volunteered to serve as master of ceremonies for the pregame festivities, and he'd arranged for a tuxedo promotion, and if it wasn't quite the same to walk out on the field in a starched shirt and cummerbund instead of a chest protector and a ball sack, it was a start, anyway. Perhaps the greatest asset Nelson brought to his new career in the front office, he thought, was his showmanship.

Once the season was under way, Nelson had quickly ascertained that it would take more than a couple of on-field promotions to liven up this ballpark. Low attendance was one problem; the general manager, Nelson concluded, was another. David Simpson was not one of those GMs who mingled easily with the crowd. Where Simpson carried himself with a visible reserve, Nelson was naturally gregarious. Where Simpson was content to let whole innings pass with little more than bingo to provide extra entertainment, Nelson preferred to make some noise. So Nelson had taken it upon himself to create the kind of environment that would make fans want to return to the ballpark. Key ring jingling in his back pocket, walkie-talkie squawking in his left hand, Nelson would work his way from one end of the park to the other twice every night, from the first-base bleachers, across the grandstand and box seats, and into the third-base bleachers, all the while holding court. He'd inform the Zoo Crew that the name of an umpire on the field was Bill, then lead them in a cheer of "Bill! Bill! Bill!" He'd tell anecdotes about his umpiring days—how once, in the ninth inning, he took revenge on an especially argumentative batter by instructing the catcher to set up a foot off the plate and call for three quick fastballs, all of which Nelson pronounced "Strike!"; or the time he got to work the plate for the Los Angeles Dodgers in an intrasquad spring-training game during a major league umpires' strike, and the other "ump" had been *Tommy Lasorda.*

One night, in the late innings, Nelson emerged from the ramp leading to the grandstand and heard . . . nothing. Not a sound. He dashed up to the press box and told the PA announcer to fill the next inning break with Gary Glitter's "Rock and Roll, Part Two" (the anthem-of-the-moment at ballparks everywhere), then recruited grounds crew and concessions staff to join him on both dugout roofs, where they led the crowd in the song's endlessly repetitious, deliberately moronic chant of "Hey!" Thus was a new nightly event born. Then, just the evening before the Comedy Night, during a downpour, Nelson had asked the PA announcer to crank up Genesis' "I Can't Dance" and to introduce the Wet Willies—Nelson and the rest of the already-drenched tarp crew parading behind home plate in imitation of the song's music video, using fungo bats for guitars.

The Waterloo Diamonds Comedy Night, Nelson hoped, would be an extension of that communal spirit. He and several of those same staff members arrived at the Sky Room Comedy Club just minutes before the scheduled 8:15 showtime. The Sky Room had been operating since the fall in what used to be the Tea Room on top of what most everyone in town still called "the old Black's building," after the department store that had occupied the ground floor of the building from its opening, in 1914, to the store's closing, in 1981. Long tables covered with white plastic tablecloths fanned away from the stage, toward the towering arched windows along one wall. Only the tables immediately ringing the stage were filled. Nelson led his party to a table away from the stage, and then spread across the far end, as if trying to create the impression of a crowd. A waitress stopped at the table, and Nelson ordered two Long Island iced teas. When she left, Nelson sat staring at the door, while the rest of the Diamonds' party sat staring at him.

"This hurts," Nelson said softly. "Inside, it really hurts." Then he looked back to the others and, raising his voice again, commended them on their performance as the Wet Willies. He said he wouldn't mind seeing them perform during every rain delay. He said they should add "Rubber Ducky" to their repertoire. He licked his lips and continued throwing out ideas: putting on a show once a week, rain or shine; scheduling regular rehearsals; scheduling a rehearsal for *this Tuesday*. "People will start coming out on overcast days hoping for a rain delay!" he announced. Then their drinks arrived, and Nelson glanced back at the door again and said softly, "Come on, guys, work with me."

"Any players here?" the nightclub's owner asked, appearing over the table at 8:30, fifteen minutes past the appointed starting time. Jim Miller was a onetime comic himself, of the one-man-band variety, as well as a former member of the Waterloo City Council. He'd opened this club the previous fall, amid considerable fanfare, in an effort to combine his two careers—presenting quality entertainment while revitalizing downtown Waterloo after dark.

"Not yet," Nelson began, "but—"

"That's okay, that's all right, I was just asking, no problem." Miller said he would hold the show a few more minutes, then, if necessary, handle the emcee chores himself.

Just as the lights went down, several players crept in and sat at the table nearest the door, bringing the customer total to around fifty. Miller took the stage and welcomed everyone to Waterloo Diamonds Night. Then a comic came out and said it was nice to be in Waterloo . . . because last weekend he'd had to work in

North Dakota. Next, another comic said he wanted to start out with his impression of a good time in Waterloo, Iowa, on, oh, a Saturday night: vomit; pause; "I'll drive." Eventually Miller returned to the stage and said that he'd just heard the Diamonds had lost both ends of a doubleheader today, and then he warned the audience that the players would be out stealing everybody's *Couriers* tomorrow morning. Just as the lights came back up, several players crept out the door.

At the staff table, the talk quickly turned to how unappreciative the manager and players were of what it took to run a professional baseball operation. Rollo performed his impression of a Class-A ball player.

" 'That ball hit a rock!' " he said in a high whine. " 'This isn't like the major leagues!' " He broke himself up.

"Sniff, sniff," said Nelson, dabbing his eyes with a cocktail napkin. Then he straightened up and glowered toward the door. "If they were winning, they'd be 'Hey, this field is *perfect*. Don't *touch* it!' " He continued glowering around the room until he saw that one player, a pitcher named Jeff Brown, was still there, along with his parents. Then Nelson sagged and sighed and said he supposed he'd better go over and thank them for coming. When he returned, Nelson stood at one end of the table and waited until he had everyone's attention. Then he announced, "All I know is Brown's parents were there for the rainout last night and they said, 'We loved your act.' "

Everybody laughed.

"We're legends," Nelson boomed. "We're *legends!*"

Then they took a vote and decided to head to the ballpark and play a little midnight baseball. On the drive back, they stopped and bought beer, but when they reached the stadium, all they could bring themselves to do was sit in the dugout and drink and talk. Every so often, one of the men would heave himself off the bench and visit the pitching mound. That night, the silence of the ballpark was broken by two new sounds: the steamy hiss of warm spill on cool soil, and, rising out of the darkness, an echoing, insistent "BOO-hahaha."

5

A certain degree of intrigue preceded the owners' meeting at the end of May, their first during the season, and the first since they'd voted not to put the ball club up for sale. For some time the behavior of the general manager had been puzzling and even enraging various members of the board. Now word had gotten back to a few of the owners that the GM, in addressing a civic organization, had spoken in a threatening manner: that the community wasn't supporting baseball, that the community didn't deserve baseball, that, if need be, the owners were ready to move the team. The information was secondhand, and the issues subtle and open to misinterpretation, so who could say how accurately the content of his words was being repeated? Still, there was no mistaking the impression the GM was leaving in his capacity as ambassador for the ball club. "Last year when he spoke to us," a Cedar Falls Rotarian told one owner over the phone, "his drawl had played well. But this year—blackmail is an extreme word, and it might not be the right one, but, really, there are *millionaires* here, you don't *treat* them this way." Not fully trusting his own reaction, he said, he'd approached four of his fellow Rotarians after the meeting. The sentiment toward their guest speaker, he reported, was uniform: "Screw you!"

David Simpson belonged to the generation of minor league general managers who had come of age during the 1980s. In the minors, the job of GM used to be relatively straightforward: "Show up at the start of the season and unlock the gate." It was a dusty position in a dormant industry. Hot dogs and beer were consumed, and baseball was played, and that was just about it for fun at the old ballpark—or at least that's how it seemed in retrospect to the generation of GMs who had grown up with a faster, jazzier, more financially sophisticated brand of minor league baseball. (They had a joke: In the old days, the only distraction at the ballpark was the organ—*and organs are for funerals.*) Over the past fifteen years, the minors had become one of the great success stories in the entertainment world, reflecting a similar vibrancy and expansion at the major league level and, in general, throughout professional sports. In fact, an entire academic discipline had arisen to meet the employment demands of this new niche in the national economy. In the late 1960s, Ohio University began offering the first advanced degree in sports management—a business program with a specialization in sports. Two decades later, at least seventy-five institutions of higher learning were offering similar programs to approximately 3,000 students. The new breed of front-office worker wasn't simply "somebody's brother-in-law"—another stereotype for the old breed—but a specialist who had trained extensively for front-office work by literally studying every aspect of a sports franchise's operation, often by serving an internship with a professional sports franchise. For the recipients of a bachelor's or a master's in sports management, pro ball wasn't a hobby, and it wasn't a pastime, and it wasn't a part-time job. Minor league baseball—professional sports—was what they'd trained to do for a living. It was a career.

Simpson didn't have the degree, but he and his peers shared a set of fundamental experiences and principles. At league meetings or All-Star games or baseball's Winter Meetings—wherever front-office folk swapped shoptalk—they would huddle in the hallways during breaks and complain about whatever state of affairs they'd inherited: "First year I came here, they set a record for attendance, and they barely made a profit. To me, it doesn't make much sense. If you set a record for attendance, you should also set a record for profits," or "On one page of the program there were four sponsors, and they all paid a different price. People had the idea, 'Well, if I buy a billboard, I should get some box seats and a program ad thrown in,' but you go down to their appliance store, you buy a washer and dryer, they don't throw in a refrigerator. Now our price is our price, and people either pay it or they don't." "Gil Hodges, Duke Snider," a Midwest League GM once said, telling about the time he'd worked for a franchise in a city that decades earlier had played host to several baseball legends. "It was all people wanted to talk about: the past, the past, the past. Nobody wanted to talk about the future." He meant no disrespect. The driving force behind the new breed of GM was a belief in the possibility of performing the alchemist's trick of mixing work and pleasure to produce a labor of love: the business of baseball. "I never thought I'd be in baseball worrying about per caps and profit margins," this same Midwest League GM said, "but that's what's fun. If it wasn't a business, it wouldn't be fun. It would be"—he stammered here, searching for the right words—"just a game!"

For six years, first at Double A Memphis as vice president of stadium operations, then at Class A Fayetteville as assistant general manager, David Simpson had apprenticed as a front-office executive, accumulating expertise on what it would take to run a minor league operation in a truly professional manner, if ever he had the opportunity. Waterloo, then, was his chance. Simpson's interview for the GM's position had consisted of a meeting with a committee of four owners, including Dan Yates, in late 1990. It was the fall of the Professional Baseball Agreement negotiations, an especially volatile and uncertain period in the history of the minors; at the time, nobody was sure even whether there would be minor league baseball the following season or, if there were, whether Waterloo would continue to be a host city. Hiring a new GM, however, wasn't simply an act of blind optimism on the owners' part. Across the country, owners of minor league ball clubs had no choice but to proceed under the assumption that the concessions stipulated by the new PBA would be manageable, somehow. Still, whatever they might turn out to be, those concessions clearly were going to require a fundamental change in the way this ball club, in particular, worked. The four owners had sat Simpson down at the Rodeway Inn and made it plain as day: They wanted someone who would run their ball club like a business.

What Simpson brought to Waterloo was a philosophy then inspiring as much fanaticism in front offices around the minors as anything happening on the base paths: respect for the ticket. The old way of doing business had been, in a sense, to "give away the store," both to advertisers and to fans, and the bedrock of that philosophy was the ballpark buyout—a game for which an advertiser or a company, sometimes for a set fee of, say, $700, or sometimes as part of a larger promotional and advertising package, received a block of free tickets to distribute to customers or to reward employees. In theory, everybody went home happy: The sponsor generated goodwill toward the product or company; ticket holders got an evening's free entertainment; and the ball club put more bodies in the ballpark, where, the assumption had been, not only would the customers spend more than enough on hot dogs and beer to offset the missing box office revenue, but they'd also create the kind of full-stands, festive atmosphere that would encourage repeat visits.

The new philosophy, however, placed a premium not on bulking up attendance figures, but on building up fan loyalty. Give something away for nothing, the thinking went, and that's what customers would figure it was worth. Fans who showed up only because they could get in free weren't desirable, anyway—weren't the kind of customers who would be likely to return on other, full-price nights, or who would have disposable incomes to spend at the concessions counter. Furthermore, too many free nights would devalue the ticket for the customers who *were* desirable— season-ticket holders or full-price regulars, which was to say those who *would* have disposable incomes.

It worked. The season before Simpson's arrival, nearly half the home dates in Waterloo—thirty of a scheduled seventy—had featured free or minimal admission. In his first season, Simpson eliminated ballpark buyouts altogether on Fridays and Saturdays, and he kept them to maybe half a dozen total for the season. Although the Diamonds compiled the fourth-best overall won-lost record among the fourteen Midwest League teams, even flirting with a playoff berth for a brief period, in terms of attendance the club came in last: 58,000—a drop of 20,000 from the previous season. Were people not coming out to the ballpark because they hadn't yet adjusted to the idea of paying full price for a seat—or were they staying home because they'd lost interest? Were the few regulars really spending more money than the freeloaders of old—or were Simpson's spending cuts making up the difference? These were crucial distinctions, but no matter: For the owners, it was enough that in the first year of the new PBA their ball club had managed to turn a profit—and a tidy one, at that. At their first postseason meeting, the owners entered into the board minutes an expression of their gratitude: "Dave is commended for a great year."

"Respect for the ticket," though, wasn't about just numbers but overall presentation of a product. It required a thorough rethinking of the organization. For that reason alone, some unpleasantness would have been inevitable, and indeed Simpson had encountered second-guessing to his suggestions from the start. He'd angered some fans by raising admission prices, he'd angered some sponsors by refusing to give away $2,000 worth of advertising for $1,000, and he'd angered a faction of the owners who contended that the ball club couldn't afford to alienate long-time fans and sponsors. Simpson's response never varied: a shrug. The ball club couldn't afford *not* to alienate long-time fans and sponsors, if that's what it took to educate them about the new status of the ball club—if that's what it took to attract a better class of customer.

Still, Simpson couldn't help noticing a growing resistance over the off-season. During his first year, some owners might have objected to individual initiatives, but the board as a whole almost always acquiesced. Now, when he made the suggestion that the ball club save expenses by eliminating the "Diamonds Notes" newsletter, the owners vetoed it. Against Dan Yates' strenuous advice, he made the suggestion that his reward for saving the ball club should be a seat on the board, and the owners vetoed it, though they did give him a raise and a second commendation: "Consensus was that Dave Simpson did a remarkably good job of running the club, especially for generating a healthy profit when the club began the year, under new terms with major league baseball, at a disadvantage costing well in excess of $25,000." Then he insisted that the ball club, as the ballpark's primary tenant, impose a fee on any baseball organization that the city allowed to use the facilities. Traditionally, the ball club had encouraged such visits as part of its community responsibility. As one owner tried to explain to Simpson during a board discussion of the issue, "It's a *big deal* for high school or Optimists to play on this field."

A second owner suggested, "Why don't we say, 'Put down a deposit for clean-up, and if you don't clean up according to our specifications, you forfeit it?'"

"Why don't we charge 'em $200?" Simpson answered.

"Because," a third owner snapped back, "this is small-town America and that ain't the way it's done!"

During his initial job interview, Simpson would have had every reason to assume that the four board members instructing him to professionalize the operation represented the sentiment of the board as a whole. It was true that a mom-and-pop operation such as Waterloo would have greater financial obstacles to overcome on the path to professionalization than a more modern organization, but it was also true that, back then, it had been this aspect of the franchise that especially appealed to him. "The people here in Waterloo—you can't even live outside of the boundaries of Black Hawk County and be an owner," he'd marveled shortly after his arrival in town, during his first appearance before the Park Board on behalf of the ball club. "That's why I think Waterloo is such a different and good and just a back-to-the-basics town. Because the people care about the baseball." (Once, at the ballpark during a game, while her husband was out of the office, Trish Simpson had confided to the box office staff one reason why her husband had taken the job in Waterloo. "Dave likes homey things," she'd said, and giggled.)

Even at the start, though, Simpson was no slave to sentiment. "They really did the trick on us," he said of the major leagues at that same early Park Board appearance. "The minor league clubs that suck it up and do the job are gonna stay in business. It's gonna be survival of the fittest." He promised to do what he could do—and he'd *done* it, making a profit that first season. But the fact was, if it turned out that Waterloo couldn't support pro ball, there were other towns out there that could. As Simpson saw the situation, the owners had three options: Keep the club for themselves, and keep it here. Or keep the club but move it to a potentially more hospitable and profitable location—Champaign, Illinois, or Evansville, Indiana, or Grand Rapids, Michigan, all cities that recently had applied for the next expansion openings in the Midwest League, should there be any. Or sell the club. These were the options that Simpson had outlined to the owners, and these were the options he had outlined when the question came up at a Rotary lunch in Cedar Falls.

Jeff Copeland, the owner who received the call complaining of the general manager's tone, paid Simpson a visit at the office and invited him on a walk around the park. Copeland had been one of the four owners who interviewed Simpson for the GM's job,

Copeland had become not only Simpson's strongest advocate on the board but also probably his closest friend in Waterloo, and Copeland had been the one other owner, at the previous board meeting, to agree with Dan Yates about putting the ball club up for sale. Now, when they'd reached a point on the field out of earshot of any potential eavesdropper, Copeland told Simpson that the owners had hired him to perform a specific job, and, as far as Copeland was concerned, he'd performed that job precisely. The problem, Copeland said, was that some owners didn't like what that job was.

One owner in particular had become especially vocal in his criticism of Simpson. Jeff Copeland and Jerry Klinkowitz were professionally and personally close. Both were professors of English at the University of Northern Iowa, and it had been at Klinkowitz's suggestion, in fact, that Copeland joined the board. Temperamentally, however, they were opposites. Copeland, round-faced, soft-spoken, was an accommodationist, a perpetual seeker of the middle ground. During a board discussion of Simpson's idea of charging fees to other users of the ball field, Copeland tried to quell tempers by suggesting that the owners form a community relations committee. Klinkowitz, by contrast, was an absolutist. He never gave ground, and he never gave up. Spread-eagling his arms at a board meeting, jackaloping up the grandstand steps during a game, Jerry Klinkowitz would press his point while pursuing his prey—who, as often as not these days, was Simpson. At that same discussion of fees, Klinkowitz waved an open palm toward Simpson and invoked the name of the owner of the Quad City franchise: "This man would be the best GM for Rick Holtzman. His bottom line is money. That's not our bottom line. Our bottom line is to keep baseball here as long as possible."

"But that takes money!" an incredulous Simpson answered him. "We've gotta meet major league statutes!"

"We've got to be sharing! Altruistic!"

"We made money last year."

"We made enemies, too. And just at the time we can least afford it."

"I thought," Simpson said, shaking his head, "you-all *wanted* me to make money for you."

"*We* don't make any money off this!"

To which Simpson replied, wearily, "Yeah, you do. You get a million. You split it fifteen ways."

It was on this point that Klinkowitz's arguments with the GM always broke down. Klinkowitz, nearing fifty, was the son of a Milwaukee beer salesman, and although he'd left his beginnings behind through a long career in teaching and writing (among his published works was a collection of short stories about minor league ball, *Short Season*), he'd immediately identified in the ball club's directors, when he met them back in the 1970s, an assembly of like-minded souls. What his fellow owners took for granted, he exalted, and over the years, he'd emerged as the board's most ardent defender of tradition by far. For Klinkowitz, selling the ball club wasn't an option. Technically, Dan Yates at the previous meeting had suggested only announcing that the ball club was for sale, in the hope of prompting emergency action from the city or flushing out a local investor or donor. For Klinkowitz, however, even *announcing* that the club was for sale wasn't an option. It wasn't even their *right*.

"We are not the owners," he'd said. "We are the stewards. We are in charge of keeping baseball here, and that's all. We knew it wasn't going to be easy, and now that it's not is no time to quit."

But, as Copeland and Yates pointed out, if the board members waited, they risked having nothing. The franchise might cease to exist; or it might revert to the Midwest League; or—who knew? The stadium renovation deadline of April 1, 1994, was going to come and go and all the owners might have to show for their noble intentions were fond memories and an empty ballpark.

"Fine," Klinkowitz said. "That's as it should be. That's how this club *should* fold—with us clawing in the dirt until the last dollar is gone."

In the conference on the ball field, Copeland advised Simpson to be on his best behavior at the upcoming board meeting—tell the owners what they wanted to hear; be conciliatry; *smile*. Meanwhile, on the phone to his fellow owners, in the days before the meeting, Klinkowitz sounded out support on Simpson's possible ouster. And on the night of the meeting itself, while Simpson was out of the office, Jeff Nelson turned to Brian Pfaltzgraff at the next desk and huffed, "Maybe after tonight we'll get to do things *our* way."

At precisely 7:00 P.M., Dan Yates positioned himself in the aisle that ran the length of the grandstand, looked up at the board members milling around the folding chairs and benches, and called out, "It's seven o'clock! That's the starting time!"

Nobody seemed to hear.

"Let's *go,* people!"

At this uncharacteristically stern admonition, the owners glanced up at Yates and began taking their seats. The weather had warmed enough that, the vote at the end of the previous meeting notwithstanding, the board had abandoned the sterility of a motel meeting room for the fresh air and familiar setting of the grandstand on the first-base side. Flanking Yates on folding chairs in the aisle, as if staking their claims to the extreme positions on the board, were Klinkowitz, the board secretary, and Copeland. The other owners arranged themselves among the folding chairs in the first set of boxes above the aisle as well as across the first bench of grandstand seating. Jeff Nelson and Brian Pfaltzgraff sat back in the benches, too. Just as the meeting was getting under way, Simpson entered, up a ramp, smiling.

Board meetings began calmly. No matter what item already might be on the agenda for the evening, no matter what plans individual owners might have for raising a difficult issue or introducing a controversial motion, a respectful hush always greeted Yates when he began speaking. In this way, Yates's introductory remarks served as a transition from premeeting bonhomie to a more businesslike frame of mind, however nominal. Tonight's informational review was exceptional only in that it seemed to be taking longer than usual: notification that the organization had established a new savings account with a local bank as a sign of good faith for advertising with the ball club; news of Midwest League approval of yet another franchise sale, this time of the Rockford club to the Chicago Cubs; reminders that the Player Development Contract with San Diego would be expiring at the end of the season, and that some time after the June free-agent draft the ball club could expect a decision on whether the Padres were planning to renew. Then Yates said, "Now I have here a letter I'll read."

As quiet as the owners had been throughout his review of old business, the stillness that descended on the group now was unnatural. No fidgeting; no coughing; no movement whatsoever. A held breath.

Yates didn't look up from the paper in his hand. "Dear Board of Directors," he began.

> I hereby give you notice in writing that I am resigning as president of Waterloo Professional Baseball, Inc., effective this night.
>
> I will continue to be an active board member and assist the organization in any way I can.
>
> Sincerely,
> Dan Yates

Yates kept his head down as he took the deliberate step up from the aisle to join the body of the board. He found an empty folding chair between two of his fellow owners and sat down. He crossed his arms. He crossed his legs. When he'd finished fidgeting, nobody was moving. None of the board members made eye contact with any of the other board members, and none of them looked at Yates. They simply stared wherever they could that wasn't somebody else—the peeling red benches of the grandstand, the thick mesh hanging between the stands and the field, the massive dead tree beyond the center-field wall.

Why? The question, when it came, was almost a howl, more an accusation than anything else. Yates deflected it with a shrug. But then all the other owners, one by one, shifted in their chairs to face him and take turns asking: *Why? Why? Why?*

"It's very simple," he said. "I'm tired of the infighting here. I'm tired of fighting City Hall. I'm tired of fighting the major leagues. It's just not fun anymore." He shrugged. "My mind is made up. And nobody will change it."

Nobody believed him. First they refused to second the motion of his resignation. Then, when somebody did agree to second it, if only to mollify Yates, the owners (unanimously) voted not to accept his resignation. They tried arguing him out of it: "For God's sake, don't strand us in the middle of the season!" ("Let's get on with it," Yates answered. "Let's get on with it.") They tried shaming him out of it: "I think it's just the worst thing from a public-relations standpoint." ("I acknowledge that," he answered. "But it's time for me to *go*.") They even tried bullying him: "The motion has failed. You're still in charge." ("Now I told you," Yates answered, *"I am not going to do it."*) Throughout it all—nearly an hour's worth of debate, if the back-and-forth, I-will-you-won't, automatic naysaying could be called that—Yates remained resolute, and so did the rest of the owners. They had reached an impasse.

If his intention had been to put a fright into them, Yates had succeeded. The ball club's dealings with the major leagues, which included not only the San Diego Padres and any other possible future affiliations, but all the considerations of the new Professional Baseball Agreement as well; with the minor leagues, which included the National Association, the Midwest League, and the other thirteen franchises in the league; with the City of Waterloo, which included the Park Board, the parks director, the City Council, and the mayor; with the ball club's business contacts around town, a lengthy list of advertisers, suppliers and supporters, present or potential; with the organization itself, which included the front office, the ballpark staff, and *them,* his fellow owners—all these responsibilities Dan Yates had navigated and executed masterfully for six years. When the owners had entrusted the future of the franchise to his care, they knew that he would proceed in a calm, orderly, logical, responsible fashion, like the Eagle Scout he appeared to be, and he had never disappointed—until now. It didn't make any sense. The worst that could be said about Yates was that he was perhaps too conscientious—unwilling to let go of the least detail, unable to delegate responsibility.

They offered a compromise. Several owners mentioned—and the others immediately said they would welcome—the possibility of setting up committees, of shouldering more responsibility among themselves, of learning more about the inner workings of baseball.

"Well, I think that's an excellent idea," Yates said. "But I'm not going to serve as president, and I think everyone's got the idea." Legs crossed, one foot wagging faster and faster, his naturally high voice pitching higher and higher, Yates said, "Now, it's going to take up a lot of your time, but if you want this organization to survive—*that's what it's going to take.*"

After a long silence, the owners reconsidered the motion to accept Dan Yates's resignation as president, effective immediately, and this time it passed.

The members of the board then set about selecting a new president from their ranks. After some discussion, and taking into account Yates's reminder that the responsibilities of the post consumed a good deal more time than they thought it might, they narrowed the field to one potential candidate: Bill Boesen, the electrician who had retired only the previous year. He puffed his cheeks and said he had a lot of work around the house that he'd been putting off for years, but, sure, he supposed he could find time for the job. "I'll tell you now," he said, softly, almost to himself, "I'll make some changes right away."

The vote was unanimous.

Boesen rose from his folding chair and moved down to the aisle, into the space between Klinkowitz and Copeland. He blew out a breath. Then he blew out another one. He looked around the ballpark, then up to the sky, as if hoping for inspiration, or perhaps divine intervention. The setting sun was showing through the chicken wire on the back of the grandstand on the third-base side.

Not only did the owners have to begin their adjustment to life after Yates, but they still had all the business of a regular board meeting to get through.

Boesen gave his head a shake and turned back to the group. He was a short, burly bantamweight with a salt-and-pepper beard, and as he paced in the aisle, he seemed to be springing up and down. He spun one way. He spun the other. He hitched up his pants. He didn't know where to begin. So he began where he knew best: electricity. For his first act as president, Boesen chose to address a vandalism problem that had developed lately with the scoreboard. Immediately he warmed to his topic. He said he wanted the ball club to build a protective fence around the scoreboard, and he wanted one soon. He wanted to figure out how to get one, and he wanted to figure it out now. "We oughta quit foolin' around here and just *do* it," he said. He called up to Simpson, in the second row of the grandstand, and asked what he thought.

"You're the president," Simpson called back.

"I say let's do it," said Boesen.

"I'd say," Simpson drawled, "that's a good idea."
He was still smiling.

The morning after, Yates woke up and told his wife, Pat, that he couldn't remember the last time he'd slept so well. He said he felt years younger, pounds lighter. He said he felt like a new man.

Meanwhile, in another part of town, Boesen was waking up, like a drunk after a blackout, to the vague memory of having done something foolish, or worse. When he remembered what it was, Boesen broke the news to his wife, Bev. Her response, as swift as it was uncharacteristic, surprised even her.

"Oh, shit," she said, her hand flying to her mouth.

The burden that overnight had lifted from the bed of Dan Yates to flock upon the house of Bill Boesen was an ancient burden. It was the same burden that Yates, in his day, had inherited from Mildred Boyenga, who, in turn, had inherited it from all her predecessors, whatever their various official titles and at whatever levels their various ball clubs had operated, going back to the beginnings of professional baseball in Waterloo. The fact was, Waterloo was always in the process of "losing" professional baseball. Worrying about losing it, losing it, working to get it back, only to worry about losing it again—the cycle perennially stood at one stage of loss or another, and those who accepted the responsibility for providing the Factory City of Iowa with a link to the National Pastime in its professional incarnation were forever preparing for the worst.

For virtually as long as there had been minor league baseball, there had been minor league baseball in Waterloo. In 1903, the year the majors and the minors formally recognized each other, an amateur team calling itself the Waterloo Lulus played an exhibition game against the professional Cedar Rapids Rabbits of the Class B Three-I League. The following year, Waterloo became a charter member of the Class D Iowa State League—along with Boone, Burlington, Fort Dodge, Keokuk, Marshalltown, Oskaloosa and Ottumwa—and the city's first home game as a professional representative of baseball occasioned a municipal holiday complete with half-day work schedule and parade.

In the infancy of the minors, the classification of an individual league as Class A, B, C, or D was determined by the league's overall attendance, and an individual ball club's license to remain within that league depended on meeting a similar minimum attendance standard. In the early years of the Iowa State League, one prairie city after another that had overestimated its entitlement dropped out, but not Waterloo. Still, as those cities were replaced by older, more established Mississippi River cities farther south, in Illinois and Missouri (and as the league reflected that shift by changing its name to the Central Association), Waterloo found itself increasingly isolated geographically—a serious consideration in an era of primitive road conditions. Every off-season, Waterloo's backers had to resist pressure from their fellow operators for the right to remain in the league, until at last, in 1910, they capitulated. They surrendered their spot in the Central Association to Galesburg, Illinois, and signed up with the Class B Three-I League. The higher league, however, carried a higher attendance standard, which Waterloo after two seasons proved unable to meet, and in 1912, through no fault of its own, Waterloo for the first time lost professional baseball. So maybe the city didn't belong in Class B, after all, but what the ball club's backers had learned was an even more important lesson: Waterloo *belonged*.

"They've done something to add to the glory of our city," a Cincinnati booster said of the Red Stockings team whose barnstorming tour in 1869 had marked baseball's transition into the professional era. "They advertised the city, advertised us, sir, and helped our business." In Waterloo, as in other communities, it was local business leaders who first saw in professional baseball a vehicle for advancing their hometown's status as an emerging manufacturing center, even naming that first team the Lulus after a locally produced cleansing powder. A new century stretched ahead, and with it Waterloo's future as an industrial and agricultural powerhouse—among all the other industrial and agricultural powerhouses arising across the prairies. As an Opening Day mayoral proclamation from an early season in Waterloo said, "It is a recognized fact that good, clean baseball is one of the greatest advertising mediums a city can possess." On any summer evening, in the hours between the five o'clock factory whistle and dusk, amateur teams of local boys might have been playing on a dozen fields in any number of towns, yet it was the presence of professional baseball that somehow had come to distinguish a community. By virtue of being paid, its ball players presumably were superior to their amateur counterparts, by virtue of charging admission, its franchises presumably presented superior entertainment, and by virtue of being a commercial enterprise, it in itself—pro ball—presumably reflected on the superior economic vitality of the host cities. In short, professional baseball distinguished a community because professional baseball existed in the marketplace.

Then as now, the ability of a community to support a pro ball team, and the level of competition at which that team played, were to some extent a reflection of the city's standing in a regional, and even national, capacity. In 1876, only seven years after Cincinnati inaugurated the era of professional baseball, a group of pro ball club owners had locked themselves in a hotel room in New York City, and when they emerged, they had christened themselves the National League of Professional Baseball Clubs and declared themselves "major"—in so doing relegating the rest of the professional ball clubs, by definition, to "minor" status. It was business as usual in the era of the robber baron. Seeing a claim, the owners staked it; staking the claim, they monopolized it. Throughout the last twenty-five years of the nineteenth century, one upstart league or player's organization after another challenged that system, but it wasn't until the formerly "minor" American League declared its intentions to become a "major league" in 1901, and made good on those intentions through superior attendance and player salaries, that the National League conceded defeat—though not before a two-year war waged largely by bidding for the services of minor league players. The National Association of Professional Baseball Leagues, the umbrella organization for the "minors," came into existence in 1901 as a protective measure against the player raids from the "majors." In 1903, those designations became official, as the National and American leagues settled their differences with each other as well as the rest of pro ball by signing the Major-Minor League Agreement. For the first time, all of professional baseball existed within a formal hierarchy. Up there, somewhere, were the cities of the two major leagues: the industrial centers of size and renown and import: the great metropolises roughly north of the Mason-Dixon Line and roughly east of the

Mississippi: Boston, Brooklyn, Chicago, Cincinnati, Cleveland, Detroit, New York, Philadelphia, Pittsburgh, St. Louis and Washington. Down here in Class D, less prestigiously perhaps, though no less notably in their own communities, were the towns in between and far beyond, the outposts that had survived and prospered throughout the latter quarter of the old century and on into the new: Beatrice, Nebraska; Paragould, Arkansas; Chehalis, Washington; Corsicana, Texas; Coffeyville, Kansas; Paris, Kentucky; Waterloo, Iowa.

In those days, the operation of a minor league club was primarily a local and independent affair. It was the proprietor of a minor league ball club who hired the manager, and it was the manager who in turn hired the players, either by recruiting from amateur teams in the area or by soliciting from a network of national contacts. If some local employers could find places on the payroll for a few of the players—as Rath Packing and Illinois Central, for instance, did in Waterloo—then so much the better. If those players should coalesce into a championship squad—as happened in Waterloo in 1907, 1908, 1914, 1924, and 1928—then there was truly cause for celebration, at least until the time came to raise money to field a team for the following season. What constituted a commitment to professional baseball—what constituted *baseball*, for that matter—would change over the decades, but not the city's commitment itself. Every so often, word would reach Waterloo: This was what it was going to take to remain in pro ball. Then, whatever it was, Waterloo did it.

Waterloo's first absence from pro ball lasted one season. By the spring of 1913, the city's business leaders had arranged with their peers in similarly disenfranchised Cedar Rapids to correct their common source of municipal shame by together re-joining the Central Association, which now was drifting back northward, away from the older Mississippi River cities, to accommodate the addition of the prairie cities that had been re-invigorated by the new rail lines through the region. With one exception, Waterloo never again had to go without professional baseball other than in times of national emergency. In 1918, Waterloo, along with most minor league cities in the country, lost professional baseball due to World War I, then regained it in 1922, after civic boosters financed a new ballclub and a new ballpark to replace the old dilapidated stands. In 1933, Waterloo lost pro ball again, due to the Great Depression, then regained it in 1936 with both another new club and another new ballpark, to replace the one that had burned down. In 1942, Waterloo lost pro ball yet again, due to World War II, and that November fire yet again claimed the city ballpark.

By now, the minor league marketplace had changed. The original system had held as long as the agreement between the majors and the minors held. When it didn't, after the economic fallout from World War I had produced another major-league bidding war for the services of minor leaguers, one innovative major league GM refined an alternative: the farm system.

Rather than engage in high-stakes skirmishes with more prosperous major league organizations, Branch Rickey reasoned, his St. Louis Cardinals could scout and develop players by owning and operating minor league clubs outright, or by contributing enough capital to merit working agreements with ball clubs. In time, the Cardinals farm system expanded to outright ownership of thirty-two clubs and working agreements with eight others, along the way feeding the multiple pennant- and World Series–winning "Gashouse Gang" teams of the late '20s, '30s, and early '40s, while, not incidentally, filling the club treasury. The competition couldn't help noticing, and it wasn't long before every other major league club was buying up or otherwise forging financial agreements with its own extensive assortment of small-town teams.

"Raping the minors" was how baseball's first commissioner, Judge Kenesaw Mountain Landis, termed the development of the farm system. In the pivotal confrontation, he accused Rickey of potentially undermining competition in the Three-I League by simultaneously holding agreements with two Illinois teams, Danville and Springfield. Such an arrangement, Landis charged, conceivably constituted a conflict of interest. "Big as a house, isn't it?" he said to Rickey.

"It is not big as a house," Rickey answered.

"I think it is as big as the universe. This is just as important in the Three-I League as it would be in the National or American leagues."

What was at stake, to Landis, was the very nature of the minors.

By buying and leasing ballclubs, the major leagues were shifting the purpose of the minors from what would benefit a local audience—winning pennants—to what would financially benefit the major league provider—developing players. Landis stripped Rickey and the Cardinals of several dozen players, but ultimately he was powerless. The farm system stayed.

In 1937, this new way of doing business—the modern era of minor league baseball, in essence—reached Waterloo in the form of an affiliation with the Cincinnati Reds. When the Reds left town, the Chicago White Sox moved in, this time as the owner. The White Sox assumed control of what happened off the field and what happened on the field. The city only had to provide the field itself.

In the beginning, Waterloo Municipal Stadium was a gift to the city. Even though the war would delay the possible return of baseball for the foreseeable future, a group of local businessmen led by Reuben Rath immediately spearheaded a drive to raise funds for a new facility. By the end of the war in August 1945, the group had raised $80,000, which it turned over to the city's Park Commission. In order to ensure the return of professional baseball for the first peacetime season, the city wasted no time in selecting a site and breaking ground, and by the following spring the present stadium had risen on a corner of Cedar River Park, abutting Fairview Cemetery, on the east side of town. Deere might have kept more people on the payroll, and its presence in Waterloo might have represented the company's greatest investment in an individual community, but its headquarters were in Illinois; Rath Packing, however, was wholly a local operation, and if a Rath himself should decree, "Let there be baseball," then there would, by God, be baseball.

Despite Landis's reservations, the arrival of the farm system in cities such as Waterloo wasn't an altogether unwelcome development. Maybe the brand of baseball had changed, but it was still baseball, and it was enough. Better yet, this brand of baseball removed from the local backers the onus of running a baseball operation. What the ball club lost in autonomy it gained in stability—a trade that worked as long as the major leagues remained flush.

The boom that followed wasn't peculiar to Waterloo. Fifteen years of a great depression and a world war no doubt contributed to the sudden resurgence in interest in the National Pastime at every level, from the majors downward. After mostly sitting out the war, the minors returned stronger than ever and in 1949 reached what would prove to be their zenith: 59 leagues, 464 clubs, attendance of nearly 42 million.

The decline that followed wasn't peculiar to Waterloo, either. In part, it was attributable to a number of broad social changes— new mobility, fresh prosperity, the movement of the middle class toward the edges of cities and into the suburbs, and, especially, the introduction of television. Previously, if fans in a setting such as Waterloo wanted to see major league caliber play, they had no choice but to travel to St. Louis or Chicago. Now, suddenly, they had a choice. They could content themselves with the lower-quality though technically professional play at Municipal Stadium or, without even leaving their living rooms, they could watch Ted Williams's Boston Red Sox slug it out with Joe DiMaggio's New York Yankees, or Jackie Robinson's Brooklyn Dodgers battle Stan Musial's St. Louis Cardinals. In part, however, the decline of the minors was also attributable to economic changes at the major league level. The competitive advantage that the St. Louis organization had enjoyed through the development of the farm system eventually was erased as other major league clubs developed their own farm systems. Once the playing field had evened, a new bidding war for likely prospects developed that, on top of all the other expenses a farm system demanded, led to a majority of big-league clubs declaring operating losses.

By 1956, only 28 of the 59 minor leagues from seven years earlier remained. In Waterloo that year, attendance dropped to 46,000, and after the season the Chicago White Sox moved their Class B Three-I affiliate to the larger market of Davenport, Iowa. By now, the minor leagues had changed once again. The division of responsibilities had reached their contemporary form: What happened on the field still belonged to the parent organization, and the field itself still belonged to the locals, but now so did what happened off the field as well—the operation of the franchise. No matter. After one season without pro ball, and once more through the efforts of local civic leaders, Waterloo in 1958 joined the Class D Midwest League. So Waterloo didn't belong in Class B, after all. Still, Waterloo belonged.

When Mildred Boyenga became president of this organization in 1984, she proceeded under the assumption that the bond between the city and baseball that had endured for eight decades was intact. In those days, the major league general manager would visit the premises personally to negotiate with the mayor as to what it was going to take to keep pro ball in Waterloo. The various parties would meet at the ballpark, tour the facilities, and agree on some course of action. Then everybody would go to lunch. In 1984, however, the Cleveland GM visited the ballpark and issued an ultimatum: Improve the facilities or lose the affiliation.

The loss of an affiliation was always a possibility. Twice in the previous fifteen years the ball club had lost parent clubs—Boston and Kansas City. Still, the timing of Cleveland's ultimatum couldn't have been worse. The city was experiencing its most severe economic crisis at least since the Depression, and possibly ever, and it would have been understandable if Waterloo at this point had let go of not just a parent club but pro ball, period. Still, the city came through. Over the 1984–85 off-season, city crews as well as baseball volunteers renovated the clubhouses and rebuilt the dugouts. "BASEBALL ALIVE IN '85!" proclaimed that year's Booster button.

Still, it was only a start. The Cleveland GM continued stopping by the ballpark and pointing around the place, ball club officials continued discussing these "suggestions" with the city, and the city continued considering which deserved highest priority in what was becoming a nearly annual three-way dance of appeasement. During the 1987–88 off-season, the city completely gutted the outfield, adding a warning track, expanding the playing surface to make it more consistent with major league dimensions by pushing back the fences and adding to their height (the ball club bought the lumber), and, as long as the ground was being torn up, laying a wiring network that would be able to accommodate whatever lighting system the city eventually might choose to install. "We could have a Rolling Stones concert out there now," the parks director crowed. "We got enough power to light up New York!"

Still, it wasn't enough. One year-end compilation of umpires' reports filed with the league office from the period included the comments: "Field needs lots of work," "Dirt full of rocks," "In-field grass is bumpy and uneven," "All grass areas uneven," and "Outside area tacky." "The ballpark rating system had us tenth or eleventh out of fourteen parks in our league," the GM at the time told the *Courier* following the 1988 season, "and those cities below us are working on big improvement projects." That September, after twelve years of affiliation, and on the final afternoon before the Player Development Contract would automatically renew, Cleveland finally made good on its threat of old and severed its ties with Waterloo. For several months the franchise floated in limbo, its directors facing the real possibility that Waterloo would be without a professional baseball team for the first time in more than thirty years. Dan Yates, by now having succeeded Boyenga as president, put out feelers to every major league organization that didn't already have an affiliate in the Midwest League, yet when he attended the Winter Meetings in Atlanta that December, the ball club still didn't have a major league parent. Not until the final night of the meetings did he learn that the president of the National Association had prevailed upon San Diego and Baltimore to send a co-op team to Waterloo. It was far from ideal—co-op teams are notorious for consisting of the dregs of both systems, and the lack of a contract with a single parent club didn't bode well for a long-term commitment from either—but this solution did have a certain skin-of-our-teeth quality that, if nothing else, might underscore the severity of the situation for the folks back home.

In early 1989, the Padres and Orioles dispatched a contingent of farm executives to Waterloo. As usual, major league officials met with the ball club president, the mayor, and other ball club and city officials, inspected the facilities, and determined the stadium's most pressing needs—in this case, in addition to the lighting renovations already under way, complete overhauls of both clubhouses. What distinguished this particular conclave, however, was the presence of the president of the National Association of Professional Baseball Leagues. Sal Artiaga was on a tour of several Midwest League cities to observe for himself the growing gap between the condition of facilities in various communities, and presumably to lend through his personal attention an institutional gravity. Elsewhere in the Midwest League, Davenport's old ballpark was then undergoing its renovation, while a year earlier, South Bend had entered the league with a new state-of-the-art park. "Our objective is to save professional baseball in Waterloo," Artiaga declared. "The city has a very strong tradition in the game that we want to see continue. But," he went on, "we are in an evolutionary period where this past year minor league baseball achieved an all-time attendance record. So many communities are reaching out for professional baseball. Many of them are putting considerable money in refurbishing or building facilities."

"We've got professional baseball in this town," Mayor Bernie McKinley responded, "and we need to keep it. I don't know what the price will be. It may be too high. But after meeting with these people, I don't think it is."

In April of that year, the City Council approved $205,000 in bonds for improvements to the stadium over a four-year period. "By the end of the summer," the *Courier* reported in the days following the vote, "work should be started on the new clubhouse." When it soon became clear that this amount wouldn't cover the cost of a clubhouse, the safety and engineering requirements, *and* new lights, the City Council, again at McKinley's urging, approved another $120,000 exclusively for lights, with the understanding that the new total of $325,000 should be enough to keep professional baseball in Waterloo at least for a few seasons.

"We need to talk, folks." City Parks Director Rick Tagtow sounded a grave note as he stood before the Waterloo Park Board one morning in September 1990. Two summers had passed since Mayor McKinley informed the board that Waterloo would be building a new clubhouse—and, in fact, it was the promise of a clubhouse that had helped convince San Diego to sign a two-year solo Player Development Contract after the end of the co-op season. The clubhouse was to be a freestanding structure behind the existing grandstand and bleachers on the third-base side, would hold both home and visitors' locker rooms, and would cost $85,000. So far, however, it existed only as an engineering study.

For once, the problem had nothing to do with baseball. The problem was the floodplain. According to government codes, any new structure built in the floodplain of the Cedar River, which was to say anything remotely in the area of the ballpark, would have to be elevated four feet off the ground. This stipulation had now pushed the cost of the clubhouse project to at least $267,-000—more than triple the original estimate. Still, it was somehow fitting, even liberating, that the rising cost of keeping baseball in Waterloo was attributable for once to something other than baseball. For years, baseball's two staunchest advocates in the city government, aside from the mayor, had had to contort themselves in their defense of public funding for the stadium before doubting Park Board members, disbelieving city officials, and an increasingly angry public at City Council meetings. As long as the problem was baseball, the subject had required some tact; it was one of the mayor's (many) pet projects, after all, and part of his vision of Waterloo's future. Once the blame shifted off baseball, however, even the traditional defenders were free to voice their frustrations.

Tagtow was one. "I feel bad because we're going to the well again," he said. "But that was out of our control. It wasn't that our estimates were wrong. It was that we didn't realize the nature of the beast. So we're going back to them [the City Council] and saying if you want it, somebody's got to pay for it, and here it is. Because, unfortunately, we live in a society—particularly it seems that Waterloo is very acutely attuned to this philosophy—but a society where everybody wants things but nobody wants to pay for them. And that, of course, is impossible."

Sammie Dell, the Council member who traditionally sponsored the ball club's interests on the City Council, had worked closely with Tagtow on ballpark funding. Twice in the past eighteen months he had gone to the Council begging, and receiving, and now he nonetheless found himself facing the prospect of going begging once more. At a Park Board meeting that fall, he delivered to Dan Yates a message on the Council's, the mayor's, and, he emphasized, his own behalf. "It's nickel-and-dimin' us!" he said. "In terms of lights, the clubhouse, the structural improvements—how much money are we talkin' about, *total?* What would it take to bring that baby up to code and up to where you wanted it? What is that figure? Let us know *what it takes* to get this thing in order, so that the city can make a decision as to what constitutes support to baseball programs or not. Because we don't *know*."

Nobody knew—not in Waterloo, not anywhere. In city after

minor league city across the country, the fundamental changes that the minor leagues had undergone in recent years had left everyone involved at every level of a franchise's tenancy in a civic ballpark—from the minor league franchise operators, through the administrators of city governments, to the general managers at the major league level—wondering how much was enough. Before the several sides in Waterloo could reconvene, however, the new Professional Baseball Agreement had taken effect, rendering the question of the clubhouse moot.

At least, the clubhouse then under review. Not so the question of a clubhouse in general, which was only one of the dozens, if not hundreds, of mandatory ballpark improvements that would have to be addressed by April 1, 1994.

So now they knew. This was what it was going to cost to keep professional baseball in Waterloo. Nobody knew the exact numbers yet; the figures would depend on the architect's report, as well as the new GM's success in holding down costs while raising revenues. On one side of that deadline were all the cities that heretofore had comprised professional baseball; on the other, the survivors. Those cities that made the cut would stay in pro ball; those that didn't, wouldn't.

The precariousness of the franchise was nothing new. It was in the nature of minor league baseball. The need for a stadium was nothing new. Without new stadiums, pro ball wouldn't have returned to Waterloo in 1913, 1936, or 1946. Geographical shift of the league? Same thing that cost Waterloo minor league baseball in 1912. Bad economy? 1933, 1934, 1935. Attendance problems? With the exception of one receding, fleeting era that you'd have to be at least half a century old to remember, when hadn't there been?

"They don't *get* it," Boyenga reported back to Yates after the City Council meeting she had attended for him in April, meaning: What was new here was the finality of it. The difference this time was that if the city couldn't succeed in keeping the ball club, it wasn't going to get it back, and Waterloo would go the way of all the Oskaloosas and Ottumwas, all the Paragoulds and Galesburgs, all the Shamokins and Larneds and Big Stone Gaps of the world that once had professional baseball, and lost it.

*

Three nights after assuming the presidency of Waterloo Professional Baseball, Inc., Bill Boesen went out to the ballpark and sat in his usual spot, on a hardwood bench a couple rows back of the railing that separated the folding chairs of the reserved boxes from grandstand seating. His view was directly down the first-base line; it had been his seat for years. He belonged to that group of regulars who had come here as a kid, neglected it during his early years of marriage, then returned when his own kids were old enough to attend games. Now the two boys were grown, well into their twenties, though they still lived at home. ("I don't think they'll ever leave," his wife would confide, back-of-the-hand, to one or another of her neighbors in the grandstand.) After all these years, Boesen couldn't walk through the ballpark without seeing the physical evidence of what he had done with his own hands: the metal plates that covered the rust spots under the seats, or the wiring that branched out of the press box and along the rafters to the speakers. The holes drilled in the seats of the metal folding chairs in the reserved boxes, to drain rainwater? His idea. The concession stand: just went in there and did it, him and a bunch of other volunteers, and nobody ever complained. And pigeons! He used to stop out here with a .22, no powder, and take care of the pigeon problem himself. Boesen had offered this service to Simpson, too, but the GM had declined; so now whenever Boesen came out to the ballpark, which was almost every night the team was in town, he had to bend to examine his bench first. Tonight, after completing the inspection, Boesen straightened, disappeared below the grandstand, and returned a minute later with a squirt bottle and a rag.

"That your job now?" one of his friends called down to him.

"Shit, you know it is."

Word of his new title had leaked to a radio station by the morning after the meeting, and now it was common knowledge around town. Just today the president of Waterloo Savings Bank had called the front office to ask whether it would help the ball club in this time of transition if he bought it for $30,000, and Simpson had said that any such inquiry would have to go through the organization's new president, and then Simpson had warned Boesen he'd be getting a call, but it had never come. Still, Boesen supposed he was going to have to start learning what to say when these situations arose. He was going to have to start learning a lot, he supposed. The past couple of nights, he had stopped a few of the other owners in the aisle and said, *You've been to some of the other ballparks in this league—how's this one rate?* Yesterday afternoon he had come out to the ballpark in the early afternoon, just to poke around a little, trying to draw a bead on the place in his new capacity as the person ultimately responsible for its upkeep. He'd found Nelson standing on the home dugout, in a white shirt and tie, tangling with the mesh. Boesen walked over, jumped on the dugout beside Nelson, and gave the mesh a good tug. A piece snapped off in his hand.

"This is rotten!" he said. "Where's that new mesh?"

Nelson flashed his full-teeth grin of obvious insincerity. "Ask the city!"

In fact, Boesen had planned on talking to the city first chance he got. This morning he had called Tagtow, who'd tried to insist that his schedule was full, but Boesen had answered, "Come on, I want to work with you," and Tagtow had relented. At 2:30 this afternoon Boesen had arrived at Tagtow's office, and he had stayed for an hour, asking about one thing and another. *We want to build a fence around the scoreboard.* Talk to the Park Board. *We could use some new infield dirt.* Last time we brought dirt out there all we got was complaints. *What about the mesh? We bought it with our own money. When are you going to send someone to put it up?* There are nine parks ahead of you.

"So what you're telling me," Boesen had said, "is you're not gonna do nothin'."

"What I'm telling you," Tagtow had answered, "is we don't have the manpower."

Boesen set the rag and the plastic bottle down on the ground now and took his usual spot at the end of the bench, next to his wife. Bev used to come out here as a kid, too, though she hadn't known Bill then. Now they had been attending games together for twenty years. During games she tended to keep up a constant current of chatter with whatever friend happened to be sitting nearest. At the moment she was in the middle of a story about the time the Strategic Air Command out of Omaha was performing maneuvers in Waterloo and she'd gone out to the airport with a friend to watch. They'd positioned themselves under the flight path; the idea was that when a jet came screaming in for a landing, they would try to stand still as long as possible, but Bev always chickened out. At the last second, she said, she'd start yelling and running in circles.

"They're coming in no higher than the top of this grandstand," she said, "and my friend says, 'It's not going to fall from there to the ground,' and I say, 'It will if it starts falling back there!' "

She burst out laughing and turned toward her husband. If he'd heard a word of her story, he wasn't showing it. He'd folded his arms, tucked his beard against his chest, and narrowed his sights at something in the distance, far down the first-base line, or beyond, in the graveyard.

"We are in a world of shit," he said, and then, blinking as if he'd just remembered something, he turned back to the ball game.

6

The Waterloo Diamonds were lost. Somewhere in southwest-ern Wisconsin the bus driver had missed a detour sign, and as the morning wore on, the scenery was growing less familiar. Usu-ally what passed outside the tinted windows of the coach was the uninflected landscape of the interstate—the straightaways, the sudden cluster of bypasses that indicates the proximity of a major urban area without revealing the city itself, the occasional exit ramp leading to an overpass where a sign says it's two miles to the nearest town and the arrow points to infinity. When civilization did present itself, it was in the peculiar form of commerce familiar to the cocooned traveler: motel chains with uniform "FREE HBO" marquees, truck stops with acres of eighteen-wheelers, bill-boards with advertisements for the next motel, the next truck stop. Only occasionally would a sign that was unmistakably in-digenous to the region appear, reminding the players that where they were wasn't home:

"BOARD? Galena Lumber Co."
"Or′•ē•ō•zŏl. A pronounced improvement in
swine-disease prevention. Aureozol 250."
"Avoid fecal fingers. Use lift-it. World's only germ-proof
toilet seat handle."

This morning, however, the bus at some point had left the inter-state behind. The lanes had to have narrowed from six to two, and the grass median had vanished, replaced by a yellow line. The road twisted. The bus slowed, barely, then more. Once, it stopped for a red light.

"Whaaat?" came a cry from the back, because the bus was idling outside a school for the deaf.

The light changed, and the bus started again. Now the players were rousing themselves. Eyes opened. Earphones slid off. The player napping in the overhead luggage compartment—the only uninterrupted horizontal surface on the bus long enough to accommodate the full human form—poked his head down. In the front seat, Champ dropped his legs from the railing and craned toward a windshield as wide as the sky. In the seat behind him, Treanor lowered the "Money" section of that morning's *USA Today,* to which he had turned a half an hour earlier in desperation.

Fields of crops were sweeping past. Furrows of tall green, followed by furrows of short green, followed by furrows of tall green. Suddenly, a cemetery. Then more crops.

"Did you see where they had an atlas for sale? Back at that gas station? Shows *every road in the state.*"

A town, four blocks long. Grain silo at one end, gas pump at the other, and in-between white clapboard houses and a school—a two-story red brick building with a jungle gym out front and a backstop out back. Then, more crops.

"There's Walton Mountain. And there's the Waltons!"

"Yuma! Next four exits!"

"John Deere Historical Museum, to your left."

And then a real sign: "Ding A Ling Supper Club." Nobody knew what to make of this, and before they could decide another cry arose:

"Big, *big* truck!"

The bus swerved. The truck swerved. The bus braked. Tires touched shoulder. A little fishtailing in the spit of the gravel, a little rocking in the suck from the truck, and then back on the blacktop. At the next intersection, the driver pulled into a gas station and said to Champ he thought he might get out here and ask for directions.

Bus trips were part of the lore of the minor leagues. *Long* bus trips, punishing bus trips, bus trips that lasted past dawn, bus trips in hundred-degree heat and no air conditioning, bus trips that separated the men from the boys, bus trips that ended with players getting out to push. Some of these stereotypes might have still been true, but for the most part, the latest Professional Baseball Agreement had relegated them to the past. In the division of responsibilities between the major league parent club and the minor league affiliate, the bus fell on the local franchise's side of the ledger. Rule 39, "Travel Standards for Minor League Clubs," Section 3, "Approval Of Vehicles," stipulated that a minor league club "must obtain the Major League Club's approval of all vehicles used for the purpose of traveling to road games." Gone were the days of a ball club buying at a bargain whatever clattertrap vehicle the local school district was willing to unload after 100,000 miles of abuse. Now a ball club either purchased a decent vehicle of its own or, like the Diamonds, solicited bids on a season's contract from the area's reputable coach companies. Still, a bus trip was a bus trip. When the players were lucky, the bus might have an overhead VCR player and a boxful of tapes. (On that memorable morning, Dean Treanor had selected for the team's viewing pleasure *Weekend at Bernie's,* eliciting a chorus of *"Awe*-some" and "Aw-*right."*) When the players weren't so fortunate, the bus lacked adequate shocks, or a driver with a keen sense of direction.

Champ clambered off the bus. After a moment, the players followed, packing the shack that served as this crossroads' convenience store, emptying the shelves of pretzels and chips and doughnuts, and no doubt providing the proprietor with his best sales day in memory. Champ stood out in the noon sun and chatted up the driver, who said he'd spent the past two days driving a gambling tour to Minnesota. He said he'd gotten back to the depot in Dubuque last night around midnight, driven the hour and a half to his house in Wisconsin, slept, driven back the hour and a half to the depot in Dubuque to pick up a new bus, then driven another hour-and-a-half to Waterloo for the 8:00 A.M. pickup at the ballpark and the theoretically six-hour drive back through Dubuque and all the way across Wisconsin to Kenosha, on the shores of Lake Michigan. He said he'd gotten about two hours' sleep, but he didn't need much. "Five, most nights," he said. He said he'd be retiring in the fall, and he said he and the wife had bought a bus they'd converted into an RV, which, after he'd retired, they planned to drive around the country. Champ got back on the bus.

"He's a nervous wreck," he said.

Despite the best efforts of the Professional Baseball Agreement and the United States interstate system, the rigors of a life on the road remained an essential part of minor league baseball. The fifteen dollars a day in meal money—distributed in one lump by the trainer minutes after the bus pulled out of Waterloo—didn't go very far, but it went farther for players who packed a cooler full of yogurt and milk and sandwiches, who slept late on the road to save the cost of breakfast, and who made a meal of the fruit-and-cheese buffet that the Padres provided in the clubhouse for every game. Which left only lunch, and so one of the players' main concerns about any motel was its proximity to fast food. The other was the availability of cheap fun within walking distance, to fill the hours between lunch and the bus ride to the ballpark, and between the bus ride back from the ballpark and curfew. The Exel Inn in Appleton, for instance, was situated at one end of a mile-long stretch of commercial development and offered plenty of fast-food opportunities, but no distractions. The Continental Regency Hotel in downtown Peoria was nowhere near fast food, though it did offer, only a block away, Big Al's, a strip club the players had heard about through interviews with the dancers on TV talk shows. And one budget motel, in Rockford, was near nothing; it was on the wrong side of the interstate. The only food within walking distance was a hotel restaurant across the street that charged nearly seven dollars for a hamburger. Before the team's first afternoon in that motel was out, Champ had gotten on the phone back to Waterloo and received permission from Simpson to move the team to another, slightly more expensive motel on the other side of the interstate.

The Howard Johnson in Kenosha, however, had it all. What it lacked in atmosphere—it lay barely a long fly ball from the blaring, grunting trucks on the interstate, and the swimming pool was full of broken blocks of concrete—it made up in location. It shared a parking lot with both a Burger King and the Congo River miniature golf course, and was across the road from half a dozen other fast-food joints as well as the Brat Shop restaurant and bar for late-night lounging. But the best part, from the perspective of a player facing a four-day stay in this spot, if not a four-game series in the waning weeks of a disappointing first half of the season, was the Factory Outlet Centre only a two-minute walk away—more than one hundred outlet stores under one roof, a series of interconnected structures so massive that the buildings themselves were color-coded.

The first afternoon the Diamonds were in Kenosha, the rosters for the Midwest League All-Star game arrived by fax at the Simmons Field front office. At the moment, the Kenosha Twins and the Waterloo Diamonds had compiled almost identical records: 25–33 and 25–35, respectively. Kenosha was in last place in the Northern Division, and the Waterloo Diamonds were in fifth place in the Southern, fourteen and a half games out of first with ten games to go, and a team batting average of .227 that in the entire league eclipsed only Burlington. During pregame warmups, Champ and Treanor stood near the fence behind home, studying the list of players on the Southern Division All-Star squad. Midwest League rules required that each team send at least one representative to the All-Star game; eventually, Champ and Treanor found the Diamonds': Jason Hardtke.

Treanor sneered. "He'll be thrilled. Haw!"

"They've got him down as a utility infielder," Champ said softly. "He's not even a starter." He shook his head, then shuffled the pages. Now he was studying the All-Star roster for the Northern Division. "It's one each," he said to Treanor, showing him the second sheet. "See, Kenosha's got just one player, too."

"So what you're saying," Treanor said, crossing his arms and resuming his usual deadpan, "is this series is going to be evenly matched."

"I don't know *what* this series is going to be." Champ folded the rosters in half, then in half again. He stuffed the tidy square of papers into his back pocket. "All I know is every other player is going to be thinking, 'I didn't make it.' "

At any moment a manager might be carrying a piece of information that will affect the trajectory of a player's career. It might be as slight as a mental note to mention a shift in a batting stance; it might be as significant as a written evaluation of a player's prospects, either immediate or long-range. This knowledge alone, or the possibility of such knowledge, endowed the manager with an authoritarian air. On the bus, Champ got the seat behind the stairwell, the one with all the legroom, and if at the end of a ride he needed to announce the bus's departure time, he said it once and once only. "Bus leaves eleven-thirty," he would bark, and a voice from the rear would say, "What time?" but Champ would already be gone, striding briskly across the parking lot of some commercial-strip motel in the middle of America, windbreaker billowing, right arm hanging straight from the weight of his briefcase and the secrets within. Even among his peers this hierarchy held; when Champ hosted a barbecue at his basement apartment in Cedar Falls one Sunday night off, it was he and the Springfield manager who sat atop the wall of what passed for a terrace off the living room, while the coaches and trainers from the two squads stood in the concrete well at their feet.

This status carried a certain responsibility. The trick wasn't to treat all the players equally, but to figure out a way to favor the genuine prospects with the extra attention they needed without their teammates noticing. "As you go up, you'll be seeing better heaters," Champ counseled a couple of sluggers; to a quartet of catchers he said, "We've got four quality players here, and there's no fuckin' reason we can't be quality every fuckin' inning"—but all the while he was thinking, *Gotta fool 'em. Gotta make 'em think they can do something they can't.* In amateur ball, every player deserved a manager's complete attention; but this was pro ball: the instruction of the few. When pitcher Cameron Cairncross, after a good outing, had been quoted in the *Courier* as saying, "All I wanted to do was shove it up their (expletive)," Champ had pulled him aside before the next game and said, "Compliment yourself, compliment your teammates, but don't say anything bad about the other team. All that's gonna do is fire 'em up for next time." Or Hardtke: Champ was pulling him aside twice a night now sometimes, stopping him on the dugout steps, or intercepting him as he trotted off the field, to whisper a few quick words: "As you move up, the players will be better, and you'll be able to count on that throw being there for you."

But the trick was getting trickier as the season progressed and the players' natural differences in ability and determination revealed themselves. In the past two weeks, Champ had lost all his other potential All-Stars to High Desert—Cole Hyson, Steve Hoeme and Shawn Whalen, the league leader in saves, arguably the league's most effective set-up pitcher, and one of the league leaders in home runs and RBI, all gone, all on the final day of May. "It's like, come *on,*" Champ had said to Treanor when he'd gotten the phone call informing him of his impending losses. "We already have almost nothing." Still, what he had was exactly what

San Diego had promised Champ in offering him the job in Water-loo; if the Padres' system weren't stacked at the position, the Dia-monds' All-Star second baseman might not be here, either.

"Everybody grab a seat real quick," Champ said before the first game in Kenosha, standing in front of the corner locker that, at Simmons Field, served as the visiting manager's office. "Okay, listen up. Anybody learn anything about the infield out there?"

He waited. "Slow?" offered a tentative voice.

"Right! *Very* slow. The grass is very long. That means it's a good field to bunt on. Outfield, you're going to charge the ball more than you would at home. Base runners, you can take the extra base—maybe.

"All right," he went on. He looked at the floor: carpeting—a surprise, considering. He looked up. "I've just found out about the All-Star team." For a moment, the clubhouse fell silent; a wave of nervous laughter followed immediately, washing over the play-ers. Suddenly they were bobbing, tittering, joshing one another, throwing fake punches all except Hardtke. He didn't move. He didn't blink. He simply poised on the edge of the folding chair in front of his locker, eyes widening, senses straining, a pointer pick-ing up the scent.

"Jason, where are you?" Champ looked around the room. Hardtke raised his hand. Champ walked over to him. "Congratu-lations," Champ said, shaking his hand. "Represent us well." While Champ returned to his own locker, Hardtke, his squarish features dissolving into a grin of relief and gratitude, received handshakes from his teammates. "If we hadn't made that trade," Champ called back to him, "we might not have anybody to send! Which would you rather do, go to the All-Star game, or spend three days in Waterloo? That's incentive right there." There was laughter. "Okay," said Champ, "let's go have a little fun."

From a far corner, a lone voice rose. "Isn't there supposed to be more than one?"

Still, it wasn't for the Burger King or the Congo River or the Brat Stop, and it wasn't for the rocky bus trip that got them there, and it certainly wasn't for the games themselves (the Diamonds dropped three of four) that Kenosha would remain memorable. Sometimes a stop on the road provided a bonus. Clinton, for in-stance, was a city of many smells. ("Potato chips," Maxwell had said one afternoon there, raising his face toward a doughy sky, "and . . . dog food?") The motel in Burlington had an indoor pool. And Kenosha had Juggsy.

It could have been anywhere, but it was in Kenosha that a woman who worked in the picnic area down the right-field line caught the attention of the team. A low cyclone fence separated the picnic area from the visiting team's bullpen, and before games Waterloo players would unstick themselves from the bullpen bench—it was flush against the outfield wall, offered no hint of shade, and faced directly west, into the setting sun: a home-team advantage—and wander over to the fence and strike up a conversation. She wore a cutoff jersey that exposed her midriff and that, when she leaned across the fence, inspired more than one player to drop to his knee and retie a shoelace.

"How big are they?" a player wondered one afternoon, sitting on the bullpen bench about an hour before game time.

"How stupid is she?" said a second player.

"The more she sees you watching her, the more she sticks them out," said a third.

"Can you imagine being married to a slut like that?" The first player spat. "Pushin' her tits out there all the time." He spat again, then got up from the bullpen bench and went over to talk to her.

They named her Juggsy, at first; then, after the number "54" on the back of her cutoff jersey, Juggsy Five-Four. Following the third game of the Kenosha series, Sean Mulligan commandeered the drivers' microphone on the team bus in the Simmons Field parking lot. Mulligan, big-browed, and with a L'il Abner nose and chin, had been sent down from High Desert to work on his catching mechanics and to replace Shawn Whalen as the designated hitter. At the moment, the driver, the manager, the pitching coach, and the equipment manager were elsewhere.

"Juggsy!" Mulligan commanded.

She didn't appear to hear. She was talking with friends, standing inside the gate across the parking lot, her back to the bus.

"Juggsy Five-Four!"

Farlow climbed aboard the bus, sized up the situation, and informed Mulligan that his voice wasn't carrying. He said he'd walked right past Juggsy and couldn't hear a word from the bus.

Farlow continued down the aisle of the bus. Mulligan raised his voice.

"Oh, you big-titted baboon! You fucking baboon, you! Excuse me, Five-Four!"

"Come on, get her, Mully!" came a voice from the back.

"Five-four! Five-*four*! *Five . . . four!* Come here, Juggsy, I'm talkin' to you, on the horn."

"Get her, Mull!"

"Five-four! Come on ovah!"

At long last, she turned to the bus.

"Ooohhh!" A cry went up on the bus. "Oh! Oh! Oh!"

She motioned to her friends to wait a minute, then crossed the parking lot. She stopped at the front stairwell of the bus.

"We want to talk to you!" Mulligan said. "Come up in here!"

She hesitated, then obeyed.

"What's your name?"

"Wendy," she said to him.

"Wendy?" Mulligan said, guiding her shoulder, turning her toward the rest of the bus. "This is Wendy, everybody."

Her eyes bulged. Sizing her up over the seat backs were the eyes of twenty young men.

"So, Wendy, what are you doing here?"

She turned back to Mulligan. "I work here."

"You work here? Where are you from, Wendy?"

"Here."

"Kenosha? Okay. Well, we were just interested because we were watching you last night, and we wanted to get to know who you were."

"How old are you, Wendy?" someone shouted.

"Do you go to school?" said Mulligan.

"Yeah."

"What grade are you in, Wendy?"

"What *grade* am I in? I'm a junior in college."

"A junior? Are you on summer break, or you going to summer school?"

"No, I'm on summer break."

"You ever been to Chicago?"

"All the time."

"All the time? Good, good. So, where are you going now?"
She named a bar.

"We'd like to go there. How do you get there from Howard
Johnson's?"

"I don't even—it's like somewhere around here."

"Is it? By chance, do you have a car?"

"Petey," she said, turning and taking one step down the stairwell and shouting from the door.

"Petey, come on ovah," said Mulligan.

"Do you know where the bar is?" she called.

"Show us your knockers!" somebody said.

"Knock it off!" somebody said.

"Three blocks?" she said. She turned back to Mulligan. She
stayed one step down the stairwell. "Three blocks south," she
told him.

"Well, we don't have a car. We're right on the interstate, and
we'd like a ride."

"Show us your Twins!" somebody said.

She shot the busload a look of shock. Mulligan eased her back.

"Are you going to the bar?"

"Yes."

"Do you have a car?"

"Yes."

"May I have a ride?"

"Just you?"

"Yes. I'm Sean, by the way." He extended his hand. "I'm the
guy who took the initiative to bring you over here to say hello."

"You've got the mike."

"I have the mike."

They shook hands.

"Well, I think I have to go. Other people are going."

"Well, are you coming to Howard Johnson's?"

She turned and shouted to her friends across the parking lot,
"Okay, I'll be right over."

"Call me."

"Huh?" She twisted on the stairs.

"You're going to call me?"

"Yeah."

"Okay. I'm in Room 210."

"All right." She stepped off the bus and turned. " 'Bye, " she said to Mulligan, then ran across the parking lot to rejoin her friends.

Mulligan stared after her. Everybody on the bus stared after her. Then Mulligan turned to his teammates.

"That, gentlemen, he said, "is how it's done."

"I respectfully request that you give your attention to all matters brought before us," Bill Boesen announced, banging a hammer against a ballpark railing and silencing the group seated before him. "I now call this meeting to order."

It was the first official gathering of the franchise's board of directors since Dan Yates's resignation, and Boesen, the new president, was presiding. The opening invocation from Robert's *Rules of Order,* which Boesen had memorized through his years of attending meetings of one sort or another as a union steward with the International Brotherhood of Electrical Workers, was a nod toward professionalism; the ballpark setting, a nod toward the organization's traditional informality. The hammer on the railing was to make sure he had their attention. Most of the owners had spent the better part of the day attending the funeral of Lefty Dunsmoor, a 75-year-old former Rath salesman and real estate broker, and fellow shareholder in Waterloo Professional Baseball, Inc., and then continuing to mourn in their own way, downtown at the VFW Hall. Lefty Dunsmoor had been suffering from prostate cancer for some time, and his death had not been unexpected. He had been in the hospital for several months, and he hadn't attended a board meeting since November. Still, the grimness of the day, greased as it was by too much sun and alcohol for several of the owners, threatened to pitch the proceedings into moroseness. Under the circumstances, Boesen's call to order served as much as anything as a reminder of why they were here.

In the first weeks of his tenure, Boesen had set about trying to mend fences—literally and figuratively. He had approached Parks Director Rick Tagtow about building a fence to protect the scoreboard, but gotten nowhere. Next Boesen had called on the Park Board member who served as the liaison to the ball club. Once, Russ Garling had been one of them. A large man possessed of a guttural growl, Garling was the son of a traveling salesman. He had never been to college, as he didn't hesitate to point out, often while apologizing for not knowing "all the fancy English that a lot of people do." Also, he wasn't "influential in the community." "I'm merely a marketing rep, I'm not a manager, I'm not a supervisor," he'd say of the position he held with Midwest Gas, comparing himself with the ball club's owners. "I'm just an employee of a firm, no different than they are."

What was more, Garling had been a member of the ball club's board, serving as secretary, then vice president, and, ultimately, president. He'd had a falling out, however, with one of the current owners, whose name he wouldn't speak, but who everyone on the board knew to be Barb Kuper, who had been influential in his ouster. His time as president, in fact, had fallen during a late-1970s, early-1980s era of contentiousness on the board, a time of personality clashes and possible scandals that ended in one president after another stepping aside. Skimming the concessions profits, charging the ball club for the whole family's trip to the Winter Meetings, stacking the board with cronies, bingo rigging, kickbacks—the specific accusations and denials of wrongdoing in the various instances had shifted and receded over the years, but not so the nuggets of the grudges. These the aggrieved parties on both sides had kept grinding away at in their conversations and then in their memories, turning them over and over, tumbling them, polishing them, until they flashed, quite unlike anything else on the gray industrial landscape of Waterloo, with the jewel-like brilliance of unforgiveness and unforgetting. "As long as that one person is still there," Garling would say to this day, "I will not be a baseball attendant. I'll work for baseball the best way that I can, outside of attending ball games. Unfortunately. And that's a personal thing. I will never in my *life* be humiliated again by people, and there is nothing any more *vicious* than the humiliation and greed of some people."

Boesen visited Garling in his office, on the second floor of the Midwest Gas headquarters downtown, a low modern building landscaped out front with a rectangle of artificial grass. Modesty aside, Garling had done all right for himself (according to speculation among ball club owners, by marrying money). He may have labored in a nondescript cubicle, but on one partition he'd hung two wide-angle photographs of his house on Silver Lake Drive, the same circle of exclusivity wherein former mayor Bernie McKinley resided. One photo showed the front of his property, the other the back, where the long lawn led to a gazebo, then past it, to a lake. The upwardly spiraling property taxes of the City of Waterloo and Black Hawk County had clipped Russ Garling especially hard, and during Park Board discussions of baseball funding, he often said that it galled him to think he might be expected to bankroll a ballpark when he knew there was private money out there. He returned to this theme during his meeting with Boesen. Garling said the ball club could have its fence.

But.

He wanted to see action. The ball club used to have access to "the Waterloo power structure," he said. He wanted to see the ball club get back those contacts, and he himself had an idea how to do it. He said that one day that past winter he'd attended a meeting at which a Midwest Gas brochure was distributed detailing the utility's role in industrial development in Iowa, and at the time he'd jotted a note to himself. It read:

> Setting Here thinking this type of approach for friends and Organizations for Waterloo Baseball to get Capital Dollars.
> 1. Have a plan.
> 2. Review Background.
> 3. Give Board Membership large Dollar Donations.
> 4. Have a plan for Structure-Stadium Development.
> If we'd put together a general outline of this type of project—could Bernie's people put together the details and total script—printed?

"Bernie," of course, was the former mayor, and his "people" were the Cedar Valley Partnership, the privately financed commercial development group where he now served as marketing director. Perhaps the Cedar Valley Partnership would be useful in planning a brochure; perhaps the CVP would foot some or all of the printing and production costs. If nothing else, "Bernie's people"—the people who could get things done in Waterloo, after all—would be aware of the ball club's plight. "If you want to save baseball," Garling said now to Boesen, "we'll work with you; we'll help you save it. *But.* You've got to do more than just exist."

Bill Boesen might have had good reason not to trust Russ Garling, but he couldn't exactly dismiss his advice. Like any student of a factory city, Boesen had learned that sometimes it was accomplishment enough just to get out—if not out of town, then at least out to the ballpark for an evening. The owners, in fact, had exceeded that accomplishment by accepting the responsibility for keeping the ball club alive, and if they had met that responsibility by doing the bare minimum, who could blame them? Boesen didn't know what to make of Garling's suggestions because he didn't what it was going to take to save professional ball for Waterloo. Still, what with the resignation of Dan Yates, Boesen couldn't deny that the bare minimum had just gone up.

At the next owners' meeting, Boesen informed his fellow board members that the time had come to share some of the responsibilities that the president of the ball club had always been able to execute on his or her own. They formed committees in the following categories: field conditions; concessions; stands; public relations; beer bar; souvenirs; relations with the mayor, council, and parks; relations with San Diego; and fund-raising. Then, after rising for a moment of silence in memory of Lefty Dunsmoor, they went home, where a few of the owners continued the meeting on a less formal basis, calling one another late into the night, their drooping, swooping voices consoling themselves over the loss of one of their own.

The Diamonds' bus pulled out of the Howard Johnson parking lot in Kenosha, immediately started the climb up the ramp to the interstate, and headed due south, along the tollways and interstates that towered over the immense rail yards on the industrial outskirts of Chicago, then due east, across the steel-mill country of northern Indiana, toward South Bend. *This was it,* the Midwest League veterans had tipped off their teammates. For four days, the team had been playing in the purgatory of Kenosha, a lame-duck franchise in a seventy-one-year-old facility. In South Bend, however, waited the promised land.

The Diamonds greeted their first glimpse of the sleek facilities from the bus with whistles and sighs.

"Wow."

"Welcome to Waterloo Stadium."

"Nothin' on the 'loo."

"Compared to this every other place is a joke."

"Welcome to the *bigs.*"

The exclamations only grew after the players and staff had walked down the long, wide concrete ramp that led into the bowels of the entertainment complex and gotten a look at their dressing room: not only carpeted, not only immaculate and spacious, but considerate. Respectful. *Solicitous.* The folding chair tucked within each locker. The separate offices for the manager and for his coaching staff. The daily stats sheet waiting on the manager's desk.

Treanor picked it up. "Well, we're last in hitting," he said. He put it back and continued unpacking his equipment bag. After a while, he pulled out a can of soda, handed it to Champ, and explained that he'd gotten it out of the vending machine at the hotel.

Champ hefted it. He looked at it. It was a can of Pepsi, only it bore the South Bend White Sox logo and the team's home schedule.

"Ho, man," said Treanor, as Champ, without comment, handed back the can.

Down the hall, players had begun congregating in the spacious trainer's room to hear Sean Mulligan tell his Juggsy story. While he and Juggsy had been inside Room 210 at the Howard Johnson in Kenosha, he explained, four of his teammates had been outside, on the balcony, working the video camera that the club sometimes used to study pitchers' motions. A space in the curtains was all the access they'd needed.

"I could hear you guys," Mulligan admonished a couple of players, lounging and laughing nearby. "And she goes, 'There's somebody there!' " He endowed her with an air of falsetto alarm. "So I got up and closed the curtains and we went back to it."

"The ultimate minor league bimbo!" somebody roared.

Mulligan laughed. "What's she gonna do to somebody who's just been inside her crack?"

Then it was time to head toward the playing field, where more wonders awaited them. The long concrete tunnel leading from the clubhouse to the dugout was as tall and as wide as a truck and led into a dugout twice as long and deep as the one in Waterloo, and the dugout led to a field where the grass was manicured so that concentric circles of mowing grace radiated from the pitcher's mound.

"Going from Waterloo to here is like going from night to day."

"Waterloo makes *Kenosha* look great."

"We'd win more games if we had facilities like this. You look better, you feel better."

"They shouldn't even *show* this to other teams. Or they'll all want this."

Exactly. South Bend—both franchise and facility—had set the standard. Even as the Diamonds' bus was pulling into the South Bend parking lot that afternoon, ground was being broken some 80 miles farther along, near the Ohio border, in Fort Wayne, on Allen County Memorial Stadium—the new home, as of the following season, of the Kenosha franchise the Diamonds had left behind just that morning. Already advance crews from Allen County had made several drives up to South Bend, partly because Kenosha/Fort Wayne was now owned by a former South Bend owner, but partly because South Bend had come to exemplify throughout the minors how to run a comprehensively professional operation. "When I greet people at the ballpark," the GM liked to say, "it's, 'Hi, glad to see you,' but in my mind it's, 'Hi, glad to see you spending money.' And if they can have a good time spending money, why not?"

The staff in South Bend now included, in addition to the president and GM and assistants, a vice president of baseball sales and promotions, a director of stadium operations, a director of concessions operations, a ticket manager, and a public relations and marketing administrator. Of the ten full-time, year-round staff members, two held a master's in sports management, and two a bachelor's. In addition, owner Alan Levin used the minor league operation as the base for AML Entertainment, which oversaw a rock and a pops concert series at the ballpark as well as the South Bend White Sox Baseball Academy. He also ran a placement bureau at the Winter Meetings, where, one year, he introduced applicants to the blunt realities of the new pro ball marketplace with this warning: "In today's minor league climate, you've got to make money. We don't need statisticians. We're not looking for lovers of sport. The perspective today is a business perspective, not a sports perspective."

If Davenport had represented the 1980s ideal of how to rehabilitate an existing market by refurbishing an existing facility, South Bend had represented the next significant advance in the evolution of the minors: how to create a market by creating a facility. Stanley Coveleski Memorial Regional Stadium—or The Cove, as the ballpark was known locally—had proven to be a godsend for both the ball club and the parent club: concession stands with full views of the field, private boxes aplenty, amenities such as executive suites and an elevator to connect them with the clubhouse level, and the capacity to expand to Triple A attendance standards (and indeed the ball club recently had bid unsuccessfully for the right to a Triple A expansion franchise). But Triple A accommodations weren't merely a matter of seating; they required that the facility be acceptable to players who had been to the major leagues. Even as a Class A facility, the Cove's 90-mile distance from the South Side of Chicago and the parent White Sox organization made it a convenient overnight stop for players on the mend. Only a week before Waterloo arrived, in fact, the White Sox had sent Carlton Fisk to South Bend for a day of rehab. (He hit a home run.)

South Bend was the facility and the franchise that, perhaps more than any others in the minors, had prompted Major League Baseball in 1990 to reexamine the assumptions that had been governing its relationship with the National Association for thirty years. From a postwar high of 42 million, annual attendance in the minors had dropped steadily until, from the early 1960s through the early 1970s, it was averaging less than 10 million. If the minors had existed only to meet the demands of the entertainment marketplace, they very possibly might have expired. But the minors, of course, also existed as a player-development system for the majors. For the majors to ensure the survival of their talent pipeline, it had become more cost-effective to divest themselves of these money-losing franchises on an individual basis, letting the local folk fret about selling fence-board space or ordering enough hot dogs for the Fourth of July, and to increase their subsidies to the minors as a whole. Since the 1950s, local owners had been returning to minor league baseball, either by reclaiming a market that the majors no longer wanted, as was the case in Waterloo, or by relieving a major league club, sometimes for the price of a dollar, of a franchise it had found unprofitable. Profits, however, didn't necessarily concern local operators. All they needed was enough to break even, and so the majors had instituted a system of subsidies. In 1956, the majors contributed $500,000 to a stabilization fund for the minors. In 1962, the majors and the National Association completely rethought the farm system, not only eliminating the A, B, C, and D classifications and replacing them with Triple A, Double A and Class A, but instituting a Player Development Contract that standardized the financial responsibilities between minor league franchises and their major league parents— who would pay what portion of the players' salaries, equipment, travel expenses and meal money. In 1967, resolving a long-running dispute about the effect of major league TV broadcasts on ballpark box-office in minor league markets, the majors began paying their affiliates a "special considerations" fee. All these subsidies were subject to periodic renegotiations, the underlying question of which was: What will it take to keep the minors alive?

What resulted was a classic case of free-market frontiersmanship. By the late 1970s and 1980s, formerly failing minor league franchises had become success stories—modest success stories, but success stories nonetheless. In the cyclical nature of entertainment, a public that had seen nothing but big league baseball for decades, and had brought major league attendance to new highs, now sought something simpler. Perhaps it was the physical distance from the field created by the new multipurpose major league stadiums of the 1960s and early 1970s; perhaps it was the psychological distance from the players created by the rise of free agency and skyrocketing salaries; perhaps it was the cumulative impression, through these factors and others, that big league baseball was leaving or had left one era behind and was entering another. Whatever the reasons, fans started attending minor league baseball games again, and they liked what they saw enough to keep coming back—some as owners.

The chance to own a piece of the National Pastime! A privilege once available to communities or major league clubs was now open to anyone. It was out there, and it could be had in those days for next to nothing, especially at the lowest levels of the minors. And if these novices couldn't believe their good fortune in being able to live out the fantasy of owning a baseball team, then they must have been overwhelmed once they had figured out the industry's financial structure, which could hardly have been more favorable to the owner. Major League Baseball paid an appreciable portion of the players' expenses. The local government provided the venue. Even the purchase cost in those wide-open days could be paid entirely with credit and no proof of net worth. A minor league ball club owner still had numerous out-of-pocket costs— the remainder of the players' expenses, often some part of the ballpark maintenance, plus all the usual responsibilities of running a business, such as salaries, inventory, insurance, licenses, and so on—and even breaking even was by no means guaranteed. But these subsidies suggested the possibility of a fringe benefit this first generation of new owners wouldn't have demanded but nonetheless welcomed: a profit.

In 1987 the franchise that was on its way to becoming the South Bend White Sox was purchased by a pair of fledgling baseball entrepreneurs named Jay Acton and Eric Margenau, a New York literary agent and a New York sports psychologist. Previously, Acton had bought a share in the Utica, New York franchise in 1983 on a lark (one of his author clients, Roger Kahn, had become a part owner in that club as research for his book about the minors, *Good Enough to Dream*). Acton sold his share after the season, then returned to baseball with Margenau in 1986 as owners of the Watertown, New York ball club. According to Acton, "That first season, we had a great time. Didn't make any money, but that wasn't really the point." The second year, the team won the division pennant for the first time in franchise history; after the season, Acton and Margenau moved the franchise because they sensed "the potential in these organizations as money-makers." They sought a better market and a better facility, and they found both in Welland, Ontario, where, Acton would later reflect in his book, *Green Diamonds: The Pleasures and Profits of Investing in Minor-League Baseball,* "the move accomplished its purpose; it made the team profitable, which it hadn't been before."

The South Bend franchise was going to require an even more substantial investment. The ball club had begun life as a piece of paper—the right to an expansion franchise—purchased from the Midwest League for $40,000 in 1984 by a Decatur, Illinois couple. Their plan had been to set up a franchise in Champaign, Illinois, using University of Illinois facilities, but a school prohibition on beer sales at university-related events forced them to look elsewhere. At that time, civic leaders in South Bend, Indiana, were starting the search for a franchise they could lure to town with the promise of a new stadium and the announced intention of the Chicago White Sox, if such a franchise could be found and a first-rate facility built, to locate a Class A affiliate there. The mayor at that time envisioned the stadium as an anchor in the redevelopment of a downtown in a city that had been devastated over the previous two decades by the losses of such industrial stalwarts as Studebaker, Singer Sewing Machine and a John Deere tractor factory. The floating, dormant franchise was the obvious choice, but wave after wave of taxpayer opposition to city funding of a new stadium delayed the process for a couple of years. By the time the mayor had maneuvered stadium financing past its legal obstacles, the couple from Decatur was ready to sell, and they found eager, if nervous, buyers in Acton and Margenau, who swallowed hard and agreed to pay $475,000.

The money was becoming serious indeed, and not only in South Bend. In the New York–Penn League, the $125,000 that Acton and Margenau had paid for the Watertown franchise only a year earlier had surpassed the previous league record by $50,000; now, the Elmira franchise in the same league was selling for more than $300,000. Throughout the minors, this pattern was repeating itself: new owners, new records—and then, as often as not, new ballparks in new cities. The South Bend White Sox joined the Midwest League in 1988, playing at the $5.95 million Stanley Coveleski Memorial Regional Stadium. By the end of Acton's and Margenau's first season with South Bend, they realized that the elaborate operation that their kind of minor league business had become required a different kind of management. Such substantial investments required substantial rates of return; often, such hefty up-front action required a hefty cash flow just to service the debt. Acton invited an old business acquaintance, a CBS television executive named Alan Levin, to invest in the business and lend his expertise. The following year, the franchise made a *profit* of

$400,000—nearly double the operating expenses of a Waterloo style of operation at that time. The year after that—1990—Acton and Margenau sold South Bend to Levin, "a fan of baseball, but not a fanatic," as Acton wrote. "He was interested in baseball as a business proposition." The price: $2.7 million.

To major league owners, a transaction such as this proved their growing suspicion that they were subsidizing the literal fortunes of their minor league counterparts. Again, South Bend was hardly alone. The market for minor league ball clubs—and a market was what the buying and selling of franchises had become by now— was yielding one Xerox-in-1952 bonanza after another: Harrisburg, Pennsylvania, bought in 1980 (in Nashua, New Hampshire) for $85,000, sold for $3 million; Peoria, Illinois, bought in 1983 (in Danville, Illinois) for $125,000, sold for $1.2 million; Durham, North Carolina, the club whose movie stardom had contributed to the near-cult status of no-frills pro ball, bought in 1979 for $2,400, sold for $4 million. In the periodic renegotiations between the Major Leagues and the National Association over the preceding several decades, the underlying question had always been the same: What are the minimum subsidies from the majors that are necessary to keep the minors operational? It was the assumption behind these subsidies, as well as the subsidies themselves, that came up for renewal at the 1990 Winter Meetings.

Or, more accurately, two sets of Winter Meetings. That fall, when negotiations over a new Professional Baseball Agreement broke down, the majors pulled out of the scheduled meetings in Los Angeles to convene meetings of their own in Chicago. A system of subsidies might have made sense when the beneficiaries were mom-and-pop operations that reinvested profits in a new tarp. But now, the majors argued, their subsidies were helping to make the minors rich, and, besides, they were spending $100 million a year on their farm systems—didn't that investment entitle them to greater authority? "We don't want to run their show," said Pittsburgh Pirates president Carl Barger, a negotiator for the majors. "But we do want to run our show. We have a huge investment in our player development pool."

The minors, for their part, suspected a more sinister motive. When the minors were struggling economically, the majors hadn't been all that eager to exercise more control. Why now? It wasn't just greater authority over their affairs that the majors wanted, the minors charged, it was a piece of the action. A few years earlier, when the major league owners were starting to question the rising value of minor league franchises, a National Association president had summarized the prevailing mood in the minors succinctly, if not diplomatically: "My answer is that you fellows bailed out long ago and missed the boat."

The majors opened the PBA negotiations that summer by threatening not to renew any of the fifty-nine Player Development Contracts expiring that year. In September, they made good on that threat. In October, they announced plans to field fifty-nine teams of their own the following year in the baseball complexes of Florida and Arizona, an alternative that some baseball theoreticians (among them Whitey Herzog) had been advocating anyway as the next logical step in the economic evolution of the minors. Finally, in November, as if to underscore just how little they needed the National Association, the majors pulled out of the Winter Meetings—the annual convention at which the two principal components of professional baseball traditionally broke bread together as if they were all one big happy pastime.

The minors, having little leverage, surrendered. The new PBA wound up changing the trend of the previous thirty-five years, not only eliminating some subsidies, but reversing others. Now it was the minors making concessions to the majors.

The "special considerations" TV fee? Gone—at a cost to a Class A club such as Waterloo of $11,000. The number of players and staff whose travel expenses a minor league club must pay? Up—at the Class A level, from eighteen to twenty-six for 1991 and 1992, then to thirty in 1993. At an average discount rate of $25 per room-night, two persons per room, and, conservatively, fifty nights on the road, the difference for Waterloo at first would be at least $5,000, eventually rising to $7,500. Then there was the contribution to the majors of 5 percent of after-tax gate revenues, which in Waterloo would amount to approximately $4,000. In the short term, what it was going to take for a club such as Waterloo to continue supporting professional baseball would be going up at least $20,000, and probably $25,000.

What it would take in the long term—a club's commitment to its future, in effect—was more difficult to calculate. "Attachment

D: Facility Standards and Compliance Inspection Procedures" ran nineteen single-spaced pages. Some of the hundreds of provisions were requirements, some recommendations. Some applied to new facilities only, some to existing facilities. Put them all together, and they spelled out the major league ideal of what a minor league ballpark should be.

The first ten sections pertained to new facilities only and covered such off-the-field concerns as seating, concessions, ticket windows, security and first aid, parking and access, the sound system, the scoreboard, media facilities, and the administration area. The final three sections pertained to all facilities (though standards for new facilities were often higher than those for old), and it was here that the new PBA really got down to business—the facilities, field and groundskeeping considerations that affected the players directly. These included: home and visitor clubhouse dimensions and locker sizes, shower and toilet distribution, training room dimensions, number of coaches' lockers, warning track width, outfield fence height, maximum grade from the pitcher's mound to the foul-territory warning track, maximum grade from second base to the outfield warning track, acceptable lighting levels, the need for a dark center-field batter's eye, field layouts that actually follow the dimensions as specified in the Official Baseball Rules, and a playing field that "shall be maintained at the highest possible professional level."

For the new generation of owners, these results presented a potential threat to an investment. For the old generation of owners, however, the PBA was a threat to their existence. In order to survive, they were going to have to meet the significantly higher demands of the new PBA; they were going to have to start running their operations as if they were the new generation of owners.

In ten years the minor league marketplace had changed again. The ownership of some clubs had shifted from locals who ran them on a virtually not-for-profit basis, to fans who got involved out of love of baseball but found they could also turn a profit, to outsiders who, however fond of the sport, considered their acquisitions in business terms only. Not all clubs, certainly, and maybe not even most clubs. But enough clubs were making fortunes and proving that cities out there were willing to build beautiful new stadiums that they changed the economic structure of the minors.

They imposed a subtle pressure on other clubs to conform to their standards, at least at first; eventually, a not-so-subtle pressure; and now, through the new PBA, a mandate.

Whose minor leagues were they anyway? Nobody would dispute that the landlords of some ballparks had been less than fastidious over the decades, or that some clubs needed subsidies like they needed a fifth base, but what the minors most objected to during the negotiations was the suggestion that it was the majors that had the right to set those standards. The numerous givebacks in the contract, while significant, even traumatic and revolutionary, were surmountable. Not so the minors' further erosion of autonomy. The majors' opening gambit in the negotiations—threatening to take control of the minors, more or less rendering the National Association obsolete—had served as a forceful reminder of the minors' traditionally subservient status. The eventual compromises kept the NA functional and necessary, but they still required the minors to surrender to the majors oversight in areas that traditionally had been all their own—all merchandise licensing (in exchange for a fee), audited financial statements of ball clubs, final approval of franchise sales or transfers and league expansions.

Finally, there was the elimination of the $35 transaction fee that a major league club traditionally had paid the National Association every time it made a minor league roster change. The loss of the fee was sure to have a practical implication for every minor league ball club. At $35 a crack, and thousands of transactions every year, the fee was a source of several hundred thousand dollars; the removal of it would reach individual ball clubs in the form of higher dues for leagues and the National Association (costing a club such as Waterloo another few thousand dollars). But it would have a symbolic impact as well. Prior to the new PBA, players had appeared on the rosters of the minor league organizations themselves. A Waterloo player was truly a Waterloo player, at least in name. This technicality clearly was an anachronism, a holdover from an era when ball clubs scouted and signed their own players, and the fee plainly had functioned as one more token gesture from the majors to make sure that the keepers of the talent stayed solvent. But it also had served as a particularly resonant symbol of what remained of the minors' autonomy. For decades the major league parent clubs might have been able to decide who went where when, yet as long as the $35 fee was intact, as long as the players' names appeared on the franchises' rosters, minor league ball clubs were still officially in the business of providing baseball players—were still *teams*. But now that fee was gone, and with it went the last vestige of what the minor leagues had been at their birth.

One Monday afternoon in June, the president of the Midwest League visited Waterloo Municipal Stadium. As George Spelius and his grown daughter Mary walked through the front gate of the ballpark, Jeff Nelson and Jerry Klinkowitz were waiting by the souvenir stand, while Bill Boesen was wandering over from the far end of the concourse, where he had been trying to fix a stopped toilet. He was gripping a toilet plunger as if it were a sceptre. Spelius's greeting was to toss Nelson a small manila packet without warning. Nelson trapped it against his chest.

"It's from Peoria," Spelius said. "I haven't even opened it."

Nelson had to stare at it for a moment before he realized what its contents must be: "evidence" of the poor field conditions that had inspired the Peoria protest the previous month.

"Aww, geez!" he said, rolling his eyes elaborately. He ripped the package open and pulled out a bunch of photographs. Boesen and Klinkowitz crowded his shoulders as he started flipping through the Polaroids. Spelius glanced over, too. It didn't take them long to figure out that what they were examining was close-up after close-up of infield dirt.

"Yep," Nelson said. "Looks like dirt, all right. Oh, this one's upside down." He tossed the photographs to the souvenir counter, reached inside the package, and pulled out several plastic bags containing presumably foreign objects presumably plucked from the infield. When he got to a metal bolt about three inches long, he gathered up the whole assortment and handed it back to Spelius.

"Get this shit out of here," he said.

Spelius turned to Boesen. "He talks this way around my daughter because he knows her."

"Hey, she talks that way around me," said Nelson.

They all laughed. Then Boesen pointed the handle of the

plunger at the bolt. "Save that," he said. "We can use it in these seats."

George Spelius, a short, bespectacled florist by trade, made a point of visiting each franchise in the Midwest League at least once during each half of the season. In 1982 he had been one of the founders in Beloit, a ball club that took as its inspiration not the limited partnerships or absentee ownerships then emerging but the all-volunteer hometown model. As recently as 1981, all eight teams in the league had been mom-and-pop operations— five in Iowa (Burlington, Cedar Rapids, Clinton, Quad City, and Waterloo), and three in Wisconsin (Appleton, Wausau, and Wisconsin Rapids). Now the league stood at fourteen teams; Wausau and Wisconsin Rapids no longer existed; and the mom-and-pop franchises were outnumbered eight to six. Spelius had risen to the post of league president partly by espousing the virtues of small-market clubs. The league office was in his home, and his daughter was accompanying him on this trip because she was one of the league president's two secretaries. The other was his wife. As the balance in the league had shifted, however, his sensibility had almost cost him his job. Every two years he came up for reelection, and every two years the vote got closer. This past winter, the owners in the league had struck a compromise; they'd reelected him, but only for one year.

"You asshole!" Spelius called. Simpson had joined the group in the infield; he grinned in response to Spelius's greeting. Spelius grabbed Simpson's hand and shook it energetically, then reached into his inner coat pocket and made a production out of handing Simpson a piece of paper. "This guy's really been after me about scheduling around the UNI games here next year," he said, jerking a thumb at Simpson. Simpson shrugged sheepishly. "Between you and Fort Wayne, I swear! Fort Wayne keeps saying they've got to start their season on the road because they don't know if they're going to have their stadium ready by April ninth."

"Fort Wayne?" Boesen whispered to Klinkowitz.

"Moving from Kenosha," Klinkowitz whispered back.

Boesen frowned.

"You're going to have to be on the road a lot at the start," Spelius said to Simpson, "and when you guys have a record of four-and-twenty after the first month, I don't want to hear any complaints!"

Simpson grinned and nodded. Boesen frowned again. Everybody else laughed.

Then Spelius indicated that he wanted to see Boesen and Klinkowitz, the only team owners present, alone for a few minutes, and the three of them headed off on a little walk, leaving the office workers behind. They could have been three landowners checking out the back forty on a warm and dusty spring afternoon. At one point, Spelius remarked that he thought he had heard there might be storms tonight; then again, he said, there might not. When they'd reached a point about midway between straightaway right and center, he stopped. Boesen and Klinkowitz turned to him, waiting for him to begin. Spelius wasn't smiling anymore.

"I just want you to know where you stand with this new PBA," he said. "If San Diego pulls out of here after this season, by contract the major leagues have to give you a team, even if it's a co-op. That's guaranteed in the PBA. Come hell or high water, you'll have a team here for the next two years, through the end of the '94 season. If they have to get *Eskimos* in here, you'll have a team. It's after that where we start running into problems.

"Now a Player Development Contract can last four years, at the most," Spelius continued. "But most of them are for one or two years. And that puts pressure on a smaller-market club like Waterloo when you go to the city looking for money, because you can't guarantee that the majors will have a team here a year or two down the line."

Klinkowitz interrupted to say that some of the operators of the gambling boats on the Iowa side of the Mississippi had announced within the past couple of weeks that they were going downriver because they could make more money in Mississippi or Missouri. "And these cities have put a lot of money into getting those boats there!" Klinkowitz said. "And there's always talk about the dog track closing right here in Waterloo."

"That's right," said Spelius. "There's no guarantees. A local club like Waterloo can't guarantee that the majors are going to keep a team here. South Bend can, because there will be four or five major league teams in line behind the White Sox, just to have that stadium as a showcase."

Boesen and Klinkowitz nodded.

Spelius advised them to wait until they got the architect's report on the PBA inspection before spending any significant amount of money, but he also advised them that a significant amount of money would have to be spent. "The day of the new-coat-of-paint, put-a-nail-in-the-board are over," he said.

"We tried to play hardball with the city," said Klinkowitz. He laughed, unconvincingly. "We tried to be Nolan Ryan."

Spelius shrugged. "Yeah, well, Nolan hasn't won one this year, either." He turned away from Boesen and Klinkowitz, toward the infield. His voice assumed a faraway tone. "I was at a ballpark recently, sitting with the owner. I won't say who, but he was one of these high rollers, and do you know what he said to me? 'Within two years, this league is going to lose four teams.' It was the way he said it." Spelius shook his head. "Now, why would anybody want something like that to happen? I just don't get it. And you know, I went and talked to his GM later, and his own GM said to me, 'Well, you know, sometimes he only thinks of himself.' People lack the compassion for other people; that's what bothers me. That's why maybe I'm not the favorite of some of the owners. And maybe someday I won't be the president, but that's neither here nor there." Spelius gave his head a light shake. Then, shaking his head again, only harder, he turned back to Boesen and Klinkowitz. "Look, I'll tell you what I told my own ball club in Beloit, and what I told Dan Yates, and what I'm telling everybody. Give yourself twelve months to try to keep the team here. Then take the money. A million dollars, whatever it is. There are people out there right now—you'd probably get a minimum of a million dollars for your team, if you sold now."

"That's not what we voted," Klinkowitz said. "This came up at a board meeting, and we voted to fight to the end. It's in our minutes that our philosophy is to go down in *flames,* to crawl through the *mud*—"

"Well, we're not going to do that," Spelius snapped. "We'll sell. If you can't cut it, get your buck for your team now. Sure, you're going to lose baseball from your community, but get it now. This is the decision; we've made our decision. Because when you get down to the eleventh hour, they'll say, 'You want a million? You're not going to get a million.' Because they know what'll happen—you'll go belly up, and your club won't be worth anything. So I say give yourself twelve months and then get your million dollars—whatever you can get for it—because that's just what's going to happen. You're going to run out of time, and it'll be a bullish market. Or bearish. It'd be a buyer's market, anyway. And you'll be stuck with something that's worthless." He turned away again. He was facing the first-base bleachers. "I never thought I'd hear myself saying this. I hate saying this. But I said this to our own board in Beloit, where I thought we'd always have baseball."

Klinkowitz and Boesen stared for a moment at the back of his green jacket, then followed his gaze, toward the bleachers, and beyond them, toward the river, and beyond it, toward where they knew the John Deere Tractor Works would be. A breeze had risen from that direction. For several moments they continued to search the horizon, but then, finding nothing, they looked up.

III

DOWNHILL

WATERLOO— Dear taker of life's wrong doings:

My husband and I try to bring up our children in the way they should go, with all of the love and understanding that a role model can give.

By you stealing our son's bicycle off the front steps, you pushed us through another door of life's unfair trials and tribulations.

At first, he was harvesting some real bad feelings and entertaining negative thoughts on what had happened to him—keeping in mind this is a real dramatic thing to have happened to a 4-year-old's birthday present.

However, he's better now and his chin is high. He's learned a lesson and I think he will be OK. But Mom and Dad aren't. We were wondering how you could justify your actions in your own mind.

The only other thing that I have left to say to you is I hope the child you stole the bike for wasn't with you. That way, at least one person in this world thinks you're a hero. As for my family and I— you are a zero.

Lisa Frost

—*Waterloo Courier,* July 19, 1992

7

The crackers were new. John Maxwell took one bite, wrinkled his brow, and reached back for the carton that the clubhouse manager had just deposited on the milk crate in the middle of the coaches' office, along with the obligatory pregame peanut butter, jelly, and bread. " 'Nouveau,' " Maxwell read aloud. Slowly he turned over the box of crackers. "Hey, even the ingredients are in French."

In one corner of the office, Champ was filling out reports. In another corner, Treanor was sitting motionless, eyes closed under the bill of his cap. In a third corner, Jack Grandy, the sixtyish clubhouse manager, was conducting an inventory of the crackers, pretzels, and paper plates he kept in the top drawer of a file cabinet. The second half of the season was now nine games old. The Diamonds had finished the first half of the season with a 28–41 record, sixteen and a half games out of first in the Southern Division and second worst in the entire Midwest League, but in a split-season format, each team started the second half with the same 0–0 slate. "Otherwise," as Champ had said of his own team, "these guys would just *stop.*"

Winning might not have been the point in the minors; the demands of player development often might have conspired to prevent it; but it was still more fun than losing. Just last night the Diamonds had returned home from the first road trip of the second half with a 6–2 record, and the PA announcer had gotten to say, as the team took the field, "And now let's welcome our first-place Waterloo Diamonds!" Technically, it was true: The Diamonds were in a three-way tie for the lead in the Southern Division. And, as it turned out, thunderstorms across the Midwest were raining out every other game in the league, leaving the Diamonds with the opportunity to claim first place all for themselves all on their own—or not. The game that followed, however, had been a hard-luck affair all around. First Hardtke went home complaining of a bad burrito. Then, in the top half of the first inning, Todd Altaffer threw two wild pitches, utility infielder Dave Adams—who wouldn't have been in the game if the team didn't need a substitute at third for Farlow, who was substituting at second for the ailing Hardtke—committed a throwing error on what could have been an inning-ending double play, and the South Bend White Sox went on to score three runs, all unearned. Altaffer threw two more wild pitches in the game, the Diamonds committed five more errors, and Waterloo lost the game 8–3, as well as a claim on first place. Now the remainder of the season—two months to the day—stretched ahead, and at least some members of the coaching staff had resigned themselves to seeking motivation wherever they could find it. Tonight it was a new kind of cracker.

"After the Fourth of July," Champ said, "it's all downhill." He pushed the paperwork away and turned from his desk. "It goes fast. You'll see. It'll go"—he snapped his fingers—"just like that." He leaned forward and picked up the carton of crackers.

"No, it won't." Treanor didn't shift in his chair. Under his cap only his mouth moved. "No . . . it . . . won't."

"Dean's one of those guys gonna be counting every minute that final week of the season," Maxwell said.

Treanor grunted but didn't open his eyes. Maxwell shook his head. Champ took a bite of a cracker. Then, he took another bite.

"These crackers," he said. He held one up before his face. "These *crackers*," he said again, chewing slowly, ruminating. "They taste—now why would I remember this?—but these crackers taste just like the crackers my kindergarten teacher used to give us. I remember this. They were these crackers, and she'd give them to us with milk. Warm white milk." He took another bite. "And even then I knew, even then I remember thinking, 'These don't fuckin' go together.' "

Captain Dynamite pulled up to the ballpark at four that afternoon in a 1979 Dodge van emblazoned on the side with both his stage name and a crude-but-effective drawing of his crude-but-effective form of entertainment: a real big explosion. He eased himself down from his van and approached the front gate with a bowlegged tenderness. There he did what he always did when he arrived in a new town: He gave interviews. He had agreed to stop at the ballpark early today specifically so that he could meet with local TV and newspaper reporters, and for their benefit he'd donned a naval cap and an emerald green jacket embroidered with skull and crossbones.

The captain—né Patrick A. O'Brien, of Houston, Texas—bore a more-than-passing resemblance to the actor Jack Palance. His features were broad and leathery, and he wore a perpetual squint, as if smoke were forever stinging his eyes. To one reporter after another, the captain said that, at seventy-six, he "had the reputation of being the oldest active stuntman in the United States"; that he'd been a stuntman for forty-one years; that he'd blown himself up 4,000 times; that the blasts sometimes knocked him unconscious for five to ten seconds; that his seaman's cap and captain's status dated back to a stint with the merchant marine, where he'd risen to the rank of chief engineer; that among the injuries he'd sustained in his line of work was the blasting cap that had lodged in his back during a performance in Chattanooga without his realizing it was there until hours later; that he'd performed stunts in such movies as *Thunder Road* and *Duel;* that he'd once staged a fake knife-fight at the Brown Derby in Hollywood that landed him and Mickey Rooney in jail; and that while running guns in South America, he'd come within six hours of death by firing squad. Between interviews, David Simpson approached him with a gentle "Hey, Cap'n," and asked if he needed anything. The captain handed Simpson a photograph of himself handling two sticks of dynamite and said he needed photocopies so that he could have something to autograph for fans tonight. As Simpson headed to the front office, the captain called out a reminder that he needed the original when Simpson was done with it. Then Simpson called back, "How many copies you want, Cap'n?"

"What?" said the captain.

"How many copies?"

"What?"

"How many copies?"

"What?"

For Fourth of July eve, Simpson had booked one of the staples on the circuit of minor league novelty acts. A general manager fortunate enough to be running a ball club playing at home on a beautiful Fourth could, with a couple of canny promotions, more than make up for any lackluster attendance figures earlier in the season, and by the first week of July, there were fewer places in pro ball where such compensation would have been more welcome than in Waterloo. Even leaving aside the early-season weather problems, the preceding few weeks would have been particularly damaging at the box office. Due to the vagaries of scheduling, the Diamonds had played only three games at home in the twenty-two days between June 9 and July 2—the potentially lucrative immediately postschool period. The club's average daily attendance now stood at 480, or thirteenth in the league, ahead of only lame-duck Kenosha. The franchise's drawing power had even become somewhat of a national embarrassment, at least among the front-office types and agate addicts who read *Baseball America:* The latest issue, listing several mid-season bests and worsts throughout pro ball, ranked Waterloo fifth from the bottom in average daily attendance among all sixty full-season Class A clubs in the country. (The Midwest League's Kane County, by contrast, was first, with a reported average of 4,027.)

The effectiveness of the "respect-for-the-ticket" strategy that Simpson had introduced to Waterloo depended, of course, on there being an audience to accord the ticket said respect. The previous season, Simpson had succeeded in eliminating much of the old audience. No longer was it possible to stop by the 7-Eleven or Hy-Vee on the way to the ballpark and grab a handful of free passes for that day's game. This season, however, a new audience would have to start showing up at the ballpark on a regular basis in order for "respect for the ticket" to be a success. It hadn't, yet—but, then, the ball club had suffered from fits of bad weather and unfortunate scheduling, and, as the league president had reminded all the clubs at a league meeting during the All-Star break, baseball's traditional "meat months" were still to come. "Things have been instituted," Simpson had reassured some nervous Waterloo owners at a recent board meeting. "That's a gamble we had to take. Or I had to take. And I took." In some ways, the season started right now—and not a moment too soon.

As of June 30, eight months into the organization's fiscal year, the ball club's net income was running more than $40,000 behind last year at the same time. With the exception of the $10,000 that the board had deposited in the fund-raising account after the end of the previous season, last year's profit was long gone—the same profit that a grateful board of directors had been willing to accept as proof that Simpson's business philosophy could work even under the new economics of the Professional Baseball Agreement. In part, however, that profit had been somewhat inflated by left-over revenue from the pre-PBA era that had happened to arrive in the post-PBA fiscal year—$11,000 in "TV considerations" fees from Major League Baseball, for instance. Even without those revenues, Simpson still would have managed the impressive achievement of turning a profit during the first PBA season, but this year the ball club was $15,000 in the red, and at one point in the preceding month the bank balance had dipped below $100.

In anticipation of the Fourth of July home stand, Simpson had placed a small ad in the *Courier*'s sports section, headlined "HAVE A BLAST THIS WEEKEND" and enumerating the four days' worth of promotions:

Thursday is 'Thirsty Thursday'
All Beverages are $1.00
Friday
*Watch Captain Dynamite Blow Himself Sky
High (Courtesy of Nestlé Foods)*
Saturday
*Fireworks Night—Fireworks after
the Game*
Sunday
*Church Day—Each Church Bulletin
worth Half Off a Ticket*

The Thursday and Sunday events were, in fact, the regular Thursday and Sunday promotions in Waterloo—and the Thursday attendance had indeed consisted of the five hundred or so Thirsty Thursday diehards. Furthermore, the event that fell on the Fourth of July itself, while always popular, required no scheduling talents on Simpson's part; fireworks on the Fourth were a tradition of long standing at ballparks everywhere. Tonight's show, however, would be truly singular. Captain Dynamite was the only personal appearance of the entire season, and Simpson's one extravagance, within reason. A Phillie Phanatic, a Morganna the Kissing Bandit, a Famous Chicken, or a Dynamite Lady might charge several thousand dollars, plus airfare; Captain Dynamite could be had for a fraction of that, plus gas.

By game time, the captain had returned to his van and added to his wardrobe a pair of slacks with red zigzag piping, like bolts of lightning. He threw out the first ball, then stood under the grandstand and gave away his handouts. On one of his past visits to Waterloo, he'd attached a caption to the photo that read, in part:

O'Brien, a 190-pound congenial Irishman who clinched three successive annual championship titles in International Crash Roll Tournaments staged over major Fair circuits by the Aut Swenson Thrillcade, performs his new thriller while encased in a coffin-like container before big league ball games, fairs, grand openings and probably weddings and wakes, providing his fee of $600 per pop is forthcoming.

On this visit, the captain was going with only a photo and, in the upper-left corner, the back of a business card, on which he had inscribed:

GOOD LUCK TO:

From:
Captain Dynamite

What the fans crowding around him in the concourse were receiving, then, wasn't exactly Captain Dynamite's autograph; it was a photocopy of his autograph. The authentic signature in the captain's uncertain hand that they got to take home was of their own name.

When he was done meeting the fans, the captain delivered a copy of the "Stuntman's Script" to the press box, then passed the rest of the game sitting on a picnic table outside the ballpark down the right-field line with his son and partner, Dusty "Fireball" O'Brien. (The captain's daughter, "Dynamite Dinah," also a stunt performer, would be meeting up with them in Peoria for a Fourth of July show at the Chiefs' game the following night.) At fifty-seven, Fireball was several teeth short of a full set, and he also bore a fresh burn scar over his upper lip, a souvenir of an accident three nights earlier before a ball game in Charleston, West Virginia. The stunt had called for Dusty to set himself on fire at second base and then streak toward home by way of the pitching mound. The assistants with fire extinguishers he had recruited from the Charleston Wheelers' staff were stationed at the mound and home plate, waiting for him to throw himself on the ground as a signal to put him out.

"Usually I'd stop at the mound," Fireball was saying now with a chuckle and a shrug. "But I decided to keep going home. I trusted the guy with the extinguisher there more."

His father motioned to him for a cigarette. During the autograph session, somebody had walked off with the captain's pack of Basic Lights 100s, as well as his "Operation Desert Storm" lighter.

"Turned out that guy didn't know what he was doing," Fireball went on, shaking his head at the memory.

The captain offered a sympathetic shake of his head, too, a father commiserating with his son about the unpredictable nature of the family business.

"I *reignited*," Fireball said. He chuckled again and said it sure was fortunate a TV camera had been there; otherwise, his mishap might not have been the lead story on the local news that night.

His father shook his head and cackled. "We'll be invited back there next year, all right."

"If that TV station has to pay for it themselves," said Fireball, cackling, too.

When the game ended—White Sox 5, Diamonds 2—players from both teams arranged themselves on the lawn in front of the dugouts, knees up, gloves on the grass. In the grandstand, giddiness prevailed. Bev Boesen started telling about the time there was a fatal car crash at the racetrack that used to be behind the Food 4 Less out on University Avenue, and everybody sitting within a couple of rows of her joined in: how the driver's helmet had rolled a great distance, how when the paramedics were putting the driver in the ambulance one of them had to run back and fetch the helmet, how somebody who knew somebody who knew the paramedic swore that he had to go back and get the helmet because *the stuntman's head was still inside it.*

The crowd quieted as the captain walked into the ballpark through the gate down the first-base line. His pallbearers—Van Sant, Rollo, Nelson, and Fireball—followed, carrying his paper coffin. In the press box, the announcer, Kelly Neff, popped a cassette of a funeral dirge into the stadium's sound system. Neff, tall, thin, silver-haired and golden-throated, hosted a morning music show on a local country-and-western station as well as a Saturday-morning sports-talk show. Now, employing his somber, "This-bulletin-just-in" radio voice, he began reading from the script:

> LADIES AND GENTLEMEN,—THE (Waterloo 'Diamonds') ARE PROUD TO PRESENT ONE OF THE MOST UNIQUE ACTS IN THE WORLD TO-DAY.—IT IS ALSO ONE OF THE MOST DANGEROUS IN THE WORLD— especially dangerous for the Stuntperson performing it.—
> MORE STUNTPEOPLE THROUGH THE YEARS HAVE BEEN INJURED WHILE ATTEMPTING THIS STUNT, THAN ANY OTHER IN THE BUSINESS. SEVERAL, THROUGH CARELESSNESS, HAVE BEEN FATALLY INJURED.
>
> -(pause)-

The funeral procession stopped at second base. The pallbearers deposited the coffin and departed from the field. The captain inspected the explosives one last time, gave the signal to the press box that the countdown should commence—both arms raised toward the heavens—and proceeded to lie down in his coffin. Neff, following the written instructions, led the crowd in the backward march toward zero.

The blast was a satisfying, annihilating comic-book kaboom that shook the stands with several waves of sound. In the press box, Neff read the instructions to himself: "(WAIT UNTIL HE STANDS—OR—STAGGERS UP.)"

Neff waited. Smoke parted. Shreds of the paper coffin coiled and rolled across the dirt and grass. Still the captain remained motionless. Then he stirred. He stood. He staggered. Again he raised his arms toward the dark heavens. Neff looked back to his script:

"HE'S OK!!!"

*

Her first morning in retirement—Independence Day, as it happened—Mildred Boyenga awakened to the realization that never again would the arrival of the weekend mean what it had meant to her since she was a little girl growing up in Stout, Iowa: chores. Nonetheless, she straightened up the kitchen, washing dishes and cleaning the sink, but she didn't touch any of the other rooms, and she didn't tend to the yard work, either. Instead, she drove to the cemetery.

Fairview Cemetery backed up to the ballpark. The morning was cool and the sky empty, save for five vapor trails that hung together like a musical staff, and once inside the cemetery's wrought-iron gates, Boyenga got out of the car and started walking. There were other cemeteries in town, but to her way of thinking most of them were characterless affairs: flat expanses bounded by chain-link fences, free of trees and hills and dignity. She preferred the contours and foliage of the aptly named Fairview: the sight of the public park and softball fields across the road, and the river beyond that, and the John Deere plant beyond *that;* the creak of ancient tree limbs; the leafy shade that swayed with the breeze; the deep shadows, even in daylight; the land itself, rising and falling and rising and falling and rising; the hints of history and continuity and permanence.

Just past the entrance, in the position of greatest prominence, stood the tall, broad tombstones that bore the names of the families that had invented Waterloo. Black. Rath. Wirt P. Hoxie. Bishop, the founder of a chain of family restaurants. Lichty, the farmer and landowner whose holdings eventually became much of what was today the south side of Waterloo. Grout, who had endowed the local history museum. Cutler, too—a less-resonant name, but known to Boyenga as a wholesaler who used to supply the machine shop and hardware store her father had operated in Stout. Boyenga followed a path to the left that kept her in sight of the softball diamonds across the road. Soon she came upon the children's section of the cemetery, and she paused long enough to take note of the large number of 1917 dates: a flu epidemic she had heard about from her mother, whose own father, a Baptist minister who'd ventured west from New Jersey, had presided at many of the funerals. She found a REED tombstone that bore two

Christian names—Verna May and Lee Evelyn—and two sets of dates, 1925–1935 and 1933–1935, and she wondered what had happened there. A little farther on, she paused to consider a couple of deflated Mylar balloons ("You're the best dad!" and "I LOVE YOU DAD!") next to a 1966–1989 tombstone and, after a moment's reflection, remembered that two weekends earlier had been Father's Day. She herself had gotten divorced in 1972, after her four children were grown—two sons who still lived in Waterloo, and two daughters who had scattered in opposite directions, one to Pennsylvania and the other to New Mexico. When she was growing up in Stout, kids used to flee the small towns in the area for Waterloo as soon as they were old enough. Now it was Waterloo kids couldn't wait to leave. She kept moving; she saw some vacant land; she wondered if it was taken. Then she came in sight of the ballpark.

When she assumed the presidency of the organization in 1984, it was the period of the ball club's greatest disorder and borderline collapse, and it was the period of the city's greatest disorder and borderline collapse. The disputes and rivalries that had been plaguing the organization for years had culminated earlier that year in the resignations of, first, the president and, within the month, the vice president who succeeded him. Boyenga, a thirteen-year veteran of the ball club who had been serving as board secretary, took charge. She extracted a pledge from the city to begin the ballpark renovations that Cleveland was demanding. She assembled an executive board that included herself as president, Barb Kuper as vice president, and a former assistant GM named Ruta Bloomfield (who later moved out of town) as secretary, marking perhaps the first time in professional baseball that the top three positions of an organization were held by women. And she oversaw a front-office effort that resulted in a profit of about $5,000 in a season when thousands of local workers were worrying about, and losing, their jobs. On the same day that November, she met with the Cleveland GM to sign a new Player Development Contract, and she got a phone call informing her that she had been named the Rawlings "Baseball Woman of the Year."

"I deserved it," she declared during her acceptance speech at baseball's Winter Meetings. "I worked damn hard this year."

A month later, she was out of a job. Rath Packing had closed.

This was where the ground shifted. She had reached the top of a gentle rise, from which the earth unrolled down toward the iron spears of the cemetery fence and, several yards beyond, the backside of the ballpark fence and the wooden beams that braced it. Once she'd inquired about purchasing a plot in this part of the cemetery, but she'd been informed that it was the black section, and that in any event all the plots were already taken. In time, the eventual addition of a second tier of advertising signs on the right-field fence had pretty much blocked the view of the diamond anyway. She drifted in that direction now, letting gravity guide her among the headstones, and along the way she recognized the names of several friends from the old days at Rath.

It would be difficult to overestimate what the loss of Rath Packing had meant to the city. Layoffs at Deere had claimed more jobs over the years, but in many ways Rath *was* Waterloo. When some nineteenth-century civic leaders who called themselves the Waterloo Improvement Syndicate had taken it upon themselves to create a city of factories, it was their success in attracting Rath Packing in 1891 that forever changed the future of Waterloo. In time, the packinghouse grew into the largest of its kind in the world. Rath provided paychecks for one in every seven Waterloo households. Jobs became family legacies; during the Depression, the company made sure that at least one person in each Rath Packing family remained on the payroll. By the time of Rath's seventy-fifth anniversary in Waterloo, in 1966, it ranked as the nation's 249th largest industry, and Rath was shipping Honey Glazed Ham, Hawaiian Ham, and Champagne Ham; was packaging 1,800 pounds of bacon an hour and 2 million hot dogs a week; was producing 1,000 meat items in all, a figure that didn't include by-products such as spray-dried blood, of which Rath was supplying 10 million pounds a year to adhesives manufacturers, intestinal mucosa, from which a drug manufacturer made a blood anticoagulant, and shortening, of which Rath was supplying 100 million pounds annually to Pillsbury, General Mills, the Doughnut Corporation of America, and the like. Each year, Rath paid more than $700,000 in property taxes to local governments, $3 million for goods and services to area businesses, $35 million in wages, and $135 million for livestock from farmers, most of them Iowans. Even after its demise, The Rath Packing Company continued to keep watch over Waterloo, its smokestack appearing around corners or through trees or over rooftops, seemingly as permanent a part of the natural landscape as the soil and sky it bridged.

It had been a long time in coming, the end of Rath Packing. Boyenga herself had started there in 1955, a young mother taking phone orders from company salesmen around the country, and even then the disputes that would follow the company to its final days and beyond were already in evidence. An industry that employed hog headers, loin pullers, and trimmers of pigs' heads lent itself to discussions of such issues as workmen's compensation or on-the-job safety and sanitation, and in 1942, the same year that organized labor arrived at Waterloo's John Deere plant, Local 46 of the Packinghouse Workers' Organizing Committee opened shop at Rath. The first major strike in 1948 cost one life and started a riot. Deere's first major strike came two years later. More strikes followed, at more or less regular intervals, at Rath and Deere and many of the other industries in town. At one point, during one of the lesser work stoppages, management had tried to send the nonunionized "office girls" into the plant to replace striking workers, and Boyenga had refused. Later she became one of the leaders in the effort to organize about 150 of her fellow office workers, eventually succeeding by a one-vote margin. She served as area steward of Local P78 of the United Packinghouse Workers, then as chief steward, and in time, toward the end, on the legal committee to protect employee rights. Had the Rath heirs squandered the family business and the community lifeblood, pocketing profits rather than reinvesting in new technology and research and development? Or were the facilities, once the most modern in the world, so outdated that any such efforts would have amounted to throwing good money after bad? Had management padded its own ranks, bloating the white-collar bureaucracy and fattening wallets? Or had the unions become unbudgeable and unrealistic in their demands, and in the bargain cut their own throats?

These questions weren't peculiar to Waterloo; they were the same battlegrounds on which any number of meatpacking cities on the prairies were waging war in those years. The meat-packing industry—and industry itself—had changed. Old machinery and high wages—at least relative to what workers received else-

where—proved a lethal combination. By the 1960s, Rath was laying off employees and eliminating lamb and veal processing. By
the mid-1960s, the company was losing $4 million a year, and a
new company president used the occasion of the seventy-fifth anniversary celebration to announce the imminent elimination of
cattle processing, too. Henceforth the company would confine itself only to what it had done from the start: pork. Still Rath bled
red. More layoffs followed, followed by more production cutbacks, followed by more layoffs. In the late 1970s, facing certain
loss of their jobs, employees conceded $17 million in wages and
benefits in exchange for a 60 percent controlling interest in the
firm. In the early 1980s, a Black Hawk County economic-devel-
opment committee recruited a couple of consultants to advise
both management and labor at Rath, and Boyenga could remember them warning even then that a new company, Iowa Beef
Processors, had perfected the slaughterhouse of the future: a hori-
zontal-kill method, modeled on the assembly line, that was more
efficient than Rath's vertical kill; significantly lower wages than
what the union workers at Rath were getting; and plans to expand
into pork. Pork! Everybody scoffed: *They wouldn't dare.*

Foreseeable or not, the closing of Rath left Boyenga with little
to occupy her time but the ball club. Which was . . . what? If she
had learned anything from her experiences on the employees' legal
committee at Rath—traveling down to the district courthouse in
Cedar Rapids, attending endless hearings on such issues as who
owned the Rath Indian-head trademark, seeing for herself what
tradition was worth in the face of greater economic forces—it was
this: Get it in writing. Already the Midwest League was changing.
Three years earlier, the league had expanded from eight teams to
twelve. Two years earlier, the Minnesota Twins had announced
that they wouldn't be renewing their affiliation with Wisconsin
Rapids, citing a longtime dissatisfaction with the condition of the
field there. A buyer from Kenosha had come along, and that was
that. Meanwhile, an expansion franchise was floating in limbo,
waiting for South Bend to sort out its legal and financial affairs
and build a stadium. And the president of the league at that time,
sensing that the minors had entered a sellers' market of franchise-
fee inflation, was preparing for another round of expansion, from
twelve to fourteen teams. Boyenga couldn't have known precisely

what form the future of minor league baseball would take—the increasing influence of outside ownership, the multimillion-dollar new stadiums, the thousandfold rise in franchise values—but she knew enough to look around the room at a meeting of her fellow Midwest League directors and ask, "Who *owns* this club?" Boyenga engaged the services of an attorney who, at that time, was helping a number of other Midwest League clubs try to answer that question for themselves—who, indeed, was helping the Midwest League get its own paperwork in order—and with her newfound free time she began the search.

She unpacked box after box in the storage areas at the ballpark, and she combed through record files at the Black Hawk County Courthouse. The search unearthed a document from the 1970s that seemed to suggest an attempt at legitimacy, but that the ball club's attorney advised her was, in fact, legally meaningless; articles of incorporation from the 1958 rebirth of the ball club that had lapsed by the early 1970s; documentation from the 1920s indicating that some people had contributed money to the ball club, perhaps even as "stockholders," though by then whatever claim they had on the ball club would have long expired; and even a box of canceled checks, some signed on the back by Carlton Fisk; but no proof of ownership. Nothing conclusive, anyway. Over the decades numerous fans and businesses had donated time or money to the ball club and the ballpark; conceivably Waterloo, the Iowa countryside, and retirement communities across the nation were inhabited by samaritans who had kicked in a hundred bucks to help open the gates of Waterloo Municipal Stadium at the start of some long-forgotten season. Did they own the club? Boyenga called one such sometime contributor, a former mayor of Waterloo who had moved to Des Moines, and confirmed that *he* didn't think he did, anyway. And yet; but still. On the advice of counsel, Boyenga drove downtown to the *Courier* offices and placed the following legal notice, which appeared in the paper three times in March and April, 1986:

NOTICE REGARDING
WATERLOO BASEBALL, INC.

Please take notice that WATERLOO PROFESSIONAL BASEBALL, INC., a corporation, the successor to all of the rights, properties, and obligations of WATERLOO BASE-BALL, INC., a dissolved Iowa corporation for profit, has been organized. All persons having claims or demands against WATERLOO BASEBALL, INC., a dissolved Iowa corporation for profit, whether as shareholder, creditor, or in any other capacity, are requested to present their claims in writing to:

> WATERLOO PROFESSIONAL
> BASEBALL, INC.
> c/o Mrs. Mildred Boyenga

Nobody came forward.

In many ways, the incorporation of the franchise required as great an act of faith in the future of Waterloo as had founding a ball club in 1904 or building a ballpark in 1946. The industrial era that civic leaders had anticipated at the turn of the century, and the economic recovery that civic leaders had predicted after fifteen years of depression and war, had come to pass; in both cases, the professional baseball team had played a role. Now, with the closing of Rath, Waterloo seemed to have reached a point in its history at least as equally momentous as the earlier two.

In the five-year period starting in 1981, about 12,000 workers in the Waterloo area—nearly one out of every five—lost their jobs. Rath was only the most visible casualty of the enormous economic contraction convulsing the area. Suddenly the city was filled with workers who had given up greater and greater parts of their paychecks, and had given up their benefits, and had given up their pensions, agreeing to live for years in a state of reduced circumstances and anxiety about their livelihood in exchange for shares in a company that ultimately had proved worthless. So extreme was the crisis that the mayor whose misfortune it was to be presiding over Waterloo during this period broke with precedent and didn't seek reelection after his single term. (His reputation would be sealed when he attempted to goose the bidding at the Rath auction and inadvertently wound up purchasing the factory's facilities and real estate on the city's behalf. He went back to City Hall and started calling Council members. "I said, 'We bought Rath Packing,' " he later recalled, "and they said, 'What do you mean, we?' I thought, 'I'm really in trouble here.' ") A month before Rath closed, a city councilwoman wrote a letter to President Reagan criticizing government funding of road construction for Waterloo, calling the city "the most depressed area in the nation." She went on: "We keep pouring money into a city that is dead, and has been dead for fifteen years. We could pour our downtown streets with gold, but if you don't have the people and business downtown, who's going to use them?" It was the five-term former mayor who had overseen the first stages of the highway construction project back in the 1970s who returned to the Council chamber and rallied to the city's defense, responding, in part, by advising her to read Norman Vincent Peale's *The Power of Positive Thinking*: "Do you think that when I went home every night and watched myself be so positive on television, saying good things are gonna happen, that I really felt that way all the time? Don't kid yourself."

These, then, were the legacies inherited by Bernie McKinley: highways and optimism. Born salesman, born-again Christian, recovering alcoholic and eternal optimist—one of his favorite expressions was "You're always just one telephone call away from that million-dollar sale"—Mayor Bernie McKinley took office as the vision of an industrial future that had sustained Waterloo for nearly a century was vanishing, and immediately he set about trying to reinvent the city as thoroughly as the Waterloo Improvement Syndicate had a hundred years earlier.

"Vision" was one of McKinley's favorite words. "This is the vision that I see of what Waterloo needs," he would say; or, speaking of one civic undertaking or another, "You've gotta have a person that could see that vision." McKinley worshiped at Sunnyside Temple, a Wesleyan congregation that, in terms of class and stature in Waterloo, was virtually synonymous with Prospect Boulevard, and that owed its philosophical bent to the teachings of the Reverend Robert Schuller. The example that guided McKinley in his vision of Waterloo's future was Reverend Schuller's Glass Cathedral: how the minister one day "sat down with a piece of paper and a pencil and determined that the cathedral would cost $10 million"; how he decided that, rather than pursue a single $10-million donor, he would solicit ten million-dollar donations; how he systematically targeted fifty individuals who "could and should" have an interest in giving $1 million each for such a worthy cause; how, when the cathedral came in $6 million over budget, he sold windowpanes to make up the difference. McKinley would tell this story with obvious relish. It seemed to offer for him a worry stone–smooth example of the combination of vision and ingenuity—of Christianity and capitalism, of optimism and highways—that just might prove to be Waterloo's salvation.

The Factory City was dead, yet within a year of taking office, McKinley issued an eight-point "Mission and Objective Statement" pledging that his administration would help make Waterloo nothing less than "the best possible place to live, work, do business, play and raise a family for all citizens." Never again would Waterloo be the industrial giant it once had been; those days were gone forever. But there was a new world coming, he'd say, a world of businesses that trafficked in information. He promised to "rebuild the downtown area by attracting service industries, i.e., insurance companies, telemarketing companies, transportation headquarters, and financial institutions." He set a goal of 1,000 new jobs a year, and he said the only way to get them here was to put Waterloo back on the map.

Waterloo had risen at the mid-nineteenth-century height of the era of river commerce. The era of rail commerce that followed half a century later had been especially kind to the city, providing the ideal network for trading corn and steel between the surrounding farmland and the outside world. The era of highway commerce that followed another fifty years later, however, had bypassed Waterloo. In part, this growing isolation was due to the city's physical circumstances. Waterloo lay 100 miles off the beaten path that had developed to the south, stringing together Chicago and Davenport, Davenport and Des Moines—a trade route that the arrival of Interstate 80 could only reinforce. The *extremity* of Waterloo's isolation, however, was another matter. When the state had wanted to build a diagonal road to connect the capital of Des Moines with the important urban center of Waterloo ninety miles to the northeast, the agricultural lobby not only blocked the effort on the grounds that the blacktop would cut a swath through the foursquare layout and displace invaluable farmland, but pushed through legislation barring the future construction of diagonal highways. This grass-roots populism found its foremost practitioner in H. R. Gross, a Waterloo broadcaster and, for thirteen consecutive terms, from 1949 to 1975, congressman from the Third District of Iowa. He earned a reputation as "The American Taxpayer's Best Friend"; each congressional term he introduced a balanced-budget bill, and he once questioned even the use of federal funds to light the flame on President Kennedy's gravesite. At a time that city and state governments across the land were lobbying for the chance to lie along the interstate system, Waterloo's most visible representative was actively refusing federal funding for his constituency in virtually any form—which, at the time, was perhaps a luxury that this prosperous city believed it could afford.

It was true that Bernie McKinley inherited the city's comprehensive highway projects from the late-1970s administration of Leo Rooff, who had identified in the Interstate Substitution Program—a federal system that would allow the city to modernize its transportation system while absorbing only 15 percent of the cost—a way to reverse Waterloo's insularity. But it was also true that McKinley renewed the city's commitment to them, making highways the cornerstone of his campaign to rehabilitate the city's economy. He could see where they led. For the first time, Waterloo was going to stand at a substantial crossroads, straddling an east-west, north-south axis of highways. Once the dust had settled, the city would serve as the midway point on the Avenue of the Saints, connecting St. Paul to the north with St. Louis to the south, and a relocated and expanded Highway 20 would provide Waterloo with four-lane access with Chicago to the east, and vice versa. Even before Bernie McKinley took office, the Avenue of the Saints had extended right up to the southern city limits, not only linking Waterloo with I-80, the national thoroughfare that cleared a path from New York City to San Francisco, but also ending forever Waterloo's dubious distinction as the largest city in the country not being served by a major interstate.

Highways, however, were only a start. They might open the city to the outside world, but what would the world find once it got here? What the city needed, McKinley decided, was an ambitious campaign of "quality of life" activities, institutions and programs that might convince an outside business to relocate to Waterloo and a native industry to stay put. It was going to cost in the short run, he acknowledged, but it was going to be worth it. "Money usually isn't an objection, if your idea is good enough," he'd say. "The money is somewhere; there's all kinds of money out there; there's billions and billions and billions of dollars out there. If the idea is good enough, it will attract the money."

Once, McKinley stood on a bridge then emerging out of the city's vast network of new highway construction, looked at one of the gravel pits lining the north end of town, and saw what wasn't there: a sports complex. Already he'd decided that the city's gravel pits—the craters being created by construction crews dredging fill material for the city's numerous new roads—could one day metamorphose into a Chain of Lakes. Now he envisioned an accompanying sports complex that once and for all would resolve the city's recreational needs: tennis courts, an Olympic-size swimming pool, basketball courts, an ice arena, a new high school football facility and—why not?—a baseball stadium.

In Bernie McKinley, the ball club had a cheerleader, though not necessarily a fan. Nor, for that matter, was he a fan of the symphony. "I could go forever without either," he'd say, "but that isn't the question." Baseball, McKinley believed, was something a city of a certain stature was supposed to have—or, at any rate, having it, wasn't supposed to lose. From his meetings with other mayors around the Midwest, he knew what was possible in the realm of baseball facilities, once you put your mind to it; he'd monitored the progress of South Bend in building a stadium and attracting a Midwest League expansion team. The cost of keeping baseball might be rising, but what baseball contributed to a city couldn't necessarily be quantified. "To lose baseball in Waterloo," he once said, "would be to me as bad as losing Rath—I shouldn't say 'as bad as,' but it falls in the same category. I think if we lose it, there'll come a time ten years from now when people will look back and say, 'Them idiots in City Hall: All they had to do was be *creative.*'"

Besides which, baseball's contribution *could* be quantified. *Places Rated Almanac,* a quadrennial comparative study of every metropolitan area in the country, was one of a handful of standard references on cities for industries and individuals thinking of relocating. The 1989 edition ranked 333 cities, placing Waterloo in 158th place overall. Those standings were based on results in nine categories, such as Costs of Living (Waterloo's ranking was a seemingly enviable 17, but it was due to the economic collapse of the 1980s), Jobs (an abysmal 311, ditto), Crime (80), Health Care & Environment (102), Transportation (264), Education (161), The Arts (153), Climate (316), and Recreation (74). Waterloo's rating in Recreation, however, depended in no small measure on the presence of a professional baseball team, without which the metro area's rating in that category would have dropped fifty places to 124. That drop, in turn, would have lowered the city's overall ranking by sixteen cities to 174—enough to nudge Waterloo from the upper half to the lower among all cities in the nation, a potentially significant psychological difference when the preliminaries are over and a prospective client is sufficiently impressed to walk down the hall to the office reference room, or across the street to the city library, and take down from the shelf a standard reference on municipal livability to try to get a rough idea on where Waterloo, Iowa, stands.

"The City of Waterloo's Leap to the Future, Year 2000 & Beyond"—devised by more than one hundred community leaders, revised by the citizens of Waterloo at a town meeting, and shepherded throughout by McKinley—was a Strategic Development Plan that enumerated everything about Waterloo that might convince an outside business to relocate, and that might convince a native industry to stay put. It was a blueprint for the future in the form of a foldout brochure, and it included Strategies for Progressive Government, Strategies for Economic Development, and Strategies for Human Relations. There it was, under the heading "Quality of Life," subheading "Strategies," right after "Promote quality of life activities as part of the Chain of Lakes complex such as boating, theme park, zoo, information center, botanical gardens, band shell, winter sports, etc.," and right before "Support and encourage a positive attitude toward the 'East' side of Waterloo": "Construct a sports complex."

So it came to pass that Bernie McKinley informed the City Council that what he liked to call "this little town of Waterloo, Iowa" just wouldn't be the same without professional baseball. The four-year, $325,000 in ballpark renovations that McKinley pushed through the City Council was designed to keep professional baseball from leaving Waterloo until the construction of that sports complex—or whatever form a permanent home for the ball club might take. But now it was McKinley who was gone.

In the cemetery, Mildred Boyenga had come to a stop. In many ways, she'd been fortunate. She had saved the ball club, succeeding with baseball where she and thousands like herself had failed with Rath. She'd made the age-fifty-five cutoff that determined which Rath employees would receive their pension benefits. Furthermore, she'd found another job within a year, at Miller Medical Service. But last month she'd turned sixty-five, and now she'd retired for good, and IBP had indeed opened a massive new plant across the northeast end of Waterloo, and when she thought of all the union people she'd gotten to know who had worked at the slaughterhouses in Ottumwa, Fort Dodge, Dubuque, Sioux Falls—all these *friends*—she had to ask herself, Where were they now?

She stood on her toes, straining, until she could see her usual seat, in the first row of boxes on the third-base side of the grandstand. She could also just make out the tops of several blue-helmeted heads on the field near home plate—a morning practice must be in session—and when she concentrated, she could distinguish the solid crack of ball on bat from the constant, ringing tap-tap-tap of kids blasting Fourth of July caps off a distant sidewalk. How many times while watching a game had she looked into the cemetery and seen the pinkish reflection of the setting sun off the backs of the headstones, the trees surrounding them already dark with dusk, as forbidding yet inviting as a forest in a fairy tale? If anyone had been sitting in her seat now, this tiny woman standing in the cemetery might have looked like an apparition, but from out here, it was the ballpark, empty yet echoing, that seemed populated by ghosts.

That morning at the ballpark, the players were working under the supervision of the director of minor league instruction for the San Diego Padres. Tom Gamboa, forty-four and mildly graying, had an open face and a ready smile, a surface affability that didn't begin to disguise his deeper competitive drive. Several years earlier, when he was managing the Toledo Mud Hens, the Triple A affiliate of the Detroit Tigers, he had explained to a writer from *Sports Illustrated* why he'd stayed in his office until 5:00 A.M. after a sixteen-inning loss: "I made a vow when I first became a manager that I'd never take a loss home with me, that I'd never leave the ballpark until I got it out of my system. Well, this was the test. I guess I failed. I couldn't leave this one. I went home just because I was hungry. I still haven't slept." This morning he pursued the least detail of the Waterloo operation with a good-natured doggedness, all the while popping sunflower seeds with an almost-compulsive fervor—splitting a couple with his teeth, extracting the meat, spitting the shell fragments to the grass, then starting over again.

Partly for Gamboa's benefit, Champ had scheduled a practice the previous afternoon and another this morning. Yesterday Champ and Gamboa had drilled the catchers on throwing out base runners. This morning they practiced relays from the outfield, the kind of game situation that might involve the defensive abilities of any number of players. First there was the throw from the outfielder to the cutoff man; then there was the trailer—a backup in case the outfielder failed to hit the cutoff man or the cutoff man failed to pick up the ball cleanly; then there was the relay to the plate by the cutoff man or trailer; then there was the catcher, positioning himself to block the plate and pick up the throw; finally, if other runners were on base, there was the trailer for the catcher: an altogether routine play, but one that regularly affected the outcome of games, and one that required the active involvement of more than half the players on the field, and potentially all of them.

Then Gamboa conducted private sessions with the players. Sometimes a player heard what he already knew: "What's the problem here, Jeff?" an outfielder named Jeff Pearce said while waiting his turn, expertly imitating the earnest, guilt-inducing concern Gamboa would lavish on a fading prospect's .228 average. Sometimes a player heard what he already knew but needed to hear again: "You're wrapping the bat," Gamboa said to Scott Pugh, who grimaced. It was the same advice he'd gotten from Gamboa the previous year. "Guess I forgot," Pugh said. And, every once in a while, a player heard something he'd never heard before.

Under the high Fourth of July sky, Robbie Beckett listened as Gamboa delivered the organization's verdict on his progress so far: "Way slower than we'd anticipated, given what your ability is." Gamboa reminded Beckett that he'd had three seasons to prove himself. He said that the time had come for Beckett to meet the Padres halfway. Gamboa said the organization wasn't down on him, and they weren't taking the ball away from him, but they were having trouble seeing what effect their teaching was having on him. None of this was anything that Beckett hadn't heard before. A long, drawling specimen of Lone Star laconism, Beckett in these situations adopted an appropriately repentant manner. He blinked heavy lids; he hung his head; he murmured assent. For his part, Gamboa popped a handful of sunflower seeds. He split; extracted; spit. Then he said something Beckett hadn't heard before.

"From now on you're not going to be on a pitch count," Gamboa said. He said that if Beckett didn't have good stuff on any given night, Champ and Treanor were under orders to pull him—*boom.* "From now on, you want the ball, you're going to have to fight for it," Gamboa said. "Got it?"

Beckett looked at him. The look in the pitcher's eyes told Gamboa something he hadn't heard before: Beckett, just maybe, got it.

Evaluations were an ongoing part of the professional baseball process. They happened all the time. After every game, the manager filed a report that detailed the performance of everyone who had played that day. Champ and Treanor would park themselves in the coaches' office with a hot dog and a beer, transcribing each batter's statistics at the plate and on the base paths, and assigning each pitcher both a numerical rating for each type of pitch he had thrown that day and then arriving at an overall performance review. "Poor location," Treanor said one night about a particular pitcher's relief performance. "Gave into the hitters in the fifth inning."

" 'Poor location,' " Champ repeated, filling in the official game report form at his desk. " 'Did not pitch to situation.' " He stopped writing. "I don't want to say he gave up."

"I didn't say he gave up," Treanor said. "He gave *in.* He can't pitch when men are on base. So. However you want to say that."

Then, every few days, someone from the front office in San Diego would call for an update—though those calls seemed to be coming less and less frequently as the season stretched on. (One afternoon in June, Champ had complained to Treanor that he hadn't heard from San Diego in two weeks. "Yeah, I know, it's draft time, and they've got mini-camps, but two weeks is *two weeks*. Plus, with our record, they know what it'd mean to us." Champ's voice was getting smaller. "Only time I heard from them is today, when I got my paycheck.") And then there were the periodic visits from scouts, instructors, and all the other professional evaluators that the Padres, like every other major-league organization, sent coursing through the farm system on a perpetual loop. Gamboa, for instance, had last visited in early May, and he'd visit again in another month or so. His wouldn't be the final word on whether the organization would renew a player's contract—that would belong to Joe McIlvaine, San Diego's general manager, or Ed Lynch, the organization's director of minor leagues, each of whom was due to pay the ball club a visit before the end of the season—but it certainly would count.

The evaluations didn't end even with the team. When Gamboa had finished meeting with the players on the Fourth, he turned his attention to the playing conditions. Champ led him to the chalk line between home and third and positioned one foot lengthwise along the base path so that half his shoe rested on the grass and the other half on the dirt. Ideally, the two surfaces—sod and soil—should run flush, but when Champ placed his weight down, his shoe listed at a good 45-degree angle.

"The lip is rising," Treanor said later, in the coaches' office. "The dirt's being pushed under, and the sod is riding up. By the end of the season, you'll be able to lay down in the base path, and nobody will see you."

"These guys think there's nothing wrong with their field," Champ said. "They think the grass is green, the dirt is brown, and everything is okay."

"There are problems," Gamboa agreed. "I remember these locker rooms from '84, when I was managing Beloit. There was talk of improving the locker rooms then, and I see they're still talking about it." He shrugged and smiled. "But the lights are better. And the infield's a lot better than last time." Smiles all around: On his previous visit, two months earlier, Gamboa had been sitting in the stands the night the Peoria manager refused to let his team take the field for nearly an hour because he considered the conditions unplayable. Gamboa shrugged. "They've mowed the grass," he said.

Still, it was only after the season had progressed past a certain indefinite point that evaluations could begin to lead to reliable conclusions. The April phenom—the player who burns up the league while burning himself out—was a common enough occurrence that nobody took early-season heroics too seriously. Even more common was the player who maintained a respectable output from April to July, only to wilt in the final humid summer weeks through some failure of conditioning or stamina. Only over the course of the season could baseball's professional observers measure progress—and the later in the season the evaluation, the more accurate the reading. As Champ remarked one night, feeding a game report into the maw of the fax machine, "That's why we play one hundred forty games, and that's why the bigs play one hundred sixty-two. All these guys are talented, but it's who can be *consistent.*"

Consistency to a great degree was a question of talent, but not only a question of talent. Beckett, for instance, was already endowed with the physical abilities of a major leaguer, but he nonetheless was advancing slowly because of his emotional constitution. Every outing he went full force, and every pitch he tried to blow past the batter, no matter how often he heard advice to the contrary. Treanor was merely the latest in a line of pitching coaches who had tried to instruct him to trust himself more. Don't try to strike out every batter, they'd tell him. Let the batter take a swing. *Let* the batter make contact. But Beckett couldn't stop himself. He couldn't help himself, and then all the coaching in the world couldn't help him either. The first solid whack of the game, and he was gone. And then Beckett would start throwing instead of aiming, and he'd start thinking about the infinite combination of possibilities that could go wrong, and he'd start thinking about how many more pitches he had to throw, and pretty soon all pitches started to seem the same—ball, strike, whatever—just as long as he threw one more on the long march toward whatever that day's pitch count was. He'd be thinking about everything but the next pitch, to this batter, in this situation: second inning, one out, man on first, 1–1 count. But this season Beckett's lack of control seemed to extend off the field as well. He was forever leaning over on a dugout or bullpen bench, on the verge of nodding off. Where was his discipline? His dedication? His maturity?

"He's nineteen going on fifteen," Treanor said one day about Beckett behind the closed doors of the coaches' office in Waterloo.

"Maybe late relief down the road," said Champ.

"A five-year project," Treanor agreed. "And even then—" He shook his head.

When they got together and talked about evaluations after a certain point in the season, what baseball veterans meant was consistency, and when they talked about consistency, what they meant wasn't only the ability to identify what was working and stay with it but to identify what wasn't working and make the adjustment, and when they talked about making the adjustment, what they meant—the word that always arose in these circumstances—was "maturity." Maturity here didn't refer to personal habits, unless they affected a player's performance or relationship with his teammates; it was pretty much assumed that kids one month out of high school were going to do pretty much what eighteen-year-olds were capable of doing, and to do it occasionally to excess. Major league organizations routinely instructed the managers and coaches at the Rookie level that they were going to have to serve as surrogate mothers, fathers, and counselors. But after a player had spent a year or two in the organization, it was further assumed that he would be able to find his own apartment, do his own laundry, be away from home; would know what habits adversely affect his performance, and would know to avoid them; would be ready to think of baseball as not just a game, but a career.

"That Jason Hardtke?" a Padres scout named Van Smith said to Champ one night. "You're absolutely right. You told me about him, but you know, the first time I saw him, I wrote him off. The second time, I thought, Hey, maybe. And the third time, I thought: He's a hitter. He doesn't overwhelm you, but he's there. He's right there. He's the only hitter on your club that can lengthen his stance but still hang back on an off-speed pitch. He'll just hold his bat back there, waiting for it."

The evaluations didn't end, period. Smith, Champ, and Treanor were sitting around a table at a bar across the street from Marinelli Field in Rockford, where the Diamonds had just suffered a particularly severe beating. Champ nodded his head thoughtfully. Hardtke had gone hitless in five at bats that evening, but his batting average was .304, and he'd slugged seven home runs and sixteen doubles. Well more than halfway through the season now, he commanded attention and respect through his consistency.

"You throw BP and you can see," Champ said. Smith had thrown batting practice that day. Smith and Champ went back fifteen years, to the time when Smith was a college coach trying to recruit Champ out of high school. Smith's pleasure in Champ's company was palpable; when Champ spoke, Smith beamed, as a teacher might in the reflected light of a star pupil. Champ said, "The batter who goes after a low and outside pitch and follows it through and does something with it—you've got yourself a real hitter."

Smith offered to throw batting practice again the next day.

"It's yours." Champ refilled Smith's beer glass. "You could be our designated pitcher."

Smith frowned. "What's that?"

Champ explained that each day's lineup card had to carry a designated pitcher: one position player who could pitch in a pinch. For the Diamonds, it was always Kevin Farlow. Farlow, in fact, had pitched that evening. Down 12–5 going into the bottom of the eighth, Champ had turned the ball over to his starting third baseman. "We should have another pitcher, actually," said Champ.

"I could be your twelfth pitcher," said Smith.

"Davila's our twelfth pitcher," Champ said. "And we only have eleven." They all laughed. After the eventual release of Billy Johnson, Jose Davila had assumed the role of battle fodder—the mop-up pitcher available when the manager wants to spare the rest of the bullpen. "Hey, I'll tell you this," Champ said to Smith. "Beckett's no better than Davila. Sure, Beckett's got better control—if he's got it. But that's a big if."

"You mean"—Smith pushed back from the table—"you've got as good a chance with Davila as with Beckett?" Smith pondered this for a moment, then pulled himself close to the table again. He picked up a toothpick tied with green cellophane and started toying with it absently. "How many of these kids know they're playing for a junkyard team?" he said.

"None," said Champ. "Maybe a few."

Treanor cleared his throat. "*Some* of them know that *some* of the team is a junkyard team."

"You know what one guy told me?" said Champ. "That this is the best team he's ever played on."

"You're kidding!" Smith pushed away from the table again.

"And he's only played on winning teams," said Champ. "But *this* is the best team he's ever played on." He laughed hoarsely.

The group grew silent. On a TV screen at one end of the room, ESPN's *Sportscenter* was showing the day's major league highlights. At the moment, Mark Carreon of the Detroit Tigers was hitting a home run. Smith broke the silence by asking what the difference was between Carreon's swing and Scott Pugh's.

"Not a lot," said Treanor.

"That's true. But there is one difference. You stay behind Pugh sometime and you'll see. His bat does this—" Using the toothpick, Smith demonstrated a miniature swing of the bat, level but for one noticeable bump.

Treanor nodded.

"And that Keith McKoy," Smith said. "He runs like the wind, huh?" He went back to playing with the toothpick. Without looking up, he said, "Does he know he's maybe two months away from being out of baseball?"

"No," Champ said. "None of them do. Well, maybe a few, but that's it. And that's because they can't evaluate themselves."

Smith nodded. He was still looking down. "Can you evaluate yourself?" he said.

Champ shifted on his stool. "Yeah," he said after a long pause. "Yes. I think I can. I think I honestly can. People don't believe it sometimes when I say what my goal is. It pisses them off, but I'm just being realistic. People say, 'You don't want to be a major league manager? Or a major league coach?' Of course! But I know I'm not going to be. Sure, I'd like to be"—he paused, searching for an example, and came up with the name of the Padres' manager— "Greg Riddoch. But I never played out of A ball, so there's no reason I should expect to manage in the majors."

"But you need goals." Smith had stopped playing with his toothpick. He was looking at Champ now. "You need to think you can improve."

"That's not what I'm saying," Champ said. "Don't get me wrong. But if San Diego called you tomorrow and said, 'You're out,' what would you do? Quit baseball?"

Smith frowned and looked down.

"*Hell,* no," said Champ. "You'd try to get a scouting job somewhere else. Or something. Same with me. If I couldn't do this, I'd try to get a scouting job or a coaching job with a major league organization; and if I couldn't do that, I'd look for a college job; and if I couldn't do that, I'd start looking at high schools. If somebody told me tomorrow that I would never manage in the majors but I could have a twenty-year contract with the Waterloo Diamonds, I'd take it. I'd *take* it. Because that way I know I'll be in baseball. Because what else can I do? Go to work for Granite City Steel?" He fell silent and took a quick sip of his beer, then another. "My goal, all I want to do—my only goal—is to stay in baseball."

By definition, the veterans who sat around passing judgment and drawing conclusions were the baseball personnel who had survived long enough to become the veterans who sat around passing judgment and drawing conclusions. For proof that it was possible to stay in baseball through a combination of a certain amount of talent and a certain amount of ambition, all they had to do was look at one another. They had demonstrated to their own satisfaction that maturity was an attainable goal—that it was possible to make the adjustment and, by making the adjustment, to achieve consistency, and, by making the adjustment and achieving consistency, to endure. For them, what it came down to was this: How badly did you want to stay in the game?

On the afternoon of the Fourth, sitting around the office at the ballpark in Waterloo, their conversation drifting from one hitter's habit of "collapsing his elbow" to another's "bullshit dry drag swing," Champ suddenly shook his head and said to Tom Gamboa, "This is the same stuff I was telling players in spring training, and it's the same stuff they've been hearing all their lives. And they'll remember it for a game or two, but you know what? When they've got an 85-mile-an-hour fastball coming at them, and they're worried about coiling and hanging back and shifting their weight, and they miss the ball, they're going to think, 'Fuck it, I'm going back to what I've been doing since I was five.' And we can't change that. They won't listen until they're really suffering."

"That's why it's a game of attrition," Gamboa answered him. "Guys who can make the adjustment, make it. And those who can't—" He smiled. He shrugged. He popped a handful of sunflower seeds.

That evening, vendors appeared. Captain Dynamite had indeed done the trick the previous evening, at least by Waterloo standards, notching the largest attendance figure so far this season: 952. For the fireworks on the Fourth, however, Simpson was counting on an even better crowd—at least 1,000, which was his informal barometer for when to bring out the vendors. For the first time all season, the ballpark would echo with the cries of "Peanuts! Popcorn!" and "Beer here!"

Fifteen minutes before the start of the game, a line formed at the front gate that just wouldn't quit—another first for the year. Even as those at the head of the line purchased their souvenir programs and surrendered their tickets and entered the concourse, the line continued to grow. Inside the ballpark, the crowd belted out the National Anthem along with the prerecorded organ. At " . . . and the home of the brave," fireworks whistled skyward from behind the scoreboard. Still the line out front grew. It wasn't a sellout; far from it. But it was enough of a crowd that after a couple of innings, the groundskeeper Jim Van Sant had to pocket some petty cash and drive off in search of a fresh supply of hot-dog buns. He returned a short while later. "Hy-Vee!" he announced, holding aloft several sacks packed with hot-dog buns, the conquering hero parading along the concourse. "On sale! Two for a buck!"

Every so often, somebody affiliated with the club—Simpson, Nelson, one of the owners—would slip into a seat near Gamboa, and Gamboa would always be welcoming. He would say how impressed he was by the crowds this visit, and what a difference it was from his last visit, and how the whole atmosphere seemed livelier, and what a good game the fans were getting tonight, and how that would bode well for return attendance on other nights. At one point—top of the seventh, tie score—a South Bend runner tried to score from first on a double, and Keith McKoy's throw from right-center missed the cutoff man. Hardtke, backing up the throw, fielded the ball smoothly and threw a strike to the plate. A slide. A pause. The ump's upraised thumb. "The trailer nailed him!" Gamboa yelled. "We worked on that just this morning! Good relay!" he called out to the field.

Around this time, cars started lining up in the cemetery beyond the right-field fence to wait for the fireworks show, their parking lights glowing red amid the trees. For the second night in a row, the home team lost but the entertainment ended with a bang anyway, sending the fans filing out of the ballpark wearing stupid, sheepish grins, as if embarrassed that something so loud could be so much fun.

"Guess *what!*" Mildred Boyenga shouted to Dan Yates, spotting him through the crowd under the stands. They were both holding their own against the movement of fans shuffling toward the parking lot. Boyenga shouted to Yates that she had spent her first morning in retirement walking around the cemetery and looking at the ballpark.

Yates looked puzzled, but willing to be pleased for her. "Well . . . good!" he shouted back.

Then Jeff Nelson shouted to them both. "Attendance," he announced. "Two thousand, two hundred and eight!"

The three of them looked at one another, or tried to look at one another, but it was difficult through that surging record-setting crowd. The concrete stank of beer, and the air was rank with cigar smoke—a not-altogether-unpleasant combination of odors. Heady, intoxicating even, when you stopped to consider that this was the smell of success.

"We done set the tone," Nelson shouted, "for the rest of the season!"

8

One evening at Municipal Stadium, between pitches, Waterloo right fielder Jeff Pearce wandered over to a bare patch in the grass and used his spikes to scratch a straight line in the dirt. Then he scratched another line next to the first. Then he scratched a third that crossed the first two, and a fourth next to that one. Then he returned to his position. After the batter was retired, Pearce returned to the formerly bare patch and scratched a symbol in a corner of the grid: X. He returned to his position; returned to his grid: O. Next inning, another X, another O. Throughout a mid-July baseball game of little consequence, Pearce continued his game of tick-tack-toe, and when the groundskeeper Jim Van Sant teased him about it the next day, Pearce suggested that Van Sant chalk the grid. One evening Van Sant did, and then every evening thereafter.

The season had reached that point where it no longer seemed quite endless, but neither did the end seem near. For all its disappointments and traumas, despite the daily addition of wins and losses, and regardless of the relentless accumulation of individual and team statistics, the season in some ways had never arrived in Waterloo—not for the players, not for anyone. First there had been the freezing temperatures and incessant wetness of April, then the blue-domed days but empty stands of May, then the virtual month-long absence during June. Where was *baseball?* With the possible exception of the Fourth of July, a platonic evening of minor league baseball—that carnival atmosphere of hot dogs and beers and cigar smoke and prizes and big crowds—had yet to appear. When the Diamonds returned from a road trip on July 12, they were completing a thirty-two-day period during which they had played only seven games in Waterloo. They were also beginning a thirty-two-day period during which they were scheduled to play only eight games away from Waterloo. There was still time—

and, for one brief spell, there was even timelessness.

On the road, time passed quickly. There was always a lunch to grab, a curfew to meet, a bus to catch to the ballpark, or back to the hotel, or to the next city, or to Waterloo. Players and coaches were in a perpetual state of packing and unpacking, of adjusting to a new place, of leaving that place behind for now or, increasingly, for good: Appleton, done for the year; Kenosha, done for the year; Beloit, South Bend, Quad City, and Rockford, by the middle of July, done, done, done, and done.

Time, at home, however, slowed. Routines developed. Sameness ensued. At 3:00 in the afternoon, the players converged on the ballpark. They opened their mail—letters from girlfriends ("I understand totally that you have been really busy and finding time to write was scarce"), or solicitations from investment brokers ("You don't need me to tell you the kind of financial success that comes from playing major league baseball. When that day arrives you will be earning more in 'meal money' than you are earning now. [That still seems incredible to me]"). They engaged in philosophical discourse ("Baseball players like sex, you think?" "Women and baseball. What else is there?" "Money"). Then they slipped into their batting practice jerseys and took the field. They stretched at the same time every day, long-tossed at the same time every day, held batting practice and took infield and hit fungoes, every day, same time. Even the sun, smudged by midsummer haze, seemed to hang in the same spot over the parking lot every day in the hour before the ball game. Pinned to the wooden bench in the public concourse just outside the clubhouse's screen door, pools of plum juice or tobacco spit collecting at their feet, the pitchers would congratulate themselves on having found a spot where they had at least a chance to catch a breeze. "Got more sense than the hitters," they'd say of their teammates in the clubhouse behind them. The pitchers' regard for the intelligence of their natural prey was not especially high. "You come inside, what the fuck's the batter think, you're going to come in again? What the fuck. You're settin' him up low and away. But can they ever figure it out? No." This was Beckett. "I just don't get it. It's a fucking mysterious game."

The extended, nearly uninterrupted stay in Waterloo afforded the players a chance to make themselves at home—or, if not home, at least home away from home. The airline industry's fare wars of that summer helped. Across the country, the players' families and friends had consulted their Waterloo Diamonds pocket schedules, noticed at a glance the solid blocks of pale green dates starting in the second week of July, and booked accordingly. Suddenly the pass list at the ticket window swelled into the dozens, and the stands started filling with familiar faces. Girlfriends showed up for brief visits, went home fiancées. (News of an engagement was duly reported over the stadium loudspeaker.) Parents arrived bearing birthday presents or, better yet, invitations to dinner. But, however welcome these visits might have been for the players, what were they if not reminders of home, and how soon they'd be there? What was happening to the season? Where had it gone?

Where was baseball?

Sometimes, in the morning, a player and his family would make the one-hour pilgrimage down U.S. 20 to Dyersville, site of the ball field from *Field of Dreams*. "If you build it, they will come" by now had entered the vernacular; it was endlessly revived in media coverage of cities building baseball stadiums in the hopes of attracting teams, and it was endlessly reprised regarding anything else. ("If you ignore it, they will come," read a headline in the *Courier* that month, about a new city crackdown on parking meter scofflaws.) Certainly it was endlessly repeated about this very plot of cropland. The two neighbors who owned separate parcels of the property had feuded briefly over whether to maintain the ball field as the filmmakers had fashioned it, or to return the land to crops. The matter had been settled by the growing number of fans who were willing to ask directions in Dyersville and follow a maze of back roads a couple of miles outside of town. Daily a line of cars rolled down the path from the road, serendipitously re-creating the final shot from the movie. Fathers and sons by the dozen climbed out with their mitts, crossed the foul lines, and played catch. And standing among them were the professional baseball players from Waterloo, sharing a literal common ground.

Here it was, the daddy of all diamonds, doing in a cornfield what baseball had done from the start: carve a corner of civilization out of the countryside, and open into the limitless frontier. Overhead, off-camera, electrical wires hummed. To one side, off-mike, a father at the souvenir stand snapped at his son, "We already got enough shit. Don't get greedy." For any visitors who wanted to find the irruptions in the illusion, they were there; for those who didn't, they didn't have to be. Most of what they remembered from the movie was still intact. The bleachers back of first base were still there, as was the ball diamond itself. At this time of year, the famous wall of cornstalks fronting the outfield was indeed tall enough to hide a team. Still, however moving it might be, what was this place if not baseball at least thrice removed: a shrine to a motion picture about a shrine to baseball?

Sometimes, long after a game, players would wind up on the sidewalks on College Hill with the ballpark staff, everyone agreeing that just because the bars were closing didn't mean their night had to end. They still had a whole ballpark to call their own. And so they would climb into their cars and race back there, occasionally receiving the attentions of the police cars that waited in the dark of the parking lot across Park Road, light-spinning to life, and then they'd have to explain, "But officers, we *work* here." Sometimes their arrival would spook Jack Grandy, the clubhouse manager, who would be trying to sneak a nap in the home locker room, lying across the washer and dryer with a baseball bat along his spine, letting the gyrations of the machines massage his back and lull him to sleep. Later, he would make an appearance in the dugout doorway and, before disappearing for the night, mutter, "*Bull Durham* bullshit."

It was, and it wasn't. True, some of what drew them here was a romantic view of ballpark life that had nothing to do with loads of laundry needing to be clean by 10 A.M., but some of it was just the joy of being young on a summer night: goose-bump breezes, a choir of crickets, a field of stars, and all of it—the universe, no less—suddenly, vaguely illicit. So they lingered, ignoring Grandy's grumpiness. They sat in the dugout and talked blurry beer talk at one another, they sang, they danced, they revved up the John Deere tractor and played Jump the Mound ("I'm not pitchin' on it anymore," said a pitcher out for the season with a sore shoulder, shrugging), and when the first faint streaks of pink appeared in the sky beyond the trees in the cemetery, they sent Courtney the ticket taker into center field, where she welcomed the new day by turning cartwheels in the dew.

But that wasn't it, either—though it came very, very close. On July 6, 1989, a game in Waterloo Municipal Stadium lasted twenty-five innings, still a Midwest League record. The day that almost ends at closing time but somehow lasts till dawn; the game that might end any second or might go on for hours. The second before sunrise; the final out. The time before the time to go home. No game has ever lasted forever, but, in theory, one could, and that—*that*—would be baseball.

"As a little kid, with my father, it was always, 'Throw one more. Just one more,' " Jeff Pearce was saying to Scott Bream in the Waterloo dugout one evening. "Didn't matter if I swung and missed. I just wanted that chance." He winced. "As a little kid," he went on, "if you swung and missed, you always had one more. It didn't bother you. The other kids laughed because they knew you were the best around. The kids laughed, you went home and got a meal in your stomach from Mom, and it was okay."

"In high school," said Bream, "you'd go in the hole and make the play, and everybody thought it was great. Now you're *expected* to do it."

Their heads were swiveling back and forth while they watched the visiting team take infield practice. Bream had been the Padres' third-round draft pick in 1989, Pearce the sixth-round pick in 1990. Each had received a sizable signing bonus; each, at some point, had lost nearly a full season to injuries. At the moment, Bream was hitting .215, Pearce .235.

"The day you sign," Bream said, "every player thinks, 'I'm going right to the big leagues.' "

" 'I can hit the ball five hundred feet,' " Pearce said. " 'I can hit a ball thrown *three times* that fast.' "

Bream bit his lower lip. Pearce tapped a bat slowly against the dugout's wooden floor. Each tap lingered, its echoes ringing hollow.

"And then you learn, 'I'm not going right to the big leagues,' " said Bream. " 'I'm not that good.' "

Professional ball required of a player not only that he come to work and do his job every day, but that he come to work and do his job at the peak of his abilities . . . every every every *every* day. One night he could perform the minor miracles of coordination and strength and strategizing that baseball routinely required, and then the next night he had to go out and perform them again. And again. And again. And if one day he woke up and realized that despite his best intentions, he hadn't gone out and done his best in several days, or a week, or a month, or all season, the effect could be devastating.

This was what Pearce's father thought he recognized in his son when he visited from California during this period. Jeff Pearce the elder began his visit by doing the dutiful divorced-dad thing: treating his son and his son's roommate, Kevin Farlow, to dinner at the Ground Round, just about the only restaurant open in Waterloo after an evening game. Afterward, the father took the son back to a room at the Ramada Inn, sat him down, and asked him what was wrong.

Jeff Pearce the younger could be his own severest critic. Once, making small talk in the shower, a visiting scout had complimented him on the Ruthian exhibition Pearce had just given in batting practice, and Pearce had answered, "A five-o'clock hitter." "Come on," the scout had answered, "you're not giving yourself enough credit." "That's me," Pearce said. "A five-o'clock hitter."

Now he told his father that he was having the usual problems. He was psyching himself out, he said. He got down on himself. He beat up on himself. If he saw two fastballs, he started worrying about whether he was going to be seeing a curve, or two curves, or a third fastball. And if he guessed *wrong*—

"Just get in there and hit." His father cut him short. "You've seen all the pitches. You've seen fastballs before. They're not going to throw a thousand miles an hour. You've already seen ninety-five, ninety-eight miles an hour. It doesn't get any faster than that, except in the majors. You've played baseball in Georgia, South Carolina, North Carolina, West Virginia. You've played baseball in Idaho, Washington, Oregon, California, Nevada, and Arizona. Now you've played baseball in Illinois, Wisconsin, Indiana, and Iowa. You've *done* that. That alone brings maturity. If it wasn't for baseball, you'd be selling tires. You know what your biggest problem is? You can't see anything all the way through. You can't make the final fold on the tarp. You'll say, 'Why? It's fine that way.' "

Jeff Pearce was nodding his head: *I know, I know, I know.* And he *did* know: His father was right. He could run, throw, hit with power, and he wasn't doing it. And the hell of it was, there was nothing else he *could* do. The Padres had drafted Pearce after his junior year at Pepperdine University, home to one of the strongest baseball programs in the country, and he was openly grateful for having missed his final year of studies. Both off-seasons since then he'd thought about going back to school and getting a degree, but he'd never quite gotten around to it. Instead, he always seemed to wind up at the beach, surfing and water-skiing. One of his favorite memories was the vacation he and a friend had spent at a cove in Hawaii, an existence that he wouldn't have minded extending indefinitely. "To wake up to that view every morning . . . ," he'd say, his voice drifting. Sometimes Pearce would try to offer himself reassurances: "I'm not like a lot of these other guys who never think about anything but baseball. I can do something else. I mean, money is freedom, but *hey.* And it's not freedom. Not really." But then he'd find himself lying awake at night wondering how much longer he could stretch his bonus or sustain his career, and worrying what he would do when he'd used them up. He knew what he was, and he wasn't afraid to say it, if only to defuse the criticism that was sure to come: "I'm a waste."

"Just *do* the *task,*" his father said now. *"Finish* the *job."*

But that was just it: It *was* a job. Not only did they have to perform miracles, and not only did they have to perform them night after night, but the players had to do so without a break in sight. From July 15 to August 9, the schedule yielded no relief, no weekends to provide release, no off days, not one. "It used to be you'd give your right arm, nut, *whatever,* to be here," Champ lectured them one afternoon. "Now you get the opportunity, and you're whining." Champ was right, of course: What they did for a living was better than the nine-to-five factory job he was always comparing it to. But that wasn't the point. The point was that every player had to take the passion of his youth and harness it— deliver it on demand at the same time every day. One game in Clinton during this period, on a Sunday afternoon after an evening game in Waterloo and then a two-hour bus ride that morning, Scott Pugh raced home from third to make the score 6–6 in the fifth inning and to cap a dramatic comeback, yet when he reached the dugout, he slammed his helmet against the ground and grunted a heartfelt *"Fuck!"* Well, it *was* hot out there, if you were the runner on third looking home, and you were staring straight into the setting sun, and you were hitting a workmanlike-but-unremarkable .252, and you had played in every single one of your team's 105 games so far this year. "I want the year to end," the *winning* pitcher said after one game, addressing the insides of his locker. "Then I want it to start again. Just take a month off, then come back. *Two weeks* off."

Yet it was at this point in the season that a player who needed to make an adjustment—and who didn't?—had to do it. Just as his inner reserve started to fail him, the rigors of the season demanded a new level of maturity: the ability to make whatever adjustment was necessary in order to maintain his consistency. After his father's visit, Pearce vowed to raise his batting average thirty-five points to .270 by the end of the season, a pace that would necessitate his having a .400 August. One day Champ approached Bream and asked if he'd ever thought about learning to switch-hit as a way to compensate for his difficulty connecting with a curveball. Bream said in fact he had been thinking about it, and Champ, sucking back a scream, said that, well, this might be a good time to do it.

Even Beckett, after his talk with Gamboa, had curtailed his after-hours habits, figuring that there might be some relation between his lack of sleep at night and his exhaustion the following day. Gone now was the all-night carousing. Well, not gone, exactly, but not there as much, either. He further resolved that he would start rewarding himself after good outings. In his first start after talking to Gamboa, Beckett had struck out eight and given up only three walks over six innings, and when he left the game, the score was tied 3–3 (though Rockford eventually won on a ninth-inning rally). The next day, he bought himself some clothes and a handful of new CDs—country and western for the clubhouse, Bach for the bus rides. But those heroics had taken place on the road. When he next took the mound at home, the last the Waterloo fans had seen of him was a far more typical three-inning, seven-walk performance. Now the catcalls started even while he was working on the first batter of the ball game; the count went to 3–1, and a voice boomed, "Ahh, throw strikes, will-ya?" Beckett threw a strike, watched the batter foul off a couple of pitches—and then surrendered the walk.

He lost it. There were times Beckett could disappear so far inside his game that he wouldn't hear anything but the grunts and pumping blood that come from throwing a baseball nearly 90 miles an hour right where he wanted it pitch after pitch after pitch. And then there were other times, like this night, when he *needed* to hear—when he strained for the voice of his pitching coach from the dugout, shouting adjustments or encouragement: "That's it!" "Right there!" "Slow down!" "Atta babe!" "We'll take that all day and all night, ba-*by!*" Of course, it wasn't just Treanor's voice that filtered through at such moments; what Beckett heard now was a stream of invective. It seemed that each misplaced pitch elicited a fresh insult. And then it wasn't just the voices in the stands or a voice from the dugout he was hearing; it was Gamboa's voice: "If you don't want to come back here next year, you'd better get to work." Beckett didn't want to come back to Waterloo next year. After all, he was a first-round draft pick; he'd been "top dog" at his high school. Of course, just about every other player in pro ball had been top dog at some high school somewhere. Beckett had learned that hard truth well enough. When he signed with the Padres in June 1990, he fully expected that in two years—now, tonight—he'd be in the majors. But here he was, in Waterloo, Iowa, middle-level *A ball,* worrying about whether he'd still be standing on this same misshapen mound of earth one year from tonight. *Damn! Another walk. How many is that?* "Number four!" came the answer from the crowd.

In the third inning, Beckett faced seven batters and retired not one, along the way surrendering two doubles, a triple, and a home run. Champ made the walk to the mound.

"See enough, Champ?"

"Where you been?"

After the game, Champ, just hours off the plane from San Diego and the Major League All-Star game at Jack Murphy Stadium, waxed philosophic to the reporter from the *Courier:* "Glavine didn't have his stuff, either"—Tom Glavine, the starter for the National League who had given up five earned runs in 1–2/3 innings, including seven straight hits in the first inning. Only a week earlier, in this same room, Champ had been raging: "This fuckin' game! Thirty or forty years from now, when I'm seventy and lookin' back at this, I'm gonna think, 'This is how I spent my time when I was thirty-two years old, worryin' about everything like it's some life-threatening thing?' I mean, I take every game as seriously as Greg Riddoch takes his. And to be honest, who gives a fuck? If San Diego really cared, they'd send some fuckin' support my way. I got guys moved up, guys injured—they don't send me nothin'. I got Davila starting today. Davila! *Wow*." Then he learned that the Padres would be flying all their minor league managers to San Diego for an all-expense-paid visit to the All-Star game. Champ had returned to Waterloo late this afternoon just in time to suit up and oversee a 17–6 loss to Kenosha, but he was still afloat on a pillow of Padres goodwill. After the reporter left, Champ turned to Treanor and pointed to his own left elbow. "Ted Williams." He pointed to his right elbow. "Ken Griffey, Jr." Left elbow: "Willie Mays." Right: "Reggie."

"*Ho,* man." Treanor hung his head and shook it.

Champ eased from a pocket of his briefcase an airline boarding pass and handed it to Treanor. With some apprehension, Treanor accepted it; it was inscribed with Bob Feller's autograph. Feller was a Hall of Fame pitcher and Iowa native who had developed his baseball skills in the 1930s on a diamond his father had cleared on the family farm. Champ explained that Feller had happened to be in Waterloo for a baseball-card show over the weekend, and that on Sunday, the two of them had flown on the same itinerary from Waterloo to Minneapolis to the All-Star festivities in San Diego. "I'll tell you," said Champ, "he hates the airport in Minneapolis, it's the worst goddamn airport in the world, right? We get to L.A. 'I hate this airport. It's the worst goddamn airport in the world.' In Minneapolis he rents a luggage cart—he puts a dollar in, but it still needs two quarters. He pulls out a roll of one-hundred-dollar bills. *I* have to pay for his luggage cart. Then he brings the cart on the moving sidewalk. There's this girl standing there, there's no room, but he can't wait, he's got to squeeze past her, right? 'Stupid bitch. All them stupid bitches are the same.' Then he goes, 'Maybe you're not supposed to bring these carts on here.' " Champ paused. "*You think?*"

Treanor had been studying the boarding pass. Now he handed it back to Champ, who replaced it gingerly in the briefcase pocket. Then Treanor said, slowly, contemplatively, "The thing about Bob Feller"—he paused—"is he could throw the *shit* out of the ball."

That was it, after all: what counted, what lasted. Feller was a native Iowan, and among the locals the tales of his behavior were legion—how to this day he would appear at a ballpark to throw out the first pitch to some lucky Boy Scout or Little Leaguer, and he'd seem to put a little something extra on the ball and knock the kid on his ass. Yet, whatever the truth of these stories or Champ's anecdote, one fact about Bob Feller remained and loomed over all others: Once he was a major league pitcher, and he could throw the shit out of the ball.

One evening in the dugout during a game, Bream was studying the opposing pitcher's patterns when he turned to Pugh and said, "If he gives me a fastball middle-in, I'm taking it over the Harley-Davidson sign."

Pugh shrugged and nodded good-naturedly. After all, Bream was still looking for the first home run of his professional career.

That inning, he found it. Left center, smack over the Harley-Davidson sign.

"Ho-ly . . . *shit!*" Pugh turned to his teammates in the dugout. "You know what?"

They knew what.

Baseball.

One night at Toad's, Maxwell told Champ that from what he'd been hearing by way of the Padres grapevine, Riddoch was on his way out as manager in San Diego, Champ's mentor Jim Riggelman was in line to take his place, getting the promotion from Triple A to the Show, and the manager at the Double A level would be jumping to the Rockies organization after the season, all of which presumably would be leaving plenty of room for advancement for managers at the lower levels of the system. "You'll be moving up," Maxwell said. "Looks like you joined the organization at the right time."

"Maybe," said Champ. "But the best part is, next year I won't be in Waterloo."

Maxwell glanced at him, then back up to the television. Some-where a major league baseball game was starting. Maxwell asked if Champ ever thought about managing in the majors.

Champ said no.

"But it's gotta be a *goal,*" Maxwell said.

Maxwell hadn't been present at the bar in Rockford the night that Champ had addressed this topic, so Champ beckoned his standard response, and the words obeyed: No, it wasn't a goal; if he found out tomorrow that he'd never manage in the majors, that would be okay; all he wanted was to stay in baseball; it was all he'd ever wanted; it was better than a *job.* Then he fell silent.

"I saw something tonight," Champ said after a while. He'd been coaching third, when a foul ball floated into the stands be-hind him. "People really went after it," he said. "You know: 'I almost had it!' 'I shoulda brought my glove!' And I remembered, 'Oh, *yeah.*' When they went home, that scramble for the ball was probably going to be the highlight of their night, and they didn't even *get* to it." He shook his head. "Even if there's only three hundred people there, that's still three hundred who paid to see this sport. This entertainment." He shook his head again, and this time when he beckoned, no standard response obeyed. His mouth worked, but the words wouldn't come. "There's something *about* this game," he finally said.

"Football!" said Maxwell.

Champ followed his gaze up to the television; a commercial for a pro football preseason game was in progress.

"You know what that means," Maxwell said.

"Yeah." A note of surprise had entered Champ's voice, and, perhaps for the first time all year, a note of regret, too. "Season's almost over."

The architect's report arrived in the mail at the front office one Tuesday morning. The report proper ran eighteen pages, the ap-pendices another five. The information of immediate concern—"Requirements Not in Compliance," stemming from Sections 11, 12, and 13 of the Professional Baseball Agreement—took up one page and the top of another. It was now official.

The home clubhouse measured 608 square feet, out of a re-quired 800. Lockers numbered 30, the prescribed number, but their widely varying sizes didn't conform to the 24″ by 72″ standard. Overall comment on the home clubhouse: "Very cramped." The training room measured 150 square feet out of the required 175, fell one whirlpool short of the required two, and lacked both required weight-equipment areas. In addition, the two "residential washers/dryers" didn't constitute the mandated "commercial quality" laundry facilities. "Does not exist," was the report's assessment of the coaches' locker room; instead, "Coaches have one long shelf & bench." The visitors' 640-square-foot clubhouse actually exceeded the required 500 square feet, but had 21 lockers rather than 28, and was short a training table, a whirlpool, and an office for the visiting manager. Outside, the playing area lacked: a 15-foot warning track anywhere but in the outfield; a bullpen mound that was "not a trip hazard"; a bat rack in each dugout that could hold 30 bats rather than 16; foul poles with "no white signs adjacent"; a "written maintenance program"; a regulation mound; legal dimensions throughout.

The lighting passed.

The day the report arrived, Simpson made a copy and drove it over to the Park Commission offices and presented it to Rick Tagtow, the parks director, who accepted it with hardly a word or a glance. For nearly two years now, the fate of the franchise had rested on the results of the architect's survey of the facilities. Here at last were the precise measurements and quantities and comments that would determine how much it was going to cost to keep professional baseball in Waterloo. Yet over time, and even as the arrival of the report grew imminent, this concern had been overshadowed by an even more pressing question: Who was going to pay?

In Rick Tagtow, the ball club had the benefit of a parks director who was a fan—though not necessarily a cheerleader. Tagtow had grown up four blocks from the ballpark, and he could remember standing in his yard and hearing the roar of the crowd. "I used to climb the left-field fence as a kid and sneak in," he liked to joke. "Now my job is keepin' kids out." These days he had sons of his own, and every so often he would bring them out to the ballpark early so they could watch batting practice and meet the Diamonds, while he went off and chewed the fat with the front-office staff. Tagtow read baseball periodicals avidly, he'd visited many of the Midwest League's parks, and every June he tried to attend the Midwest League All-Star game. Personally—Tagtow had said this again and again—he'd love to see pro ball stay in Waterloo.

Professionally, however, was another matter. As the parks director, he was responsible for administering the facilities and the paid staff of the Park Commission, and for executing the policies set by the Park Board. A forester "by vocation and by avocation," he now occupied a desk job. Sad-eyed, full-cheeked and fortyish, Tagtow had been chosen for the post by Mayor McKinley in 1988 from a field of four foresters. His jurisdiction included twenty-four basketball courts, thirty tennis courts, twenty-nine restrooms, twenty-eight shelters, five concession buildings, nine maintenance structures, three pro shops, and a boathouse. It also included fifty-one baseball diamonds, of which Waterloo Municipal Stadium was only one. Sometimes David Simpson or Dan Yates or, now, Bill Boesen would visit him in his office to discuss the future of the ballpark, and Tagtow would point to a cabinet in a corner and say, "To you, it's your life. To me, it's one of those files."

Once, his personal concern and his professional responsibility had dovetailed. In the early years of his tenure as parks director, Tagtow had been able to join Bernie McKinley and argue in good conscience for ballpark funding, secure in the belief that he was helping professional baseball stay in Waterloo, that he was adding to the city's quality of life.

It was true that some of the complications that arose, almost as soon as the four-year commitment had cleared the council, were the result of government regulations regarding construction in the floodplain. As Tagtow himself said at the time, accepting responsibility, apologizing to the Park Board and, by extension, the public, "I thought we were building a big bathroom, folks. We build bathrooms all the time. Foolish us. When you get into locker rooms, you get into a whole new ball game."

But some of the complications were purely the province of baseball. The initial $205,000 in funding for the clubhouse had grown by $120,000 when San Diego indicated that lights should be a priority, too. Then the Padres changed owners, and Tagtow had to worry whether the requests and demands of the new front-office regime in San Diego would be the same as those of the old regime. Even before he'd gotten an answer, the time had come for Tagtow to worry whether the Padres would even be renewing their Player Development Contract with Waterloo, and whether a new parent club's front office would impose yet another set of priorities. Then the new Professional Baseball Agreement had rendered the city's clubhouse plans obsolete—even if the city had had the money to build one that met code—and had raised the standards for Class A lighting, but fortunately only to levels for which Tagtow, by now having learned to anticipate changing rules, already had solicited bids. At least Waterloo had been spared the fate of Clinton, where the city had bowed to the pressure of the major league parent and built a spacious, carpeted, $125,000 clubhouse that would have been the envy of any other club, if it hadn't fallen several square feet short of the PBA standards that arrived while the facility was under construction.

"Time after time, page after page of stuff they want out of us, and I'm just afraid of getting sucked down a big rathole," was how Tagtow described the new baseball agreement to the Park Board a week after it was reached. "We've tried very hard—you folks, us, Bernie, everybody in this room and Bernie—to say, 'We've given you a pile of money, and that's it.' But you just feel constant pressure. 'Well, when we get that pile, where's the next one?' That's what makes me nervous. Because there won't *be* a next one."

Whose responsibility was the ballpark, really? Officially, the city was the landlord, and the ball club a tenant at the token rent of $1 a year (and, in fact, not even that), but Municipal Stadium was simply where the professional baseball team in Waterloo played—and had played, for nearly half a century. It was some measure of the informality of the arrangement that when the ball-club leaders decided several years earlier that their organization had outgrown its business office, which at that time occupied a cubbyhole adjacent to the visitors' clubhouse, and that the ballpark furthermore could benefit from a new concession stand, a group of volunteers had gotten together and stuck a cinder-block bunker under the grandstand, without so much as a single permit.

Part of the problem in fixing responsibility for the ballpark in Waterloo, as in other cities, was the landlord's neglect. Except for the occasional coat of paint and some restrooms in the 1970s, that addition of a combination front office and concession stand had constituted the first significant improvement to the ballpark since its opening in 1946—and it had been an off-the-field improvement at that. Even after the city started making repairs in the 1980s, the ballpark still suffered by comparison with other Midwest League facilities, generally rating ahead of only decrepit old John O'Donnell Stadium in Davenport in the hearts and minds of players, managers, farm directors and other baseball personnel.

But part of the problem was that some improvements were for the benefit of one tenant only. New lights Tagtow could justify because they would benefit anyone who played at the ballpark. Even if pro ball left town, he once joked to the Park Board, "we'll have the best-lit Pee Wee League baseball field on the North American continent." But a new clubhouse and the dozens of other PBA-mandated improvements would satisfy the demands of professional baseball and no one else.

For most of the century, the civic contribution of professional baseball had provided all the justification the community needed: Whatever it took to keep pro ball, Waterloo did. The benefits ultimately might prove to be economic, but such considerations were left implicit. As the local economy declined, and as the demands of baseball grew, however, the ball club for the first time found itself needing to address the question explicitly: What was professional baseball worth to the city?

First the ball club prepared a study of the economic impact of professional baseball on the city, based on figures worked out with the Chamber of Commerce. Using a multiplier of seven—the number of times a dollar would turn over in a community—the study argued that $145,000 in team salaries (29 employees times $1,000 a month times five months) was worth $1.015 million to Waterloo's economy; that the visiting players' meals and salaries were worth $572,000; that the ballclub's own expenditures were worth $725,000; and so on. The grand total came to $2.495 million.

Still, it was only a start. One morning Dan Yates had appeared before the Park Board and said Waterloo Professional Baseball, Inc., was organizing a not-for-profit arm, Waterloo Diamonds Baseball Association, to raise money for the purpose of renovating the stadium. A modest fund-raising campaign brought in about

$10,000 during the first year, and that fall, after weathering the first PBA season with a profit, the owners had designated another $10,000 from the for-profit ball-club ledgers for the not-for-profit account.

Still, it wasn't enough.

If the fate of professional baseball in Waterloo for most of its existence had relied on city boosters, and then for much of the 1980s on the vision of Bernie McKinley, in the 1990s it came to rest in the accounting ledgers of the city—and in particular, that corner of the municipal budget presided over by the Park Board. An advisory panel of seven volunteers appointed by the mayor, the Park Board convened one Wednesday a month at 7:30 in the morning in a conference room in the Park Commission headquarters. The City Council and the mayor made final decisions, but the Park Board members could make recommendations and set policy and certainly force an issue. Month after month, the issue that the Park Board tried to force was what to do with Waterloo Municipal Stadium. It wasn't always even the board members' money at stake; the $325,000 in municipal bonding, for instance, hadn't come out of the Park Commission budget. But, of course, as Waterloo taxpayers, it *was* their money—or, as one of them, speaking in the heat of a Park Board debate about ballpark funding, once described it: "More money, and more money, and *more* money."

More so than in most communities, taxes were an especially sensitive topic in Waterloo. A combination of factors, all of which were taking their tolls singly or doubly in any number of cities, had hit Waterloo one right after the other. When the factories closed, thousands of jobs disappeared. When thousands of jobs disappeared, so did thousands of workers. As the population dropped, the individual tax burden on those who remained in Waterloo grew. And *grew*, as federal funding cuts to states trickled down to counties in Iowa in the form of residential property devaluations. In all, Waterloo in recent years had experienced a $250 million property-valuation loss—a quarter of a billion dollars suddenly not subject to city and county property taxes. If only to approach previous, prerecession levels of income, both the city and county had raised property taxes dramatically. (Russ Garling, the Park Board member who once served as the ball club president, often complained that his property taxes had tripled in one year.) A *Consumers Digest* survey of real-estate taxes related to home-market value that listed Waterloo's as among the highest in the nation only confirmed what local taxpayers already suspected, though the specific ranking might have come as a shock: number five.

The problem—a major factor, anyway—was the highways. The significance of the highway funding wasn't only in the overall dollar amount—perhaps $15 to $20 million, and maybe more, by the time all the construction was done. It was in the *pace*. Because the city's commitment to highways had been so furious and fast— a lot of money over a relatively short period of time—highway bonds dominated the budget every year, taking the lion's share and leaving the scraps. If, by law, the total amount the city could bond in a given year was, say, $4.5 million, then $3 million to $3.5 million might have been going to the highways. All the other programs in the city would have to make do with what was left over, or not—and McKinley called those shots, too. Naturally, professional baseball had made the cut.

When Bernie McKinley had embraced highways and "quality of life" projects as the path to Waterloo's prosperity, he had set a goal of 1,000 new jobs a year. In fact, he surpassed it— 9,000 jobs in six years. Some of the jobs, however, were part-time, some were minimum-wage, and many were obtained, at a time of skyrocketing individual taxes, by offering corporate tax breaks to companies willing to locate in Waterloo. In 1990, the modern IBP meat-packing plant opened on an industrial site in the middle of farmland on the far northeastern side of the city, effectively replacing the Rath plant that had closed six years earlier, right down to the number of employees on the payroll—2,000—only this time workers would be starting at $6.50 an hour, about one-third of what they might have been earning at Rath. Critics charged that their taxes were going up to build the roads so they could drive to a job where they would be making less money. In the end, the outcry was as loud as the line of applicants was long.

"We're not back in 1985," McKinley would answer his critics, his voice thinning with impatience. Maybe the jobs at IBP or in the service sector didn't pay as well as the assembly line or vertical kill had in the old days, but they were jobs just the same; and, like it or not, they were Waterloo's chance at prosperity in the century to come. McKinley knew what lay beyond the horizon—he could *see* it—and those unfortunates who couldn't see it, or wouldn't, suffered from what was, for McKinley, perhaps the most crippling affliction of all: "absolutely zero vision."

"See, another problem we have is the mayor," a Park Board member said one morning, during a discussion of stadium funding. "Maybe one thing we can do is have the mayor come to a meeting and sit down and discuss how we feel about all this."

"We, over the years," another member of the Park Board moaned, "we've had such crying needs and other priorities here that we've just been absolutely neglecting because we're cranking in the kinds of funds that we're cranking into baseball." And another: "Something that bothers me is if you take $500,000, look at what we could do to the rest of our facilities."

"Oh, yeah," Tagtow agreed. "I've discussed that with the mayor. That would make a heck of an impact with the rest of our facilities." Once, wistfully, he'd listed what the $325,000 could have bought the city's parks system: "All new playgrounds, all new restrooms, and everything handicapped-accessible. Golf courses? Major problems solved: irrigation system. Two restroom/shelters at each course. *Bridges.*"

So why, the question would come up at Park Board meetings, can't the city just take the money out of the ballpark and distribute it elsewhere?

"The mayor," Tagtow would answer, "made it abundantly clear that commitments had been made."

"In spite of what the mayor thinks," a Park Board member said at the October 1991 meeting, "I think that the mayor better— either you convey to him at your meeting with him this time, then also ask him here, and let us be real emphatic about it, and let us have a little battle here if necessary."

There was a photo of Bernie McKinley on the front page of the *Courier* three weeks later, on the morning after the election, that showed him at his "victory" celebration: eyes wide, lips thin, one lock of hair uncharacteristically marking his forehead. If in hindsight his defeat came to seem remotely possible, at the time it did not. It was shocking. It *shocked.* For years McKinley had been talking about improving the city's "quality of life," and Al Manning had stolen the issue. While waiting for a future with a brighter quality of life to arrive, voters had endured significant cuts to library hours, garbage collection, parks mainenance—to say nothing of the inconvenience of every other street being blocked with bulldozers. The paper summarized the situation three weeks later: "A number of respondents to this week's 'Call the Courier' question said they were just shelling out too much of the green stuff in property taxes and fees while seeing a decline in the services they received in return." The "Call the Courier" question was "Why do you think Manning won?" but what most published respondents seemed to be answering was "Why do you think McKinley lost?": McKinley was associated with the businesses and the wealthy." "He lost track of what the working class in Waterloo can afford." "Voters in Waterloo were tired of Bernie McKinley being a puppet for so-called city fathers."

Bernie McKinley and the ball club might have made strange bedfellows, but it had always been the "city fathers" who sponsored pro ball in Waterloo. When Al Manning won the election, the ball club lost not only its most powerful sponsor but perhaps the last backer who would proceed under the same assumption as did the ball club owners—that the bond between the city and baseball that had endured since the turn of the century was still intact.

One month after the election David Simpson showed up at a Park Board meeting to say that the ball club wanted to make three improvements to the ballpark that would enhance revenue: six new outfield signs, a new window for the concessions stand, and a finer mesh behind home plate. He said that the total cost would be about $3,000, but he emphasized that it would be the ball club's money, not the city's.

More advertising signage—the Park Board members could understand how that might enhance revenue. But a new window on the concession stand? At a time when they were waiting to hear how the ball club was intending to raise the money to renovate the ballpark? And *mesh?*

Simpson explained that a finer mesh would provide a more enjoyable viewing experience than the present heavy mesh, and therefore more repeat customers. "It's gonna improve the stadium," said Simpson. "So instead of sittin' dead in the water, waitin' for something to happen—which I don't know what's gonna happen, I don't know if we're gonna get money from John Deere, I don't know if we're gonna get a hundred thousand, I don't know if we're gonna get a hundred and fifty thousand, I don't know if we're gonna get two *million* dollars."

"Or anything," a Park Board member said.

"Exactly!" Simpson said. "At *least* we're makin' these improvements and at least we're tryin'."

The Park Board said Simpson could institute his $3,000 worth of changes provided that he show up at the next Park Board meeting and submit a written plan as to how the ball club proposed to raise $100,000. Simpson didn't show up at that meeting, due to a scheduling error on the Park Commission's part, but he promised to appear at the next meeting. ("I'd *like* to see him here," one member said, hooting with laughter. "Make him squirm again. We're gonna get our money's worth in a pound of flesh!") The following month, however, Simpson again was absent. In his stead, he had sent what amounted to "the written plan." It was a letter on the stationery of the Waterloo Diamonds Baseball Association, the fund-raising arm of the organization, and it was addressed, "TO WHOM IT MAY CONCERN:"

> The Waterloo Diamonds Baseball Association, an Iowa Non-Profit Corporation (C163105) has $20,000 in an account for Capital Improvements at Municipal Stadium.
>
> The Association will release this money to the City, when an agreement is reached between the Parks Director and the Diamonds, as to exactly what project or projects the funds will be used.
>
> The Association will continue to raise money, but will not commit to any dollar figures, until the City Council approves a yearly $75,000 Capital Improvement Bond for the perpetual improvement of Municipal Stadium.
>
> Sincerely,
> Dan Yates, President
> Waterloo Diamonds Baseball
> Association

"Hardball," they called it. It was a bargaining tactic that in the minors previously had been associated primarily with operators such as Rick Holtzman. It was a tactic that the majors had perfected, most recently, and most notoriously, in Chicago, where the White Sox had been threatening to leave town for a $140 million stadium in St. Petersburg, Florida, until the Illinois State Legislature delivered funding for a new, $150 million Comiskey Park. Now it was a tactic that Yates and Simpson were willing to try. Yes, the ball club faced a significant and potentially fatal fiscal crisis; yes, the ball club was willing to contribute to the funds; yes, it would be nice if pro ball in Waterloo were self-sufficient—and maybe one day, Simpson had told Tagtow, it would be. But for now, the ballpark would have to remain a part of the city's responsibility.

First the ball club sent a letter to its mailing list asking fans to write and call the mayor and City Council. Then Dan Yates sent a letter to the *Courier* responding to news coverage of the most recent Park Board meeting, which Simpson had decided to attend. "Park Board Says Baseball Team Not Cooperating," read the headline; the article mentioned the flyer with the addresses and phone numbers of the Council members and mayor, and quoted a Park Board member as telling Simpson, "It appears as if you want to sidestep us. I don't believe that you folks should be bypassing the park board." Yates's letter ran in late March under the headline, "Baseball as usual?"

> WATERLOO—Waterloo Baseball disputes charges by the Park Board that we are not cooperating with them. The record will show a long history and cooperation with many Waterloo park boards.
>
> The Diamonds are not interested in leaving Waterloo. However, the stockholders of the Diamonds must do what is necessary to protect the franchise. The Diamonds do not own Municipal Stadium. The city of Waterloo does.
>
> We have a good working relationship with Parks Director Rick Tagtow and the City Council. We cannot say the same for the Park Board.
>
> There will be baseball as usual this year (the home opener is April 11, against our arch-rival Cedar Rapids), and we are

confident the city will do all possible to make sure professional minor league baseball continues for the citizens and fans of Northeast Iowa.

Dan Yates, President
Waterloo Diamonds

"Advice to City: Pay or Lose Ballclub" read the banner headline on the front page of the *Courier* on the Sunday of opening weekend, six days after the owners' meeting at which Yates had suggested announcing that the ball club was for sale. What Yates's board wouldn't allow him to do, this article did. *More.* It delivered more background information on the PBA, put the case of Waterloo into the broader context of what other cities had funded, and carried far greater credibility than could any number of ball club owners at a press conference.

"If you don't rebuild it, they will go," the article began, and it went on to suggest that the fate of Kenosha, Wisconsin, might await Waterloo. As recently as 1983 the Kenosha franchise had been located in Wisconsin Rapids, a town of 18,000 even farther north than Appleton. After that season the Minnesota Twins had announced that they would not be returning due to the condition of the playing field; a plumber and former minor league player then bought the club and moved it to his hometown of Kenosha, a city of 77,000 in the southeastern corner of the state. But Simmons Field, situated in a residential neighborhood only blocks off Lake Michigan, was a liability from the start. Early in the season, it suffered frequent snowouts. Later in the season, it suffered fog and cold. The new PBA had simply sealed the franchise's fate.

Enter Eric Margenau. Two months before the article appeared, he had purchased the franchise for approximately $1 million, hoping to perform the same feat of franchise magic in Fort Wayne, Indiana, as he had several years earlier in South Bend. It was a no-lose proposition: Either Kenosha would build him a new stadium, which was highly unlikely, or Fort Wayne would, in which case he would have a new franchise in a city of 175,000. Margenau did extend to Kenosha the courtesy of choosing whether to fund a new facility, but in fact the city's decision was a foregone conclusion: Kenosha was still reeling from the loss of the Chevrolet plant that had sustained the local economy for years, and was struggling to build a new jail, police station and nursing home. ("Kenosha," Waterloo Park Board member Russ Garling had commented at a meeting, "is a sister city to us like you wouldn't believe.") So Margenau announced that the franchise would be moving the following season to Fort Wayne, where local officials had made clear that they could put together a $5.6 million financing package. The 6,000-seat Allen County Memorial Stadium, complete with eight skyboxes and the potential to expand to the 10,000-seat Triple A minimum, and located in the same complex as the Allen County War Memorial Coliseum & Exposition Center, a combination sports arena and convention hall near the interstate on the outskirts of the city, at one end of an enormous commercial strip that already included Indiana's largest mall, would be ready for baseball by the following Opening Day.

"It's a dollar war," Tagtow told the Park Board, "that I'm not sure we can win."

"It's a real sorry state of affairs for baseball," Russ Garling agreed, "and that is that there are too many cities that have come up with angels that have laid out tens of millions of dollars that they've built into grandiose ballparks. Now the majors think that they can bite that hand anywhere they want to go. And they can start dictating. Well, that puts us in a very precarious position. We can't get half a million, let alone ten million. So here we are. See, when you come up with a 1994 idea, that is, that's, boy, that's— unless you get John *Deere's* or someone to shell out ten million for a new ballpark, you're not gonna git *anywhere*."

Shortly after he took office, Al Manning asked Tagtow how much revenue the Diamonds actually generated—not in some long-range, Waterloo-in-the-year-2000 fashion but right now, in a way that registered in the city coffers. For years the ball club had been claiming a local economic impact of $2.495 million based on a dollar turnover rate of seven; could that amount, the new mayor wanted to know, possibly be accurate? Tagtow said he had his doubts but the only way to be sure was to ask an economist. To Tagtow's surprise, the mayor did. Manning met with the director of the Small Business Development Center at the University of Northern Iowa, who wrote back that if the ball club's argument "is based on a multiplier of six or seven, I would strongly argue against using the dollar benefits quoted from such a study as representative of the actual increase we should expect from this project." A multiplier of 1.2 to 1.7, he wrote, would be consistent with reliable studies of baseball franchises. Based on these far more conservative figures, the ball club's annual contribution to the local economy would be, at the most, $600,000—not an insubstantial amount, but in terms of what would actually reach the city government in the form of taxes, and thereby offset what would have left the city government in the form of further ballpark funding, negligible.

Late one afternoon in that dreary season of fiscal bloodletting at City Hall, at a City Council work session—an informal meeting immediately preceding the official City Council proceedings—the City set a preliminary budget for the five-year period that would follow the final installment of the $325,000 in ballpark renovations. Dan Yates attended the meeting, and for the first time in his tenure as president of the ball club, he found himself bearing witness to a long-range budget plan for the City that included no mention of Municipal Stadium.

The first city budget passed under the Al Manning administration had managed to avoid any additional cuts to essential city services while also keeping taxes at the same rate. The day that David Simpson walked the PBA results into Rick Tagtow's office happened to be the day before this new city budget would take effect, yet already the city was projecting a shortfall of $500,000.

In late July, Rick Tagtow was a guest on Kelly Neff's Saturday-morning sports-talk radio show. At one point, Neff asked what work still needed to be done at the ballpark. Tagtow said, "Two big things facing us are, one, a new clubhouse in order to meet the requirements of the Professional Baseball Association [sic], and, second, new rest rooms. We do not met the requirements of professional baseball—nor do we meet the requirements of our fans," he added, laughing.

And how much would this cost?

That question again. It was the question that had been hounding the franchise for as long as Rick Tagtow had been parks director, it was the question that the Professional Baseball Agreement was supposed to settle, and now he had the results of the architect's survey, and he still didn't know the answer. There was no way to tell what it would cost short of authorizing a study—but the last one he had authorized, at a cost to the city of upwards of $15,000 for a clubhouse that would never be built, was sitting on a shelf in his office. What was more, the last of the $325,000 would soon be gone on safety and other structural renovations. Still, he could hazard a rough estimate: "$800,000 to $1 million."

And where was this money going to come from?

Off the air, what Tagtow was saying about the ball club these days was, "Nobody cares about baseball. Even I—'Mr. Baseball Family'—even I don't care. Laying off police officers? I'm callous: $325,000—that's all we can give you. That's the best we can do." Professionally, however, he was more diplomatic. "The City Council has indicated that they don't have that kind of money available," he told Kelly Neff. "That money, I would expect, would have to come from private sources."

"What's messed up baseball in this town," one old-timer in the Zoo Crew said several days later, when conversation turned to Rick Tagtow's appearance on Kelly Neff's show, "is baseball." He tugged his cap decisively. A Grateful Dead logo decorated the front face of the cap; below it, on the bill, he had affixed a Waterloo Diamonds logo. He'd been coming to the park since the 1930s, and he could remember an era when local ball clubs weren't beholden to the major leagues. "Every time we get good prospects, they send 'em up. Let 'em play the year here, 'stead of bouncin' 'em up right away. Then you wouldn't have no"—he glanced at the scoreboard to see how badly the Diamonds were suffering at the moment—"10–4 games. We still had good teams, you'd see crowds out here then. *Then* you wouldn't have to worry about no clubhouse."

From Major League Baseball to the National Association to the Midwest League to the Waterloo front office to the Park Commission to the fans—the business of baseball worked its way down, down, down, until, at last, it reached the bleachers. It communicated itself in radio broadcasts, in newspaper articles and letters to the editor, in appeals for donations arriving in the mail. It communicated itself in the empty stands, in the owners' animated and often-vocal discussions about policy matters in full public view, in the increasingly diverging public personas of the general manager and his assistant. "Hey, Hollywood!" the fans would shout to Jeff Nelson, parading through the stands in his designer shades, and he would throw open his arms and yell back, "My people!" The louder Nelson got, the quieter Simpson grew. The GM had developed a smile that just wouldn't quit. It first appeared around the time of Dan Yates's resignation, and over the months it had grown unsettlingly masklike, exuding an other-worldly calm and inspiring no end of speculation among fans and owners alike as to whether he knew something nobody else knew, or knew nothing and was scared for his job. One band of grand-stand regulars tried to get a little action going on who would come out on top at the end of the season, Simpson or Nelson, but had to abandon the idea because nobody wanted to bet on the GM.

"I hate coming to work in the morning!" Nelson announced one night. He was standing in the aisle between the box seats and the rest of the grandstand, addressing Jerry Klinkowitz and a fan named Tim Wiles. Wiles was a graduate student at the University of Northern Iowa and, it so happened, a former librarian at the Baseball Hall of Fame in Cooperstown. Some nights he would sit with Jerry Klinkowitz and Mildred Boyenga behind home plate and rhapsodize about what it was like to watch the sun set from the empty stands at Cooperstown's Abner Doubleday Field. Wiles grew up in Peoria and had often attended Chiefs games there, but he had been introduced to minor league ball in Waterloo by Klin-kowitz, and tonight Wiles was trying to perform the same favor for a couple of his own friends. They planned to take in a minor league game, go for a walking tour of the field, then head back to Wiles's apartment and watch a video of *Bull Durham*. In the ninth inning, however, as they were preparing to head down the foul line to the gate to the field, they were approached by the assistant general manager, who, in a voice loud enough to reach the back row, described a slight he said he'd suffered from Simpson.

"Hey," Nelson said, "I can make more money than this manag-ing the bar back home."

"You have one of the best jobs in the United States," Wiles said.

"I know I have one of the best jobs in the United States. But I'm working for one of the biggest jerks in the world!"

"You have to be above all this," said Klinkowitz.

Nelson said that everybody he had talked to was behind him. Even the concession workers had pulled him out to the parking lot tonight to tell him that if he goes, they go. Klinkowitz said that running around talking to everybody behind the GM's back might not reflect well on Nelson in some quarters.

"Hey, *they* came to *me*," Nelson said. "Sportschannel Night," he went on, walking away, "he just sat up in the press box. Let's see if he gets any help from me on Funny-Nose-and-Glasses Night!"

"*Be above it*," Klinkowitz called to him, scrambling up to the aisle. He trotted after Nelson.

Wiles watched, then turned to his two guests. "In Peoria," he informed them, "it was an honor when the owner would sit down next to you and talk. Of course, that honor depended on there being a big crowd. Here," he went on, "if you can't get to know one of the owners, you must be completely lacking in social skills."

The game was over by now, and the threesome made their way to the low wall down the third-base side and the gate that opened out to the field. They started down the left-field line at the home bullpen, studying the bench there and the pitching rubber, then continued in a clockwise direction along the warning track. When they reached straightaway center, they paused to shade their eyes, squint into the lights that bracketed the grandstand, and gaze back at the glowing green diamond. Then they headed for the parking lot. As they were cutting across right field, however, they stopped. In a bare patch of grass, they'd discovered what appeared to be a crudely painted grid. They stared until their eyes had adjusted to the contrasting light paint and loamy soil, and they could discern the Xs and Os of a tick-tack-toe match played to a draw.

"I guess," Time Wiles said, ending the dumbfounded silence, "that's what they mean by the game inside the game."

One morning Bill Boesen got up at 3:30 to drive to Indianola because his wife Bev wanted to see a hot-air balloon launch. They arrived by 5:30, in time to watch the balloonists start their day's work. Despite Bill's objections to spending money on a bed when their own was less than two hours away, Bev insisted that they check into a Days Inn. They rested a few hours before returning to watch the balloon launch in the afternoon, then stayed the night.

First thing the following morning, they drove back to Waterloo, but before he could allow himself to address the problems at the ballpark, Boesen had to get to work on a plumbing emergency at home. He soon discovered that he needed a new washer on a faucet in the upstairs bathroom, and he drove over to Cashway, one of the warehouse-style hardware stores that in recent years had appeared on the edge of town. When he couldn't find the kind of washer he needed, he asked a clerk for help. After some searching, the clerk informed Boesen that the store didn't stock the washer he needed. At this point, Boesen found himself shouting. "That's the problem with you big guys! You come along and run the little guys out of business, and they're the ones who carry every last thing!"

The extent of his responsibilities as board president—a post that Dan Yates had filled for years with seeming effortlessness— had lately been dawning on Boesen. It was no wonder that Yates had finally chosen to resign; the presidency had become a job suitable only for somebody who didn't already have one. Even in retirement, Boesen was finding it increasingly difficult to fulfill all the ball club's obligations. Twenty years earlier, he had suffered a heart attack; three times his heart had stopped. Ten years earlier, there had been no work for an electrician in the Waterloo area; Boesen had spent weeks at a time on the road, often out of state, taking work where he could find it. Throughout all these ordeals he'd made promises to Bev and to himself about what his life would be like once he'd reached retirement age. And now that the time had come, he felt a responsibility to set aside at least most mornings, as well as an occasional off day, to his personal life, because Boesen had come to understand that if he let it, the presidency of the ball club could easily become a more than full-time occupation.

He was on the phone to George Spelius nearly every day now, and to Yates, too, seeking advice, gathering information, trying to figure out whether San Diego would be renewing its affiliation with Waterloo and what to do if it didn't. Then the rest of the owners were on the phone to *him,* complaining about Simpson or Nelson or one another. Afternoons he spent running errands for the ball club. From the hardware store he drove over to a lumber-yard to discuss the construction of a protective fence around the scoreboard, an expense that he supposed the ball club was going to have to absorb after all. Then he headed to the ballpark, where fresh worries always waited—the stands in need of sweeping, the fans complaining because the advertised gate giveaway on "Baseball Card Day" had turned out to be last year's surplus. Today it was a letter from the National Association reminding all its members that according to the new Professional Baseball Agreement, every ball club had to submit a copy of its stadium lease, a document which, in the case of Waterloo, didn't exist.

"Come on, Jason!" Boesen bellowed from the stands that evening, trying to encourage Hardtke at the plate. "Put it in the graveyard!" He gave his beard a furious scratching. "We can't bring nobody home," he muttered.

After a moment, Bev said, "Can't bring *any*body home."

The ball games themselves Boesen was lucky to follow these days. Arms crossed, beard sunk deep against his chest, a roosting bird puffing its plumage at nightfall, Boesen would sit on his customary grandstand bench and monitor the comings and goings of his fellow owners, his GM, his assistant GM, and however many fans there were, not filling the rows and rows of empty seats. Not that he was above the fray. When the scoreboard blinked out during one game in the ninth inning, and the PA announcer joked, "Okay, who forgot to pay the electric bill?" it was Boesen who yelled, "Simpson!" When Captain Dynamite and Dusty Fireball made a return appearance at a discount rate and only 400 fans showed up because Simpson had neglected to take out an ad in the *Courier,* it was Boesen who, even as the waves from the blast were still rebounding and rebounding between the grandstand and the outfield fence, turned to face some fellow owners on the back benches of the grandstand, raised four fingers on each hand, and shouted, *"Four hundred dollars!"* He didn't need anyone to remind him—though Bev often did, anyway—that he didn't want to be remembered as the president who was running the ball club when Waterloo lost professional baseball.

The more he thought about it, the more Boesen had come to accept the inevitability—if not the wisdom—of Russ Garling's idea. He had concluded that if the ball club were going to raise money for the stadium, it would have to seek money outside the city government; and if he had any doubts, they were dispelled by a newspaper article that appeared two days before the most recent owners' meeting. On Monday of that week, a local lumber merchant had appeared before the City Council to announce that he was donating $200 to the city and to challenge 5,000 other citizens to follow his lead and contribute $100 each to offset the city's new budget deficit. By Friday of the same week, an article on the front page of the *Courier* reported, the city had received more than $2,000 in donations, and the lumber merchant had announced plans to reward donors with a bumper sticker reading, "I ♡ 'Loo, so I gave $100 too." Three weeks into the new fiscal year, the City of Waterloo had become a charity.

Boesen outlined his plan for his fellow owners one evening at the ballpark while the team was out of town. He started the meeting by passing around copies of the PBA inspection results. "We got this big sheet, which is—what it is," he said. "A big sheet." Then Simpson arrived. The board had disinvited front-office staff from recent meetings, other than for brief appearances, and now Simpson provided a business update. As he spoke, the distinct popping of gunfire started sounding from somewhere beyond the outfield wall. Simpson forged ahead. He said that he'd been thinking about the board's request to put more bodies in the seats, and that he'd been hoping to schedule several promotions: UNI Night; Mug Night; Funny-Nose-and-Glasses Night; Baseball Card Night. Simpson said, "I wanted to see what your-all's feeling was."

There was a silence, except for a report from somewhere beyond the center-field fence. Simpson flinched.

"This year's cards," Boyenga asked, "or last year's?"

"Them people were hot," Boesen chuckled.

Simpson's smile froze. "The ad *said* '1991.' "

After Simpson left the premises, Boesen introduced his plan: hiring a full-time fund-raiser. What he was proposing was a departure from the way the board usually considered the matter of fund-raising, which, beyond petitioning the city for money, consisted of every once in a while dispatching Dan Yates or David Simpson to talk to a person or group. Instead, he said, what the ball club needed was someone who could manage the stadium renovation fund on a full-time basis—producing a promotional brochure, identifying and meeting with every likely individual or corporate donor in the vicinity, cultivating contacts throughout the business community. In short, someone who could develop a fund-raising campaign that was truly professional. "It's gonna cost us bucks," Boesen said. "But it takes money to make money."

He went on. He said he thought that Jeff Nelson might be just the man for the job. Boesen acknowledged that some tension existed between Simpson and Nelson, but he suggested that by dividing their duties so they didn't overlap, the board could salvage both their jobs. Under his plan, Simpson would continue to run the ball club while Nelson would handle the fund-raising program. "So," Boesen said, "what do you think?"

Boyenga was sitting to one side, shaking her head. "I'm confused here," she said. "Are we talking about donations?"

"Yes, yes," said Boesen. "To feed that capital-improvement thing. So what we got to do is get someone who can go into these places and spend some time. This isn't a five-minute deal. You know Jeff's got a good palaver. He's no five-minute-meeting guy."

Now it was Lana Morgan's turn. She was one of the owners who had come out to the ballpark as a kid, drifted away, then returned once she had kids of her own. Every so often she'd register a complaint about one thing or another at the ballpark with her friend Bill Boesen, who was involved in the organization. "You don't like it," he'd tell her, "*you* get up there"—referring to the next meeting of the ball club's directors. Once, she did, and that was that. She was one of them. "So Dave would be"—she paused now and hazarded a guess—"out of the picture for advertising."

"*No,*" said Boesen.

"So this would be"—another pause—"just fund-raising."

"*Yes.*"

"And Dave would still do advertising."

"Yes! We're not *talking* about advertising." Suddenly Boesen spun toward the outfield. "The hell *is* that?"

Dan Yates said, "I think somebody's shooting birds."

"I wish they'd get over here," Boesen said, turning back to the board but regarding the rafters with some suspicion.

The discussion ended some time later with the board deciding that the public-relations committee should meet that coming Sunday to discuss Boesen's idea. At Yates's suggestion, Boesen agreed that he should first set up a meeting to explore these possibilities with Simpson and Nelson alone—both of them, at the same time, in order to avoid any appearance of favoritism. Then Boesen sighed mightily. "And if this doesn't work out?" he wondered aloud. He answered his own question. "Then I'll have to talk to them," he said. "And I'll hate that."

After the meeting had adjourned, several owners stayed behind, standing in a small circle under the grandstand. Boesen rolled up the window on the beer-vending station, grabbed a stack of blue plastic cups, and started running them under the tap, angling the flow expertly to avoid too large a head. When he'd handed everybody a full cup, he reached into a cardboard box and tossed some bags of peanuts on the counter. The board members roared their approval and started shredding plastic. The shouts and the shell-snaps ricocheted from every direction, bouncing around the ancient concrete and steel. Boesen came out from behind the counter and scraped a metal trash barrel across the concrete to catch the droppings.

Boyenga mentioned that since her retirement she'd been studying her Social Security information. "My last year at Miller Medical," she said, "I made half what I made at Rath at the end."

"That's right," said Boesen. "I'm not surprised. People around here used to make good money. Seventeen dollars an hour. Twenty."

"And they *spent* it *here,*" Boyenga said gloomily.

"Aw, hell." Boesen picked up his valise, plopped it on the counter, and started clawing through it. He said that lately he'd been looking into methods of clearing the pigeons from the ballpark rafters, and he'd brought along some brochures he had wanted to discuss with the board, but he'd forgotten about them until now. He located the flyers in his bag. From one he read aloud about a device using ultrasonic signals. Another he held up so that everybody could see a picture of the product: a model of an owl—an especially glowering owl, judging from its likeness—that purportedly would spook its natural prey. Above the owl were the words "Terror Eyes."

His fellow owners burst out laughing. Boesen's shoulders sagged, and he turned the flyer so he could see it, and then he laughed, too. Then the discussion turned, boomingly, boisterously, back to business.

"I think Dave's doing a terrible job," one owner said.

"I'll tell you this," said another. "Jeff has wanted Dave's job from the first day he walked in that office."

"Jeff wants to be a GM this September—if not here, somewhere."

"Ol' Dave lost his spirit in April."

"He lost it last year!" This was Klinkowitz. "He came in here when we were going bankrupt—"

"We were never going *bankrupt*," Boyenga interrupted.

"We were! Don't you remember when Dan laid out the PBA guidelines for us? We thought we'd be broke! And Dave performed an economic miracle. And in business you reward somebody who comes in when you think you're going bankrupt and turns it around and makes a profit—you reward that person with a piece of the company."

Then somebody said that if Jeff Nelson or any other fund-raiser found someone willing to contribute a substantial sum toward the renovation of the stadium, then the board might have to surrender a seat anyway.

"*Now* it's gettin' down to the nitty-gritty," Boesen said. He'd been silent for some time, letting the others speak with a lack of inhibition he only wished they would show during the meetings themselves. Now his fellow owners turned to him. He cocked an eyebrow. "Do you want to give up a share of one-point-two-five million dollars?"

Boesen allowed the question to hang in the air a moment. After all the shouts and echoes and peanuts and beer, the sudden stillness under the grandstands seemed unnatural. The silence hummed. Then Boesen broke into a broad grin, gripped a flyer in both hands, and raised the piece of paper high over his head. At the end of his arms, the sheet was shaking with his laughter and his rage.

"Terror Eyes!" Boesen yelled.

Everyone looked at the owl. The owl looked back.

9

Rumors of his arrival preceded Joe McIlvaine into Waterloo by several weeks, as befit not only a baseball dignitary, but a potential shaper of destinies. He walked through the ballpark gates on a Monday evening, and he wouldn't be leaving town until Saturday morning, and the promise of the presence of the executive vice president of baseball operations and general manager of the San Diego Padres in a box seat behind home plate for such a leisurely stretch signaled the possibility of an imminent resolution to at least two questions—for the players, *How am I doing?*, and for the owners, *Will we have an affiliation next year?*

Joe McIlvaine was then in his second season with the Padres. After spending ten years in supporting positions with the New York Mets, in part helping to assemble the formidable teams of the mid-1980s, including the 1986 World Champions, McIlvaine had taken the job of general manager with the San Diego Padres following the 1990 season. That summer, Tom Werner, a television producer who had hit the jackpot with syndication sales from *Roseanne* and *Cosby,* had led a group of fifteen investors in purchasing the Padres from Joan Kroc, widow of McDonald's magnate Ray. They hired McIlvaine to work the same magic in San Diego that he'd helped work in New York, and they communicated to him through his own three-year, multimillion-dollar contract, and through the generous salaries of other Padres executives, that money was no object.

For McIlvaine, the new job and new title at the start of a new regime was an opportunity to remake an organization in his own image. That December, during his first Winter Meetings as a GM, McIlvaine had provided spectacular relief from the otherwise all-consuming negotiations between the majors and the minors on a new Professional Baseball Agreement by engineering an old-fashioned, four-player, superstar-for-superstar swap: the Padres'

Roberto Alomar and Joe Carter for the Toronto Blue Jays' Fred McGriff and Tony Fernandez—the kind of talent-for-talent deal, McIlvaine liked to say, that general managers used to make all the time. That trade, however, turned out to be less a harbinger of a new era than the last hurrah of the old.

In recent years, the GM's job at the major league level had changed as surely as it had in the minors. Major league baseball had reached a point in its evolution where ownership had passed from the original, family-business style of management to the modern corporate structure. Billion-dollar broadcast and merchandising revenues, hundred-million-dollar expansion franchise fees, and lavishly favorable stadium leases had irrevocably altered the industry. Unlike the old generation of owners, who regarded baseball as an exclusive club and a hobby, the new generation treated it as a business that had enormous profit potential but was laboring under an antiquated philosophy and methodology. The extent of specialization that front offices in the minors had undergone—the addition of departments, and department heads, to handle ticket sales, marketing, stadium operations, media relations—represented a fraction of the expansion of responsibilities among front-office executives at the major league level. Along these lines, the GM's responsibilities had both narrowed and deepened. Once former players or owners' cronies who prided themselves on masterminding shrewd deals, major league GMs now needed legal or business backgrounds as well as similarly educated support staffs just to interpret all the fine points of a contract—salary disbursements, incentive clauses, no-trade restrictions, arbitration eligibility, and so on—even before they could begin to take a player's ability and health into account. (The collapse of the reserve clause and the rise of arbitration and free agency had revolutionized salary structures for the players, but it was the new revenues that determined what the limits of the salary structures would be.) McIlvaine continued to place his faith in an old-fashioned ability to spot talent, and in March of 1992 he engineered a deal that had the makings of one of the all-time great highway-robbery trades, and that should have been cause for season-long celebration: pitcher Ricky Bones and two minor leaguers in exchange for Milwaukee's Gary Sheffield, a heretofore .194 hitter currently contending for the Triple Crown with a .327 average, 18 home runs and 64 RBI. But by the time of McIlvaine's visit to Waterloo, it was already a bittersweet memory, because the owners recently had put him on notice: Money was an object, after all.

"Money," McIlvaine was known to moan, "is the bane of our existence." A former seminarian and still a devout Catholic, McIlvaine had a mystical, overtly religious faith in baseball; he believed that baseball was like the Church: built to last. He felt that baseball had grown on a foundation so strong that it could withstand anything that any of his contemporaries might do to it. McIlvaine had ended his playing career in the Midwest League, in Clinton in 1973, after four years as a pitcher in the Detroit organization, and when he walked into the ballpark in Waterloo, what he remembered was how the Midwest League had "the longest trains in the world"; how players in Clinton learned to arrive at the ballpark early to catch the bus for a road trip because the railroad tracks cut off the stadium from the rest of the city; how Jim Leyland, then the twenty-eight-year-old manager at Clinton and now the manager of the Pittsburgh Pirates, would order the team bus to pull out of the parking lot precisely on time even if some of the players were only across the tracks, stuck, waiting for an endless freight train to pass. *That* was baseball, McIlvaine believed. Lately, in what was being widely interpreted as a veiled reference to a group of owners in San Diego who learned too late the costs of running a major league organization, McIlvaine had been saying that he wanted to see people getting involved in baseball "because they love this game," and what he saw at both the minor and major league levels was people buying clubs for "the wrong motivations"—but that he thought baseball could withstand that, too. "Baseball," he'd said, "is bigger than all of us."

The All-Star Game at Jack Murphy Stadium earlier in the month, an event that far in advance had seemed to hold the promise of a public-relations triumph—a national showcase for the new San Diego Padres and their new GM—had degenerated into a travesty, a cavalcade of doomsday scenarios, on television and in newspapers, for the organization and McIlvaine's job: that the Padres had lost $6 million so far this year, that the organization stood to lose a total of $9 million for the year, that McIlvaine was under orders to start cutting the payroll. But cut . . . what? His team was in contention. By the final week of July, the Padres were in second place in the National League West, two and a half games behind Atlanta. But cut he must, and so McIlvaine wound up spending most of his time in Waterloo holed up in a Holiday Inn, short-shrifting his family and his farm club for the sake of the 11:00 P.M. Friday, July 31, interleague trading deadline.

McIlvaine arrived in Waterloo on a Monday evening and he left on a Saturday morning but all he saw were two games in their entirety. He skipped batting practice on the days when he did go to the ballpark, and he skipped the ballpark altogether on the night of the trading deadline. The Diamonds lost both games McIlvaine did attend, including a 14–1 blowout in which Jose Davila's ERA hit 9.99 and Kevin Farlow once more moved over from the infield to the pitching mound to finish the game. Every evening the players stole glances toward the box seats, waiting for a sign of any kind from the person most responsible for their professional future. (For John Abercrombie, it came on the evening of a rainout, when McIlvaine passed him on the way out of a restaurant where they both had happened to be dining, clapped him on the shoulder, and said, "Good to see you, Derek"—apparently mistaking him for Derek Vaughn, another African-American on the team.) And every evening Boesen approached him, either at the ballpark or over the phone, with a dinner invitation for the following night, but every night McIlvaine had another excuse: he had already promised to take his wife and three children out to dinner; he would be working on the phone all evening in his hotel room; he'd be gone.

Still, it would have been a mistake to assume that McIlvaine's seeming inattentiveness meant that he didn't have a chance to reach at least cursory conclusions. McIlvaine's reputation as a front-office tactician rested in no small part on his scouting prowess. After finishing his pro career with Clinton, McIlvaine had spent much of the 1970s working for three major league organizations as a Latin American scout, and in 1980 he had joined the Mets as director of scouting. In his estimation, scouting and player development constituted the bedrock of a strong organization. When he used to scout high school or amateur games, he would sit near the players' parents, or, better, their girlfriends. One-on-one, playing dumb, he'd ask questions such as "That guy over there, you know anything about him?" Sometimes he didn't even have to ask. On a good day, he could leave a ballpark knowing everything he needed to know without having said a word. McIlvaine, sitting with his wife and kids behind home in Waterloo, could make do with two games, if he must.

One night during his visit, a Cedar Rapids runner was leading off third with less than two outs when the batter hit a pop fly to center. The runner on third tagged up.

"Here we go," McIlvaine said.

It was a situation that, depending on what happened next, might reveal all manner of insights into the defensive abilities of any number of Waterloo players. Almost imperceptibly, McIlvaine leaned forward. The ball carried to medium-deep left-center, where Keith McKoy—an eighth-round pick from the June 1990 draft—caught it. If the fly had carried to the wall, McKoy could have conceded the run and lobbed the baseball back to the infield; but the ball had traveled only midway out on the outfield grass. There might be a chance for a play at the plate, but only if McKoy could throw a strike to the shortstop Scott Bream, who had edged onto the outfield grass in anticipation of McKoy's throw, and then only if Bream could relay a strike to the catcher. It was McIlvaine's belief—and among baseball observers, he was far from alone in this contention—that it was a rare player today who knew how to throw. McIlvaine once had said that the Dominican Republic was his idea of the best place in the world to spend a week. Down there, he said, they play baseball with anything, everywhere, and all the time. And that was the only way to learn how to throw, he'd said: throw, throw, throw.

Now, McKoy threw. The ball reached Bream on a bounce.

"Okay," Joe McIlvaine said, leaning back in his seat. "McKoy—no arm there."

One hazy Monday afternoon, two of the ball club's owners made the two-hour drive to Des Moines to inspect the new Sec Taylor Stadium. Ken Bergmeier and Don Blau had joined the board (along with Jeff Copeland) during the owners' latest—and presumably last—recruitment drive, in 1987. At that time, the old ownership was looking for new blood, and Dan Yates held a meeting in his basement to weed out those hopefuls who wanted to be involved in baseball "just for the glory," as he put it, from potential owners who took their baseball to heart. (Interlopers were to be further discouraged by being required to pay $1,000 for their shares of ball club stock, as a gesture of good faith.) Both Blau and Bergmeier collected baseball memorabilia for fun and profit, and they passed a good deal of time on the drive this afternoon trading genial boasts, like baseball cards, about sports legends they had each encountered personally. Their voices, hard and hollow, carried them along the corn-bordered county roads that honored the endless gridwork of cropland between Waterloo and the state capital, first due south and due west, then south and west again. It was what they had in common: an appreciation of baseball as partly pleasure, partly business, and partly the pleasure of business: the sound of their own voices.

They were entrepreneurs. As such, they represented a new way of thinking about Waterloo and about baseball. For them, the city had never smoked. They had never owed their livelihood or their life to Rath Packing or John Deere, and memories of an era when the ballpark sold out night after night didn't cloud their judgment of what professional baseball in Waterloo could and should be today. Bergmeier ran a salvage company and flower business; at the ballpark, he preferred to sit with the scouts behind home plate, trading gossip about front-office politics in the big leagues. Blau, in addition to teaching at a junior high, was a partner in a sporting-goods store in downtown Waterloo; he bought every book he could find on the business of baseball and subscribed to magazines such as *Skybox,* whose slogan was "The Business of Baseball." They might not always agree, but Bergmeier and Blau proceeded under the assumption that if any members of the board were qualified to traffic in the commercial considerations necessary to save the ball club, they were.

A week earlier, they had prevailed upon the Des Moines box office to set aside free tickets to tonight's doubleheader for some visiting owners of the Waterloo club. Now they convinced a guard to let them park in the VIP lot by the ballpark entrance. Bergmeier did the talking. Blau did the driving.

"Yeah, I'm a friend of the owner." Bergmeier flashed his National Association membership card.

"And I'm a friend of Phil Wrigley," Blau muttered as he stepped on the gas. "I chew his gum."

The new Sec Taylor Stadium had risen during the off-season on the site of the old Sec Taylor Stadium, and it had succeeded in attracting not only the usual Iowa Cubs crowd, which came to see Class AAA players only a phone call and a one-hour plane ride away from Wrigley Field, but baseball fans from a several-hundred-mile radius whose interest lay more in the stadium itself. The Kansas City firm of Hellmuth, Obata and Kassabaum—or HOK—had emerged as baseball's architects of the moment, if not the decade. Unlike the previous generation of architects, which had favored giant, generic, artificial-grass, multiuse facilities, often in suburban settings, HOK and its kind designed stadiums that harkened back to an earlier era of ballpark architecture, preserving the awkward dimensions of old, providing seating close to the action, respecting geographical idiosyncrasies, and utilizing building materials complementary to neighboring architecture. In the Midwest League, HOK's projects had included the renovation of John O'Donnell Stadium in Davenport and the design of Coveleski Stadium in South Bend; in the majors, the new Comiskey Park, renovations at Wrigley Field, and, most notably, Baltimore's Oriole Park at Camden Yards. Then in its first year of operation, Camden Yards already was famous for drawing record crowds that were as curious about the facilities as the ball games. On a smaller scale, the same phenomenon was happening in Des Moines.

When Philadelphia's Shibe Park opened on April 12, 1909, it signaled the end of the nineteenth century's makeshift-wooden-park era and the start of a new concrete-and-steel, multitiered, built-to-last era for a new century. Three other examples of the style followed that same year—Forbes Field in Pittsburgh, League Park in Cleveland and Sportsman's Park in St. Louis—and then nine more over the next six years—Comiskey Park, the Polo Grounds, Ebbets Field, Fenway and Crosley and Wrigley: all the names that, in time, would come to evoke a distinctly urban, industrial, northeastern, predominantly blue-collar setting, oases of green in landscapes of gray: diamonds in the rough. The next generation of stadiums arose at a time those same cities were starting to show their ages, and the architecture reflected one widespread sentiment toward urban decay: Pretend it wasn't there, either by fleeing to the city limits and looking like a mall, or, if a structure needed to be located in the old downtown for political reasons, by having as little to do with the surroundings as possible (often by looking like a mall).

Sec Taylor, like many examples of the new generation of stadiums, was a throwback to the old urban ballpark. It was part of a conscious effort to reinvigorate the center of the city, serving as an economic anchor for a neighborhood on the skids. Despite the Des Moines metropolitan area's population of 350,000, small by Class AAA standards, the new Sec Taylor in its first season was outdrawing almost every other Class AAA franchise and had become one of the city's major tourist attractions. In reconceiving Sec Taylor, HOK had been working with a site in one of the city's oldest districts, at the confluence of the Des Moines and Raccoon rivers. The building's putty and red brick echoed the look and feel of the warehouses in the area as well as the downtown office buildings in the near distance. As at most ballparks, the front gate faced west, but at this ballpark the plaza immediately inside the gate was broken by pillars of pinkish brick that soared to a substantial height, so that on summer evenings the setting sun created an effect that architects call "God's fingers." The interplay between the ample light and solemn columns in fact suggested the entrance to a cathedral, a place to stop and collect oneself before passing from the secular world into the house of worship.

"If people in Waterloo could see this," Blau said.

"Yeah," said Bergmeier.

"It would have to be scaled down—"

"Yeah, yeah."

"—and you don't need that"—Blau pointed to the Hall of Fame shop—"and those food courts over there are nice, but . . ." He shook his head. "It's too bad we got all that damn politics and crap to get anything done. Hell, we can't even get our mesh up."

A young woman holding an ice-cream cone drifted past, and the two men marched off to buy some food.

The debate that preceded the construction of Sec Taylor had not, in fact, been free of politics, but in the end the approximately $13 million cost had been divided among the ball club's owners, private investors, and, mostly, government funds that voters had

approved as part of a countywide referendum on overall improvements to the area's parks system. Under the referendum, a vote for
the playground down the block counted as a vote for the new Sec
Taylor Stadium as well.

It was a strategy that had been under consideration in Waterloo. For some months now, Sammie Dell, the alderman who lived
in the ballpark's ward and who served informally as the ball club's
advocate on the City Council, had been urging that the fate of the
stadium be put to a public vote. Two years earlier, before the new
PBA came along to complicate matters, Dell had told Dan Yates at
a Park Board meeting, "I honestly feel—and I'm not speaking for
the Council, I'm speaking for me—that if you want to do something, you've got to get it done within the next year. Because you
don't know *what* council's going to be here two years from now."
He had been wrong about the Council—who would have guessed
it was Bernie McKinley himself who was politically vulnerable?—
but he had been right about the public mood. Now Dell had been
making much the same argument again, though with even greater
impatience: that the next city elections would reflect an even more
pronounced shift in the public sentiment, and therefore that the
time for the ball club to act was now—though this time not by
going through the mayor and Council, but by taking the case directly to the voters themselves.

If the election of Al Manning had come to symbolize anything,
at least in the hindsight his half a year in office afforded, it wasn't
a flat-out rejection of taxes. Rather, it was a rejection of who had
gotten to decide what those taxes would be and where that money
would go. Over and over, this was the message of the protesters at
the City Council budget hearings in the spring; it had been the
message of Kathy Oberle at the City Council meeting in April,
where she used the debate on stadium improvements to wave a
long list of municipal bonds in the air: Let the voters decide, issue
by issue. Highway construction—yes or no? Decorative street
lamps downtown—yes or no? Ballpark renovations, or even a
new stadium—yes or no?

No—at least, not the ballpark alone. In the present political
climate, it wasn't realistic to expect that a referendum to bring a
playing facility up to the standards of professional baseball would
pass. For Dell, however, the question of the ballpark wasn't a mat-

ter of saving pro ball, anyway. "That's where I disagree," he once said about the ball club's owners' insistence that they would never willingly relinquish the franchise. "If somebody came along and offered them the right amount of money, they'd sell. This is America. Hell, we used to be into selling people. Don't tell me they wouldn't sell a *baseball team.*" Given the changes that the business of baseball and the economy of the city had undergone even in the past couple of years, as he'd said both at City Council meetings and in private conversations with the ball club's directors, he'd resigned himself to the possibility of Waterloo losing professional baseball. Like everyone else, he was always quick to say he'd hate to see it happen, and, as much as Rick Tagtow and maybe even Bernie McKinley, he'd been responsible for making sure the City Council passed the ballpark funding that had ensured the ball club was still in town. Even then, though, it wasn't pro ball that had concerned him so much as the ballpark itself: the city's showcase baseball diamond, and one that happened to be located on the northeast side of town. "If that facility is gone," he'd say, "that's another blow to our community."

In 1955, at the age of eight, Sammie Dell and his mother and six brothers and sisters took the train from Phillips, Mississippi, to Waterloo to join his father, who two years earlier had come north looking for work, and finding it, at Rath. Now Dell had a degree in sociology and a seat on the City Council, and he'd become one of the severest critics of the city's distribution of wealth. (He was also dean of student affairs at Hawkeye Tech, where, that summer, he'd hung a quote from the movie *Unforgiven* on his office wall: "Okay, so what did these guys do? Cheat at cards, cut up someone, or spit on a rich fellow?") In recent years, he'd watched as the highway projects along the southern end of town had fueled a mini-industry of construction and development—shopping centers, hotels, restaurants, fast food joints, the dog track, an industrial park—while, by comparison, the Northeast Side got nothing. Or less: The tax money that fed the building boom at one end of town, sending greater advantages to the side of the city that already had more, was money that didn't go toward city services elsewhere.

"That's a hell of a lot of money," Dell once said about the city's $15 million (so far) commitment to highway construction. "I'm thinking we could have spent some of that on recreation. The city doesn't have a recreational plan. There is no plan for how do we link together the pools, the golf courses, the riverfront, the baseball, the hockey. Every year at budget time the same discussions come up—for years, for *years*."

Sammie Dell's suggestion was a vision to rival Bernie McKinley's, one that placed as high a premium on Waterloo's "human infrastructure" as the former mayor's had on the "physical infrastructure." The ballpark would be only a single element (along with any number of other worthy projects, on the northeast side and elsewhere) in a comprehensive overhaul of the city's parks and recreation facilities, which, Dell argued, had deteriorated to the point that voters might willingly spend money on them. "They want to know: 'If we spend $15 million, what are we going to get? Am I going to be able to take my boat down to the river? Is my kid going to be able to go to a water slide near Waterloo without having to drive up to Cedar Falls? Are my golf courses going to be maintained? Will I have adequate tennis courts? Are the park bathrooms going to be safe and clean?' If you tell them that, people want that type of stuff. They want that more than they want the damn highway comin' through town." Then, softly, "But I'm the only one who thinks that."

Certainly the new mayor, the Park Board, Rick Tagtow and the ball club owners didn't. A simple majority of the voters might be difficult enough to muster, but a referendum would need 60 percent to pass. The owners had discussed the possibility of supporting such a measure during their April debate on the future of the franchise, but the failure of a referendum was too great a risk to contemplate. In the absence of public support—or, more to the point, in the presence of public rejection—what possible justification could they then mount if the time ever came that they had to approach private sources for stadium funding?

Now that the time had come. "A de facto referendum" was what Rick Tagtow often called the idea of a private fund-raising campaign for the ballpark and, especially in an era when public funds were no longer available, it did serve the same issue-by-issue, once-and-for-all, yes-or-no function. It also presented the same hurdle, one as wide as the river. From their vantage point twenty or so rows up on the first base side at Sec Taylor, Blau and

Bergmeier could study the giant quilt of faces fanning to their left, around home and down the third-base line. They passed the first game of the doubleheader pointing out the plentiful young couples, pointing out the huddles of young men in suits, pointing out the whiteness almost without exception.

"In Waterloo," Blau said, "nobody wants to come downtown."

"Yeah," said Bergmeier.

"Nobody wants to come to our ballpark. We're in a good spot for the blacks, and even they don't come out."

"Yeah, yeah."

The ballpark in Waterloo occupied a twilight zone in the city. It was close enough to downtown to suffer by association for those who never went there anymore, yet far enough upriver to seem remote for those who did. A location that used to be considered central had become practically, if not geographically, peripheral when the city spread to the south and west in the decades after World War II. Waterloo Municipal Stadium now stood on a neither/nor patch of land that rendered it not so much a common meeting ground between both sides of the river as an outpost for either. Bounded by a cemetery, a railroad track and, on two sides, a city park that itself ended at a river, the ballpark was isolated physically even from those who lived and worked nearby. For those who didn't, the ballpark suffered from a psychological isolation that was even greater.

Throughout the state, "Waterloo" was a euphemism. In Waterloo, "the East Side" served much the same purpose. The Negroes who migrated north to Waterloo from Mississippi to act as unwitting scabs in a railroad strike had settled originally in a small triangular district next to the tracks on the east side of town. As other migrants from Mississippi followed over the next few decades, especially after Deere and Rath started hiring blacks, this settlement inevitably spilled over its narrow borders. Yet even when the percentage of the city's population that was black had grown sufficient to distinguish Waterloo as having the highest black concentration in the state (12.1 percent, according to the 1990 census), the settlement stayed, almost without exception, in one area on one side of the river. Whether the widespread assumption was true that squalid living conditions, vice, and violence proliferated on one side of town with the tacit approval of the other—"It was always very convenient for the power structure," as one progressive civic leader once said of the city's problems, "if you know you're going to have them, let's keep them *there*"—the resulting division couldn't have been starker. A recent city study had found that in the two-square-mile area east and north of downtown, 46 percent of the houses were "dilapidated" or "deteriorated." Prostitution and gambling were problems that confined themselves primarily to the East Side. Gangs and drugs were problems that confined themselves primarily to the East Side. When National Guard helicopters and choking black smoke, twin symbols of big-city unrest in the 1960s, filled the skies over Waterloo, they were East Side skies.

"The East Side" as euphemism, of course, didn't refer to the entire area east of the river—a side of town, after all, that at one time included the city's main department store and still housed such downtown institutions as the old Black's building, the Chamber of Commerce, the county courthouse, and City Hall, and that contained neighborhoods that were white or racially mixed. It didn't even always refer only to the black population; sometimes the East Side meant the rough side, or the poor side. Still, the East Side was "the East Side," and that's where the ballpark was, nearly a mile up the river from the downtown business district, and two blocks over from the St. Vincent de Paul Thrift Shop and the Broadway Pawn & Gun. To the East Side of town, the ballpark might be merely inconvenient or even unaffordable, but to the West Side, it was invisible.

Between games of the doubleheader, Bergmeier and Blau talked their way past the usher guarding the private elevator to the Sec Taylor luxury boxes. Slowly Blau and Bergmeier strolled down the carpeted hallway that ran past the doors to the private suites. Trying not to look conspicuous, they stopped every so often to press their faces against a door window. They saw sofas, stools and neon sculptures, wood paneling and wet bars, menus and mini-fridges, and, at the far end of the rooms, rows of cushioned seats that looked down on the box seats and the field. They strolled on, and when a young waitress holding a tray of drinks drifted past, they took the elevator back down, bought a couple of ice-cream cones, and hit the road.

Throughout most of its history, baseball had enjoyed its greatest popularity among the working class, making the sport a natural match for the industrial towns of the prairie. It was in Des Moines, in fact, in early May of 1930, that this match grew even more intimate with the installation of lights for professional baseball's first night game. Waterloo followed suit only six weeks later, on June 16, and for the next fifty years an evening at the ballpark remained a staple of factory family life. When the factories cut back or closed and people left town; when those who stayed had to take new jobs at lower pay; when both halves of a couple went to work and took home less than what one person would have made in the old days—when fans by the thousands stopped having time or money for the ballpark, the stands emptied. The "respect-for-the-ticket" philosophy that David Simpson espoused, and that the ball club owners embraced, however reluctantly, had succeeded in eliminating much of whatever audience remained from the lower half of the economic spectrum. The question now was not simply whether new fans would show up, but whether new fans from the upper half of the economic spectrum would show up. They hadn't last year, and they hadn't in the first half of this season—and, as the second half of the season reached its midpoint, they still hadn't. Were they not there, or were they not there in sufficient numbers, or were they there in sufficient numbers but unreachable? And what if they *were* reached?

"We need the money people," Blau said on the drive home, "but if we're going to get them interested, we have to bring them out to the ballpark, and what are they going to see but this decrepit thing? They don't want to put their money into something that looks like that."

"It scares me," Bergmeier said, "what's happening to this club."

They drove on in the dark, retracing the route home along the lonely roads of central Iowa, their voices keeping them company, soft yet insistent, like a weak radio signal. In time a glow appeared on the horizon, then fanned across the sky, announcing a city: Waterloo. Just south of town, in Hudson, Blau pulled off the highway and bounced his van down a side street until he was even with Bergmeier's house.

A light was on. Crickets were humming. In the front seat, Berg-meier hesitated, shaking his head.

"Aww, baseball will change," Blau said. "But as long as it has that ice cream, it won't be so bad."

One morning, Champ received a phone call at home from the brass in San Diego. The previous evening he had neglected to in-clude the next day's starting pitcher on the report he had faxed to the front office. Now San Diego wanted to know who that pitcher might be. Champ still didn't know. He didn't want to call Treanor at the hotel where he was staying with his mother and two kids, but Champ had no choice: the pitching situation had deteriorated past the crisis point, and San Diego wanted answers. Lately Champ had been spending a lot of his time in the dugout during games asking Treanor which pitchers they could push today, but it almost didn't matter, because all the pitchers were beat now, they were all suffering abuse.

Later that day, at the ballpark, Champ tried to tell Treanor that the pitching problems weren't his fault and that San Diego knew he wasn't to blame, but Treanor shrugged off the manager's assur-ances. The pitching coach had sunk into a chair in a corner of the coaches' office, as he did every day just before the game, but for once he'd dropped his usual grim demeanor. "You know," Treanor said, "if it wasn't for knowing my kids would be coming in, I don't know how I would have gotten through this season. The next off-day, we're all going to Adventureland." He allowed himself a smile. "And tomorrow I'm taking my son over to see the Field of Dreams."

The office had entered the ritualistic part of the day, that imme-diately pregame period when each creature involved himself in some private habit. Champ was rubbing black polish into his shoes. Maxwell was checking supplies on the upper shelf in his dressing stall. Jack Grandy, the clubhouse manager, was sitting, legs crossed, trying to thread dental floss through a needle—an old clubhouse trick. Floss was the same color as a home uniform, and sturdier than thread. Beckett's uniform rested on Gran-dy's lap.

"Usually it's good when the San Diego personnel come out here," Champ was saying, "because it means more to see what's goin' on for yourself than to hear about it from me every day over the phone." He held one shoe out at arm's length for inspection. Then he placed it on the carpeting and picked up the other. "But McIlvaine didn't get the true picture, because we had that one rainout, and he had one night in his hotel room on the phone. So he only had two nights at the ballpark. I just hope Lynch and Gamboa will see enough." He shook his head. "We've got twelve pitchers on the staff because San Diego knows how hurt we've been. But when you look at it, we've got two pitchers injured, and Beckett and Davila don't really count. So that leaves eight and a half pitchers, maybe, when you're supposed to have at least ten." He held out the second shoe for inspection, then lined it up on the floor next to the first. "I'm not worrying about how to win a game lately. I'm just trying to figure out how to get through the nine innings. How to get the starter to go four innings, because otherwise it backs up the bullpen for three days down the line. And when a starter is shelled in the first, who knows what to do?"

Grandy looked up from his needle and floss. "You think they have sewing machines in Triple A?" he said. Nobody answered. "I know they have dry cleaning in the big leagues," he said.

Maxwell turned from his locker. "Really?" He turned farther, to face Champ. "Really?"

Champ had finished tying his shoes. Now he stood up and started tucking in his jersey. "Triple A?" he said.

"No," said Maxwell.

"The bigs?"

"Yeah," Maxwell said.

"Yeah," said Grandy.

Champ gave a quick nod.

"You think they have two uniforms?" Grandy said.

Champ belted his pants. "Three. At least. And new ones every month."

Grandy and Maxwell shook their heads. Then Grandy bent closer to his darning, and Maxwell returned to rummaging in his locker. Champ put on his cap and adjusted it, then turned to the rust-spotted mirror on his shelf, as he did before every game, and gave himself one last look.

"So it's Beckett tonight," he said. "And I'm going to have to push him one or two at-bats longer than you'd think, just because

I want to spare the bullpen." Satisfied with the tilt of his cap, he turned to face the other men in the office. "I feel like a factory worker who's a month away from retirement, but he's still got to work his dick into the ground. 'Ahh, he's been workin' here forty-seven years. He'll be gone in a month. Then we won't have to listen to him. *Get out there and dig that ditch!*'" Treanor, still sunk in a chair in a corner of the room, raised his eyes at the outburst. Champ turned to him to perform the final pregame ritual, but this one time it came out different.

"Go"—and here Champ erupted with a sudden, uncontrollable, massive yawn. When he'd recovered, he shook his head and completed his thought—"get 'em."

Bill Boesen walked into the conference room toward the back of the Waterloo Chamber of Commerce offices on Fourth Street and thought: *We are in a world of shit.* The invitation to attend this meeting had come by phone from someone whose name Boesen hadn't quite caught; the call had interrupted Boesen's shower, and, wet and penless, he had agreed to show up Tuesday at noon at the Chamber offices, but when he'd hung up he was at a loss as to why. When he called Dan Yates for help he realized he couldn't quite be sure even of the name of the organization he would be addressing, but after some discussion Boesen and Yates arrived at the most likely scenario: The Cedar Valley Partnership wanted to know what had become of the $5,000 the CVP had donated to the nonprofit arm of the ball club. The donation was one of only a few that Yates had managed to elicit from the business community last year, but it was an important one. The CVP represented the interests of local leaders who were trying to attract commercial development to the Waterloo area; it was an organization that Bernie McKinley had helped establish when he was mayor, and it was where McKinley had landed, as marketing director, after his election loss. All season the ball club's owners had been hearing that they needed to reach out to the business community; now the business community was reaching out to them. Boesen had asked Yates if he'd like to make the presentation, but Boesen could have predicted Yates's answer before he gave it, because it was the same answer Yates had given whenever Boesen's nerve started to fail:

He wasn't president of the ball club now. Bill was.

Boesen had prepared some notes on the topic, and he'd put on a dress shirt and slacks, but when he walked through the door of the conference room, he couldn't help noticing that every man there was wearing a suit. That, and eating lunch; any meeting they might be holding here would still have to be some minutes away. Boesen checked his watch: noon. Satisfied that he was on time and his hosts were not, he waited for any of the seventeen men and one woman who had gathered around the tables in the center of the room to step forward and greet him. After several long moments, he crossed the room himself, sat in a plastic chair in a corner, and set his IBEW Steward valise on the floor beside him.

Who are these people? he wondered. Lawyers, probably. Lawyers and . . . lawyers. All eating sandwiches and chips, and drinking from bottles of Mountain Dew, and flipping through copies of this meeting's agenda, which was something else, in addition to a bite to eat or a drop to drink, that Boesen wouldn't have minded having. He didn't understand how businesspeople could keep up with all their meetings and reports, plus their own businesses; he, in retirement, couldn't keep up with Waterloo Professional Baseball alone. If the ball club had a full-time fund-raiser, he supposed, that person would be sitting here now instead of him. *All these businessmen,* Boesen thought, *they probably got their own PR people.*

At a quarter past the hour, the meeting began. Somebody got up and introduced Boesen by name and title, which did nothing to disabuse him of his suspicion that all along everybody here had known who the guy sitting in the corner of the room was. Boesen stood and approached the near end of the conference table.

"I'm here from Waterloo Professional Diamond Baseball," he began, not looking up from a sheet of notes. "I became president a couple of months ago, so I don't really know what's goin' on. Over the past winter"—he caught a quick, deep breath—"our lights was installed. We had volunteer help from IBEW, which was good. We heard from professional baseball about all the things we got to do out there. The clubhouse, for instance, got to be 800 square feet, and ours is 600. The training room's supposed to be 175 square feet, and ours is 150. We got a sheet from baseball, and another sheet. Two sheets." He glanced up from his notes and laughed, then looked down again. "Anyway, we got to do these things by 1974."

The murmur from the crowd caused him to look up again.

"Nineteen seventy-four?" somebody offered.

"Nineteen ninety-four," he said. "Did I say seventy-four?" He laughed. "Anyway, your money's safe. We got it put away. But the thing is, I feel like we're in left field dealin' with the Parks." He described how this past off-season the club had paid for new mesh, which the Park Commission had refused to install. He described the scoreboard fence—another short, sharp breath—and the runaround he thought the Park Commission was giving him there, too. Boesen's breaths were coming in briefer, shallower bursts now, but he plunged forward, skimming his notes. He mentioned a promotion with the local cable-television company that he hoped would bring the ball club $2,500. He talked about the need for new "latrines." "If you've been out there on a night we got a crowd, then you know what I'm talkin' about, 'cause you've had to stand in line." He tried to describe the frustration he felt in dealing with the Park Commission on setting priorities. "Parks keep talkin' about the handicapped. We got to widen the aisles, even though nobody uses 'em, because of this OSHA deal, for people that are crippled or what-have-you."

By this point, some members of the Cedar Valley Partnership had started consulting their copies of the agenda again. When Boesen did look up from his notes, he was seeing fewer and fewer faces, and those he did see were wearing the bunching eyebrows and rapid blinking that betray a growing bewilderment. Finally a man halfway down the table spoke up: "What exactly is it that you're looking for? Or is this just an update?"

Boesen cocked his head; as if he weren't having enough trouble up here, now they were speaking too softly. "No," he said. "This is—what we're lookin' for is a couple hundred thousand." Everybody in the room took advantage of this moment to break the tension by laughing hard. "We're goin' to be satisfied with a lot less," Boesen went on. "What we're doin' is, after the season, we're goin' to get a PR person, and that person will go to the city, but not just Waterloo. He'll go to all these other towns around here—Hudson, Cedar Falls, Dike. The city, we know it's strapped. But don't worry"—he laughed again—"your money's safe."

The man who had introduced Boesen—very possibly the man who had phoned Boesen, too, though Boesen had no way of knowing for sure, and wouldn't have recognized his name with any certainty, anyway—now spoke from the far end of the table. In a tone that suggested he might be trying to prompt Boesen, he said, "Do you have a formal fund-raising committee? Anything in the way of a program?"

Boesen cocked his head again. "As I said, I came aboard a couple of months ago, so I'm the new kid on the block here. I don't know anythin'. I mean, I been on the board twenty years, so I do know some things. But for fund-raising, we already had one meetin' about that the other night, Sunday night. It was a fiasco," he added, dropping his voice, "but we're workin' on it."

The man at the far end of the table adopted a new tone now: one that suggested the guest's time here was drawing to a close. "If you get a formal fund-raising proposal together, we'd be happy to entertain specifics."

Boesen blew out a breath of relief. "Well, we got a couple English professors from UNI on our board. Maybe they can write somethin' up." He laughed.

The man at the far end of the table thanked Boesen, Boesen thanked the group and, after assuring the group one last time that their money was safe, he retrieved his IBEW Steward valise from the floor beside the chair in the corner of the room. As he walked down the hallway of the Chamber offices, he was nearly stampeded by a phalanx of men and women approaching from the opposite direction, marching with purposeful strides and armed with an easel, blueprints, and leather briefcases. Boesen flattened himself against the wall.

Outside, on Fourth Street, the sidewalks were shadowless in the noontime sun. Across the way, four storefronts stood vacant. At the corner was Fourth and Sycamore, once the busiest intersection in Waterloo, but when Boesen headed in that direction now, he was the only soul on the block. As an electrician, Boesen sometimes used to get jobs downtown, and from where he was walking he could see one building where he had installed charged wire along the top to keep the pigeons off. *It used to be a nice building,* he thought, *and now look at it.* He walked on, and he kept walking until he reached the intersection, where he turned the corner, found a restaurant, and treated himself to lunch.

"I've got a bad feeling about San Diego's decision," Jack Kuper said one evening, up in the Zoo Crew section of the bleachers behind first base. He leaned forward, resting his elbows on his knees. His large meat-packer's hands hung, useless, between his legs. "I'm trying to tell myself otherwise, but I can't. Keokuk, Dubuque, Danville, Quincy, Wausau—all the small markets are gone. Wisconsin Rapids would love to get minor league baseball back, but they won't. Once it's gone, it's gone forever. I retire in four years, and there won't be anything here." He spread his hands to indicate the game in progress tonight and all the games to come, then clapped his hands together and shook them, as if in fervent prayer. "It'll take a miracle," he said.

Behind him, another member of the Zoo Crew leaned forward, laid a hand on Kuper's shoulder, and said that last week he had gone to Des Moines to see the new Sec Taylor, and some fans approached him about his Midwest League All-Star Game T-shirt from Cedar Rapids last year. They said they had been thinking about seeing some Midwest League games, and he told them they should try out Waterloo. "Well, the other day, they showed up here. And you know what? They said they loved it. They said it reminded them of Sec Taylor twenty years ago." He lifted his hand off Kuper's shoulder and leaned back. His voice rose; he was reporting his findings to the whole of the Zoo Crew now. "People have nostalgia for baseball, and this is it. It's right here: This is what they have nostalgia for."

On his next visit to Toad's, Champ sat at a table in a corner rather than on a bar stool. While he was waiting for Jack Grandy, he ordered his usual vodka. He blinked at one of the TV screens hanging soundlessly from the high-beamed ceiling; on a cable channel, *Minor Leagues, Major Dreams,* a documentary about a Class A team in California, was just starting. Champ looked away. He looked around the bar. He looked back at the screen. He looked away.

"This place is depressing," he said when Grandy showed up. "Half the people always in the bag."

A waitress stopped at the table to take Grandy's order, and Champ asked for another vodka. Grandy, nearing sixty, was a former salesman at Sears who had been divorced for eight years. She got the house, he got the stock, which he promptly, "foolishly," spent on women and Florida. Now he was back in Waterloo, doing custodial work for a church in the winter and serving as the clubhouse manager for the Diamonds in the summer. When he told the story of his life, which he would if he sensed someone wanted to know why a man of his age was doing laundry and buying fruit for nineteen-year-olds, he did so without evident embarrassment. "My *friends* are embarrassed for me," he explained. "They'll say, 'What are you *doing*? You used to be a *salesman!*' " Then he'd shrug and grin and say, "I haven't got a pot to piss in." Now Grandy was talking to Champ about his pre-Sears career, some work he'd done more than thirty years earlier for a television station in El Paso, Texas. He told Champ about the time he was the cameraman on the tarmac for the first airplane hijacking. He told Champ about the time he was the cameraman on the Rio Grande for the first round-the-world satellite transmission. Champ's expression never changed. He'd settled on staring at the screen beyond Grandy. Young men on a baseball diamond somewhere were going through their daily stretches. Eventually the drinks arrived, and Grandy stopped talking.

"Ed Lynch is coming in tomorrow," Champ said.

Grandy nodded his head. The news was not surprising.

"You think San Diego will renew?" Champ said.

"I've just got a feeling." Grandy leaned forward, spreading his elbows against the table and looking at Champ with great earnestness. "I don't know why. I've just got a feeling that they will."

Champ continued staring at the screen beyond Grandy. He sipped his vodka, swallowed hard, cleared his throat. "Let me ask you. If you were San Diego, would you renew?"

"No," Grandy said softly, lowering his eyes.

"No," Champ said. "And let me tell you why. It's the field." Now he looked at Grandy. "San Diego can't get an accurate reading on a field like this. You think if you had a golf course out there in the infield and the outfield that anybody would care about the clubhouse or the press box or any of that other shit? But these people here sit in the stands and think the field looks good. Because they don't know any better. They need somebody who's played ball—a college player or pro or semipro or somebody who's played on a field and knows what it needs. Those other things are nice, too; don't get me wrong. They're part of it, too: You got a South Bend or Kane County, and you think Waterloo can compete with them? And that's the thing: Waterloo is out here thinking about how they're going to fix this place up, and what they're doing is trying to ride a horse and buggy down the middle of the street, and that time has gone. It's not sad. It just is. It's just change. It's business. Baseball is a fuckin' business. You give somebody a choice between South Bend and here, and they're going to take Waterloo? You give them a choice between a new Mercedes and an old pickup, and they're going to take the old pickup because it's got charm or tradition? Fuck, no! Baseball is changing. And Waterloo isn't. Waterloo is living in the past. Now, I don't want to see Waterloo lose professional baseball. They've had it for, what, fifty years or something? It's going to be a real loss. I don't want to see Burlington or Clinton or Waterloo or any of these towns lose pro ball. But they will. They all will."

"I don't want to see it either," Grandy said.

"But it's too late," Champ said. "It's too late for '94. They've waited too long. Waterloo has made their decision. And if San Diego doesn't come back, you think somebody else is going to want to come here?"

He looked away from Grandy, back to the screen. Young men on a bus were playing cards, or napping. Champ raised his glass and took a long swallow. When he spoke again, it was without inflection.

"Fuck, no," he said.

Ed Lynch arrived in town reading the David McCullough biography of Harry S Truman, which might explain why Waterloo on this trip struck him as a city straight out of the 1930s. Twice he had gotten himself lost on what should have been the ten-minute drive from the hotel to the ballpark, and both times he'd received the same chortling response to his request for directions: "You can't get there from here." The extent of the road construction confounded Lynch. It seemed to him how Kansas City, Missouri, must have looked in the depths of the Depression when Truman stood up to the citizenry and insisted on building highways as a way of investing in the future. It took a kind of visionary, Lynch thought, to spend money on roads when people couldn't afford to eat.

His first game in Waterloo was a loss to Appleton. If Champ had wanted to impress upon Lynch the depths of desperation that the pitching situation had reached, he couldn't have imagined a better first game for Lynch to see on this visit. At first it seemed to be shaping up as merely one more textbook illustration of the kind of predicament Champ had outlined in his office the previous day: what to do when the starter doesn't have his stuff. Jeff Brown, the staff's only healthy starting pitcher with a winning record, struggled all night. His fastball was off, and he was having trouble hitting his spots, and he wasn't helped by a second-inning, run-scoring error by Jeff Pearce, in right field. After six innings— ten hits, four walks, and eight earned runs—Brown left the game down 9–1. Jose Davila replaced him, but after an inning and two-thirds of no-run, one-hit relief work, Davila left the game complaining of a sore shoulder. Once more Kevin Farlow trotted over from shortstop to mop up, giving up no runs and one hit over an inning and a third, and even earning a strikeout, but it was the loss of Davila for the foreseeable future that suddenly put the pitching situation into a new perspective. If it was ridiculous to have to turn the ball over to the starting shortstop for the third time in ten games because the pitcher of last resort couldn't finish the job, it was unthinkable not to have a pitcher of last resort in the first place.

The next day, Champ activated his pitching coach. Dean Treanor, now forty-four, volunteered for roster duty. "We need bodies," he told Champ. "We need bodies," Champ told Lynch. "Waterloo," Lynch, with any luck, would tell McIlvaine, "needs bodies."

Lynch's second day in Waterloo, there was no game. At 7:00 P.M., under a cloudless sky, in ideal shirtsleeves-and-shorts weather, and on what would have been "Funny-Nose-and-Glasses Night," the assistant GM was standing at the front gate turning away a steady stream of would-be customers. It had stormed during the night, and apparently nobody had thought to put down the tarp.

Lynch's third day in town was "Jamaica Me Happy Night" at the ballpark. The members of the ballpark staff had spent much of the day trying to transform the place into a tropical paradise, dumping sand at the stadium entrance, fitting a few makeshift palm trees with black balloons, which was as close as they could come to coconuts in Waterloo, and covering the concrete between the metal standards by the concessions stand with a miniature lagoon of sand and water and cocktail umbrellas. The combination of reduced-admission vouchers that Nelson had been leaving on cashier counters and cigarette machines all over town and the prospect of going home with a genuinely valuable door prize—a couple of airline tickets to Jamaica, courtesy of a travel agency and an airline—had attracted a crowd of more than 1,000. The night was exceptionally humid—the first punishing humidity of the year, really; the close air kept sounds near to the ground, as if the sky had truly lowered to the level of the dense cloud cover of bugs around the ballpark lights. The noise fed the noise, and before long the stadium had amassed the atmosphere of a crowd enjoying the sound of a crowd enjoying itself.

"The hammers are here," Cameron Cairncross said before the game, sitting on the dugout bench. He raised his eyebrows and pointed with his chin toward the two men consulting behind the batting cage; Lynch and Tom Gamboa, who had returned to Waterloo for one final visit of the season. "You make it or they'll hammer you." Cairncross was to have been the starter for the previous night's "rainout," so by now he'd had an extra twenty-four hours to ponder the present game. His record stood at 4–7, he was coming off a couple of disastrous starts, having given up six earned runs in each of his last two outings while lasting only two innings and three innings respectively, and his ERA over that period had ballooned precisely one whole run, from 3.18 to 4.18. As tonight's starting pitcher, he was exercising his right not to participate in the pregame warm-ups and, rather, do whatever he needed to do to summon his motivation—in this case, plop down on the dugout bench and chat up anyone who happened to pass within striking distance. He winked at one player. He nodded to another. He raised his eyebrows. "I'm going to try to stick it up their asses," he announced to nobody in particular. When Lynch himself stepped down into the dugout, Cairncross greeted him with a "How ya doin', lad?" Lynch, looking slightly startled, stopped and nodded back before ducking and disappearing down the tunnel to the clubhouse.

On the mound that night, Cairncross wasn't overpowering. If anything, the Burlington pitcher was, providing an impressive mix of fastballs and offspeed pitches, and holding the Diamonds to no hits until two outs in the fourth inning, when he got behind in the count 3–1 on Hardtke, who guessed fastball and was right. Hardtke sent the pitch for a home run, and then the next batter, Shawn Robertson, took advantage of the pitcher's lapse in concentration and did the same. What Cairncross was, however, was efficient. He scattered his hits with intelligence and guile, holding the Astros to one run. In turn, the crowd responded to the strong pitching with appreciation, applauding both pitchers' performances, even—for the first time the entire season—rising to its feet and yelling in anticipation of particularly important pitches. Without a doubt it was one of the better ball games of the season before one of the better crowds. Even the Jamaica vacation added a touch of prosperity to the proceedings. It was possible to interpret the entire enterprise as reflecting well on Waterloo the franchise as well as Waterloo the city, and indeed, when Boesen visited the box seats during the game, Gamboa said, "I'm really impressed. Last year, the team was in contention and they couldn't draw a crowd. But this—this is great."

"What was that last pitch?" Lynch said. "Fastball?"

"Fastball in the happy zone," Gamboa said.

"You know what he said to me today? 'How ya doin', lad?' First time anybody's ever called me 'lad.'" Lynch offered a faint smile. Then he rescinded it, turned to Boesen, and asked to meet him at the ballpark the following afternoon.

Unlike Joe McIlvaine, Ed Lynch was anything but absent during his four days in Waterloo. If McIlvaine was a general manager in a transitional era, then Lynch was one of the department heads making the transition possible. He and McIlvaine knew each other from Lynch's stint as a pitcher with the Mets in the 1980s, and Lynch had assumed many of the duties that traditionally had belonged to a GM. His preparation for the role included degrees in finance and law, and he routinely applied both disciplines to his work. As a player, he had sat out the 1981 strike, and now he was management; but he was equally at home arguing either side—though he preferred to argue that there were no "sides." There was only an "entertainment business" that had experienced a "gradual upward spiral" and was now undergoing "a sudden upswing"—Lynch would demonstrate by circling his forefinger in the air—that he felt was sure to be corrected by the "sudden drop" of a "work stoppage."

When Lynch looked around the ballpark this evening, he didn't see 1,000 fans as an especially strong turnout for a professional baseball game on a midsummer Saturday night; and when he looked around Waterloo, he didn't see a factory town that simply had endured more than its share of hardships. It was Lynch's opinion that the best reflection of an ailing economy's health was the entertainment dollar. When an area's economy goes bad, movie and amusement-park and baseball attendance continue to do well at first because they're inexpensive diversions. But when an economy goes bad and stays bad—when even the minimal expense of an occasional diversion starts to weigh heavily, when diversions themselves start to seem frivolous and pointless, when people are struggling simply to survive—everything suffers, including entertainment. When Lynch looked around Waterloo, what he saw was a city that was having trouble supporting even minor league baseball, one of the cheapest buys in the entertainment business.

And this at a time when the minors had become "the place to be." Lynch certainly thought they were, and so did all the people who over the past decade had pushed minor league attendance to record levels, had spurred expansion in league after league, had sent the sheer number of franchises and players to their highest levels since the pretelevision heyday of minor league baseball. Not that it was going to last. It couldn't. It *wouldn't*. Lynch knew this for a fact. Last year, as he'd made his rounds of minor league parks in the Padres' system, he'd had to think about which two or three players to cut from each roster. This year was different. This year he had to figure out how to eliminate an additional twenty-five or so players from the organization because—following a series of discussions at the highest levels of the San Diego organization, and anticipating what everyone in the organization agreed would be a similar measure adopted by other major league organizations—the decision had been made to cut expenses by eliminating one affiliation next season at the Class A level. The industry's expansion was over; the contraction was about to begin; and it was about to begin now.

Which was why one afternoon in Waterloo, Iowa, during the final month of the season, when he had finished pacing the base paths with the manager, Ed Lynch could plant his feet in the firm soil behind home plate, cross his arms, regard the sight of his boys stretching and hitting and throwing under an immaculate blue sky, and say with some authority, "Here, today, is the height of minor league baseball in America."

On August 9, summer finally arrived in Waterloo. The humidity that had first surfaced Saturday evening now settled on the stadium for a Sunday matinee. From the lip of the dugout, Champ took one look around and canceled infield. On the field, a couple of players crawled inside the tarp roll to curl up among the only available shadows. And in the grandstand, five players gathered on folding chairs to listen to the sermon that the Reverend Mike Nemmers of Cedar Heights Baptist Church had prepared for today's baseball chapel service, taking as his subject the fires of Hell: "You know, a little while ago out here, I said to somebody, 'Sure is hot today.' And they said, 'You know what it's as hot as.' That's right. It's hot as Hell. Now the place of Hell was never prepared for you and I. It's not you or I who is expected to dwell there. God prepared the place of Hell for the Devil and his angels, and that's it. So if you go there, it's not God's decision. And it's not the Devil's decision. Whose decision is it?"

The players shuffled a bit. Spikes scraped concrete. "Ours?" a voice offered.

Meanwhile, under the grandstand, in Champ's office, Lynch was meeting with Boesen and Bergmeier. If Boesen had learned anything from his years as a union steward, it was to bring a backup witness to any official meeting, but what Lynch had to tell them that afternoon left little room for ambiguity.

It was a brief, cordial meeting. Lynch informed Boesen and

Bergmeier that San Diego would not be renewing its Player Development Contract with Waterloo. The Padres organization would be cutting $10 million in expenses; the minors would take a $600,000 hit, including the elimination of one club at the A level. Waterloo had been the last A club to join the system; it therefore, in all fairness, would be the first to go. He assured them the decision was no reflection on the city and no reflection on the facilities. He said it had nothing to do with the press box or anything else. "It's simply a question of economics," he said.

Then he gave them a tip: One of the expansion teams wanted into the Midwest League. He didn't want to risk accusations of tampering, so he couldn't be any more specific. Then he said that the Diamonds could expect confirmation of the Padres' decision in writing by the end of the month. Lynch thanked Boesen and Bergmeier for their hospitality, Boesen and Bergmeier thanked Lynch for the courtesy of the early notification, and that was that.

It was John Deere Credit Union Day—a ballpark buyout that traditionally produced the biggest turnout of the season—and Boesen and Bergmeier didn't have time to dwell on the news. They agreed, hurriedly, that it would be in the best interests of the ball club to keep the decision a secret, except among board members, until San Diego made it official; maybe by that time the club would have lined up another major league parent. Then they set to work. Bergmeier volunteered to act as an usher by the first-base grandstand entrance, and Boesen opened the station that would be supplying the beer vendors. He teamed with Lana Morgan for a couple of innings, until it became clear that for some reason the crowd wasn't buying beer in any significant quantity today—certainly not enough to justify keeping vendors on the payroll in addition to the bartenders in the beer booths under the bleachers. Boesen and Morgan told the vendors to take the rest of the afternoon off, poured a couple of beers to bring back to their own seats, and slammed the metal gate on their vending station shut.

Bev was waiting for them in their usual spot. Immediately she fell to telling Morgan about how difficult it was to paint or wash one of her kitchen walls because it was covered with shelves that she'd stocked with pigs. Saltshaker pigs, pepper-mill pigs, creamer pigs, ceramic pigs and pewter pigs and paper pigs, pigs she'd bought at antique shops and pigs she'd found at flea markets and garage sales and pigs she had purchased at department stores. She didn't know why she collected pigs, she said. She just did.

Bill Boesen didn't say a word. He sat at the end of the bench and sipped his beer. The Diamonds were losing big, as usual. The crowd was quiet. Somewhere a plane was buzzing. Boesen didn't need to see the box-office figures to know that the attendance was well under 2,000—a good crowd on any other Sunday, but by far the lowest turnout for any John Deere Credit Union Day in memory. And what crowd there was, wasn't drinking. Was it because of the humidity, stunning the customers, stilling them, sticking them to their seats? Or was it because the kind of customer who came to the ballpark for free wasn't the kind of customer who spent money? What a season: The biggest attraction of the year, and they couldn't draw a crowd; the hottest day of the year, and they couldn't sell beer.

"If we want to paint the wall," Bev was saying to Lana Morgan, "we have to take the shelves down in sections, or we'll never know where anything goes."

She let out a whoop. Her husband gave his head a violent shake, as if a fly were bothering his beard.

"Pigs pigs pigs pigs pigs pigs pigs," said Bev.

Late in the game, Bergmeier and Blau retreated to one of the top rows in the grandstand on the third-base side, out of any eavesdropper's earshot, up near the chicken-wire mesh that overlooked the dusty parking lot below and the softball diamonds in the distance. The sun pressed against the backs of their necks. The afternoon was still warm, but already the sun was low in the southern sky. Days now were shortening noticeably. Shadows were lengthening. It wasn't yet five in the afternoon, but when the two men leaned together to talk, so did their silhouettes on the field.

"He said it didn't have anything to do with the facilities," Bergmeier said.

"That's good," said Blau.

"Yeah, yeah."

"Yeah."

"He made *sure* to say that." Bergmeier nodded his head vigorously. "And he said there's an expansion club that wants into the Midwest League, but he didn't want to say which one."

"Yeah?"

Bergmeier looked around, then bent closer to Blau. "You know," he said, lowering his voice, "I talked to this Marlins scout who was out here early in the week. I asked him if they'd be interested in affiliating here."

Blau lowered his voice, too. "Marlins, huh? What'd he say?"

"He said he had to be careful about what he said because he didn't want it to seem like tampering, but, yeah, they might be looking."

"Marlins," Blau whispered. "Marlins. Marlins. You know,"— he let his voice rise—"if we had an expansion club, we could sell memorabilia and souvenirs up the butt."

"Yeah, yeah." Bergmeier nodded his head with added emphasis. "It might be a blessing in disguise, San Diego not renewing."

"Yeah," Blau said, nodding his head now, too. The two men straightened in their seats then. They sat that way for several seconds, nodding their heads, facing the field but not absorbing the game. Then their nodding slowed. The fact was, the ball club's standing in the community was already precarious. The loss of an affiliation had affected that position under less-critical circumstances in the past; who could say what such an absence might communicate now?

"Or," Blau said slowly, after a long silence, "or it could be the kiss of death."

IV

KISSING THE PIG

WATERLOO— Special thanks to the city for picking up leaves and what you might call unneeded junk.

Also, thank you for the new city busses. Whoever make it possible to purchase them, they ride wonderfully well

The new street will soon be completed on Fifth Street. It truly shows the skills of mankind.

Waterloo is a great city—hats off.
Lenora M. Happel
303 Denver Street

—*Waterloo Courier,*
November 15, 1992

10

Every Friday morning that summer, several area residents gathered in a temporary office in the Waterloo Recreation Arts Center, a modern structure that occupied an otherwise unremarkable stretch of weeds and warehouses along the western bank of the Cedar River, between the downtown business district and the John Deere Waterloo Works. There were ten in the group—nine locals and one outside consultant—and for three hours every week, they discussed their findings from the previous week and received their marching orders for the coming week: what to research, whom to contact, where, on occasion, to travel. They called themselves the Waterloo Reinvestment Group, and what they had conceived, over the course of dozens of such meetings dating back to the previous autumn, was a way that they would accomplish what Bernie McKinley could not: the reinvention of Waterloo for the next century. "History," McKinley had said, addressing the group three weeks after losing his bid for reelection, "will tell us you were the ones that made it happen."

History, in this case, began with a pink house. A few years earlier, a couple of young real estate speculators had purchased and renovated a seventy-two-year-old home on West Fourth, at Prospect Boulevard. Situated as it was on a slight promontory overlooking the intersection of the city's main thoroughfare and its most prestigious street, and sandblasted to a shade of salmon quite unlike anything else in the neighborhood, the house had announced the arrival of a new way of thinking about Waterloo as surely as any strategic-development plan or eight-point mission and objective statement. The message was unmistakable: Here was a property that everybody had been driving past every day for years without really seeing, and just look at it now.

Primarily through that house and the publicity it generated, the two developers soon established contact with other like-minded locals, and together this collection of acquaintances brought aboard an urban planning consultant, who found what anyone who had taken Urban Planning 101 would have seen in Waterloo: the lack of a natural crossroads, a predominantly working-class population, a city that for decades had lived beyond its predictable means. But as a New Yorker who had never before set foot in Iowa, Tom Gallaher also couldn't help being struck by the apparent anomaly of a city of factories standing tall in the heart of the nation's breadbasket. Now the weekly meetings began in earnest. The subject: What would it take to reinvigorate the center of the city? Forget about the old days, Gallaher advised: "There is not a downtown community in the world that will ever have a department store again." What Waterloo needed was something distinctive, an attraction that would intrigue outsiders the same way the city had first struck Gallaher. An Agricultural Hall of Fame? A John Deere Museum? One day their research uncovered something called the National Heritage Landscapes, a relatively recent innovation of the National Parks Service. National Heritage Landscapes were the first national parks to feature no forest or mountain or fruited plain. Instead, their subjects were urban— parks that preserved not the country's natural beauty, but its human history. Lowell, Massachusetts, was one such park, as the home of the Industrial Revolution. Johnstown-Altoona, Pennsylvania, was another, as the home of mining and railroads. What if Waterloo, Iowa, were to become the home of the American Agricultural/Industrial Heritage Landscape? They dubbed it "Silos and Smokestacks," and on the wall of their office at the Recreation Arts Center they mounted a map marking likely focal points: Deere plants, the remains of Rath, a railroad depot that might serve as a visitors center, a power station that Gallaher liked to describe as "two Gothic cathedrals just made for IMAX," libraries and Baptist churches and the tavern where packinghouse workers used to spend their paychecks. "The whole thing," Gallaher reminded his colleagues, "is to realize what's before your very eyes."

Already "Silos and Smokestacks" had developed into a vision equal in ambition to Bernie McKinley's. Whether his failure in fully executing his own vision was attributable to his philosophy or to his personality; to a philosophy that had proved unworkable in Waterloo or to an electorate that had removed him from office before he could see his plan through to completion; to the mayor at all—all these issues were debatable and, in fact, were debated throughout the city in the weeks and months following the election. But in the end they were secondary to another concern: What was Waterloo going to do now? For the area's most influential citizens, "Silos and Smokestacks" presented an answer, a new vision of Waterloo's future: its past.

Bald and bearded and bouncing with enthusiasm, Gallaher started making the rounds of community leaders. (It was Gallaher and friends who had passed Bill Boesen in the hall at the Chamber of Commerce.) Gallaher would recite statistics: Iowa had 1 percent of the U.S. population yet produced 10 percent of the food; 19 percent of the hogs; 26 percent of the red meat. "Twenty-four percent of the world's Grade A soil is in Iowa!" he'd say. He'd show a map of the city and walk his audiences through the Waterloo of the future. He'd blue-sky a bit. He could see a conference center that would become a meeting place for international symposia on food technology, he'd say, or a museum with interactive displays—maybe a room full of images of everyday products, and those items manufactured with corn would slowly disappear, one by one. "It would be everything!" he'd say. "You couldn't have an *automobile* without corn!" He'd acknowledge that other communities might have excelled in meat production or farm-equipment manufacturing. "Others might have done it first, or better," he'd say, shrugging and offering his upraised palms. "Paterson, New Jersey, would have been a more appropriate place to tell the story of the Industrial Revolution, but Lowell thought of it first. It's just a matter of getting the claim in. We want to put the trademark on Waterloo–Cedar Falls as the home of *this* story."

The project rapidly became an open secret among the city's civic leaders. Members of the Waterloo Reinvestment Group met with the local congressman's wife ("She went bazonkers!" Gallaher reported back) who, in turn, opened the door to her husband who, in turn, agreed to steer the project through the House of Representatives if, in exchange, he got to make the official public announcement. (It was an election year.) The editor of the *Courier* planned his family's summer vacation to include a stop in Lowell, Massachusetts, so that when the date of the official announcement came, he'd be able to file a positive background story on how a similar project had succeeded elsewhere. "Silos and Smokestacks" held out the possibility of a boom the likes of which Waterloo hadn't seen since a similar group of leading citizens had recruited Rath Packing a hundred years earlier; it could easily drive the local economy for the *next* hundred years—and this, here, now, was the ground floor. For their part, several members of the Waterloo Reinvestment Group had been buying properties in downtown Waterloo by the dozens; at one committee meeting Gallaher had chastised his charges for letting a riverfront lot slip through their hands, breaking the contiguity of what they owned along that particular stretch. "Put your mind toward acquiring property," he said. "Because unless you own the property, you don't have many rights."

The start-up costs for "Silos and Smokestacks" were to be $25,000. Gallaher spoke twice and raised $34,000. By the end of the summer, as the project grew in scope and gathered momentum, the group had raised more than $100,000. A sudden shortfall of $10,000? No problem. A local bank delivered the money that day—and when committee chairwoman Terri Walker, the wife of a prominent attorney, arrived at Gallaher's office to drop it off, she invited him out to the parking lot to see her new candy-apple-red Jaguar. Gallaher followed her to the curb and whistled approvingly. It made an impressive statement, for a can of corn.

One Friday morning, at their weekly meeting, representatives of the Waterloo Reinvestment Group heard a presentation from a publicist who hoped to work on the project. She left the office with a list of the advisory committee members and the organization's contributors, which she passed along to her business partner who, in turn, happened to show it to a friend, Jerry Klinkowitz. Although the project was an open secret among the city's civic leaders, it remained largely unknown to the general public, and it was only now that any member of the ball club's board of directors first heard of the existence of the group. Klinkowitz took one look at the list and immediately understood its significance.

The sky was falling.

*

"Now we come to the"—Bill Boesen hesitated, trying to figure out what to call the next item on the board of director's agenda. "Dave," he decided.

By this point in the season—only four home dates remained—the outcome of the vote on whether to renew the general manager's contract for the coming year was in little doubt. By any measure of front-office performance, the season had been a failure. Attendance was down; revenue was down. Whether these failures were attributable to the general manager's philosophy or to his personality; to a philosophy that had proved unworkable in Waterloo or to owners who had persuaded the GM to abandon his policy before it had a chance to work its magic a second time; to the general manager at all—all these issues were debatable and, in fact, were debated by the owners over the course of two meetings in August.

The first had been an emergency session called by Boesen when he realized that the single scheduled meeting before the end of the season wouldn't give the board a fair opportunity to assess a front-office situation that was quickly turning nightmarish. As a concession for the last-minute inconvenience to the board, Boesen had called the meeting for the VFW Hall downtown, a frequent site of board meetings in years past, and a favorite haunt of his as well as several other board members. For their meetings, the owners took over the back half of the hall, a reception room beyond a folding partition. The front half of the hall was taken up by a tavern, where a crocheted American flag hung behind the bar. From time to time during their proceedings, the jukebox in the bar would kick in with a country-and-western tune, and the music would float past the divider and carry to their table, against a far wall. One advantage of the VFW Hall was that drinks were available during the meeting, rather than only afterward, and Boesen had hoped that this circumstance would help lubricate the discussion among the owners—or, as he'd come to think of them, the "mummies on the wall."

Boesen, the old union hand, didn't relish his new management role of being the one responsible for letting an employee go, and it wasn't a decision he had any intention of having to make alone. He had tried to devise a compromise whereby both the GM and his assistant could stay—but then he'd met with them. One evening while the team was on the road, he'd invited Simpson and Nelson to join him in the visitors' locker room, and even before he'd had a chance to ask if they thought they could set their differences aside and work together, one as an administrator, the other as a fund-raiser, the two of them had fallen into a shouting match. Accusations, recriminations, obscenities rebounded from the low concrete ceiling. The gathering of the board's public relations committee at Lana Morgan's house didn't help matters. Boesen had asked in advance that there not be beer, but there was, and fried chicken as well, and before long the meeting had become little more than an excuse to socialize. "I think we have to get rid of one or the other," Boesen told the owners at the emergency board meeting. "Or get rid of both and start from scratch, which I don't want to do. But we gotta do something, and before the end of the season. Come on!" he suddenly shouted. The owners started. "Do I hear anything?"

After a moment, Mildred Boyenga accepted the challenge. "I want people in our *ball*park," she said.

It was a simple enough declaration on the surface, but none of the other board members could have failed to miss the implication. Klinkowitz, too, had been talking about drawing crowds again, invoking *Field of Dreams* and the line of headlights stretching to the horizon, and saying that's what he wanted to see outside the ballpark every evening. Others seconded these sentiments: how having just about the lowest attendance in the league wouldn't help their credibility in the community or around the minors; how they should be drawing 100,000; how, if they weren't going to be making money anyway, they might as well go back to having fun; how even when the city was falling apart in the early 1980s, the ballpark still could draw 4,000 on a fine night—"and *that* was Waterloo baseball!" "I don't *care* if we don't make a million bucks," Boyenga concluded.

"I want *people* in the *ballpark*."

Throughout these discussions, Jeff Copeland had remained silent. At one end of the group, he sat staring down at the table. Earlier, Boesen had turned to him and asked if he had anything to say, and Copeland had said only, "I promised myself I wasn't going to say anything tonight." But now he raised his face toward the rest of the group and, slowly, began speaking.

"Everybody knows I'm a good friend to David," he said, "but I'll tell you: This has ruined my season. I've never seen us so miserable as a group. Remember how it used to be? Remember how we used to go out to the park and look forward to seeing each other, and how we'd buy each other beers? I'd like to see us go out there and have a good time again. Now I know Dave personally. I've walked him around the park and chewed him a new orifice. And that worked—for about two days. And then it was back to the same old thing. You're right. He should be fired. He doesn't walk on water. He's not the second coming of Christ. We're more important than he is. When all of this is over, we're still going to be here. Let's have *fun* again." He made a face of disgust and pushed himself away from the table. "And I promised I wasn't going to say a darn thing tonight."

After a moment, Boesen said, softly, miserably, "I'm sorry I had to interrupt all your evenings out."

By the time of the next meeting at the VFW Hall, three weeks later, one answer to the question that so recently had seemed so pressing—Who will run the front office next season?—was a foregone conclusion: Not Dave. Things were moving fast now. Events were starting to overtake them. In the interim, the owners had learned that San Diego wouldn't be renewing the affiliation with Waterloo. (When the TV over the bar flashed the score Cubs 6, Padres 0, Mildred Boyenga said, "Good!" and a small cheer rose from the owners' table.) This news not only meant that they would have to devote themselves to finding a new parent club, but it complicated the already formidable task of fund-raising that awaited them during the off-season. More immediately, it rendered suddenly expendable the services of a GM whose policies had alienated fans and advertisers alike. The owners now dispatched him in short order, scribbling their votes on scraps of paper and passing around a plastic mesh popcorn dish to collect the ballots. The verdict was 8–5 against renewing Simpson's contract, with Boesen being delegated the task of telling him the day after the season ended. The GM question, however, would have seemed secondary anyway, and, in fact, it *was* secondary. The first hour of the meeting was dominated instead by discussion of the list of Waterloo Reinvestment Group donors.

Over the past several weeks, as the possibility that the owners would be approaching the area's most prominent citizens had grown more likely, Klinkowitz had been sounding warnings at the ballpark. Once word got out that the franchise was in trouble, he told the other owners, it wouldn't be exceptionally difficult for an outsider to step in and "squeeze us out." For Klinkowitz, this list now offered all the proof he needed. Why else would pillars of the community be gathering, other than to strong-arm the ball club away from its rightful stewards? *"Look* at these people," Klinkowitz said, holding up a copy of the list at the board meeting. "A cement contractor, engineers, land developers—all the people who would profit immensely by a new stadium being built. These are multi-multi-megabucks people. They make their money by picking pockets. They're into every one of your pockets. They *love* people like us. This is the same thing they did in the nineteenth century, how all those people made money. You go to them and say, 'Are you planning something?' and they say, 'Yes, but *shhh.* It's a *secret.'* "

Among his fellow board members, Klinkowitz had cultivated a reputation as a prevaricator. He was a writer, after all, and usually the owners indulged his embellishments with an open roll of the eyes or, in the case of his good friend Mildred Boyenga, a swat at his arm and a dramatically mouthed, "Not true!"—all of which seemed only to encourage him. That summer, a fight broke out at the ballpark between a security guard and a patron, and by the time Klinkowitz was repeating his version of the events (which he hadn't witnessed) at a board meeting several days later, the scene had spawned a *Courier* photographer documenting the whole sordid affair and a crowd chanting, "Rodney King! Rodney King!"

Yet even if the owners didn't trust Klinkowitz's interpretation of the list's significance—"paranoid" was one of the kinder terms they found for his behavior—neither was it entirely unrepresentative of their own worst fears. If nothing else, the names on this list served to remind the owners how formidable their next task would be.

Having accepted that they wouldn't be receiving any more money from the mayor or City Council for the foreseeable future, and having rejected a public referendum, the owners had resigned themselves to trying to raise the funds for stadium renovations from private sources. How they were going to go about that task, they couldn't say, especially now that the front-office upheaval had compromised Boesen's plan. All they knew for sure was that whatever fortunes still existed in Waterloo were the ball club's last chance at survival—and now here they were. This list was them: a Who's Who and a What's What of those individuals and institutions inevitably called by everyone else "the movers and shakers."

The widespread impression that Waterloo, like many communities, was run by a relatively small circle of prominent citizens was a reasonable one. To be sure, the ranks of the wealthy and powerful had thinned. Some had died, a few had lost their fortunes, and others had joined the exodus after the local economy collapsed in the early 1980s. But, overall, those who remained could still alter the course of the city's destiny simply by getting together in a room and agreeing to. In 1985, for instance, about fifty prominent citizens gathered at a local hotel for what they would call, in retrospect, "The Meeting." The topic under consideration was a pari-mutuel track for Waterloo. At that time, the state legislature was legalizing gambling, and the construction of a greyhound racing track seemed to offer, in that era of economic hopelessness, hope: the hotels, fast food places and restaurants that surely would follow, the engineering and construction and concession contracts, all the benefits of becoming a regional tourist attraction. The track would be a way to jump-start the local economy; not coincidentally, it would also be a way to salvage a future for themselves. The chairman of the National Cattle Congress, an annual event in the city dating back to the early years of the century, outlined the proposal, saying that he was willing to mortgage the NCC in order to get this project off the ground. Then he asked for donations of $25,000. "Seventeen hands went up," he later told the *Courier*. "A month later, we had forty-two investors and the eight hundred seventy-five thousand dollars we needed. Nobody thought we could do it." Based on the strength of those commitments, the organizers then lined up $3.9 million in loans from local banks and a $750,000 loan from the city, and when they later informed the contractors and subcontractors who submitted winning bids that it would cost a donation of $25,000 in order to actually get the jobs, they received even more money. "The Meeting" remained the model for how the city's most prominent citizens conducted business among themselves: Get together, raise money.

Once, the ball club had enjoyed their patronage. Except in its earliest, Elysian Fields incarnation, and especially at the lowest levels of what developed into the minor leagues, baseball had always been primarily a blue-collar entertainment that depended for its sponsorship on civic leaders. They were the ones who brought pro ball to town, who made sure the team had a manager and a ballpark season after season, who ensured that the treasury had enough in its coffers for the club to survive the winter. What Russ Garling always said was true: The board did use to have more movers and shakers—but, then, so did Waterloo.

Some had gone out of business. The Raths were no longer around to spearhead a ballpark drive, and according to one common estimate, only ten or fifteen old-money families still resided in the Waterloo area—and even that number might have been generous. Some had changed with the times. The *Courier* stopped functioning as the ball club's unofficial house organ after it was purchased from a local family by a national chain that took a dim view of a sports editor serving on the board of a sports organization he himself covered.

Some influential supporters, however, the ball club had lost because of what it was becoming. The attrition rate reinforced itself. The more the responsibility for running the club shifted away from the movers and shakers, the more it fell to the rest of the board, a development that, in turn, made the club less attractive to whatever influential individuals remained. One of the last to go was a Waterloo Savings Bank official who used to invite players back to his house for postgame pizza, and who used to make sure the bank took out ads and sponsored promotions and bought out the ballpark once a season, but who eventually resigned from the board because, he explained, "I *like* organization."

It was at this point that the contributions of the city had become essential to the ball club's survival. The city could do for the ball club what the ball club could not do for itself. For years Bernie McKinley had acted as a buffer for the organization, running interference at City Hall, and representing the interests of baseball to a business community that otherwise regarded the organization warily, if at all. Even now, every so often, an owner would muse that if Bernie McKinley were still in office, the ball club would get the godsend it needed to survive—if not from the city, then from the private sources that a mayor with his kind of connections could tap at a moment's notice.

The owners, however, were on their own. They had no such connections. None. When the board members looked over the Waterloo Reinvestment Group's list of contributors, they saw name after name that Dan Yates had approached during the previous year without results. Mildred Boyenga looked at the list, named one name, the head of a trucking firm, and said that during her tenure as president, he'd called her to see if the ball club might be for sale. It was not, she'd informed him, and that was *it*—the full extent of his interest in supporting a civic institution from which he wouldn't be seeing a profit. In all this time, not even an *ad*. Everything the ball club hadn't been able to accomplish in ten years, the Waterloo Reinvestment Group had done in ten months.

The question reverted to Klinkowitz. What did he suggest?

"Put the club up for sale, publicly, in a big way," he said. "By threatening to sell, I guarantee you we won't have to sell." Klinkowitz explained that a public announcement would draw any nefariously interested parties into the open, and then the ball club would know whom to avoid in the future. "But by not threatening to sell," he said, "I guarantee you the club will be owned by these people in less than a year."

"This is the same thing I was saying five months ago," Dan Yates said several days later. He and Boesen were walking together across the parking lot outside the Recreation Arts Center. If only to appease Klinkowitz and calm any stray doubts among the others, they had agreed to meet with the leaders of the Waterloo Reinvestment Group and feel out whether the ball club was in imminent danger of being taken over—somehow, by someone. Yates didn't believe it was; he'd said so, emphatically, at the owners' meeting. But he agreed with Klinkowitz that there was only one way to find out whether any local interest existed in rescuing professional baseball in Waterloo. He'd said it at the owners' meeting in April, he'd never stopped saying it, and now he was amused to hear his most outspoken critic saying it, too: To save the ball club, they had to put it up for sale.

Boesen sighed. He agreed with Yates insofar as not taking the threat seriously. He didn't know what to believe about announcing that the ball club was for sale. For the time being, he was content to table the matter. Now he told Yates that during the past few days he had been fielding phone calls from owners who had gotten nervous, after all, and who wanted him to call an emergency meeting to discuss this takeover threat further. *He* didn't want to call one, he said.

"Then don't," Yates said. "It's up to you." He laughed, and his voice rose. *"You're* the *boss."*

Boesen sighed again.

Yates and Boesen met with Tom Gallaher and Terri Walker that morning and learned about the plans for "Silos and Smokestacks." Although Gallaher emphasized that the project was perhaps a decade from completion, that in fact it would have to overcome one congressional hurdle after another for years, and that even if the funding could somehow encompass ballpark renovations—not an impossible scenario, given the scope of the project—the money certainly wouldn't be available by 1994, Yates nonetheless, for the first time in months, saw a possibility that excited him. For years Yates had been dutifully packing up ball club memorabilia and carting it off to the Grout Museum, the semiofficial repository for material relating to the history of professional baseball in Waterloo. When Gallaher had finished his presentation, Yates said he could envision visitors spending their days at "Silos and Smokestacks," then their evenings at a baseball game. He said he could imagine a display area at the ballpark that showed the history of the local pro ball club: a mini-museum all its own, yet an integral part of the Waterloo story, and deservedly so.

Gallaher smiled.

"You gotta have dreams," he said. "You gotta have goals. Otherwise a city will die"—a shrug; upraised palms—"or a team will die."

"Don't die."

Champ was standing in the visitors' clubhouse of the Kane County Events Center, delivering his final pep talk of the year. Lately his team had been playing as if the season were over— which, in a way, it was. With eleven games to go, the Diamonds had fallen fourteen and a half games out of first place. Their current four-game losing streak had eliminated them mathematically from postseason competition. Not that anyone had been harboring hopes for a miracle finish that would catapult the team into the playoffs. On the contrary: The Padres had promoted Hardtke to Class A-Advanced a week earlier, then pitcher Jeff Brown several days later, because the High Desert Mavericks were battling for a championship—the second-half, Southern Division, California League championship—and the Waterloo Diamonds were most decidedly not.

Still, the season *wasn't* over. Every so often a manager had to remind the players why they were here. Champ had done it the first week of the season, on a bitter night in Burlington, when he told the players that although they had to work as a team, they had to think about themselves first. He'd done it again just before the midseason break, on a humid evening in South Bend, when he told the players that, yes, they had to work as individuals, but that they shouldn't forget they were part of a team, too. Now he was doing it again. As recently as the previous Thursday, the Diamonds had been riding a five-game winning streak, and had compiled a respectable second-half record of 26–27. But now, with less than two weeks to go, and slightly more than midway through an eight-game road trip, Champ had to remind them that the season wasn't over. That they still had a job to do. That they were still on the payroll of a major league baseball organization, for now.

The news that San Diego would be dropping its affiliation with Waterloo and, more to the point, eliminating one of its Class A clubs next year, had only confirmed rumors that the players had been hearing all season. Some players were secure, of course; a Robbie Beckett wasn't going anywhere. Most, though, had no assurances. They'd have to wait through the off-season for a letter that, if it were bad news, would come in November or, if it were good news, around the first of the year. Yet even for the fortunate ones, there would be no guarantees: They'd have won only an invitation to spring camp, where they'd then have to earn a spot on a roster, and the whole process would start all over again.

Even so, it was still possible for even a marginal player to deny that the end of the season might also bring an end to a career. One evening trainer John Maxwell idly asked outfielder Keith McKoy what his batting average was. McKoy answered that it was .206. "Fucking sucks," McKoy added, before launching into a lengthy discourse on how he had hit .256 last season and then spent the winter working out, and how now that he'd had a miserable year, he had to wonder whether he should be working out this winter, but how either way it would be important to go to San Diego just before the start of spring training and work out at Jack Murphy Stadium. *"Definitely* gotta come in ready," he concluded.

It was even possible for players to deny that the end of this particular season, with its impending loss of approximately twenty-five extra roster slots from the organization, was more likely to bring an end to a career than any other. The players didn't discuss it much; but once, when they did, it was to speculate that the Colorado Rockies and Florida Marlins, the National League expansion clubs, would have to stock their own minor league system next year, so even though the Padres were dropping one whole club there'd still be a place to go . . . right?

Still, Champ had nailed it. They'd "shut it down." They said as much, standing around the motel lobby on a rainy afternoon, standing around the foul area before a game, standing around. Not every player, and not all the time. But whether it was because of the news of the cutbacks in the Padres' system, or simply because it was getting to be the end of a long, losing season, the change was unmistakable.

The game the following night, for instance—it would have been such a sweet victory: come-from-behind; first of the year against Kane County; soon enough after Champ's pep talk that a charitable soul could have attributed it to the skipper's powers of inspiration. In the top of the ninth, down by three runs, the Diamonds loaded the bases for Derek Vaughn, whose double cleared them. But in the bottom of the ninth, the relief pitcher walked the first batter on four pitches, then surrendered a fly ball to right that landed over Jeff Pearce's head to score the winning run. The scene in the locker room afterward was a scene that had played itself out for the Diamonds seventy-three times previously that season, yet tonight was different. No histrionics now; no glove-slamming player or curse-spewing manager. Now, the room was alive with averted eyes; clenched jaws; silence, save for the steady, steamy hiss of the shower heads. In one corner, the losing pitcher, a gentle, soft-spoken teaching major named Bruce Bensching, had started getting undressed, had gotten as far as removing his jersey.

There were players in professional baseball who secretly wanted to get their release—to be relieved of the burden of baseball, which for them had become the burden of deciding whether to do for themselves what an Ed Lynch could accomplish with one phone call, the only difference being that if Lynch did it, they could tell themselves for all time, "At least I gave it my best shot." Now Bruce Bensching counted himself among the secret quitters. Earlier in the day, back in Washington state, his wife had registered him for fall classes. LaShel already had completed five years of study herself, earning a degree in social work, though her full-time job these days was as a checker at a grocery store. She'd postponed her career so he could pursue his. In fact, he'd had a strong season, leading the club with seventeen saves and posting a 2.19 ERA. But he also knew that he was a twenty-eighth-round pick in 1990—he'd spent his $1,000 bonus on an engagement ring—and that he was completing his second season at the same level. His broad, bare shoulders blocked the locker. He was bowed forward on the folding chair, holding himself perfectly still as he stared into the ninety-degree angles of nothingness.

The change in clubhouse atmosphere, however, wasn't apparent only when the Diamonds lost. The game the following night, for instance—a scene that had played itself out fifty-four times previously this season, but this night, too, was different: the end of a six-game losing streak, the first victory against Kane County in their final meeting of the season, and the end of a long road trip at the end of a long year. "It feels good, ye-ahh!" One player was singing. Over the final five innings, three Diamonds pitchers had held the Cougars hitless. Bensching picked up the save, his eighteenth. Beckett got the win—his third in his last four outings, including two seven-inning one-hit performances. Now he was sitting before his locker. He had started to get undressed, had gotten as far as his jersey. He was facing out, away from the locker, into the clubhouse, rocking himself on the rear legs of his chair, his fingers cocked in his belt loops. A silly smile was playing at the corners of his mouth, as if it were an impulse he needed to resist. So, somebody asked, how was he going to reward himself this time?

Beckett considered. "I don't know," he finally said, the grin winning. "I bought myself a lot this second half." Then he threw his head back in a gesture of absolute surrender. "Eh-*ha!*"

"A Vision of Baseball's Future" was how the Kane County franchise billed itself, and in fact the slogan was accurate in more ways than one. On their arrival, the visiting Waterloo players had accorded Kane County the nearly obligatory appreciation and respect with which they now greeted any new stadium, but such praise was beside the point here. The Kane County Events Center was yet another product of the HOK architectural firm, but one with few frills. It had no architectural flourishes to complement the neighborhood, which was a landfill. It had no restaurant. No *roof.* It was a straightforward, no-nonsense, modern minor league ballpark, but the point here wasn't *what* it was, but *where* it was. As one Waterloo player said to another in the locker room after a game, "It's a good facility, and I wouldn't mind if they were all like this. But I got a friend in Naperville who comes here not just because it's a good facility and it's got a family atmosphere, but because it's closer than the big leagues."

If Quad City had demonstrated the possibilities in taking a large market with an old facility and making it new, and South Bend had demonstrated the possibilities in taking a large market with no facility and building one, then the significance of Kane County was the market itself. Kane County belonged to a new generation of minor league ball clubs beginning to migrate to a new generation of minor league territory—in this case, one it shared with the two major league baseball clubs of Chicago.

Prior to 1991, the franchise that would become Kane County had resided, uneasily, in Wausau, Wisconsin. Athletic Field was small (318 and 316 feet down the lines, 360 to center), rendering accurate player evaluations difficult, if not impossible. The stands were small (3,000 capacity), compounding the already formidable cold-out and snow-out problems that came with a location even farther north than Appleton or Wisconsin Rapids. And the market was small (35,000 population). In the end, the Wausau franchise single-season attendance record stood at 63,461, set in 1975, its first year in existence.

In retrospect, the mounting pressure of the minors' new economics to move ball clubs to larger markets had doomed that franchise as surely as any. In 1984 the local owners received and rejected an offer of $200,000 from a group that wanted to move the club to Evansville, Indiana. In 1987 they sold the ball club for $505,000 to a group of medical professionals who wanted to move the franchise to Fort Wayne, but city backing there for a new stadium failed to materialize. These new owners then sold the franchise again, this time to a group that had hoped to move it to La Crosse, Wisconsin, until that city's voters rejected a referendum for a new stadium. It wasn't until the Forest Preserve District of Kane County, Illinois, delivered on a long-standing effort to build a minor league baseball facility—years of debating, then rejecting, then approving funding for a stadium on a former landfill site—that Wausau lost professional baseball, presumably forever.

As recently as twenty or thirty years earlier, the area around what was now the ballpark in Kane County would have consisted of nothing but farms, and the nearest towns would have been considered, if anything, exurbia—bedroom communities beyond the outermost ring of suburbs, good places to get some sleep. Now the landscape was awake with corporate campuses, with light-manufacturing plants and office parks, with cellular-phone centers and pool-and-patio emporia, with fresh streets lined with uniform curbside mailboxes on one side and bulldozers and surveyor's stakes on the other, and when farmland occasionally did appear, as it did just blocks from the ballpark, it presented itself in the form of a Harvest Shoppe. All this activity, however, wasn't simple suburban sprawl. As surely as Waterloo was a century earlier, these were cities in the process of being born.

Technoburbs, they were sometimes called, or edge cities, or perimeter cities. In the nineteenth century, cities typically began at water's edge and expanded outward, eventually growing a ring of suburbs. Unlike the suburbs, however, these new cities weren't merely one more ring of urban growth, places to live and shop while continuing to work in the old cities. Instead, their primary social and economic relationships were with themselves and among one another: places to live and shop *and* work. Technically, they were satellites to the old central cities, but they spun in their own orbits ("galactic cities," they were also called), and when the time came for them to advertise themselves to the world—to spread the word that here was a new and vital urban organism worthy of economic development—they turned to that venerable promotional tool, baseball. In Kane County, that campaign was begun in 1985 by a forest-preserve commissioner named Philip B. Elfstrom, in whose honor the Kane County Events Center was renamed in a pregame ceremony during the Diamonds' visit. "Cities don't chase teams because they think it'll make a big profit," he once said, echoing a sentiment that could have come from a turn-of-the-century Waterloo mayor or an 1869 Cincinnati Red Stockings booster, though his business jargon was distinctly contemporary. "The synergy that press and professional athletes have creates a lot of publicity for the team's home base. I hope that happens here."

Here was the future that Bernie McKinley had envisioned for Waterloo: the service industries, the corporate headquarters, the research laboratories. Here, too, the audience that David Simpson coveted: first, a core of more than 150 corporate sponsors to buy blocks of box seats and provide the franchise with a substantial and stable attendance base, from American Express to Zenith, with stops along the alphabet for national names such as Amoco Oil Company, Armour-Swift Eckrich, McDonald's Corp. and Stroh Brewery, as well as dozens of locally influential sponsors including financial institutions, law and medical practices, media outlets, insurance companies, government agencies, architectural firms, data-resource and computer centers, even a resort; then, to fill the rest of the seats and the lawn through advance-sale and walk-up purchases, the employees of all these businesses and the thousands of others lining the access roads and crowding the cul-de-sacs in a fifteen- or twenty-mile radius; and finally, and especially, their children—and all of them, from CEOs to six-year-olds, with bountiful disposable incomes. The Kane County Events Center might not have a roof, but it did have a walk-in gift shop—not a simple souvenir stand where a kid would have to peer over a countertop and point, but a proper shop where customers could stroll among the merchandise, rummaging a little, mulling an item over, hefting it or trying it on, allowing themselves to be seduced by that perfect gift or keepsake: not only the inevitable assortment of Cougars caps and Cougars cups, but high-end purchases such as Cougars jackets, Cougars clocks (all four varieties) and Cougars sweatshirts (the embroidered-logo kind). The people who worked *there* (the "Illinois Research and Development Corridor" along the tollway five minutes to the south, or the "Golden Corridor" along the tollway fifteen minutes to the north) would go home *there* (a subdivision two, or ten, or twenty minutes in virtually any direction), then, with the whole family, drive over *here*.

"Families. Kids. Inexpensive." This was the mantra of Kane County publicity. Again and again the club's GM, who had worked in the marketing and sales end of book publishing before going back to school for his master's in sports management, repeated this refrain everywhere he went on behalf of the ball club. He and his sales staff had visited one Chamber of Commerce after another, spoken at business breakfasts and lunches and dinners, talked to any Rotary, Jaycee, or Knights of Columbus gathering that would have them. And in every sales pitch, all thoughts led to one theme: A family outing to the ballpark that might cost $100 or even $150 at Wrigley Field or Comiskey Park could be had in Kane County for $25—and without the commute.

But Kane County didn't stop there. If all the franchise had done was position itself smack in the middle of a new kind of city, it would have earned the right to bill itself "A Vision of Baseball's Future." But, as it happened, it was in the nature of this new kind of city that it cropped up on the outskirts of the country's largest metropolitan areas. Midwest League publicity—the yearbook, for instance, that the league published and sold at member ballparks—listed Kane County's "metro population" as 52,194. It was not. Possibly this figure referred to the populations of towns in the immediate Fox River Valley vicinity of the ballpark— Batavia, St. Charles, or Geneva, its actual hometown. A more accurate figure might have been the several hundred thousand or so residents of the nearest western suburbs. A *meaningful* figure, however, would have been how many potential customers could hear or read about the Kane County Cougars through the media in Chicago, whose city limits lay only thirty miles to the east: 7 million.

Kane County was part of the third-largest metropolitan area in the country, and within its first two seasons the franchise had saturated that entire market with a deft blend of a little advertising and a lot of publicity. From the start, the ball club had advertised on WGN radio, a mainstream AM outlet perennially among the metro area's ratings leaders throughout the day. The ads themselves merely laid the groundwork; the promotional visits from announcers, followed by enthusiastic on-air recommendations to head out to Kane County and give Cougars baseball a try, reinforced the impression that a new form of entertainment had arrived. Articles in the *Chicago Tribune* and *Sun-Times* pushed the momentum further. When the *Tribune*'s sports section started running the Cougars' schedule in the daily calendar of the upcoming week's sports events, the franchise instantly attained a level of legitimacy that few minor league clubs could match. Not only did such coverage correct any mistaken impression that the minors were simply glorified American Legion ball—not only did it validate the Cougars as a *professional* sports team—but it elevated the entire enterprise. Every day during the season, there they were, right alongside the Cubs, White Sox, Black Hawks, Bears, and Bulls, as if Chicago had suddenly sprouted one more team for area sports fans to call their own: the Kane County Cougars.

For fans who knew pro baseball only from its Wrigley Field or Comiskey Park incarnation, the differences between big league and minor league ball were immediately apparent. Seats close to the action, the hunger of the players, the hokum—all the traditional virtues of minor league ball were on display, and Kane County quickly gained a highly favorable reputation through the media and word-of-mouth for presenting "baseball the way it used to be."

Not that it was a brand of entertainment that fans in, say, Wausau might have recognized. The differences started outside the gate, with a $1 parking fee (which went to the county). Beers began at $2.25, about double what they cost in Waterloo. The outfield area featured three electronic scoreboards—a line-score board sponsored by a beer, a message board for greetings and more ads, and Diamond Vision, on which the Rally Meter, a cartoon invocation, implored fans to top their previous loudest cheer of the game. "MAKE SOME NOISE: RALLY METER 118," it read. (Pause for ad.) "BREAK THE RECORD. TONITE'S RECORD 119." "You say I prompt 'em?" the GM once answered his critics. "Damn right I do! So what? It keeps them from sitting on their thumbs!"

Then again, it wasn't a brand of entertainment that fans in Wausau had to worry about anymore, anyway. Ten or fifteen years earlier, what the minors had sold was baseball and little else. The gimmicks or giveaways or contests had been few and not intentionally corny; but as the industry expanded, it had to present a brand of entertainment that the new customers would recognize. Nowhere was this phenomenon more evident than in the name and logo craze of recent years, which tried to satisfy the nostalgic cravings of the new fans through faux-homespun nicknames and insignias: Albany Polecats, Carolina Mudcats, Kane County Cougars. (Waterloo Diamonds, chosen in a name-the-team contest after the club lost its Indians affiliation, represented an early and restrained effort.) The mechanical bull that the makers of *Bull Durham* had added to an outfield wall to suggest minor league authenticity eventually returned to the wall to meet the demands of fans who showed up thinking they knew how an authentic minor league park looked: life imitating art imitating life; kismet become calculation. The vision of baseball's future, it turned out, was baseball's past, only different.

In its first season, Kane County's attendance had been 240,290—second in the Midwest League only to Quad City's record-breaking pace that year, and even then only by 2,000. That summer, Kane County averaged 3,670 fans in a facility with 3,600 seats (though lawn seating raised that capacity to approximately 6,000). Early the following season, the Forest Preserve District added 1,200 seats, and by the time the Diamonds had arrived, with eight home dates remaining in the season, the franchise already had left the Midwest League record far behind and was on a pace to draw better than 300,000 easily, averaging 4,863 fans in a 4,800-seat arena (5,600 with lawn seating). Thanks to season-ticket and advance sales, even on a chilly, thunderstorm-threatening evening following a full day of rain, Kane County's attendance was *better than average*—and more than double what Waterloo's would be on its best night: 4,869.

"Day like this in Waterloo?" Robbie Beckett said, sitting on the dugout bench before the game that night. "From that light pole, to the fence." He was pointing down the first-base line to a lawn-seating area currently populated by three people.

"Good day in Waterloo?" Dave Adams pointed to a section of

the grandstands that had a smattering of customers. "That crowd there."

"Unless there's a promotion," said Beckett. "Then you get five hundred."

"That's the only time they come," said Adams, "is when they can get something for free."

The two players laughed softly, shaking their heads. Throughout their exhange, a third player, a pitcher named Tom Paskievitch, had been sitting down the bench in silence. Now he spoke.

"Day like this in Waterloo," he said, "wouldn't *play*."

The Diamonds entered the final two games against the Cedar Rapids Reds, on the last weekend of the season, needing to win both in order to tie the series between the two teams for the year. What would happen in that case the front offices hadn't agreed upon; Jeff Nelson had called Cedar Rapids with the suggestion that perhaps both staffs should kiss a pig, but the answer he'd gotten was "You're way wrong on your thinking." The only way, then, that the pig kissing was certain to take place was if the Diamonds were to lose one of the two games—preferably the first. A Reds victory on Saturday not only would clinch the season series, but would allow for a suitably elaborate and publicity-garnering ceremony before the final game between the two clubs Sunday afternoon in Cedar Rapids.

And if that turned out to be the case, then the weekend would be nearly as complete a triumph for Nelson as he could have imagined. Kissing a pig would represent the culmination of his various promotional efforts all season long, but it recently had come to represent for him the methodology and business philosophy that one day soon would bury "respect for the ticket." On Friday evening, at the ballpark in Waterloo, Mildred Boyenga had approached him and asked, "So what do you *think?*"

"About what?"

"About Dave's *con*-tract not bein' re-*newed*."

It was true that the owners, in voting not to renew Simpson's contract, had delayed a decision on filling the GM's position until after the season. It was also true that there existed among the owners a faction that didn't exactly approve of Nelson's style. But

Nelson felt sure that his ascension to the GM's post would amount to little more than a formality. After all, as he had reminded Boesen just the other day, the fans loved him, he livened up the place, and he worked hard. "You ask me to, I'll climb a mountain and eat horseshit, then laugh all the way down," he told Boesen.

More to the point, he'd kiss a pig. On Friday, some fans in Waterloo presented Nelson with Chap-Stik, while another fan took to wearing a plastic pig's snout on the front of his Diamonds cap. On Saturday, the batboy in Cedar Rapids, who knew Nelson from his umpiring career, blew him kisses, while Nelson, sitting in the first-base bleachers with a group of ballpark workers from Waterloo, got to act aggrieved all afternoon long—when John Abercrombie failed to run out a pop fly that started foul but blew fair, or when Jeff Pearce failed to throw out the go-ahead runner from medium-deep center in the bottom of the eighth. "God-fucking-damn it," Nelson roared in the top of the ninth, the Diamonds down by one, his torso twisting away from the field in a parody of anguish, "let's go!" Finally Keith McKoy struck out swinging to end the game, and Nelson, standing up, pointed toward home and screamed, "Arghh! Release him!"

The next day, Nelson arrived with a camcorder of his own. Two television crews already were waiting in the parking lot outside Veterans Stadium. Nelson complained that the wager had been made "in bad faith" because the rival front office personnel had neglected to inform him before the season that the Cincinnati organization would be treating Cedar Rapids as the Red's Class A-Advanced club this year. He complained about the play of the Diamonds in Saturdays' game. "Abercrombie can't run out a fly ball!" he moaned. "Pearce can't make a throw from medium-deep right field!" When the crews had shut off their cameras, he hinted that this stunt sure would make a swell "Play of the Day" on ESPN's *Sportscenter* that night. As the crews turned and trudged off toward the stadium to record the ceremony itself, and as a group of fans and staff from Waterloo trailed behind him, Nelson stopped and shouted to the sky, "I got it! Next year we'll call it 'Kiss It Good-bye,' and it'll be a big pig, and the next day we'll eat it!"

"Next year," the radio announcer Kelly Neff said, "take it to dinner, then give it flowers."

"Oh, God!" Nelson rolled his eyes and adopted an expression of indignation. "Why didn't I think of that!"

The pig—actually a piglet, four weeks old, and slightly larger than a loaf of bread—had been procured from a local farmer, and the ball club staff had dressed it in a Cedar Rapids Reds bib before carrying it out to a microphone stand in the grass behind home. David Simpson was there, grinning. Brian Pfaltzgraff was there, shrugging and wincing. A reporter asked him if this was the stupidest thing he'd ever done in the line of baseball duty, and Pfaltzgraff thought about it a long time before answering that once he'd had to change bulbs in the scoreboard during a game. "That was stupider'n this," he said.

But it was Jeff Nelson's show now. The "Give It a Spin Bat Race," the Gary Glitter chant-along, the home run-contest—almost every stunt that Nelson had introduced this season at Waterloo Municipal Stadium was a variation on, if not an exact duplicate of, a promotion he had seen at other ballparks as an umpire. In challenging the Cedar Rapids staff to a pig-kissing wager, however, Nelson had happened upon a promotional bonanza all his own. It was a natural. It *worked*. And, to some extent, the degree to which it worked was a credit to Nelson's public-relations skills. As a broadcast-journalism major, he'd served an internship with a TV news program in Salt Lake City, and he understood what newspaper editors and television producers wanted to hear. Even so, a pig-kissing promotion contained a certain something, an indefinable quality that captured the imagination. He had first discussed the idea publicly on Kelly Neff's Saturday-morning radio show back in March, and Neff's uproarious response had told him he was on to something. He'd plugged it at "Meet the Diamonds," to similar effect from the fans. In May he mentioned it to a *San Diego Union-Tribune* reporter who had called one day looking for items for a column on the Padres' minor league affiliates, and the result was a full article ("Losers of Wager Must Pucker Up for a Porker") that quoted Nelson as saying, "All I know is that I don't plan on eating any pork in August." Then *Sports Illustrated* ran an item on it, in the magazine's "Between the Lines" section ("Porky and Buss"), with this Nelson quote: "I can't even look at a package of bacon without shuddering." The *San Francisco Chronicle* had picked up that item ("Prelude to a Kiss"), and similarly it had led to telephone interviews with sports-talk radio programs around the country. When inspiration had struck Nelson one cold morning back in the winter, he couldn't possibly have guessed where his intuition had led him: a promotion that reinforced precisely what everyone wanted to believe about small-town life in the Midwest, and precisely what everyone wanted to believe about the minor leagues.

"That's a baby pig," somebody called to him from the crowd. "You're robbing the sty."

Nelson guffawed.

"Pig don't want to kiss *you*, Jeff!" Rollo called.

Nelson guffawed again.

The cameras were filming. Reporters were scribbling.

"This is about as Bill Veeck as you can get," Nelson announced. "To me, this is what minor league baseball is all about. Nothing is too far out. You can go to the big leagues to watch a baseball game, but you come to the minor leagues to be entertained."

When the time came for his lips to meet the pig's, Nelson paused long enough to deliver the punch line: "I'm not looking for a long-term relationship."

Then the ballpark sound system cranked up the Looney Tunes theme music, and the voice of Porky Pig was heard throughout the land: "Th-th-th-th-th-th-that's all, folks!"

11

The threat that the *Courier* had sounded at the start of the season—that September 1 might mark the last game of professional baseball in Waterloo history—seemed remote when the date arrived. By the time of the final home stand, a pair of games against Clinton on a Monday and Tuesday before a season-ending road trip to Peoria, school was back in session, and the stands had returned to their mid-May intimacy. The number of seasons that professional baseball would be played in Waterloo, a number that fans once would have thought to be inexhaustible, might yet one day turn out to be finite; but those who came to the ballpark these last two nights were saluting nothing more than the end of a season, not an institution.

"First part of the year," someone in the Zoo Crew observed about Beckett, after he had struck out five batters in the first two innings of the first game, "he couldn't *throw* a strike." The Diamonds won that game, thanks mostly to a ten-run, eighth-inning barrage. They dropped the next game, 3–2. Jeff Nelson let the bat race go on longer than usual, then awarded the contestants the bats. The public-address announcer reported the winner of the Roth Jewelers "Player of the Year" contest: "By a large margin, it's Jason Hardtke!" "Come on," a fan shouted at the press box after the announcer said that a third and final winner had claimed bingo, "it's the last day of the season. Let's have *six!*"

In the clubhouse afterward, Dean Treanor spoke in a tone even more measured than usual: "That . . . is the first time . . . I've ever seen . . . the home crowd . . . not bring back the team . . . for a final ovation . . . at the end of the year." Long pause. Glance to Champ. "Says something, don't it?"

"Yeah, it does." Champ didn't look up. He was sipping a beer and flipping through a scrapbook that a longtime fan had presented him before the game. The scrapbook contained every *Cou-*

rier clipping on the club throughout the season. Sipping, flipping, he said that he'd been told he'd be accepting the "Player of the Year" watch on behalf of Hardtke in a ceremony, but that was the last he'd heard of it. Then he said, " 'Diamonds Suffer Another Beating,' " barked one quick laugh, and slapped the book on the 1992 Waterloo Diamonds shut.

That night, after the manager and staff and players of the Diamonds had vacated the ballpark, and after they themselves had finished sorting ticket stubs and counting money and taking inventory, the ballpark workers gathered one final time—everybody but Simpson, who holed up in the front office to watch *Star Trek.* They stood around the front of the first-base bleachers and talked, but on this occasion they didn't leave the stands for the field, and their voices rarely rose above a whisper, as if their purchase on this place had expired. There would be no late night here tonight, no long talks or midnight softball games, no waiting for the dawn.

The lights were out.

The season was over.

When it started to drizzle—a cold rain, unmistakably autumnal—everybody glanced at the tarp roll across the field, against the third-base wall, but nobody made a move toward it because there would be no point now. Nobody made a move, period. They stood there, rain misting their beer, unwilling to relinquish just yet the season or the night. Their voices faded, then revived, then faded, then stopped.

Still, nobody moved.

Then Nelson spoke. He said he wanted to propose one last toast. He raised his blue souvenir cup in the rain. Jacket sleeves squeaked and sweatshirts swished as his coworkers obediently raised their blue souvenir cups in the rain.

"To the boxes and boxes," Nelson said, "of Funny Nose and Glasses!"

The season expired in Peoria on an ideal evening for baseball: cloudless, bugless, breezeless, a shirtsleeve-only seventy-six degrees, complete with an endlessly inventive sunset that spanned the middle innings. Had an infield ever looked greener, or base paths whiter? No. It was that kind of night.

The game itself stood for nothing but a game of baseball. In terms of team achievements, nothing was at stake now. Depending on the game's outcome, the Peoria Chiefs were going to complete the season anywhere from twelve to fourteen games out of first, and the Waterloo Diamonds from fifteen-and-a-half to seventeen-and-a-half, but their ranks in the standings wouldn't change. Peoria currently occupied fourth place, Waterloo fifth, and no miracle that either team could perform tonight on this field would affect that final reckoning.

This, then, was the end. In fact, "The End"—the Doors' song— was playing over the loudspeakers at Pete Vonachen Stadium as the players straggled out of the clubhouse an hour before game time. There would be no stretch tonight, no long-toss, no BP or infield. Lolling along the foul line, strolling around the outfield lawn, the players broke into small groups and talked among themselves, making jokes about everybody swinging at the first pitch tonight, jokes about getting run by the umpires in the third inning. In the dugout, Treanor sank into a corner of coolness and pulled his cap over his face. The previous evening most of the team had spent enjoying themselves at Big Al's, though no one quite to the same extent as Treanor. Now he could manage to open his eyes only long enough to inquire of the trainer what his system needed. "Salt?" Treanor guessed tremblingly.

"Fluids," said Maxwell.

"Those strippers at Big Al's," a player said, flopping next to Treanor on the bench, "what do they think about?"

"Gettin' it over," said Treanor, and he closed his eyes again.

More so than most, this final game would take place in a hangover haze of contractual obligation; more so than any other, this game would hinge on the pursuit of individual achievement. It would have been the case anyway, this being the final road trip, final series, and final chance for a player to affect this year's stats, but a couple of recent developments had exacerbated the process—had dominated conversation, in fact, since the team arrived in Peoria the previous afternoon. One involved Willie Greene. Willie Greene, a first-round 1989 draft pick, had started the season with the Cedar Rapids Reds and, even by the Class A-Advanced standards of that ball club, had immediately distinguished himself; at the time of his promotion to Double-A Chattanooga, barely a month into the season, he was leading the Midwest League in home runs and RBIs by such wide margins that the name Willie Greene had continued to appear on the daily stats sheets of top-five league leaders in both those categories for weeks to come. And now, as of Tuesday night, he was a major league ball player. On September 1, major league clubs could expand their rosters to forty players, and the Cincinnati Reds had promoted Greene as a replacement for the injured third baseman Chris Sabo.

"Hear about Willie Greene?" Scott Bream said when Champ approached a group standing in the outfield before that first game in Peoria.

"What?"

"The Show."

"No shit!"

"Went three for four."

Champ, grinning, took one step back, nearly staggering. "You're fuckin' shittin' me!"

It *happened,* and it happened *here,* sort of.

The other development—and one with greater potential significance for the members of the organization—was a quote that had appeared in print. Monday evening, on the final day of the trading deadline, the San Diego Padres had traded pitcher Craig Lefferts to the Baltimore Orioles for a minor league pitcher and a player to be named later. Wednesday morning, the *USA Today* sports section carried the following item:

> GM Joe McIlvaine said the Lefferts deal had to be made because of finances. By trading Lefferts, the Padres dropped the rest of his $1.75 million salary. "It's just that the whole financial situation in San Diego is difficult. We're in deep financial trouble. This was one of the toughest decisions to make. But it should not be taken as a signal that we're giving up."

"First time," trainer John Maxwell said, passing the paper around on the bus into Peoria, "I can remember Joe saying he made a move just because of money."

The financial problems in San Diego certainly had been no secret around the team. The absence of a hitting coach this year had been a sure sign that something was amiss. So had the apparent distractedness at the highest levels in San Diego regarding the situation in Waterloo, an impression that McIlvaine's visit had done nothing to dispel. Then, in recent weeks, the players had learned that the Padres were cutting back on the fall instructional league; rather than operate its own camp and invite the usual thirty or so players from throughout the farm system, the organization would be sharing facilities with the Colorado Rockies and sending only eighteen players (including two from Waterloo, Bream to work on switch-hitting and Beckett to work on breaking pitches). And then there had been the rumor, all season long, that the Padres would be dropping one entire club at the A level next year, and then had come the reality that it would be Waterloo. This week's turn of the screw—a report out of San Diego that the Padres' A-Advanced affiliate in High Desert was dropping *them*—more than underscored the severity of the situation. Not only did the players belong to an organization that a highly desirable minor league club could feel free to divorce, but, as a result, the Padres might have to retain Waterloo after all—as next season's A-Advanced-equivalency club. As Beckett said, the possibility dawning, his jaw dropping, " 'You're movin' up. You're goin' to Waterloo.' *What the fuck.*"

Among the players, a consensus already had formed. Ray and Joan Kroc had known how to run a major league organization, and Tom Werner and the rest of what they called his "Hollywood people" didn't—didn't understand, or at least had come to understand too late, that the purchase price of a big league ball club was only the beginning of the financial commitment, that it took considerable cash flow to keep a Craig Lefferts on the mound in San Diego and a hitting coach in the dugout in Waterloo. One night on the bus, during the dark hum of a long ride home, Maxwell regaled a small circle of players with tales of the Kroc era—how whenever a roving instructor would come to town, he would take the manager and coaches and trainer out for dinner at the best steak restaurant in town, a meal that would last long into the night, that would entail considerable quantities of food and alcohol, that would end with the instructor slapping the corporate plastic on the tablecloth and all the guests regarding it with deep satisfaction and gratitude, and solemnly intoning, "Thank you, Joan."

"That is perfect," Pearce said, shaking his head, breaking the respectful silence that followed. "That is *exactly* the way it should be."

Still, the McIlvaine quote caught everyone by surprise. In part, its significance was what he did. When he closed the Lefferts deal that Monday evening, the Padres were eight and a half games out of first with more than a month to play—long shots, perhaps, but not yet out of the running. In the annals of baseball comebacks, there were precedents aplenty. In fact, comebacks were an integral part of baseball mythology; the length of the season and the open-endedness of each game were what made baseball the sport where it wasn't over until the fat lady sang—where it ain't over till it's over. McIlvaine could insist all he wanted that "it should not be taken as a signal that we're giving up," but the meaning of his actions was unmistakable: cutting the payroll was more important than winning the pennant.

It was one thing for minor leaguers to know that winning wasn't everything. Whatever effect it once might have had on morale, the change in the minors' primary purpose from winning games and pennants to developing potential major leaguers had long ago been absorbed into the fabric of the sport and business. What was more, that change could be justified as serving the cause of winning. Even if a player had to watch promising teammates vanish through the chutes of an organization and leave him behind, or even if he had to adapt to a new assignment himself, he could content himself with the knowledge that every roster change was part of a plan intended in some way to serve the ultimate goal: to build a better organization, and therefore a better ball club at the top, where winning *was* everything. But if *that* weren't true, it wasn't something anyone ever acknowledged—unless that was what Joe McIlvaine had just done.

But partly the significance of his quote was simply that he said it. His willingness to discuss the organization's financial situation openly seemed itself an indication that he expected it to deteriorate further. In that case, the cutbacks so far wouldn't have been aberrations—regrettable but inevitable economic corrections—

but indications of much worse to come. And if *that* were true, then the worry that would follow a player forever wouldn't be simply whether the end of a season had brought the end of a career, or even whether the end of one cost-cutting season in particular had meant the end of a career. It would be whether, in what was most likely his one chance at a professional baseball career, he'd found himself hobbled to an organization with dwindling support resources and shrinking job opportunities.

At the start of the season, Champ had told the Waterloo Diamonds that they had to think about themselves. At the middle of the season, he had told them that they had to think about the team, too. Toward the end of the season, he had asked them to try to strike a balance. But as the end drew near, and the news from the highest levels of the Padres organization acquired a steadily more foreboding cast, the players might have been forgiven for suspecting that Champ had gotten it right the first time: This was the only game in town, and the way to play it was every man for himself.

After the first game in Peoria, Jeff Pearce paid Champ a visit in the coaches' office. With his performance at the plate in that night's win, Pearce said, his batting average had passed .270, the goal he'd set for himself at the start of August. He asked whether Champ was planning to start him the following night, in the final game of the season, because if it was all the same to Champ, Pearce said, he'd prefer to sit it out.

This was a new one on Champ. It wasn't unusual for a ballplayer hoping to improve his stats to ask his manager for a chance to play; questions of pride and professionalism Champ understood. Even he—with his guarantee of a job next season, an invitation to coach in the instructional league, and the assurances from above that the team's performance was no reflection on his managerial abilities—wasn't impervious to how his performance this year might look to a prospective employer at some future date. Just the other day, in his office in Waterloo, Champ had complained, "It's easy to say I don't care about winning and losing, that we're here for player development and all that, but you know what? Years from now, nobody's going to know that San Diego was dumping players here, or that Jason got moved up, or that San Diego was planning to cut the club anyway. All they're going to see," he'd said, getting up from his chair, "is a won-lost record and my name." Despite what he always said, baseball *was* a job, and he'd done it.

On the bus back to the hotel from the ballpark, declaiming from the royal distance that the front seat afforded him, Champ tormented Pearce by wondering aloud whether to start him the next day. Then, the following afternoon, Champ joined a circle of players idling in the outfield about an hour before the start of the final game of the season and announced, "I found breakfast waiting for me this morning at the hotel, on a tray outside my door."

The players nearest him hushed.

"With a twenty-dollar bill," Champ went on. "And a note on the napkin: 'To the best manager ever. J.P.' "

Jeff Pearce's perpetual wince deepened. First thing this afternoon he'd checked the line-up that Champ had posted on the clubhouse wall, and his name wasn't there. But apparently Champ wasn't going to let him off that easily.

"I hoped," Pearce said, "we could conduct this in a professional manner."

"I got my fuckin' coffee right there." Champ's hands described the topography of his imaginary room-service tray.

"I came to you yesterday in *private*," Pearce said. "Asked you as a *favor*—"

"Fuckin' *eggs*."

Laughter was beginning to whisper through the players. To Pearce, his request made perfect sense. Shortly after his father's visit, while his batting average was still languishing in the .240 range, he had vowed that in the final month of the season, he would raise it to .270. As recently as a week ago, he'd managed to push his average only halfway there—.255. Since then, however, he'd been on a tear, going two for three in four consecutive games, including the first game against the Chiefs. He'd *reached* his *goal*.

"In the off season," he told Champ now, folding his arms and staring at the outfield grass and lowering his voice, "when everybody in the organization gets together and makes the decisions, they're going to look at my stats, and they're going to see .270."

Champ dropped the tray pantomime. Now his withering smile vanished and his voice hardened and his pitch lowered and his words tumbled out in a rush. "They don't look at numbers. I'm telling you right now. They'll look at it and say, 'Yeah, he hit around .270, somewhere in there. But, hey, what we want to know is' "—Champ paused—" '*is this a guy who wants to play every day?*' "

Pearce snorted. "Release me, Champ. Get me out of this organization. That's *fine*. I said at the beginning of August, my goal is to hit .270. Now what happens if I hit the ball hard four times tonight—good hits, but right at somebody?"

"What if you *get* four hits?" Champ answered quickly. "Then you're .275, and they're goin', 'Hey, he's almost .280.' Hey, Vaughn!" he suddenly called.

"What," said Pearce. "What are you doin'."

Derek Vaughn had been standing outside the circle, away from the discussion. He glanced at Champ now, saw his manager waving him over. Players parted; a path appeared. As Vaughn approached, he wore a look that said he didn't know what this was about, but it couldn't be good.

Champ folded his arms and pointed his chin at Pearce. "Pearce says he wants to play tonight. He's back in right."

"*Why?*" Vaughn said, more a cry than a question. Such a scenario would bounce Vaughn from the lineup; he had his own agenda to pursue tonight, his potential hundredth hit of the year. Vaughn grabbed at the lineup card in Champ's hand, but Champ twisted his torso just in time. Then Vaughn looked around and saw from the expressions of his teammates that some sort of joke was playing itself out. He smiled with relief.

"What would you do?" Pearce asked him. "In my place?"

Vaughn was still beaming. "I'd shut it down."

Champ blinked. Then he said, "Where's Beckett? I'll talk to you about improving. I'll talk to you about fuckin' improving. Where's Beckett?"

Beckett was standing maybe ten feet away. Like everyone else in the immediate vicinity, he'd been watching while trying to appear as if his thoughts were elsewhere—in Beckett's case, in examining a bat that he, as a pitcher, would never have to swing in this league. But even before Champ could draw Beckett into the discussion, Pearce was dismissing him with a wave of a hand.

"He's got 'first-round' around his neck," Pearce said. "That'll follow him forever. The Padres have got $150,000 in him"—

Beckett lowered his eyes to the lawn and started swinging the bat idly, self-consciously—"and that's another number."

The laughter among the players had stopped.

Pearce could hold his own. Champ might not have pursued the issue—or at least not so publicly—if he hadn't thought that Pearce could defend himself. Pearce might not possess the physical skills or emotional discipline of a future major leaguer, but at least he had the intellectual ability to articulate his circumstances—if not a glibness that could show up anyone, even his manager. Champ had understood all this going in.

"What about the pitcher?" Champ said. "What about him? You don't think he's think' about *his* fuckin' stats? You don't think he'd like to have you in the lineup tonight?"

"I didn't think about that," Pearce said.

"He's gotta go out there without a hot bat fuckin' backin' him up."

"I didn't think about the pitcher." Pearce began studying the ground.

Champ waited.

By now, all activity on the field had ceased. The silence and tension from this small circle had radiated outward.

Champ pressed his advantage. "You know, it's a first for me—a player coming to me, telling me he doesn't want to play."

"I *want* to play," Pearce said softly. "I would *love* to play. But the game's changed. Free agents and signing bonuses have made this a different game. As a businessman, I have to look at my own best interests." At last Pearce looked up at Champ. The two men were squinting at each other in the early evening sun. "I'm *twenty-three*. And there's *another* number."

Pearce didn't play in the final game of the season, and the ambition of the other players settled into more familiar patterns. In the fifth inning, Vaughn got his hundredth hit. "There it is!" came the chorus from the dugout as the ball dropped in. Then, as Vaughn stood on second: "Quit smilin'!" In the eighth, Bream bent over a piece of paper on the dugout ledge, doing the long division on his 90 hits in 392 at-bats, the numbers staircasing down the page: 900 minus 784, 1160 minus 784, 3760 minus 3528, 2320 minus 1950. Bream turned to the bench. "What's .2296?" he called. "Is that .230?"

Nobody knew for sure.

Then Bream and Farlow together bent to the math on Farlow's 91 hits in 407 at-bats, so far, and came up with .2231. So far. But if Farlow were to bat in the ninth and get a hit, they figured, he'd be 92 for 408, or .225, the next plateau on the entirely arbitrary five-point-increment psychological scale.

Robertson led off the ninth with a double. Abercrombie struck out, and Mulligan walked.

"Pugh!" Bream shouted from the dugout. *"Pugh!"*

Pugh stepped out of the batter's box and squinted toward the dugout. For his part, Pugh had established a personal benchmark tonight as well: the only Diamond to appear in every one of the season's 137 games.

"Farlow's gotta get *up,* man!" Bream shouted to him.

Pugh nodded his understanding: Don't hit into a double play. He stepped back into the box, tried to hit the ball up, and struck out.

Then came Farlow. He took the first pitch for a ball. "Walk ain't gonna do it!" called Altaffer. Then Farlow slapped the ball to the shortstop, who tossed it to the second baseman for the force on Mulligan. Three outs.

With a 5–1 lead, Champ sent Davila to the mound in the bottom of the ninth, his first appearance since his injury early in August. He had been well enough to pitch for about a week now, Maxwell thought, but the opportunity hadn't arisen. If one player seemed certain of receiving his outright release in the off-season, it was Davila; but to release an injured player might be "controversial"—a euphemism that the organization had come to use in discussing the situation. Like a surgeon attending to a condemned prisoner, the organization needed to establish, for its own possible legal protection, that Davila was healthy enough to pitch—*then* release him.

He was. Three up, three down. The final out of the season, for the record: a fly ball to left, caught by Robertson.

The fireworks started even as the team was heading for the clubhouse. The ballpark lights blinked out; directly overhead, the Big Dipper blinked on. Some players continued across the field in the sudden total black, feeling their way, but some stopped where they were and dropped to the ground. They were together then, alone in the darkness, fans and players and constellations. For the past five months almost to the day, the players had been the collective center of attention, the source of well more than a hundred separate events in an expanding sector of the American entertainment industry. Now they lay themselves down in the grass, content for once to be the ones watching, surrendering to the sudden anonymity, allowing the sparks from the fireworks booming and blossoming overhead to shower them, burning brightly, burning briefly, like falling stars.

In the clubhouse, Champ was attempting a farewell address to the troops—"Everybody grab a seat real quick. I know it's been a hell of a year. We've been in *Waterloo*. But the day we've been waiting for is here. . . . We've had some fun this year, maybe not as much as you'd like. . . . Some of you are going to make it. Some of you aren't. . . ." But the barrage of fireworks kept shouting him down, as did the outbursts of players barging into the clubhouse ("Holy fuck! The fireworks landed in the back of a truck out there!"), and then a green flare dropped directly outside a window above the lockers, and when several players scrambled up on chairs to get a better look, Champ gave up. He stepped aside and let Treanor attempt a few words of farewell, then walked into the coaches' office and shut the door. Players shook hands with one another and dispersed, some for a long drive home on their own, the rest to make one final bus ride for the season.

That night, about 2:00 A.M., the bus pulled off the interstate an hour south of Waterloo and traveled the mile or so along the two-lane blacktop through the cornfields to the Cedar Rapids airport. Kevin Farlow had to catch an early flight, and rather than travel to Waterloo and double back to Cedar Rapids before dawn, he had asked to be let off here. From the road the terminal appeared dark, and somebody said playfully, "Hey, Farlow, grab some sidewalk," but then the bus cruised past the first entrance to the terminal, and the lights inside the airport were dim, and then the bus slowed at the second entrance, and the lights were still dim, and then the bus stopped. By now, the players were silent.

For a moment, nobody moved. In 1990 the Padres had drafted Farlow in the fifteenth round; it was understood that the organization didn't have much of a financial investment in his future. Furthermore, he had played in college; he'd had the head start the high school players hadn't. Yet over the course of his three-year professional career, he'd never finished with a batting average more distinguished than .243. This season, even though it was his second at the same level, he had actually fared worse than the previous year—not reaching even .225. Kevin Farlow might not be the first player that the San Diego hammers would pound out of the system, but he wouldn't be far behind.

Now Farlow stood up quickly, shook the hands of the players sitting nearest him, gathered his bags from the overhead luggage compartment, and fairly jumped off the bus. He tested the doors to the terminal. Locked. So he dropped one bag to the sidewalk and the smaller one at the head of a bench, for a pillow. As the bus pulled out, he climbed aboard the bench.

"There it is, man," a lone voice rose from the back of the bus. "There's pro ball."

Farlow didn't look back.

But then they'd already said their farewells to one another, the season, and maybe pro ball. The previous evening, after the first game in Peoria, Champ had invited everybody out for pizza and beer on him—or, more accurately, on the players who had paid fines during the season. Sully's was a sports bar, a staple of downtown Peoria nightlife. Signs on the wall commemorated the Peoria Chiefs who had made the majors: Mark Grace, Rafael Palmeiro, Joe Girardi, Dwight Smith, Greg Maddux. A mammoth TV screen was suspended at one end of the room, tuned to ESPN. A giant shrimp dripping drawn butter floated into view. Champ ordered half a dozen pizzas and half a dozen pitchers of beer, for starters. He announced that he had considered using the fines for car payments. "It was gonna be that, or this," he said. "I flipped a coin, and both times I lost." Pitchers of beer arrived. Pizza arrived. A player did his impression of Treanor coaching third: windmilling a base runner home, then going "Oh, shit!" and trying to call the runner back. Everybody laughed. Then Treanor did his impression of this same player playing third: cocky confidence, widening eyes, handcuffed hands. Everybody laughed, though not as much. ESPN showed the major league highlights for the day. The clips got to the Cincinnati game, and the room hushed when a ground ball rolled to the left side of the infield. "This'll be Willie!" several players shouted, unnecessarily. On the big screen, Willie Greene booted the ball. Then a card came up on ESPN showing the year's minor league leaders, and there was Willie Greene again, right at the top: 27 home runs for the season. Somewhere in that saloon in Peoria, a voice moaned, "He's made more money in two days than we've made all year."

And then everybody was chanting, "Shots! Shots! Shots!" as Beckett delivered the first two to Champ and Treanor, who dutifully downed them. Then another round found its way to Champ and Treanor's table. And another, and another, and another, until the shot glasses were backing up two by two, and Champ, ever the manager, was calling it quits with an authority that brooked no opposition. "I'll drink Davila's," he said, " 'cause I *like* ouzo." And he did, and he was done, and if the liquor was affecting him he wasn't going to show it—but not so Treanor, who was pounding back whatever anyone handed him, his face flushing, the sweat caking his weathered face from the newly gelled hair at the top of his forehead to the now-browning collar of his white dress shirt, buttoned all the way up to his bobbing, bobbing Adam's apple.

"Hey, Cam," Champ shouted across the room to Cairncross. "You got an ID?"

Cairncross stood up. "Here's my fuckin' ID," he said, undoing his belt and turning around and reaching back to grab a cheek in each hand so that everybody in the room had no choice but to gaze, glassily, at the anus of Cameron Cairncross.

And then, after the whooping and laughter had abated, it was "Big Al's! Big Al's! Big Al's!" and suddenly everybody was scrambling up, knocking over chairs, herding out the door into the rain to make the two-block weave to Big Al's, where the players joined the men in business suits in arranging themselves ringside to exercise the privilege of slipping dollar bills into the G-strings of topless women who alternately scissored themselves on faux firepoles and peddled photocopies of their 8×10 glossies, and where Pearce got tossed out bodily by a bouncer for touching the shoe of one of the models walking the floor, and where Willie Greene made one more appearance, this time on a screen even more mammoth than the one at Sully's, distracting the attention of the ball players from Farlow, who had accepted the challenge of his teammates to take the stage and sit in a chair while a stripper paraded before him, and who occasionally, as if suddenly remembering that he was supposed to be having fun up there, managed half a smile, but who mostly just sat motionless, mouth open, jaw slack, eyelids shuttering, the look on his face the uncomprehending but not uninterested expression a fatted beast might have in the instant it catches the glint of the ball-peen hammer.

Every so often that off-season, Bill Boesen fielded a phone call from a prospective buyer of the ball club. Sometimes he didn't catch the name; usually he didn't wait for the details. The new Professional Baseball Agreement had created for speculators in baseball franchises—those who already had traded in franchises before the adoption of the new PBA and those who hadn't but recognized an opening when they saw one—a golden era of opportunity. Even during the headiest stretches of the 1980s, a potential investor would have had to research almost the entire inventory of minor league franchises just to isolate the handful that might be vulnerable to a reasonable offer at that moment. Now, with the April 1, 1994, deadline only a year and a half away—and, implicitly, the outside date by which a franchise would have to secure financing either to renovate or to replace a ballpark maybe six months away—the vulnerable franchises numbered in the dozens. Owners of organizations that previously wouldn't have come on the market for years, if ever, now had little choice but to listen to any remotely reasonable offer—or, at least, to not slam down the phone.

The battle for the ball club had begun in earnest and, in a way, the owners in Waterloo were fortunate that they still had a franchise for which they could refuse offers. Toward the middle of September, Dan Yates called Ed Lynch, who confirmed that the Padres at the moment had no full-season Class A teams. Not only had High Desert divorced the Padres, leaving San Diego without a Class A-Advanced team, but so had Charleston, leaving San Diego without a slow-A team. Even so, Lynch told Yates, the Padres were still dropping one club, and that club was Waterloo. "Gee, do you think it had anything to do with our facilities?" Jeff Nelson deadpanned at the news.

That September, eighty-eight Player Development Contracts were expiring in all the minors, and seven in the Midwest League.

Yates drafted a letter to potential major league parent clubs listing the franchise's virtues, which Boesen read aloud at a board meeting. This list included: "stable local ownership" (laughter), an "experienced front office" (more laughter), "excellent player facilities" (hacking laughter and one "Oh, shit!") and "first-class bus transportation" (*"That's* true"). On September 20, the first day the rules for reaffiliation in the Professional Baseball Agreement permitted a minor league club to contact a major league organization other than its former parent, Boesen faxed this letter to the teams that were looking for farm clubs in the Midwest League: California, Florida, Houston, Kansas City, Montreal, and Seattle. At least California and Montreal called back. The Expos GM asked if Waterloo had an airport, and Boesen chuckled and said, "I think so," and they kidded around, but in the end nobody came—not one representative of a major league organization visited Waterloo and its professional baseball stadium. Appleton, Burlington, Cedar Rapids, and Quad City all found new affiliations. Kane County not only found an affiliation, but hit the jackpot: the expansion Florida Marlins, whose merchandising tie-ins were sure to perform briskly at the Cougars' gift shop. By the end of the month, only six clubs remained without affiliation in all the minors; in the Midwest League, two: Rockford and Waterloo.

By this point, only two major league organizations were still eligible to affiliate with farm clubs in the Midwest League. One was Kansas City, Waterloo's parent club back in the 1970s. The other was San Diego. The Padres had succeeded in finding a new affiliate in the Class A-Advanced California League, but not in the slow A South Atlantic League, leaving them one full-season Class A club short and nowhere to turn but the Midwest League. In early October, Jeff Nelson called National Association headquarters in St. Petersburg, Florida, and told the president's secretary that the Padres hadn't wanted Waterloo, and now Waterloo didn't want the Padres. Furthermore, he explained, the club had a history as well as a geographical kinship with Kansas City. Every so often during the next few days, the fax machine in the Diamonds' front office would whir to life, and Nelson or Pfaltzgraff would rush over to see if there was word on the club's affiliation for 1993. After three weeks, the Royals announced that they would be affiliating with Rockford. This time Nelson called the commissioner's office in New York and was told that Waterloo would be receiving notification of its affiliation with San Diego once the World Series was over and officials from Major League Baseball and the National Association had returned to their offices. The World Series came and went, however, and still the fax in Waterloo brought no such confirmation. Boesen called George Spelius, the Midwest League president. It's going to be San Diego, Spelius told him, but don't call them. You don't want to appear too eager, Spelius counseled; let San Diego call *you*. "We're suckin' hind tit," Boesen observed.

Of the eighty-eight minor league clubs whose PDC's had expired that September, Waterloo was now the last not to have a new one. In the old, pre-Professional Baseball Agreement days, the refusal alone of a parent club to renew an affiliation might have left a ball club vulnerable to pressure to release the franchise to a more hospitable environment, most likely by selling it. It had happened in the Midwest League in 1983, when the Minnesota Twins refused to renew the PDC with Wisconsin Rapids because of the field conditions there; both franchise and affiliation promptly packed off to Kenosha. When Cleveland threatened to leave Waterloo year after year, it wasn't the loss of the Indians affiliation that worried the ball club's owners and various city officials, it was the potential loss of pro ball, period. While it was true that the new Professional Baseball Agreement had heightened and accelerated the process by which a city such as Waterloo two years later would become the least desirable territory in the land, it was also true that without the PBA's guarantee that the majors would stock every existing minor league franchise through 1994, a ball club that couldn't attract a parent club on its own very likely would have lost the right to host pro ball anyway.

On November 16, the owners convened for the ball club's annual stockholders' meeting. The stockholders and the owners were the same fourteen individuals, so the distinction between the board's regular meetings and the stockholders' meeting was, to some extent, a formality. The regular meetings had continued since the end of the season, first at the Heartland Inn, where Boesen had tried to pacify a segment of the board by stocking a picnic cooler with Old Milwaukee Light and Diet Pepsi and hanging a hand-printed sign on Diamonds stationery, "50¢ beer or pop"; then, when the board's free use of a room at the Heartland Inn expired, back at the VFW. At those meetings, the owners had attended to such standard off-season matters as discussing the paint damage that vandals had inflicted on the ballpark and rejecting a proposal to keep the beer stands open until the last out. The stockholders' meeting, however, presented an opportunity to review one year and preview another—to take the long view of the entire operation, the for-profit bottom-line business and the not-for-profit fund-raising charity—and it was conducted at the office of the ball club's attorney, on West Fourth Street.

For the fiscal year ending October 31, the ball club lost $30,155.21. This loss represented a difference of $54,264.13 from the previous year's $24,108.92 profit and effectively wiped out the organization's reserves. Part of the $54,000 difference between the two years was attributable to nearly $11,000 in lost "TV considerations" from the major leagues; part to a $26,000 increase in wages, mostly the assistant GM's and an intern's; and much of the rest, said Yates, to the drop in attendance. The ball club had finished the year with an official attendance of 48,074 over 63 dates, or an average of 763, which placed Waterloo second from last in the league, ahead of lame-duck Kenosha.

Discussion then turned to the not-for-profit part of the operation, which was to say the fate of the franchise. The answer to the question that last year at this time had seemed so pressing—Did the ball club turn a profit for the year?—now seemed secondary, and that fact itself did nothing to dispel the growing sense among the owners that events were continuing to overtake them. The day after the season ended, Boesen had visited Simpson at the ballpark to inform him that the ball club wouldn't be renewing his contract. ("He had a smile, if you can believe that," Boesen later reported to the board.) The loss of the GM complicated Boesen's plan for hiring a full-time fund-raiser; the club's deteriorating financial condition foiled it. In the end, the responsibility remained right where it was, under the general manager's burgeoning job description.

Even so, a formal campaign couldn't begin until the ball club secured an affiliation with a new parent club. In 1988, when Cleveland finally did drop Waterloo and Dan Yates returned from the Winter Meetings with the last-minute reprieve of a co-op team, the urgency of the situation had provided powerful testimony to the need for city funds, but now, four years and $325,000 later, a similar sense of urgency could have the opposite effect, by seemingly attesting to the futility of such rescue efforts. Donations of money and labor and materials, let alone a sudden windfall of $500,000 to fix the ballpark, or $2 million to build a new stadium, were even less likely to be forthcoming if the ball club gave every indication of being on the brink of extinction.

The fate of the franchise had moved out of the city ledgers and into the realm of private funding, where the competition promised to be no less fierce. Fear of throwing good money after bad, the questionable professionalism of the operation, the fact that once renovations were complete baseball still offered no guarantee that the city would have a farm club beyond 1994—all the concerns that ultimately had militated against the ball club receiving more public funding would apply in the private sector as well, only more so.

All along Boesen had emphasized to the owners the importance of keeping San Diego's decision a secret, and a secret it had remained, probably for as long as it possibly could. On October 1, the day the responsibility for finding parents for unaffiliated farm clubs reverted to the National Association and the baseball commissioner's office, an article on the front page of the *Courier*'s sport section began, "Waterloo Professional Baseball has taken its final swings at trying to secure a big league affiliate for next season." Although the article went on to say that "the city will host Midwest League baseball for at least two more summers," the issues were confusing and the news itself unambiguously disappointing.

Any doubts that Jeff Nelson would succeed David Simpson diminished as the ball club's need to establish an appearance of stability and continuity grew. After waiting several weeks for official word from the Padres, Boesen decided to take everyone at the higher levels of baseball at their word, and he authorized Jeff Nelson to hold a press conference. The man had kissed a pig; surely he could manufacture enthusiasm for the return of San Diego. On November 2, Nelson stepped before a microphone at the Ramada Inn, offered his best bare-teeth grin, and announced, "I'm excited that the Padres are coming back."

It was too late. A week later, the *Courier* Sunday editorial took the form of an open letter to the fourteen individuals most responsible for the ball club. "Attention, Waterloo Baseball, Inc.," it began. "Look around. Things are happening. Plans are being made, money is being raised. Everywhere but at Municipal Stadium." After mentioning several other major fund-raising projects in the area, the editorial continued:

All the while, officials of the Waterloo Diamonds are wondering when something will be done about upgrading Municipal Stadium.

Sitting and wondering when things will get done is a never-ending and no-win proposition.

As the other projects indicate, if you want something done, do it yourself.

Complaining about not getting any help is counterproductive, and going to the City Council every year with your hand out won't get the job done.

What the Waterloo Diamonds need to do is look at what is going on around them, figure out what other groups are doing and emulate their actions.

There is no copyright on any of these other projects. And while they are all different, there is a common thread: If you want to get something done, like raising money and awareness, the right people must be involved.

The "right people" may not be the biggest baseball fans in town or even regulars at the ballpark, but they are the people who know what it takes to raise the funds that are needed to keep professional baseball viable in Waterloo.

They are the people who care about the area and keeping recreational and entertainment options available to its citizens.

The Diamonds may carry the name Waterloo, but professional baseball is really a treasure that the entire Cedar Valley should want to protect.

The Diamonds need to get some new blood involved on their board of directors.

When P.A.S.S., People Advocating a Student Stadium, wanted to build the new football-track facility and had trouble getting it off the ground, it turned to a professional fund-raiser and Waterloo Savings Bank President Dan Watters.

They went to people who know what it takes to get a project moving and who are willing and able to direct such an effort.

Waterloo will have baseball for two more years, regardless of what is done. San Diego didn't want to negotiate with the Diamonds to continue its affiliation here. But the Padres were assigned Waterloo's Class A Midwest League team by the president of the National Association of Professional Baseball Leagues and a representative of the commissioner's office.

However, if something isn't done to bring Municipal Stadium up to Major League Baseball's standards or to replace the facility completely, that will be it.

In the current climate, that would be curtains. Once baseball leaves an area, it is unlikely to return.

Baseball has had a long and successful history in this area and can play a strong part in the revitalization effort that is going on. Along with the other projects in the works, it should be one more reason for folks traveling the Avenue of the Saints to stop here.

The Diamonds need to do something to make coming to the ballpark more appealing to residents of the Cedar Valley and get moving on raising some funds on their own to either improve or replace the stadium.

It won't be easy. Nothing worthwhile ever is.

But there is abundant proof out there that it can be done.

Klinkowitz wasn't the only owner speaking of a conspiracy now. Despite the rally-the-city tone of its headline—"Time to go to bat for baseball in Waterloo"—the *Courier* editorial did little to enhance the credibility of their cause. If anything, all the talk of the ball club adding "new blood" and "the right people" rang ominous. Maybe this wasn't the kind of sinister master plot that Klinkowitz had envisioned (just before the end of the season, he'd submitted his letter of resignation as board secretary "because my feelings about the organization's future are not those of the great majority of the board of directors"). But then, it didn't have to be.

As Ken Bergmeier said, he'd read the editorial, and read it, and read it, and the more he read it, the more he thought, "Somebody knows what's going on and is sitting back waiting."

The fact was, the ball club was vulnerable. The operation of any minor league franchise (with the exception of a few independent organizations) was contingent on three documents: a Player Development Contract with a major league ball club to cover what happened on the field; a franchise charter from a National Association–sanctioned minor league to cover what happened off the field; and a lease for the field itself. The absence of any one of these elements could render the remaining two more or less meaningless. In Waterloo, a PDC for the franchise was guaranteed by the Professional Baseball Agreement at least through 1994, and the Midwest League paperwork had been in order since the mid-1980s. The absence of a lease, however, provided a loophole.

"This is the one thing that frightens me," Mildred Boyenga had said during the board meeting where the owners discussed the "Silos and Smokestacks" list of donors. "We do not have a lease." Without endorsing Klinkowitz's theory that nefarious forces wanted to squeeze the ball club away from them, she said she couldn't deny that the ball club was vulnerable to outside interference, whatever the motivation. "If they got to Park Board or City Council members—and their names are here—they could make the lease out of reach for us. Then what would we do?"

Since the late 1980s, the ball club had been operating out of Municipal Stadium without a written agreement from the city. Rather than bring the matter of rent before the Park Board and risk not only the usual criticism of ballpark funding but a rent adjustment requiring the ball club to contribute more than it could afford, Mayor McKinley and the ball club had arrived at a division of responsibilities that was informal and even open to interpretation yet mutually satisfactory. The lack of a lease had always seemed a technicality, but in the wake of McKinley's defeat and in the face of the ball club's uncertain future, that technicality could loom as large as had the lack of a PDC in 1988 or the absence of a franchise charter in 1984.

Boesen had shown up at the next Park Board meeting hoping to put this worry behind him, but Parks Director Rick Tagtow explained that the commissioners could address only those matters already on the agenda. So Boesen waited. The meeting started late, and nobody introduced him; Boesen sat to one side until the meeting was over, nearly two hours later. Then he approached Tagtow and Russ Garling and asked how the ball club could go about securing a lease for the following year. He said that there might be people looking to take over the ball club, or there might not be, and he didn't think there were, but he wanted to be sure the ball club had itself covered. Garling asked what would happen if in fact a local group were trying to take over the ball club. Boesen then said that the owners would have to start thinking about offering an interest to a sympathetic outsider in order to protect themselves from a hostile local. The ball club, Garling informed Boesen, could have its lease, all right. He had "no objection."

But.

During his tenure as ball club president, Garling had done what any president had done, including oversee crises that conceivably had saved the franchise, but he wasn't going to see a penny from a sale of the ball club—nor did he necessarily think he or anyone else should. "I just don't think fourteen people have the right to take a volunteer-run-organization and incorporate themselves as the owners," Garling said. "It borders on thievery!" If the members of the board conducted themselves as a volunteer-run organization, then the city owned the club and the money from a sale would go back to the taxpayer. If the members of the board wanted to believe that they owned a million-dollar franchise that was solely theirs, however, then they would be charged accordingly. No more dollar-a-year charity. A commercial lease. And Garling reminded Boesen that he knew from his ball club background that the park board had the leverage to make good on his threat—that if the city refused to lease the ballpark the ball club would have no place to put a team, and without a place to play the ball club would not be a viable franchise, if it weren't a viable franchise the club would have to sell or move . . . or negotiate the lease.

Despite Garling's frequent assertions that he could separate his private animosity for the board (or at least for one member in particular) from his public responsibility to the ball club, Boesen always had his doubts. Not that it seemed likely Garling would deliberately try to disenfranchise the owners. In fact, Tagtow later assured Boesen that he didn't think a lease under the usual terms would be a problem. Still, Garling's tirade did serve as a reminder for some owners, and a revelation for others, of just how tenuous their hold on the ball club was.

Notwithstanding the condescension of the *Courier*, the ball club's leaders couldn't help being aware of the area's other fund-raising drives. After two years of fund-raising, the group support-ing a new high school football and track facility had all but dis-banded before enlisting the support of a bank president. The drive for a new ice arena was being led by a prominent attorney who also happened to be the city's labor negotiator as well as the chair-man of a committee on the reorganization of city departments. And then there was "Silos and Smokestacks." In the competition for private funds, where were the rich and powerful going to in-vest their money and efforts, in an organization that stood to make them wealthier if only through the appreciation in the value of real estate they already owned, or a dumpy ballpark on the wrong side of town?

Still, comparisons between the stadium's renovation fund and the other major sports projects in the area didn't hold. A new high school stadium would provide the community with something it had never had—a track facility. A new ice arena would provide the community with something it would otherwise lose—an in-door rink, once the always-failing machinery at the Cattle Con-gress facility finally died. Renovations to Waterloo Municipal Sta-dium, however, would provide the community with neither. Waterloo had a ballpark, and that ballpark was sound. As Rick Tagtow never tired of mentioning, even if Waterloo lost pro ball, the city would still own a facility that was suitable for Little League, high school and college games, and that would remain structurally stable for the foreseeable future. The only party de-manding improvements to the facility, or a new facility altogether, was professional baseball—which was to say, a business.

And a valuable business, at that. If the phone calls from pro-spective buyers over the past few months had taught them any-thing, it was that quite by accident they had found themselves in possession of a property whose value extended far beyond the source of civic pride they found in it or the force for economic development others saw in it. The ball club carried an intrinsic valve on the open market. It always had, but it was one thing for an owner to show up at a board meeting and listen to Dan Yates say that Kenosha or Rockford or some other club looking for a buyer had found one; it was quite another to do nothing, solicit nothing, yet attract no end of offers. They owned a valuable business, they owned a vulnerable business, they owned a business— and they were going to have to proceed with all the care and caution a business deal involving a property worth in excess of $1 million deserved. And if they had any doubts about the need to proceed carefully and cautiously, the tone and content of the *Courier* editorial that appeared a week before the stockholders' meeting dispelled them.

The evening before the meeting, Dan Yates called Mildred Boyenga to solicit her support for a motion he was thinking of introducing. He said he wanted to specify a deadline by which the owners would either raise the money to save the franchise or put the ball club up for possible sale. Boyenga said she didn't understand: Hadn't he already made a motion to that effect the previous month, at the October board meeting? Well, yes, he had, but it had arisen almost on an impulse in the middle of a discussion about the number of calls Boesen had been receiving from potential buyers, and it had entered the minutes of the meeting as follows: "Dan motioned—now that we've voted not to put our franchise on the market, when the '93 season starts if the city don't move he'll vote to sell. Kuper seconded and it passed unanimously." Something more formal seemed appropriate for such a potentially momentous proposal, and the annual stockholders' meeting seemed an appropriately formal setting.

Around an hour and a half into the meeting, Yates introduced the motion: "Move that Waterloo Professional Baseball, Inc. put the franchise on the market for possible sale after May, 1993. New owners could assume ownership around September 25, 1993 and would be required to play the 1994 season in Waterloo unless ordered to move the franchise by the Commissioner's office, the National Association or the Midwest League. After the 1994 season the new owners would be free to move the franchise if desired." The purposes of his proposal, he said, were pretty much what they had been seven months earlier: not necessarily to mandate the sale of the ball club, but certainly to leave open that possibility; to "get the board off dead center" by stimulating further discussion and action; and, if May came and went and the ball club hadn't raised enough funds, to signal to any potential angels in the vicinity sooner rather than later that pro ball in Waterloo had reached the point of no return—literally. This time his motion passed unanimously.

At least now Boesen would have something to say when prospective buyers called with offers to take the ball club off his hands: Wait until May. And call they did. Some pledged to keep the ball club in Waterloo through the 1994 season before moving it. Some didn't bother to disguise their eagerness to take it elsewhere. Over the course of the off-season, each new expression of interest in the Waterloo franchise seemed to bring another addition to the list of potential relocation sites. The names were massing. The owners were beginning to talk in terms of gathering storms; to speak of vultures. The collective map in the owners' heads was crowding with possible future homes for their franchise, if only they chose to sell it: just outside St. Louis; just outside Chicago; Bloomington, Illinois; Grand Rapids, or Kalamazoo, or Lansing, Michigan; somewhere in Indiana; Ohio, even.

Anywhere but Waterloo.

12

Tommy Lasorda was standing in the hotel lobby as if he belonged there—as indeed he did. Everywhere Jeff Nelson looked, there lurked another baseball luminary, and elsewhere in the hotel, the hallways and meeting rooms were clogged with baseball executives, but it was Tommy Lasorda who, by his very presence, transformed the gathering. Perpetual manager of the Los Angeles Dodgers, legendary TV pitchman for a weight-loss regimen, Lasorda had become the closest thing to a living monument still active in the game. Right here, right now: this hotel lobby suddenly, unquestionably, had become the center of the baseball universe. Nelson approached him. Nelson just walked right up as if he belonged here, too, and extended his hand and said that Lasorda probably didn't remember him, but a couple of years earlier, in spring training, during a major league umpires' strike, they had both worked a Dodgers intrasquad game.

"I do! I do remember you!" Lasorda engulfed Nelson's hand in his own and pumped hard. His famous basset-hound features brightened. He asked Nelson what he was doing now, and he congratulated Nelson heartily when he heard. Then the two baseball veterans reminisced about that long-ago afternoon in Florida, how Nelson had handled the plate while Lasorda had worked the field, how they had been partners then.

After Nelson excused himself, he continued making his way across the lobby. He brushed past Lou Piniella. He saw Tony LaRussa. He spotted Joe Torre returning from a workout at a downtown athletic club, a white towel warming the back of his neck. And there was the White Rat himself—Whitey Herzog, none the worse for having spent a frigid, swampy spring afternoon in the primitive press box of Waterloo Municipal Stadium so many months ago. Throughout the reception area and the adjoining bar, baseball people were standing shoulder to shoulder enjoying the fellowship of other baseball people, talking baseball, trading baseball stories and, presumably, making baseball deals. Nelson moved among them, and then he rode a glass elevator up to his room. A year ago Nelson had been an unemployed ex-umpire, freshly mourning his departure from the game; now he was the general manager of a professional baseball club, staying in a suite. It was true that all the rooms at the Galt House East in Louisville, Kentucky, were suites, but still: a *suite*—and under the same roof as Tommy Lasorda.

It was the 91st annual baseball Winter Meetings, and Jeff Nelson was there. The Winter Meetings dated back to the founding of the National Association, and over the course of the twentieth century, they had established themselves as the single occasion, midway between the end of one season and the start of another, at which every level of professional baseball could gather together in a show of, if not quite solidarity, at least similarity of overall purpose.

At the Winter Meetings, as in professional baseball, it was the major leagues that captured the popular imagination and made most of the news, and, as it happened, this year's Winter Meetings fell at an especially newsworthy moment in the history of major league baseball. Three months earlier, the major league owners had forced the resignation of commissioner Fay Vincent. The record $1.5 billion, four-year network television contract was coming up for renegotiation. Partly in anticipation of sharply reduced TV revenues, the owners voted to reopen collective bargaining agreement negotiations with the Major League Players Association. Free-agent signings collectively set a record, as thirty-five players divided $225 million, including onetime Waterloo Diamond Greg Swindell's four-year contract with the Houston Astros for $17 million and, most notably, Barry Bonds's individual record-setting six-year deal with the new owner of the San Francisco Giants for $43.75 million. The *old* owner of the Giants, who was still the owner of record, threatened to block that deal in part because his fellow major league club owners had blocked his team's sale to a Florida buyer who would have set up shop in Tampa–St. Petersburg, while the city of St. Petersburg was threatening to sue because its $140 million stadium was still standing idle five years after taxpayers had authorized its construction in an attempt to attract a major league franchise. As such baseball dealings periodically did, these attracted the attention of the U.S. Congress, and Senator Howard M. Metzenbaum, Democrat of Ohio, had announced that the day after the end of the Winter Meetings the antitrust subcommittee of the Senate Judiciary Committee would be holding hearings in Washington to reconsider baseball's exemption from antitrust law—specifically, to air grievances over owners who expect their stadiums to be financed by "people who are hard-pressed to find the tax dollars to keep their kids in school, or to pay sufficient salaries to their police and fire personnel."

It was entirely possible for minor league representatives to attend the Winter Meetings and remain ignorant of all these proceedings until they returned to their hotel rooms at the end of the day and flipped on ESPN to watch the satellite feed from across the street, or woke up the next morning and read about them in the *USA Today* waiting outside the door. It wasn't just possible; it was preferable. In conducting their affairs at the Winter Meetings, the minors adopted an air of aloofness, a vague superiority that arose out of a conviction that what they represented, and what the major leagues did not, was "the pure game"—or, as Jeff Nelson once described it: "Baseball! Promotions! Hometown!" Television lights might whitewash the Galt House lobby, satellite trucks might line the sidewalk down the block and around the corner, and the occasional big-league news couldn't help intruding on anyone who happened to be in the right place at the right time— the sudden crushing convergence of media and entourage, for instance, that announced Jesse Jackson's arrival at the hotel to protest the alleged racism of Cincinnati Reds owner Marge Schott. But primarily what the majors lent the minors was what they always had, a magnificence by association, even a legitimacy (not to mention a system of subsidies), that wasn't unwelcome, though hardly essential for the business at hand. In 1990, when the PBA negotiations broke down and the majors moved their share of the meetings to Chicago and the media followed, leaving the NA meetings in Los Angeles to carry on under ominously cavernous conditions, it was the trade show that stayed put.

The Waterloo Diamonds contingent this year also consisted of Ken Bergmeier, Don Blau, and Bill Boesen, who drove down with

Bev, but it was the new general manager who was in charge of lining up the promotions and souvenirs for the season to come. "The way I try to look at it," Nelson would say to the owners, summarizing his business philosophy, "is it's a big toy and you've invited all your friends over to play with it. Hey, we're gonna make it so much fun people will *want* to pay." At the Winter Meetings, Nelson spent most of his days at the trade show, which was housed in a vast exhibition space inside the Commonwealth Convention Center, a couple of blocks from the hotel. He signed up Morganna the Kissing Bandit. He signed up Max Patkin. He signed up the Famous Chicken. He didn't sign up Captain Dynamite, but he did sign up The Dynamite Lady. ("She's got hooters," he told Boesen afterward. "Hey, sex sells.") He stood in front of a wall of caps and ordered a dozen each of the Florida Marlins and Colorado Rockies, because they would be the new major league franchises for 1993 and therefore sure to generate interest on that basis alone; and a dozen each of the Atlanta Braves, Chicago White Sox, and Chicago Cubs, because they were all available on superstations on Waterloo's cable system; and then a dozen each of the Durham Bulls, Carolina Mudcats, and Charlotte Lookouts, because any reader of *Baseball America* knew that these distinctive logos were perennially among the most popular in the minors; and then a dozen of the Iowa Cubs. "Local team," he explained to the sales rep. "We're in Cubs country."

"Lord, yes," the salesman answered.

One morning, he stopped at the Midwest Embroidery booth and introduced himself to Dean Himelick. Nelson asked the salesman if he remembered the unsuccessful visit to the Waterloo front office he'd had last winter. Himelick said he did. Then Nelson informed Himelick that he was now in a position to authorize purchases, and he placed $1,428 in orders.

Nelson carried the kind of beefy physique that could accumulate bulk with ease if he let it, and in honor of the occasion he did. He went to the awards luncheon and the closing night banquet, promotional receptions three evenings running, a Midwest League cocktail party and a San Diego Padres cocktail party (the call officially confirming San Diego's intention to renew its PDC with Waterloo had come, at last, five days before the start of the Winter Meetings) and then one more Midwest League cocktail party, as well as daily stops at the Topps hospitality suite, upstairs from the trade show at the convention center, and nightcaps at the bar off the hotel lobby, where he saw Chuck Tanner stand at the piano and croon "White Christmas" under the rising and falling elevators festooned with red and green lights—and everywhere he went, he was a general manager. He could walk into any room and experience a swell of camaraderie. He'd look around, find another GM, and talk shoptalk. One night the GM from Salt Lake City, Nelson's hometown team and the franchise that had helped make his parents' tavern a success, described a promotion that his club was planning for the following season: When a player for the home team crossed the plate after hitting a home run, he would be presented with a teddy bear that he, in turn, would then present to a young fan in the stands. Nelson listened, nodding his head solemnly, then said, "Oh! You know what'd be great? If the kid was in a wheelchair."

"That's great," the other GM agreed, nodding his head solemnly now, too. "That's *perfect.*"

And sometimes Nelson wasn't just any GM. Already, thanks to the accounts of his exploits that he had provided to *USA Today, Baseball Weekly,* and *Baseball America,* he'd become the GM who used to be an ump, or the GM who'd kissed a pig. The night that Joe McIlvaine and Ed Lynch took the GMs and presidents from every level of the Padres farm system out to dinner, Nelson sat in the backseat of a car next to Jim Riggelman, now the manager at the major league level, and when Nelson told Riggelman a little about himself, Riggelman said, "That's you?" The GM laughed and leaned back and let the car carry him to another free meal. Jeff Nelson was expanding.

His head humming with Bud Lite and big-league gossip and a juggled budget, Nelson would return to his suite well past midnight and lie awake in the dark to reflect on his good fortune, and then he would reflect on the limits of that fortune, which were the limitations of the owners. It was Bill Boesen shadowing him at the trade show, wearing suspenders with the words "Crabby Bill" emblazoned lengthwise and whispering, after each of Nelson's big-ticket orders, "It'll never sell. It'll never sell." It was Ken Bergmeier leaving the trade show with two shopping bags bulging with giveaway goodies and claiming it was all for "research." Don Blau possibly had a clue; when Nelson had said he'd just bought two thousand caps, Blau hadn't missed a beat: "That's what I would have done. You've got to walk down to the convention and spend $6,000 just to get us in the ballpark." But that was it. *Fuckin' Joe Farmers* was how Nelson figured San Diego saw these owners, and how he feared the Waterloo organization would reflect on him. By the end of his first full day at the Winter Meetings, Nelson had reached the conclusion that he'd be in Waterloo for two more years, or *one* more year—until there was no more Waterloo Diamonds.

Two years after the negotiations, the PBA continued to drive the minor league agenda at the Winter Meetings. In the hallways and meeting rooms, minor league operators were looking around at one another and wondering how many of them would survive. (The most common estimate of vulnerable clubs seemed to be thirty to forty.) The seeming aloofness and borderline superiority with which the minors cloaked themselves turned out be rather transparent disguises for a profound fear of the major leagues. That year, the National Association announced a total attendance of 27,180,170 for the season, up two percent from the previous season, and the eighth consecutive year of growth; yet even as the NA was releasing these optimistic statistics, it also was issuing to its members a list of "Talking Points for Minor League Franchises," including: "Millions of dollars lost through higher player salaries and lower television revenue cannot be replaced by squeezing nickels and dimes out of the minor leagues," and "We need to stop thinking about self-interest and focus on the interest of the game of baseball. If we don't, we will assure disaster for the game we love," and "The minor leagues contributed about $16 million to major league baseball in 1992, consisting of $13.5 million in team-related expenses, $1.9 million in ticket sales, and between $250,000 and $500,000 from licensing major league products." "There are those who say the minor leagues do not contribute," the National Association president said during his annual address. "I say they are wrong."

For two years now, the new PBA had been providing the minors with a common, even conveniently clownish, enemy. When the list of new stadium standards had started to make the rounds in the immediate aftermath of the negotiations, the same outrages had been cited again and again in the same sarcastic tone in front offices around the country. An elevator to the press box! A phone from the dugout to the bullpen! A field clock! Wrigley Field wouldn't meet all these standards. *Fenway* wouldn't meet all these standards. When South Bend underwent its PBA inspection in 1991 (two facilities in each league were tested a year earlier than all the others), the result was widely repeated throughout the minors as definitive proof of just how absurd the new standards were. As the minutes of an owners' meeting in Waterloo reported, "even South Bend's multimillion dollar, AAA standard, state of the art facility was found lacking in twenty-five respects."

Actually, a careful reading of the new standards would have shown that the elevator reference came from a passage that said, not unreasonably, "Facilities shall conform to all applicable local, state and federal codes and regulations for accessibility to the press box," that the bullpen phone was only a recommendation, and that the field clock applied to new facilities only. Still, the rhetoric of the past two years had served its purpose. It had allowed the minor leagues to persist in behaving as if the only threat to their existence came from without.

Would a city be able to continue supporting professional baseball? Would a city be willing to back up that commitment to pro ball by renovating or replacing its playing facilities? The Professional Baseball Agreement didn't create these questions; the changes that minor league baseball had undergone over the preceding decade had been exerting these economic pressures already anyway. During the PBA negotiations, the minors had tried arguing that license-to-print-money franchises were still the exception, and that many clubs still needed subsidies to survive, but the majors had argued back that they were simply responding to what the marketplace presented. However justified the animosity of the National Association toward Major League Baseball now and always, and however merited the sarcasm in the case of the on-field clock—many minor league general managers wouldn't want a clock in plain sight, reminding customers that it was 9:30 on a school night, and having to put one there was indeed an example of what can happen when the majors try to tell the minors how to run their own business—by the time of the Winter Meetings two years later it was becoming increasingly difficult to ignore not only the changes in the minor league marketplace that originally had influenced the major leagues' negotiating strategy, but the fact that the changes were continuing apace.

The disparity between clubs at either end of the minor league spectrum was only growing. The Midwest League was typical of what was happening in league after league. Ever since Quad City had redefined the Midwest League marketplace by breaking the 200,000 barrier, a trend in attendance had been evident from one season to the next: The surviving clubs at the lower end of the spectrum would hold steady or weaken slightly, while those at the upper end would play leapfrog with one another, racing to set ever more astronomical league attendance records and leaving the rest of the league farther and farther behind. The previous year, for instance, eight clubs in the Midwest League had drawn below 100,000, including two under 60,000; this year the same eight had drawn below 100,000, but now four fell under 60,000, including three under 50,000—Appleton, Kenosha, and, of course, Waterloo. Meanwhile, at the other end of the league, the previous year four clubs had drawn over 200,000, while this year one had broken the 300,000 barrier—Kane County, with a final total of 323,769, a robust 33 percent improvement over Quad City's record-setting pace of only one year earlier. And the gap between the two ends of the league promised to widen yet further during the upcoming season, once the lowly Kenosha Twins opened up for business as the Fort Wayne Wizards. All of which was good news, if you were among the owners whose clubs were moving in the right direction—though apparently not good enough.

"We're fightin' two groups," Don Blau said to Jeff Nelson one night at a restaurant a couple of blocks from the Galt House. "The city, and the other owners in the league. Half the people we were drinking beer with and were friendly to us last night would love to see us gone." He was referring to a Midwest League reception the previous evening in George Spelius's suite, and he was basing his observation on the events of the day, first the Midwest League meeting at the hotel that morning, then a conversation he'd had at a Major League Baseball Properties reception that evening. Blau had gotten to talking with Clar Krusinski, owner of the Peoria club and a Chicago real estate developer, about the future of the league, and Blau had wondered whether the league might expand again. Krusinski smiled thinly. "I'd rather see a strong fourteen," he said, "than sixteen with a weak four."

The "weak four" the Peoria owner didn't need to name: He could choose among Appleton, Beloit, Burlington, Clinton, Waterloo. And his reasoning he didn't need to sum up in one word, either, though he did so anyway. It had been the dominant topic at that morning's Midwest League meeting, it had been a recurring topic at league meetings for some time now, and it threatened to remain on the league agenda for the indefinite future, as voting control in the league continued to shift from one generation of club ownership to the next: marketing.

Or "bullshit marketing," as Bill Boesen had come to call it. The first time Boesen spoke up before his fellow Midwest League directors was to address this subject. ("Didn't know they was so many lawyers," Boesen reported back to his own board, " 'til I saw 'em taking notes.") At the league meeting immediately after the end of the season, some of the owners had argued that the Midwest League needed to bring its marketing structure up to date—that already the league was lagging behind other leagues. When they started talking about hiring a new president, Boesen decided he'd heard enough. "You're not going to get a marketing guy who knows baseball, too!" he said.

The other owners could hardly hide their amusement. Didn't he *know*? Whole graduate programs at major universities across the land had been founded on precisely that principle! What was more, a "marketing guy" wouldn't need to know baseball. He'd need to know marketing: promotions, advertising, licensing, broadcasting, media relations, corporate sponsorship, and on and on. These were the skills that had revolutionized their own organizations. South Bend was marketing itself so successfully that the club didn't sell advertising space on its dugout roof for fear of oversaturating the customer with commercial messages. These were the skills that had revolutionized the entire sport. Annual sales of Major League Baseball merchandise alone had increased nearly one hundredfold since 1979, from $25 million to $2.4 billion. These were the skills that had revolutionized sports in general. That year, the San Jose Sharks—a first-year, last-place hockey team otherwise deserving of obscurity—sold $150 million in souvenirs solely on the basis of a logo showing a shark chomping a hockey stick in half. And these were the skills that Major League Baseball had made the centerpeice of a campaign during the PBA negotiations to win a joint licensing agreement from the minors. In theory, what the minors lost in control of their merchandise on the local level eventually would be more than compensated by a higher return from the expertise and national exposure of Major League Baseball Properties.

Now, a few of the Midwest League owners were suggesting, these were the skills that could take a league with some of the strongest Class A territories in the country, wrap it up in one tidy package, and present it to sponsors. If "Manwich Presents" a family section of seating in one ballpark, then "Manwich Presents" a family section in every ballpark in the league; if Federal Express underwrites the All-Star game, then Federal Express gets to slap its logo everywhere and anywhere it wants; if General Motors advertises on one outfield wall, then General Motors advertises on every outfield wall. "We can't even get *Deere's* to put up a few signs," Boesen had gone home and moaned to his board of directors.

What was implicit in these discussions, and what Krusinski had made all but explicit to Don Blau, was a simple question: Which would be easier and more profitable to market—a league full of 40,000 or 400,000 attendance figures, a league full of Clintons or Kane Countys? Even if this particular sponsorship program should never get off the ground, the owners still had learned that they would prefer to have their own club's products (and their 9 percent royalties) being distributed in markets where they can reach hundreds of thousands of potential customers, all with significant disposable incomes. From the perspective of a Quad City or South Bend, a mom-and-pop shop was no longer merely a harmless remnant of a bygone era. It was an impediment to potential profits.

On the final night of the Winter Meetings, at the National Association banquet in the hotel's Grand Ballroom, Jeff Nelson sat next to an employee from a club in one of the larger Midwest League markets. For most of the meal and the entertainment afterward—The Lou Rawls Show, flanked by Budweiser banners— Nelson sat with his head inclined toward this informant. What the employee had to say wasn't especially shocking—that his employer was in financial trouble, that employees had learned to cash checks right away because they'd been known to bounce, that some insurance coverage he'd assumed he had he didn't, because the owner had missed payments. Nelson had heard as much about this owner simply by asking Midwest League suppliers at the trade show which clubs hadn't settled the season's bills. Yates often had said as much about several of the owners in the league: "Some of these guys are in debt up to their on-deck circles." It was entirely likely that what Nelson's friend George Spelius said was true, too: that the need of certain owners to generate ever greater amounts of revenue from their prosperous ball clubs was to subsidize the parts of their business empires that were failing. Still, this conversation had a paralyzing effect on Nelson. Only occasionally, and only with a great expenditure of effort, would he push himself away to exchange a pleasantry with Bill or Bev Boesen. "The man can sing," he'd say, nodding vaguely at Lou Rawls. Then he'd go back for more.

Jeff Nelson didn't think he was naive. He'd come into this weekend—had come into front-office life—knowing full well that baseball was a business. He'd gotten his education in a tavern that catered to the baseball crowd in Salt Lake City; he'd seen for himself the relationship between a good turnout at Derks Field a couple of blocks away and the revenues in his parents' cash register. More specifically, he understood that what happened off the field was the responsibility of the minor league franchise, and what happened on the field the responsibility of the major league parent. But Nelson had thought it was possible to inhabit a common ground, to stake out a space on the hallowed playing surface for home-run hitting contests, for give-it-a-spin bat races and rainout dances and nightly chants from the roofs of dugouts—and, in fact, nothing he'd heard or witnessed this weekend had convinced him otherwise.

Still, coming into the meetings, he'd expected that he'd find himself among people who thought about minor league baseball just as he did—that "what we're doing is selling fun, and you should have fun while you're doing it," that "the bottom line is baseball." Instead, what he found was that he was in the "vast minority." It was a realization that he'd been having trouble avoiding, and it had crystallized for him one morning at a Midwest League meeting, his first as GM for the Waterloo club. He'd sat and watched as a group of owners outlined their strategy. Rather than entrust their financial security to a florist in Beloit who ran the league out of his house, they wanted to hire a $70,000-a-year marketing pro and move the league office to Chicago. Toward that end, they were going to start collecting resumes. They were going to recruit applicants. And they were going to ask these potential league presidents point-blank, bottom-line: Would you encourage franchises in smaller markets to sell or move?

On stage, Lou Rawls sang, "When you say Budweiser, you've said it—*what?*"

"*All!*" roared the 91st annual Baseball Winter Meetings.

After the show, Nelson joined the long procession of big men clutching miniature Louisville Slugger souvenir bats as they shuffled along the corridor. When he got to the elevator, he went up. He decided he didn't want to go back down to the bar. He decided he was tired of eating, tired of drinking, and tired of smiling.

In the morning, Nelson turned on the cartoon channel and flipped absently through that morning's *USA Today:* The Giants had signed Barry Bonds after all. Then he carried his bags down to the lobby. While he was waiting for the courtesy van that would take him to the airport, he witnessed one last media crush. This time the photographers and reporters and camera crews were hustling alongside a gurney, which, Nelson learned from nudging one of the cameramen, carried the body of Carl Barger, president of the Florida Marlins and, in his days with the Pittsburgh Pirates front office, one of the chief architects of the Professional Baseball Agreement, who had collapsed and died outside an owners' meeting upstairs. Nelson watched the stretcher disappear into the back of an ambulance, and then he climbed into the courtesy van.

The Louisville airport that morning was full of familiar presences carrying bags overflowing with pennants and souvenir cups and foam-rubber tomahawks. As Nelson deposited himself in a plastic bucket seat near his gate, an announcement came over the PA asking for volunteers to take a later flight in exchange for a $200 voucher. Nelson leaned his head back. He didn't even consider the money. His eyes were heavy. His belt was tight. He wanted to go home.

Waterloo, he corrected himself.

It was the year of the flood. Throughout the Upper Mississippi Valley, downpour followed downpour until the Mississippi and its many tributaries had risen to their highest levels of the century. The Cedar didn't quite reach a record high, but it did leave its banks long enough to creep across the parking lot and through the chain-link fence of Municipal Stadium and along the concourse and under the door of the front office and inside the clubhouses and down the dugout tunnels back to daylight, where it saturated the playing surface. The ballpark, of course, lay in the floodplain, and so every few years the staff would have to pile all the front-office belongings on desktops and shelves, and afterward the owners would organize a mop-up party. This year's flood was worse than usual, to be sure, but it was hardly unexpected. The question was never whether the ballpark would one day be swept under a "hundred-year flood." It was only a matter of when.

Opening Day against the new Fort Wayne Wizards was washed out, and so were a number of other April dates as inclement weather continued to press down on the city and the ballpark grounds, but in time the waters receded and the games returned, the fans returned, and even one of the previous season's players returned, pitcher Joe Waldron. So did pitching coach Dean Treanor. Every fifth inning, Treanor continued to trudge to the mound, throw three quick pitches to that day's contestant in the Sky Room Comedy Club Home Run Contest, and trudge back to the dugout. The Waterloo roster was otherwise free of familiar names from the preceding season. Dave Adams, Todd Altaffer, Bruce Bensching, Jose Davila, Kevin Farlow, Keith McKoy, Kyle Moody, Shawn Robertson, Derek Vaughn, Shawn Whalen—all were gone from professional baseball by opening day. Trainer John Maxwell had received his release from the Padres organization as well. In all, less than half the preceding season's squad remained in professional baseball. John Abercrombie had leap-frogged out of Class A to Double A Wichita. Robbie Beckett, Scott Bream, Jeff Brown, Cameron Cairncross, Jason Hardtke, Sean Mulligan, Tom Paskievitch, Jeff Pearce, and Scott Pugh all graduated to Class A-Advanced, where they were joined by manager Keith Champion. One day that off-season, after an organizational dinner in San Diego, Ed Lynch had pulled Champ aside and told him he was being promoted to Rancho Cucamonga. After a moment's reflection, Champ said, *"Where?"*

Within the week he found out. Rancho Cucamonga was the latest addition to the California League (replacing San Bernardino, a city that had failed to fund a new ballpark), and when he showed up for a press conference announcing his appointment as the first manager in the history of the franchise, he received a briefing on what to expect: fourteen skyboxes, an elevator to the front offices, a receptionist to lead visitors through the carpeted suites. Champ looked out at the grape arbors across the road, and he imagined the subdivisions that were sure to emerge there by the turn of the century. Rancho Cucamonga lay forty miles east of Los Angeles, had been one of the nation's top twenty-five fastest growing communities of the 1980s, and promised to become the Kane County of the California League. "I've died and gone to heaven," Champ said.

Nothing like a shroudlike silence descended on Waterloo Municipal Stadium, of course. New blood replaced old. Bobby Bonds, Jr.—son of Bobby, Sr., and brother of Barry—was one name on the roster that created a stir in the stands, if only for its lineage. Another, for its glorious, improbable—no, *impossible*—yet undeniable perfection, belonged to Homer Bush. And even as fans searched this year's roster for the player who might make the season indelible, who might elicit the ultimate whispered encomium, *The kid has a shot,* last year's top prospect lived on. "Judge a baseball team by numbers alone," an article in the 1993 souvenir program read, "and the Diamonds can hardly call 1992 a rousing success. They finished 59–78 and ranked near the bottom of most league statistic categories. But judge a summer at the ballpark by the clutch hits, aggressive wheels, and spectacular defensive plays provided by one Jason Hardtke, and last season suddenly seems memorable." For the new season, the ball club had commissioned a local commercial artist to create a likeness of Hardtke taking a mighty cut in the sky above Municipal Stadium, and this giant Jason now graced the pocket schedule, commemorative poster and cover of the souvenir program—gentle reminders that history, sometimes, happened here in Waterloo, Iowa.

It would be an inaccurate and unfair depiction of this period in Waterloo's history that included only what went wrong, or at least what didn't go right. There was cause for optimism. The first elevated roadway through town opened, relocated U.S. Highway 218, which was renamed in honor of Leo Rooff, the five-term mayor whose late-1970s commitment to road construction had earned him the nickname "the father of Interstate Substitution." Every so often the *Courier* would publish a business supplement featuring prominent citizens citing a rise in new housing starts or a dip in bankruptcy filings as evidence that the area's economy was continuing to recover from its early-1980s collapse. Even Lenora Happel remained optimistic. The morning her letter to the editor praising Waterloo as "a great city—hats off" appeared in the *Courier,* she was knocked down and robbed of her purse and the bag of groceries she was taking to her church's needy box. Happel, seventy and a "four-time grandmother," nonetheless reassured a reporter from the paper a few days later that she hadn't changed her mind: "Waterloo is a great city," she repeated— though she was starting to have her doubts about some of its citizens. "At 7:30 in the morning," she said, "what were they doing? I was going to church. Why weren't they in church?"

Even in the area of vital concern to the local professional baseball franchise—the availability of private funding for large-scale civic improvement projects during an era of cutbacks in public funding—there was cause for optimism. " 'Quality of Life' Projects Abound Locally," read the headline on a *Courier* editorial. The high school football and track stadium had rallied $1 million in private pledges, while the ice arena had raised another $600,000, enough to persuade the City Council to agree to designate public funds in excess of those already set aside for repairing the old ice hockey arena to building a new one. Later, community opposition to the arena site (the proprietors of two new businesses there had received keys to the city only a month earlier for choosing to locate downtown) prompted the city to withdraw its offer and left the project, in the words of Parks Director Rick Tagtow, "really, really dead"—but then one of the heirs of a local nineteenth-century coal fortune appeared with a donation of $3 million and real estate along the Cedar River.

No local project, however, could rival "Silos and Smoke-stacks," not in the potential breadth of its support nor in the potential depth of its funding, and certainly not in its overall potential impact on the community. By the end of the year, and despite a growing sentiment that the group's leaders were, as consultant Tom Gallaher once described the popular perception, "just a bunch of rich people with public funds," the project had received $171,000 in donations from more than sixty private sources, had expanded to include more than seventy sites throughout the Cedar Valley and northeast Iowa, and had received congressional approval for a $150,000 reconnaissance study, the first major step in what increasingly was looking to become a ten-year, $10 million project. That winter, after voters approved a 2 percent motel/hotel sales tax that would specifically benefit projects that encourage tourism, "Silos" received $50,000.

The ball club, however, received nothing, because nobody associated with it knew to apply. Still, it would be an inaccurate and unfair depiction of this period in the ball club's history that included only what went wrong. Here, too, there was cause for optimism. Club owners designated $10,000 from the not-for-profit organization to buy the ballpark a new infield. The Parks Commission used the last of the $325,000 in city funding to install a PBA-mandated warning track around the perimeter of the playing surface, as well as a new press box, and to tear out the condemned second set of bleachers down the first-base line and replace it with a picnic area. Shortly after the New Year, the ball club got itself a one-year, $1 lease with the city, in writing.

Even in the area of fund-raising, there was cause for optimism. "Nelson is optimistic about Waterloo's chances of keeping minor league baseball beyond the summer of 1994," the *Courier* reported during the off-season, citing Nelson's plans for what he promised would be "a massive fund-raising effort." Working mostly after business hours, Nelson prepared the kind of brochure that Russ Garling had long argued would be an indispensable selling tool for the stadium-renovation fund. The American Legion donated $500, the Weyerhaeuser Paper Company $750. The day after the *Courier* published its open-letter editorial to the ball club, Nelson received a call from Jim Miller at the Sky Room Comedy Club, who said he wanted to offer the use of his facilities for a fund-raising event. Nelson started throwing around ideas for a nightly lottery in the stands, a country-and-western benefit concert, even egg-toss contests. "There aren't enough eggs in Iowa to fund this stadium," Parks Director Rick Tagtow said. "You still have to get Deere or IBP or the UAW or *somebody*." Still, in light of the new GM's can-do attitude and the recent successes of the Waterloo area's other major fund-raising projects, even Tagtow was guardedly optimistic. "I felt completely pessimistic about baseball last year," he said. "Now I feel there are at least possibilities out there."

Nelson designated the Sky Room Comedy Club fund-raiser as the kick-off for the stadium renovation drive, figuring that even if the $25-a-plate donation wound up covering nothing but the evening's expenses, the fact of the event would demonstrate that the ball club took seriously its commitment to its non-profit arm, the Waterloo Diamonds Baseball Association. The faces in the crowd that assembled one evening in February on the top floor of the Black's building, while frost spiderwebbed up the cathedral windows and, beyond, a 6:00 P.M. sunset flared orange, spread purple and died black in the sky over Waterloo, were by and large the same faces that might have graced the stands on a Thirsty Thursday in May: Zoo Crew stalwarts, *Courier* retirees, several of the ball club's owners. There was nobody from the City Council, nobody from the Parks Department, not a single member of the Park Board, no bank presidents or prominent attorneys, no politicians with pull on Capitol Hill or even in Des Moines, no scions or heiresses or magnates. The speakers adjusted their remarks accordingly. "You'll probably laugh when I say it," Midwest League president George Spelius told the crowd, "but there *is* money here in Waterloo."

"This—the group in this room—you—this is the core," Jeff Nelson said in his own after-dinner speech. "You people are the heart and soul of this ball club. You've got the information, now you've got to share that information. Don't let it stop here. Spread the word. Take it with you tonight. I'm *begging* you." He was, too. He'd cupped his hands and pushed them forward. "I know it's hard to think about baseball when it's thirty-five below with the windchill, but believe it or not, it's only forty-nine days to the start of the baseball season. If this kid from Salt Lake City, Utah, can get enthused about keeping baseball in Waterloo, I know you can, too. Thank you, and God bless you." In all, 117 people attended the dinner, and the non-profit corporation's take, after expenses, was $1,700.

Early one morning in the middle of March, in the same conference room where Boesen had addressed the Cedar Valley Partnership the previous summer, Nelson met with a committee of the Chamber of Commerce for what he thought would be a standard cheerleading appearance. "I can't believe how wrong I was," he reported back to the ball club owners. "No offense, but no one knows you." It wasn't just that the members of the Chamber weren't aware of who was on the board of the baseball club, he said; it was that even when Nelson told them, they still didn't know. Here they'd been reading about the plight of pro ball in Waterloo, they said, and hearing about the need for a proper fund-raising effort, and now it turned out that the operation was being run by, as one of them put it, "a bunch of nobodies"? They hinted that there were people in this very room who could help. The catch, they informed Nelson, and Nelson informed the owners, was that they'd want something more for their efforts than "their names on a plaque."

The owners immediately suspended their self-imposed May 1 deadline and appointed a Stadium Renovation Committee to pay a call on Dan Watters, the president of Waterloo Savings Bank. It was Watters who had salvaged the high school stadium project when all hope seemed lost, it was Watters the *Courier* had singled out as a potential contact for the ball club, and it was Watters who had approached the organization in the immediate aftermath of Dan Yates's resignation nearly a year earlier to explore the possibility of purchasing the club. Now, he wrote out a check on the spot for $1,000. Then he said he'd been giving the matter of the ball club some serious consideration, and he'd arrived at a possible solution: seats on the board of directors for himself and two of his associates to endow the ball club with guidance and legitimacy and access to what the *Courier* open-letter editorial had called "the right people."

The challenge that Boesen had issued one night the previous summer under the grandstand—*Do you want to give up a share of one-point-two-five million dollars?*—had never stopped echoing.

For legal reasons, they had divided their operation into a not-for-profit corporation and a for-profit corporation, but over the off-season they had resigned themselves to the realization that one had been created to protect the hide of the other. Anyone pledging a donation significant enough to make a difference wouldn't be simply saving pro ball for Waterloo, but salvaging a valuable property for fourteen individuals, no matter how altruistic their personal feelings about the nature of ownership. That person might reasonably request a piece of the action in return. (Hadn't David Simpson done just that after his first year? And hadn't they marveled at his impertinence? And where had his efforts gotten him? As of Christmas, Wal-Mart, doing seasonal work.) Jerry Klinkowitz, for one, amended his earlier warnings about the form that outside interest in the ball club would eventually take. He shouldn't have spoken of a conspiracy theory after all, he said now; it should have been an "inevitability theory." Barring a stroke-of-midnight reprieve of the kind that had salvaged the ice arena project, the ball club owners had come to accept that in order to save pro ball for Waterloo they were going to have to surrender the franchise—certainly part of it, and possibly all.

But then, a night at the ballpark had lost something already, anyway. "Go out to the ballpark this year," Don Blau observed one night, "it's like a gallows and somebody's dyin'." In seasons past the ballpark had provided a safe haven from the troubles of the day. Now the place had never looked better, and it was where the troubles resided. The press box and picnic area: The owners couldn't look at them without thinking that the city had built them not because they addressed any demands of the PBA (they didn't), but because they would benefit anyone using the park even if pro ball left town. The infield, too: The ball club had bought it primarily as a good-faith gesture to convince the Padres not to exercise the option in the new PDC to leave after one season. Even the pocket schedule, commemorative poster and souvenir program came to carry unfortunate associations. At one owners' meeting, Barb Kuper passed out copies of a newspaper article that a friend had sent from the West Coast about the arrival of professional baseball in Rancho Cucamonga. "There's really nothing to do there. The field's bad. There's really bad fan support," the article quoted one Jason Hardtke as reflecting on his previous season, in Waterloo, Iowa. "I didn't like it at all."

At the annual stockholders' meeting in November, the owners had discussed raising money for the ballpark renovations by selling board seats at $20,000 each—then realized that even five seats at that amount would get them only one-fifth of the way to their goal. What was more, if the ball club did wind up being sold, then $20,000 would have been an absurd undervaluation of a seat's worth. More recently, the owners had discussed setting a price of $500,000 for a seat—but then that price seemed an absurd overvaluation. The owners now arrived at a new approximation of a fair price for membership on the board of directors of Waterloo Professional Baseball, Inc.: three seats in exchange for a pledge to raise $500,000 by August 1. The three new members, furthermore, would receive no stock for three years, in order to protect the organization from opportunists trying to make a quick killing. "There's people who want to buy this franchise and keep it here, fine," Mildred Boyenga said. "They've got two million dollars, fine. I have no problem with selling it. But I'm not going to *give* it away."

Dan Watters had conveyed to the owners a business proposition, and the owners responded in kind. Several days later, Watters' secretary sent word that the bank president had withdrawn his interest.

The wingbeats over Waterloo were multiplying. Speculation about the eventual disposition of the franchise had spread from the relatively rarefied circles of pro ball front offices into the mainstream media. An article in a St. Louis newspaper explored the possibility of a minor league franchise moving to an outer suburb there. Articles began appearing in Chicago newspapers touting far north suburban Lake County as a possible future counterpart to far west suburban Kane County, and they rarely failed to mention the apparently imminent availability of the Waterloo franchise. ("If not for a good seventh-inning stretch or the solid crack of a bat every now and then," read one typically sunny account, "many collar-county residents might never need to venture into Chicago.") A Lake County representative even showed up in the Waterloo grandstand, chatting amiably about her home territory's virtues. One day Boesen took a call from Clar Krusinski, who said that he was planning to turn over the operation of the

Peoria Chiefs to his son, and that he was now thinking about buying another Midwest League team for himself. He said he thought he'd read that Waterloo was for sale. *"Not,"* Boesen answered with labored emphasis, *"yet."*

It was now late May. Nearly a year had passed since George Spelius had visited the ballpark and walked into the outfield with Boesen and Klinkowitz, advising them to give themselves a year to raise money, then put the ball club up for sale. Now he visited again (having survived the challenge to his presidency), this time to attend a meeting of the owners in the new press box as they tried to figure out their options. The owners told him that they were thinking of waiting until August 1 to announce that the ball club was for sale, partly so as not to taint the season with a lame-duck status and hurt box-office revenues, and partly to allow more time to explore the possibility of other local interest. *Don't,* Spelius said. If in fact no local funding were available, waiting until August 1 wasn't going to change the outcome; they'd still wind up selling the ball club. The only difference was that the price was going to drop, and some buyer was going to wind up walking away with more money, and they with less. If you're going to put the ball club on the market, Spelius advised, do it now.

Over the summer, in a flurry of meetings sometimes only days apart, the owners put their effects in order. On June 7 they held a press conference to announce that the ball club was for sale and that they'd set a deadline of July 15 for finding local interest. They fielded a couple of inquiries, and they heard a few rumors, but nothing substantive emerged, and when the deadline passed, the owners retained a professional sports broker, Bob Richmond of Baseball Opportunities in Scottsdale, Arizona, a firm that advertised in the back pages of *Baseball America* under the banner "Invest In Diamonds," and that previously had overseen the sales of dozens of other professional sports franchises, most of which were baseball. The owners projected the ball club's earnings and expenses for the fiscal year and arrived at a staggering loss of $60,000, due in part to the record rains and flooding, and in part to the country-and-western concert promotion, which alone lost between $15,000 and $25,000. They secured a short-term loan to see the club through the end of the fiscal year. Then, on August

28, they learned that the National Association and Major League Baseball had agreed to extend the deadline for stadium renovations by one year.

By then the old deadline had served its purpose. It had loomed forbiddingly on the calendar long enough that it had effected a wholesale change in the structure, texture, and future of minor league baseball. All the new deadline did was eliminate the ambiguities of the old deadline, not its intent. Now it was April 1, 1995, that would serve as the dividing line between one era of minor league ball and another. Any franchise not in compliance with the PBA by that date would be out—and by the end of the 1993 season, the owners of those clubs knew who they were.

On the final night of the season, September 2, 1993, the Waterloo owners said farewell. By then it was virtually certain that by opening day of the following year, the ball club would be under new ownership, just as it was almost virtually certain that the new owners, whoever they might turn out to be, would have no choice but to move the franchise after the final night of the 1994 season. When the owners gathered together now, pro ball in Waterloo seemed more endangered than ever, but they were not yet saluting the end of an institution, only their involvement in it. After the game—the Diamonds lost 5-1, for the record, though Homer Bush won the Midwest League batting title with a .322 BA—the owners stood for a moment in their various seats, looked out to the field, looked to one another, and then, as one, wandered onto the diamond. Mildred Boyenga walked the bases going one way, Barb Kuper the other, and when they met at second, they collapsed in each other's arms for several minutes, hugging, sobbing.

A few weeks later, the owners said farewell again. Again they gathered at the ballpark, this time for a board meeting to decide which of three offers to accept. In the press box, Dan Yates outlined the advantages and disadvantages of each, and in the end the owners voted to accept the offer from a limited-liability company out of the Chicago area calling itself Take Me Out to the Ballgame, led by Tom Dickson, a senior vice-president at the Leo Burnett advertising agency, and Tom Rubens, a former commodities and options trader who was now the president, general manager, and part owner of the Continental Basketball Association team in Grand Rapids, Michigan. The sale price was $1.8 million, and although the final three contenders had included one offer equal to that amount and another for $2 million, the Waterloo owners had chosen Take Me Out to the Ballgame both because that group's proposal contained the fewest contingencies, and because the group promised to play the 1994 season in Waterloo, at least providing pro ball in Waterloo with a suitable ninetieth-anniversary sendoff. At 6:00 P.M., the appointed hour, Boesen disappeared below the stands to call the broker from the front office and give him the board's decision. When Boesen returned, the owners pounced: *Well, what did he say?* " 'All right,' " Boesen said, shrugging, leaving it at that. So they wandered out to the field again, bringing along some fungo bats and balls they confiscated from the souvenir stand. They pitched to one another, they played catch, they tried to reach the fence on a fly, and they kept pitching and catching and batting until they started losing the ball in the dark.

As the next season approached, however, they were still saying farewell. The payments and paperwork that would complete the transfer of ownership were repeatedly slow in coming from Dickson and Rubens, as the prospective owners discovered that finding a territory for the franchise in 1995 was proving more difficult than they had imagined. First they tried Lake County, Illinois, in the far northern suburbs of Chicago. But by now the Chicago Cubs had completed the purchase of the Midwest League franchise in Rockford, apparently hoping to duplicate in a market only sixty miles from the Chicago city limits by tollway, and less than half-an-hour's drive from many of the city's northwest suburbs and satellite cities, the success of Kane County. Why would the Cubs now approve a new minor league club north of the city to siphon off major league fans from the North Side and near north suburbs and to provide competition with their minor league interests in Rockford, to the west? So Dickson and Rubens tried Lake County, Indiana, just across the Illinois border. But why would the White Sox want a minor league club siphoning off fans from the South Side and the near south suburbs and providing competition to their affiliate in South Bend, to the east? The major leagues, invoking a veto power they had won as part of the PBA, let the commissioner's office know, and the commissioner's office let the National Association know, and the National Association let the Midwest League know, and the Midwest League let the prospective owners of the Waterloo franchise know that neither move would win approval. By January 1994, the old Waterloo owners had begun making contingency plans for what their legal and financial responsibilities would be if they were still officially the owners as of Opening Day. They directed Yates and Boesen to instruct Jeff Nelson not to "go overboard with promotions," and then they tried to secure a lease.

Boesen paid a call on the Park Board, and he walked away thinking he had "a done deal" on renewing the ballpark lease at the old rate. But the Park Board, after all, was merely an advisory body, and once the lease reached the City Council, the scenario that Bernie McKinley had long feared, and had long avoided by neglecting to commit the rental terms to paper, transpired: A City Council member said he'd like to set a rent of $1 million.

By now, the prediction that Sammie Dell had made two years earlier to the ball club's representatives, that the next election would bring yet another brand of government to the city, had come to pass. The first budget of the Al Manning years had held the line on taxes without cutting services. Nonetheless, the following year had seen police layoffs, fire fighter layoffs, social service cutbacks, a record pace for homicides, and citywide austerity measures that included dousing every fourth street lamp, making the old joke about the last person to leave Waterloo turning out the lights look prophetic. At the next budget hearings, the decision had been relatively swift: higher taxes, fewer services. Soon thereafter, Al Manning announced that he would not be seeking re-election, accepting instead the position of circulation manager for the *Courier*. Sammie Dell himself, citing health problems and overall fatigue, also didn't seek reelection. The slate of council candidates that took office in January 1994 was led by a new mayor with an old name, John Rooff, nephew of the father of Interstate Substitution, and living proof that the city was back in the hands of business interests, with a vengeance.

The same month Rooff took office, an article in the *Courier* about the new edition of the *Places Rated Almanac* reported that Waterloo rated 157 out of 343 cities but that the high Recreation standing of 74 "could be substantially affected" by the sale of the ball club. "I want baseball in our city," the new mayor said in an accompanying article, "and I think everyone that is interested in our city will agree." But where Bernie McKinley had vowed to keep baseball, whatever the cost, and Al Manning had supported baseball, as long as it didn't cost, John Rooff was soon saying that pro ball was welcome to stay—for a price. And that price was half a million.

If the owners really were sincere about wanting to keep pro ball in Waterloo, he said, and said again, then they should be willing to donate at least $500,000 of the sale price toward refurbishing the facility. "I really have a problem giving them that facility with no income for the city," one City Council member said, adding that if the ball club were a not-for-profit operation he'd think otherwise. Another Council member said that if the sale went through, he wanted to "zap them for the rent." The tone was infectious. "Where's the arithmetic come in," said a member of the audience one Monday evening, addressing the Council and, via cable, the city, "if we're giving them a lease of a dollar a year and they turn around and sell that thing for $2 million? Does the city get any of that? If these guys are going to take us to the cleaners, I think maybe we ought to do the dry cleaning." A letter to the editor in the *Courier* said that "if somebody made off like a bandit, there should be an uprising." In another letter, a longtime fan wrote, "If Professional Baseball, Inc., wants understanding, admit some blame and show further commitment by pledging reinvestment of $1.8 million, as opposed to taking your piece of the pie from a $50 to $1,000 investment, slamming it into your pocket and walking away like a junk bond salesman."

In less than two years the ball club's owners had gone from being stewards of a public trust, at least in their own estimation, to objects of public ridicule on the editorial page of the *Courier,* to villains seemingly everywhere. They questioned the motives of the new mayor, who had nothing to lose and everything to gain by casting aspersions on a group of fourteen "nobodies." They questioned the motives of their severest critic on the new City Council, who was yet one more former president of their organization from its turbulent past and who, it was said by some of the owners, had stormed out of his last baseball meeting vowing, "I'll get you back!"

Finally, they questioned their own motives.

Nobody doubted that the money would ease the pain of their loss. Even during the Sky Room fund-raiser, Boesen and Blau had retired to a corner to discuss that day's latest Midwest League news: the sale of Madison to a group planning to move the franchise to Grand Rapids, Michigan. Boesen said that already he'd gotten a call from the group's leader, who previously had contacted him about buying Waterloo: " 'Well, we're not interested in your club anymore.' No fooling. But I asked him how much Madison sold for."

"How much?" said Blau.

"I can't say."

"Supposed to be one-point-three."

"More than that."

"One-point-five?"

"I can't say."

"Just say if it's more'n one-point-five."

"It's more than one-point-five."

"Two?"

"I can't say. He told me he'd tell me only if I promised not to repeat it."

"More than two?"

"No!" Boesen looked shocked at the thought.

"So I say we ask for one-point-seven-five for our club and see what happens."

"You don't want to sell," Boesen said. It was almost a question.

"No!" Blau answered quickly. He took a sip of beer. "But when we *do* sell," he said, "that's what we want."

Human nature being what it is, certainly it was possible that in the end some, if not all, of the owners had been guided more than a little by greed. "Just how much money do you *have* in this ball club, besides coming out to the ballpark and putting in a little time or having a few beers?" Boesen had yelled during one board discussion about the asking price, the thought of the likes of them making $2 million off a labor of love apparently offending him as much as it soon would his fellow residents of Waterloo. "All she sees is that one-point-five million," Boesen said on another occasion of Boyenga, and she in turn once mocked Copeland's attitude as "Sell the club! Sell the club! Sell the club!" "*I* don't need the money," Copeland answered his critics. "*They've* all got dollar signs for eyes." To which one answered back, under the cover of the darkness of a parking lot after a board meeting: "Asshole!"

"A rift has opened up," Copeland declared, "that will never be healed."

Their critics had a point—Russ Garling, Mayor Rooff and everyone else accusing the owners of betraying a public trust. It was the point that Garling had made when Boesen approached him about a lease, and it was the point that the assistant sports editor of the *Courier* had brought to public attention in a column on the front page of the sports section in the days following the announcement that the ball club was for sale: "Legally, 14 members of the Waterloo Diamonds' board of directors own a minor league baseball franchise that may be worth as much as $2 million. Morally and philosophically, the Midwest League club belongs to the city of Waterloo and its citizens, who have as much invested in minor league baseball as a board that did little to address the problems until they became too large to overcome."

It was, in fact, the point that the club's board of directors had made throughout the years. The owners had assumed legal control of the ball club on moral and philosophical grounds—"without remuneration and for the sole purpose of preserving baseball for this community." Over the past two years they had pursued a set of priorities that would allow them to fulfill that commitment: First, to keep the club for themselves, and to keep it in Waterloo; failing that, to find a local investor, buyer, or angel who would keep the ball club here; failing that, to sell the club to an outside buyer who would make the necessary stadium renovations to keep the club in Waterloo; failing that, to sell the club to an outside interest that would keep the club in Waterloo at least for the 1994 season. And they had succeeded, if only with this last, least desirable option.

Even then they had tried to figure out a way they could still keep pro ball in Waterloo. Despite the new mayor's repeated accusations to the contrary, they *had* debated selling the club and setting aside $500,000 from the sale price for ballpark improvements. The problem with that solution, one which Mayor Rooff never seemed to grasp, was that in order to get the $500,000, they would have to sell the club—and thereby surrender any say in the matter of franchise location. Dan Yates arrived at an alternative solution: offer the ball club at $500,000 off the market price, with the stipulation that the buyer would contribute the difference to stadium renovations. But the market price of a franchise that had to stay in Waterloo was going to be considerably less than one that was free to move elsewhere, and that difference was going to exert a powerful economic pressure on a new owner to turn around and sell the club for a quick profit. "It would be naïve," Klinkowitz said, "to think that anybody coming in here could dictate whether the ball club will stay, however honorable their intentions." Mildred Boyenga not only agreed, but for once she staked out a position more extreme than Klinkowitz's. In business matters, she argued, the potential honorableness of the intentions of strangers didn't deserve consideration. She called Yates "too naïve," and she said that she used to be naïve, too. "Promises don't mean anything. I'd have to have it in blood to believe it." Then she added, more softly, "I don't *like* believing bad things about people."

They even considered giving the proceeds to charity. When Davenport's local owners sold their franchise in the mid-1980s, they used their windfall to establish a charitable trust to fund various sports enterprises around town on an ongoing basis, and at one point Boyenga and Kuper did discuss with Yates the possibility of the Waterloo board committing itself to a similar venture. Given the recent dissension among board members, maybe such a proposal wouldn't have attracted the unanimous endorsement it would have needed to survive. But the mayor's public vilification of them, not to mention his demand for $500,000, had arisen before they had a chance to find out. Already an era when it was possible to feel charitable toward the city—to feel a commonality of purpose and destiny—seemed remote, even quaint. Mildred Boyenga, for one, had rallied for Rath, and she'd rallied for the ball club, but nowadays what she was saying was "I feel like Waterloo is not my town anymore."

Who owned this ball club? They did—these fourteen residents of Black Hawk County who held stock and sat on the board of Waterloo Professional Baseball, Inc. At some point they had crossed the same line that an Alan Levin or Rick Holtzman had in the history of minor league baseball proprietorship, between an era of community ownership and the era of individual ownership—and if the precise moment of passage had to be pinpointed, it was when they issued their articles of incorporation. The ball club had been a for-profit enterprise before then, however haphazard the paperwork; and if they'd wanted Waterloo to remain in the Midwest League, they had no choice but to incorporate. They had acted out of the purest of motives, and with the best intentions. Still, that was the moment. From the outside, Klinkowitz reminded his fellow owners at a meeting during this period, they could understand each step they'd taken since then and justify it to themselves, but from the outside, all anyone would see was the first step and the final step and, not unreasonably, condemn them.

That winter Jack Kuper suffered a mild heart attack, which his wife Barb attributed to anxiety about the ball club. Jack had become the ball club's groundskeeper after he lost his job at Rath, and he always said he'd still be the groundskeeper if he hadn't lost his Rath pension, too. It was widely assumed among the owners that the possibility of losing a second chance at an annuity had contributed to his condition. A couple of weeks later, during a meeting, Barb Kuper burst into tears.

"Let's get this settled," she said, "or I'm going to lose my husband!"

But what about the money? the others asked.

"We don't *care* about the money," she said. *"Let's end this."*

When the mayor said that, if nothing else, the ball club owed the city $325,000 as compensation for the funds spent supposedly to guarantee the future of pro ball in Waterloo, the owners couldn't entirely disagree. In the end, whether out of moral and philosophical considerations, or out of fear of losing the franchise—the league could revoke the charter if Waterloo didn't get a lease before the start of the season—or simply out of fatigue, the owners agreed to give some money from the sale to the city. A delegation from the ball club met with city representatives and offered to donate $255,000 to Waterloo—the $325,000 from the four-year improvements that the city had recently completed, minus $70,000 in renovations that the city would have had to make on the ballpark regardless of the presence of the Diamonds' demands. Once more, Bill Boesen thought he had "a done deal." The following morning Boesen drove to Beloit. The Midwest

League owners were meeting that day in part to determine what to do about Waterloo; meanwhile, the City Council was meeting in Waterloo to determine what to do about the Midwest League. George Spelius had been monitoring the developments in Waterloo closely. Already that off-season, the league had seen a franchise flee a city over a rent dispute—the Springfield club, now residing in Madison, whose own franchise had relocated to Grand Rapids. As much as Spelius didn't want Waterloo to lose professional baseball any sooner than it must, he also had made clear to Boesen that he couldn't have Waterloo setting a precedent for the league and for all of minor league baseball by charging $500,000 in rent. That afternoon, Boesen took a call from Boyenga, Yates, and the ball club's lawyer, all of whom had been conferring with the mayor and Council back in Waterloo, and now Boesen relayed to Spelius that the franchise had itself a dollar-a-year lease.

Spelius let out a whoop.

The catch, Boesen added, was that if the ball club did leave town after the season, the owners would have to make a $500,000 contribution to the city.

"That's it!" Spelius said. "We're taking it out of your hands!"

The following Tuesday, a Ryder van backed up to the gate at Waterloo Municipal Stadium. The movers walked into the home manager's office and loaded up the desk, three chairs, even the two milk crates; into the umpires' room and carried off four chairs and a box fan; along the concourse collecting contest boxes and metal stanchions; into the groundskeeper's cage to retrieve rakes, shovels and the John Deere AMT 600; and into the administrative office, where they packed up the air conditioner, answering machine, fax machine, copier, three telephones, three padded swivel chairs, a bar stool, a filing cabinet, three desks, a couple of trash cans, and a clock. When they were done, they pulled out of the dirt parking lot, found the nearest ramp up to the Leo Rooff Highway, and headed out of town.

"Maybe I was fooling myself to think that people cared about baseball," Nelson told the *Courier* afterward. He was on his way out of town, too; once the ball club's sale had appeared imminent, he accepted the GM position in Helena, Montana. "The bottom line," he went on, "is no one stepped forward with the money to save this team. The movers and shakers in this town thought the

Diamonds were for the little people. They didn't care. Sure there are some exceptions, but how often did you see people in suits out at the ballpark? Almost never. Ultimately, that's what cost this city baseball."

The moving van landed in Springfield, Illinois, where a San Diego Padres' Class A farm team began play barely three weeks later as the Sultans. What the van left behind were 80,000 tickets, 10,000 poster schedules commemorating the 90th anniversary of pro ball in Waterloo, and plans for a 90th-anniversary celebration at the Grout Museum, which went ahead and mounted the exhibit that summer anyway because 1994 still was, after all, the 90th anniversary of professional baseball in Waterloo. In the end, $500,000 was deducted from the sale price to compensate Take Me Out to the Ballgame for the extra expenses incurred from the move, not the least of which was the revenue loss that was sure to come from trying to sell tickets and advertising in a new market starting three weeks before Opening Day. The city, having misjudged its negotiating strength and having lost a quick $255,000 in the process, threatened to file a lawsuit against the ball club; the ball club responded with the threat of its own lawsuit to recover the difference in the sale price. Neither side pulled the trigger, but when the sale finally was completed several months later, the ball club's newly-former owners, on the advice of counsel, put the lion's share of the proceeds into escrow for five years, just in case. Throughout it all, the owners took whatever grim humor they could find in the occasional pronouncements by the mayor or other city officials that Waterloo one day might secure another Midwest League franchise. As Mildred Boyenga once marveled, "How naïve are people to think the threat of a lawsuit is an enticement to come back?" More to the point, however, was the answer that the directors of Take Me Out to the Ballgame had given, on the control interest transfer application to the National Association, to the question of why they were planning to relocate the club—an answer that couldn't have provided a more succinct summary of what cost Waterloo pro ball: "Playing facilities and market."

Pro ball in Waterloo was a ruin, and the stadium a relic. The ballpark could get a new clubhouse, new bat racks, and even a phone from the bullpen to the dugout, if a new PBA should come

along to upgrade that particular recommendation to a require-
ment, and the ballpark would still be an anachronism. Waterloo
Municipal Stadium belonged to a school of sports architecture
that dated back to the first decade of the century. It was now at
least two generations out of date. Although still functional, the
stadium not only was showing its age through missing seats,
cracking concrete and rusting girders, but its amenities were woe-
fully antiquated. All it could deliver was nostalgia, though not in
the commercially negotiable form that would have been necessary
for the franchise to remain economically competitive.

Even a new state-of-the-art stadium might not have done the
trick, because the issue wasn't whether the fans in Waterloo
would show up and spend money. The fact was, they weren't
going to show up in the same numbers and spend money to the
same degree as those in Grand Rapids, Michigan, where the West
Michigan Whitecaps in their inaugural season set an all-time Class
A attendance record of 475,212, and sold twenty luxury boxes at
$15,000 each and outfield signs at an average of $5,000 each; as
those in Rancho Cucamonga, California, where the ball club retained the advertising agency D'Arcy Masius Benton & Bowles,
the same company that handled many Budweiser ads as well as
marketing for the San Jose Sharks, and that created for Rancho
Cucamonga a team name (the Quakes), a logo (the scrawled word
"Quakes" with a fissure running through it), a mascot (Tremor),
and a nickname for the ballpark (the Epicenter), all of which
proved so popular that during its first year the ball club did $500,-
000 worth of souvenir business; as those in any of the four collar-
county cities in the New York City metropolitan area where franchises arose one year where once there were none, and were hailed
by newspaper, radio and television outlets in the largest market in
the nation, especially after the major league players went on strike
late in the 1994 season, as "baseball the way it used to be."

It was coincidence that the major changes in the minors had
arrived just as the factories were closing in Waterloo. It was coincidence that a new Professional Baseball Agreement had arrived
just as the city had exhausted its capacity to provide public funding for anything but the most essential services (and sometimes
not even those), just as it was coincidence that the PBA survey
results had arrived just as the city discovered an unprecedented

budget deficit, and that San Diego's decision not to renew its Player Development Contract with Waterloo just as the ball club turned to private fund-raising, and that the 1994 season and the need for a new lease at what turned out to be the worst time of all. But it wasn't coincidence that all these coincidences had occurred in such a linear fashion so as to all but guarantee the demise of the franchise.

Baseball was as old as the century—in many ways, *was* the century, springing from the new opportunities of an expanding nation as surely as any smokestack. It had risen to prominence at the onset of an industrial era partly as a way for countless towns such as Waterloo to promote themselves and their industries, and partly as a way for the employees of those industries to entertain themselves. The arc of its existence followed the arc of these towns, their industries, and their workers, and when the forces of the marketplace shifted, so did baseball—toward new markets, where a new arc no doubt would soar in tandem with the social and economic developments of a new century.

Baseball wasn't alone in Waterloo. In a eulogy for the Diamonds shortly after the owners announced the club was for sale, the *Courier*'s sports editor had written:

> Alone, the loss of professional baseball wouldn't be so hard to stomach. But look around.
>
> It's another real, or perceived, blow to the image of Waterloo, to say nothing of the lost entertainment and financial benefits.
>
> This from a city that makes negative news seemingly every day.
>
> Troubled schools . . . racial problems . . . crime . . . no money for streetlights.
>
> Last month it was the dog track. The Cattle Congress could very well be next. If baseball is the [sic] on the next train out of here, what's left?

Indeed, shortly afterward the Sky Room Comedy Club went out of business. Chamberlain Manufacturing went out of business. The 1994 Black Hawk County 4-H Fair was held at the Buchanan County Fairgrounds. The dog track eventually filed for bankruptcy, owing $3.2 million to local banks, $750,000 to the city,

$887,000 to businesses, and more than $500,000 to the original investors, and taking down with it the National Cattle Congress, which, in 1994, for the first time since the early years of the century, didn't accompany the arrival of the fall harvest. Such was public opinion of the movers and shakers who'd gotten themselves and the city involved in the dog track fiasco that even the impending demise of the Cattle Congress, undoubtedly a greater source of civic pride and community identity over the decades than any local sports enterprise, wasn't enough to convince voters to bail out gambling. Twice in 1994 a referendum to that effect went before the voters, and twice it failed—the second time by only 70 votes out of a record turnout of 40,000.

And Waterloo wasn't alone in baseball. "We're unique!" Rick Tagtow used to tell David Simpson, and he was right. The dependence on two industries in particular, the geographical isolation, the extremity of the economic collapse, the need to reverse the isolation to attract new industries to restore the economy— Waterloo *was* unique. But it wasn't anomalous. Waterloo merely joined Sumter, Georgia; Glens Falls, New York; Pulaski, Virginia; Kenosha, Wisconsin; Gastonia, North Carolina; and all the other cities that once had professional baseball, and lost it.

In late 1994, around the time that the City Council in Lansing, Michigan, was authorizing the construction of a $14 million ballpark to house the Sultans of Springfield starting with the 1996 season, Waterloo was signing a lease with the college-player Northwoods League for the following summer. The other cities in the league included fellow former Midwest League franchises Kenosha, Wausau and Dubuque. Waterloo's entry into the league represented the culmination of efforts by a Waterloo sports commission that had been appointed in the wake of the Diamonds' departure, and that was chaired by Dan Watters, to bring pro ball back to Waterloo. The Northwoods League, however, was not pro ball but amateur ball, and the commission members vowed to continue their search—if not in the Midwest League, then perhaps in one of the independent upstarts that had arisen in the wake of the Professional Baseball Agreement, leagues that operated outside the jurisdiction of the National Association, that didn't impose restrictions on ballparks, that supplied their own bats, balls, and other equipment, and that were responsible for hiring their own managers, who in turn were partly responsible for scouting and drafting their own players—in short, a return to minor league baseball before the inauguration of the farm system. All of which raised the question: What *was* professional baseball, anyway?

What was this enterprise to which Waterloo had pledged its allegiance? Baseball was a business, but baseball had always been a business; baseball was changing, but baseball had always been changing. Fans had accommodated themselves to managers and players who bore no relation to the city they represented; they had accommodated themselves to a system that often sacrificed quality of play and competition. The owners of this club even had accommodated themselves to competing with franchises that functioned more like miniature versions of their major league counterparts than anything resembling the minors of old. Yet all these participants had been able to pass years here without questioning the nature of the operation. And if they couldn't help questioning it from time to time, they at least had been able to distract themselves from the answers. But what a distraction! Boys in white on field of green under sky of blue! It was easy, in a sleepy ballpark in a modest town in the bountiful heart of a gentle country, to see players as playing only for the honor of winning, to believe that the heroics on the field in some way reflected on the glory of the city. *Had* been easy, anyway. And that was it: what had been different about going to the ballpark during what had turned out to be the final season in Waterloo. The rest of the owners, and maybe a few of the other fans as well, had learned what Dan Yates had known the previous year, what Bill Boesen had been learning since then, and what Jeff Nelson had discovered for himself over the course of the Winter Meetings, which was that minor league baseball had reached a point in its history where for the first time it didn't need—in fact, would fare better without—the Waterloos of the world.

On Monday, June 7, 1993, at just past 9:00 A.M., while four of the ball club's owners were sitting at a conference table in the new press box, the skies over Waterloo opened. The day had never dawned, really; headlights had announced the arrival of the procession of cars that had been pulling into the stadium's parking lot for the past quarter of an hour. As thunder boomed and the new press box roof leaked, Blau read the prepared statement:

Waterloo Professional Baseball, Inc., owners and operators of the Waterloo Diamonds franchise in the Midwest League, today wish to discuss the future of professional baseball in Waterloo, Iowa.

With deep appreciation to Mayor Al Manning, the City Council, and Parks Director Rick Tagtow, the Waterloo Diamonds Board of Directors and all baseball fans express a sincere thank you for the improvements made at Municipal Stadium.

However, amidst many rumors circulating recently within both the city and league, specific issues and details need to be addressed here today. Due to the inability to obtain a commitment from the City of Waterloo to upgrade and maintain Municipal Stadium, our franchise is unable to meet the requirements set forth by the National Association of Professional Baseball.

The statement then explained the evaluation process that the stadium had undergone over the past two years and listed the history of franchise movements out of Wisconsin and into "new municipal stadiums costing up to $10 million" in Illinois, Indiana, and Michigan. It continued:

Throughout its history, Waterloo Professional Baseball, Inc., has never received compensation for their investment other than to keep baseball alive in Waterloo. All revenue raised has always been put back into stadium improvements.

It is with deep regret that due to non-compliance by the City of Waterloo fulfilling requirements of the Facility Standards set forth in the PBA, the Waterloo Diamonds Midwest League franchise is today seeking new ownership or possible relocation.

The owners then distributed the two-page list of the PBA requirements in sections 11, 12, and 13 of the PBA that the ballpark didn't meet. Then they spoke, raising their voices over the steady drumming of the rain and the occasional thunderclap, in a more informal fashion. "Our sole purpose," Blau said, "is gonna be tryin' to keep baseball in Waterloo, Iowa, and that's gonna be to try to find an owner that will come in and hopefully renovate and put some money into the stadium and that also will keep the ball club here for many years." "We're gonna be leanin' toward anybody that's gonna be interested in keepin' it in Waterloo," said Boesen. "This is where we want to hold it yet. But if we can't"— he caught his breath—"then it's up to the highest bidder." Then they led the camera crews on a tour of the facility which, at that moment, was springing leaks seemingly everywhere. Water was rising up from the drains; water was rushing down through the cracks.

The owners met at the ballpark that afternoon, officially for the purpose of setting an asking price for the ball club, but unofficially because such an occasion seemed to call for a gathering. One of the reasons they had held the press conference first thing in the morning was to beat the deadline for the *Courier,* and by the time the owners convened that afternoon, they'd seen the front-page banner headline: "Waterloo Diamonds Are up for Sale."

As the owners pulled into the parking lot under threatening skies, the team bus was pulling out, heading for I-380 and a game in Cedar Rapids. Klinkowitz walked up to the ticket window and called inside to Nelson, "One ball club, please."

"Is that for here," Nelson said, "or to go?"

The primary order of business that afternoon was to set a price for the ball club. The owners took into consideration the sale price of Madison and settled on the pleasantly round figure of $2 million. The meeting adjourned and everybody filed out of the press box, down the steps of the grandstand, turning right along the aisle, toward the first-base ramp, past the seats where they used to hold their meetings, then around the railing and down to the concourse, moving at the slow, deliberate pace that the occasion seemed to demand, though, truth to tell, there was nothing especially mournful in their manner: no hugs, no tears, no scenes. Nothing.

"Happy birthday."

The march halted. Boyenga turned around. It was Boesen, addressing her. The owners were all standing near the concession counter under the grandstand.

"How did you know?" she said.

"I *know.*" He smiled slyly.

Then she remembered: They had made plans to drive down together to the game in Cedar Rapids tonight, she and Bill and Bev. It was to have been a birthday celebration; but, in the rush of recent events, as the date of June 7 had assumed a new significance, the celebration had slipped from her mind.

"Happy birthday to you," Copeland began, and the rest of the board joined in then. A song rose. Her fellow owners were serenading her, their voices angling awkwardly, thunderously, off the girders, and she was turning from them, twisting away under their scrutiny. She surprised herself by how little emotion she felt at that moment. She had to ask herself if she were feeling sad, and her answer was: No.

No.

There it was: No.

It's just—she started, then: No.

It wasn't as if she hadn't cried over the ball club already, many times. But what she felt today was nothing, and she wondered if that came with age. The moment had been so long in arriving that, now that it was here, she couldn't summon the appropriate remorse. In a way, all they had done today was complete the series of events that had been unfolding since that one evening at the Heartland Inn some fourteen months earlier, when Copeland and Yates had tried to convince the board to put the ball club up for sale. Of course, even then it was an eventuality against which she had been girding herself for years. Still, it hadn't seemed altogether possible, either—plausible, anyway—until another owners' meeting last year, the one in late October, in the back room at the VFW Hall. There had been a moment, fairly early in the meeting: Bill discussing whether San Diego would be back in 1993, saying that he'd heard they would but that he'd received no official confirmation. And Dan Yates had said then, simply, that if by May 1, 1993, the ball club hadn't found the funding to renovate the stadium, then he personally would vote to put the franchise up for sale—nothing much different from what he had said six months earlier, but this time nobody objected. Nobody commented. Everybody simply accepted it, as if it confirmed what they had been thinking anyway, even if they hadn't known it until that moment. That was true for Boyenga and, in that moment, she knew that it was true for the others, too. It was a casual remark and barely left an impression—the motion at the stockholders' meeting would come the following month—yet, in that moment, *this* moment had become inevitable.

After that meeting, back in October, Yates had pulled a chair beside hers. They sat alone then, the two former presidents who, for better or worse, had delivered the ball club to its present circumstances. They talked about how ridiculous it was that some members were bringing up measures about beer sales at a time like this. Then Yates sighed and said that he supposed he'd better be getting home; as a member of his church's search committee for a new minister, he was expecting a call from another applicant. The minister who'd previously accepted the job had backed out; he was from a Kansas town of 200 and a congregation of 700, and Waterloo had scared him off. "Too great a culture shock," Yates said.

Boyenga laughed. "He probably read the papers." Then she said, "Did I tell you I've been shopping for a burial plot?" She said she had given up on the idea of buying a plot just beyond the right-field fence at the ballpark; she said she had given up on the idea of there being a team to watch from over there. "Waterloo has really let me down," she said. "Deere is laying off again. Who knows how long Chamberlain will be around?" She opened her mouth, as if to add to the list, then thought better of it. Then she said nothing. Yates nodded his head sympathetically, joined her in her silence, then excused himself again and took his leave.

Boyenga didn't budge. Some of the other owners were pulling up their chairs in a circle a few tables away, and she supposed she would join them soon, but for a moment she remained off to the side of the room, not moving from her chair. One morning, a beautiful morning, she had driven to Waterloo Memorial Park Cemetery, on the southwestern edge of town, and not far from the entrance had stopped at an unmarked spot under a tree. It had been a memorable autumn, slow and lingering, a gradual surrender of one season to the next. The trees in the cemetery blazed the color of pumpkins, plums, gourds, and figs. A breeze reached her. She turned her face to the sun. Autumn in these parts could be so brief, hardly a pause at all between the two long hauls of summer harshness and winter fierceness. But this year fall was taking its time. She bent to the earth next to the tree. The dirt was still soft: no first frost yet. She rested her hand against the soil and surveyed the view from here: grass, the Veterans Memorial monument, the tree. It was an ideal spot, and she had to wonder why it was still available. It occurred to her that it might have something to do with the roots of the tree, that their entangling, consuming growth would lend whatever rested underground here a certain impermanence, but then she decided that she simply didn't want to think about it, that she was, in fact, tired of thinking, and that she wouldn't allow her doubts to intrude upon and spoil such a perfect specimen of an autumn day in Iowa: a gentle breeze, and whispering trees, and the open sky.

She stood up. Mildred Boyenga brushed the dirt from her hands and, for now, walked away from her grave.